D0149415

Ethics and the Pharmaceutical Industry

Despite the pharmaceutical industry's notable contributions to human progress, including the development of "miracle" drugs for treating cancer, AIDS, and heart disease, there is a growing tension between the industry and the public. Government officials, physicians, and social critics have questioned whether the multibillion-dollar industry is fulfilling its social responsibilities. This doubt has been fueled by the national debate over drug pricing and affordable healthcare, and internationally by the battles against epidemic diseases, such as AIDS, in the developing world. Debates are raging over how the industry can and should be expected to act. The contributions in this book by leading figures in industry, government, NGOs, the medical community, and academia discuss and propose solutions to the ethical dilemmas of drug industry behavior. They examine such aspects as drug pricing and marketing, the role of intellectual property rights and patent protection, and the moral and economic requisites of research and clinical trials.

Michael A. Santoro is Associate Professor with tenure at Rutgers Business School, where he teaches courses on business ethics, multinational corporations and global social issues, labor and human rights, international law, and ethical issues in the pharmaceutical industry. He has lectured and published widely on these topics. Professor Santoro is the author of *Profits and Principles: Global Capitalism and Human Rights in China* (2000). He holds a Ph.D. in Public Policy from Harvard University, a J.D. from the New York University School of Law, and an A.B. from Oberlin College. He was also a Fulbright Fellow at the University of Hong Kong.

Thomas M. Gorrie, Ph.D., is Corporate Vice President, Government Affairs & Policy, Johnson & Johnson, with responsibility as Corporate Officer for all federal, state, and international government affairs and policy. Dr. Gorrie has more than thirty years of worldwide healthcare experience. He has worked with various Johnson & Johnson companies in research and development, marketing and sales, business development, strategic planning, general management, international, venture capital, and health policy. Dr. Gorrie received his Bachelor of Arts degree from Rutgers University and Masters and Doctorate degrees in chemistry from Princeton University. He completed post-doctoral studies at the Swiss Federal Institute of Technology in Zurich. He serves on numerous non-profit boards, including Duke University Health Care System, the Dean's Advisory Board of the Rutgers Business School, and the Hun School of Princeton.

Ethics and the Pharmaceutical Industry

Edited by

MICHAEL A. SANTORO

Rutgers University

THOMAS M. GORRIE

Johnson & Johnson

CAMBRIDGE UNIVERSITY PRESS
Cambridge, New York, Melbourne, Madrid, Cape Town, Singapore, São Paulo

Cambridge University Press
40 West 20th Street, New York, NY 10011–4211, USA

www.cambridge.org
Information on this title:www.cambridge.org/9780521854962

© Cambridge University Press 2005

This publication is in copyright. Subject to statutory exception
and to the provisions of relevant collective licensing agreements,
no reproduction of any part may take place without
the written permission of Cambridge University Press.

First published 2005
Reprinted 2005, 2006

Printed in the United States of America

A catalogue record for this book is available from the British Library.

Library of Congress Cataloguing in Publication Data
Ethics and the pharmaceutical industry /
edited by Michael A. Santoro, Thomas M. Gorrie.
p.   cm.
Includes bibliographical references and index.
ISBN-13: 978-0-521-85496-2 (hardback)
ISBN-10: 0-521-85496-2 (hardback)
1. Pharmaceutical industry.   2. Drugs – Marketing – Moral and ethical aspects.
3. Drugs – Research – Moral and ethical aspects.   4. Medical innovations –
Social aspects.   5. Social responsibility of business.   I. Santoro, Michael A.
II. Gorrie, Thomas M.   III. Title.
HD9665.5.E85   2005
338.4'76151 – dc22   2005012018

ISBN-13   978-0-521-85496-2 hardback
ISBN-10   0-521-85496-2 hardback

Cambridge University Press has no responsibility for
the persistence or accuracy of URLs for external or
third-party Internet Web sites referred to in this publication
and does not guarantee that any content on such
Web sites is, or will remain, accurate or appropriate.

Contents

Tables

Figures

About the Editors

MICHAEL A. SANTORO

Michael A. Santoro is Associate Professor with tenure at Rutgers Business School, where he teaches courses on business ethics, multinational corporations and global social issues, labor and human rights, international law, and ethical issues in the pharmaceutical industry. He has lectured and published widely on these topics. Professor Santoro is the author of *Profits and Principles: Global Capitalism and Human Rights in China* (2000). He holds a Ph.D. in Public Policy from Harvard University, a J.D. from the New York University School of Law, and an A.B. from Oberlin College. He was also a Fulbright Fellow at the University of Hong Kong.

THOMAS M. GORRIE

Thomas M. Gorrie, Ph.D., is Corporate Vice President, Government Affairs & Policy, Johnson & Johnson, with responsibility as Corporate Officer for all federal, state, and international government affairs and policy. Dr. Gorrie has more than thirty years of worldwide health care experience. He has worked with various Johnson & Johnson companies in research and development, marketing and sales, business development, strategic planning, general management, international, venture capital, and health policy. Dr. Gorrie received his Bachelor of Arts degree from Rutgers University and Masters and Doctorate degrees in chemistry from Princeton University. He completed post-doctoral studies at the Swiss Federal Institute of Technology in Zurich. He serves on numerous nonprofit boards, including Duke University Health Care System, the Dean's Advisory Board of the Rutgers Business School, and the Hun School of Princeton.

Contributors

Thomas Abrams is Director, Division of Drug Marketing, Advertising, and Communications at the U.S. Food and Drug Administration. He received a Bachelor of Science in Pharmacy and M.B.A. from Rutgers University. In addition to his experience at the FDA, he worked as a pharmacy manager and in sales and marketing in the pharmaceutical industry.

Charles L. Bardes, M.D., is Professor of Clinical Medicine and Associate Dean at the Weill Medical College of Cornell University, where he teaches and practices general internal medicine. A graduate of Princeton University and the University of Pennsylvania School of Medicine, he is the author of *Essential Skills in Clinical Medicine* (1996) and of articles related to medical education.

Valentine J. Burroughs, M.D., M.B.A., is the Chief Medical Officer and Chairman of the Department of Medicine at North General Hospital in New York City. He holds an academic appointment at the Mt. Sinai School of Medicine. He is the Medical Director and Endocrinologist at Health Care New York IPA. He is a past Associate Medical Director and remains a consultant to Group Health Insurance of New York. Dr. Burroughs has authored several landmark articles on racial and ethnic differences in response to medications and on cultural and genetic diversity in America, highlighting the need for individualized pharmaceutical treatment. He headed the Manhattan Borough President's Commission to Close the Health Divide (2004). Over the years Dr. Burroughs has served with distinction as State Medical Association President and City Medical Society President for both the National

Medical Association and the American Medical Association in New York.

Glenna M. Crooks, Ph.D., is President & CEO of Strategic Health Policy International, Inc. She was a health policy advisor during the Reagan administration, policy director at Merck & Co., Inc., and Worldwide Vice President of Merck's Vaccine Business. She is the author of *Creating Covenants: Healing Health Care in the New Millennium* (2000) and *Covenants: Inspiring the Soul of Healing* (2002). Dr. Crooks assists government and healthcare businesses in integrating policy and politics into their research and business operations. She was awarded a Ph.D. from Indiana University in 1977.

Norman Daniels is Mary B. Saltonstall Professor and Professor of Ethics and Population Health at Harvard School of Public Health. He was formerly Goldthwaite Professor, Chair of the Tufts Philosophy Department, and Professor of Medical Ethics at Tufts Medical School, where he taught from 1969 until 2002. Professor Daniels has written widely in the philosophy of science, ethics, political and social philosophy, and medical ethics. His most recent books include (with Allen Buchanan, Dan Brock, and Dan Wikler) *From Chance to Choice: Genetics and Justice* (Cambridge, 2000); (with Bruce Kennedy and Ichiro Kawachi) *Is Inequality Bad for Your Health?* (Beacon, 2000); and (with James Sabin) *Setting Limits Fairly: Can We Learn to Share Medical Resources?* (Oxford, 2002). He has consulted with organizations and governments in the United States and abroad, including for the United Nations, WHO, and the President's Commission for the Study of Ethical Problems in Medicine, on issues of justice and health policy.

Scott D. Danzis is an associate at the law firm of Covington & Burling in Washington, D.C., where his practice concentrates on food and drug law and healthcare compliance for the pharmaceutical and medical device industries. He received his J.D. from the University of Virginia School of Law. He holds a Master's Degree in Health Services Administration from George Washington University and an undergraduate degree from Cornell University's School of Industrial and Labor Relations. Mr. Danzis has worked for U.S. Healthcare and Aetna–U.S. Healthcare Health Plans and as a Legislative Analyst for the U.S. Department of Health and Human Services, Agency for Health Care Policy and Research.

Martin Delaney is the Founding Director and public voice of the non-profit AIDS foundation Project Inform (founded in 1985). He is co-author of *Strategies for Survival: The Gay Men's Health Manual for the Age of AIDS* (1987) and editor of the *Project Inform HIV Drug Book* and other Project Inform materials. He serves on the Department of Health and Human Services HIV Treatment Guidelines Panel. Mr. Delaney is a leader of the movement to accelerate FDA approval of promising drugs and was a key player in the development of Accelerated Approval regulations and the Parallel Track system for providing experimental drugs to the seriously ill prior to formal approval by the FDA. Mr. Delaney was one of the founders of the community-based research movement and through Project Inform led the way to the unprecedented level of HIV treatment education available to both physicians and patients.

Don E. Detmer, M.D., M.A., is President and CEO of the American Medical Informatics Association; Professor Emeritus and Professor of Medical Education in the Department of Health Sciences at the University of Virginia; and Senior Associate of the Judge Business School, University of Cambridge. From 1999 to 2003 Dr. Detmer was the Dennis Gillings Professor of Health Management and Director, Cambridge University Health at the Judge Institute of Management. Prior to that he was Vice President for Health Sciences at the Universities of Virginia and Utah and on the faculty at the University of Wisconsin-Madison. Dr. Detmer received a medical degree from the University of Kansas with subsequent training at the Johns Hopkins Hospital, the National Institutes of Health, Duke University Medical Center, the Institute of Medicine, and Harvard Business School. He was awarded an M.A. from the University of Cambridge.

Julie M. Donohue is an Assistant Professor in the Department of Health Policy & Management in the Graduate School of Public Health at the University of Pittsburgh. Dr. Donohue received her Ph.D. in health policy from Harvard University in 2003 and completed a post-doctoral fellowship in Pharmaceutical Policy Research at Harvard Medical School. Dr. Donohue's research interests span the areas of pharmaceutical policy, mental health policy, and the politics of policy development in healthcare. Her research has focused on the effects of pharmaceutical promotion, cost containment, financing and organization of mental health services, federal drug regulation, and public opinion on health policy issues.

Jürgen Drews, M.D., is Chairman of the Board at Genaissance Pharm. Inc. and Director and Partner of Bear Stearns Health Innoventure Fund LLC, a company that manages capital investments in the healthcare industry. In 1998, Dr. Drews co-founded International Biomedicine Management Partners, Inc., a venture capital company, of which he also served as a Partner and Chairman of the Board of Directors until April 2001. He was formerly President of Global Research and Development at Hoffmann–La Roche Inc. and member of the Corporate Executive Committee of the Roche Group, a healthcare company. Dr. Drews is the author of *In Quest of Tomorrow's Medicines* (1999) and *Immunopharmacology: Principles and Perspectives* (1990), which have been translated in English, among many other publications. He also served as a professor of Medicine at the University of Heidelberg and adjunct professor of Genetics at the University of Medicine and Dentistry in New Jersey. He holds an M.D. in internal medicine from the Free University of Berlin.

Sev Fluss is Senior Adviser at the Council for International Organizations of Medical Sciences in Geneva. Educated at the Universities of Edinburgh, Cambridge, and Wisconsin, he worked for five years in the United Kingdom before joining the Health Legislation Unit of the World Health Organization (WHO) in Geneva in 1965. He was Chief of that unit from 1984 until 1995, concurrently serving as Administrative Officer to the Director-General from 1988 to 1995. He then worked on human rights issues in the health sector in the Office of Health Policy in Development until 1997, when he retired from WHO. During his career in WHO, he published numerous papers in the field of health legislation, bioethics, and cognate issues, and he served on the editorial boards of several journals. Among other honors, Mr. Fluss is an Honorary Member of the Czech Medical Association and was a Special Professor at the University of Nottingham from 1996 to 1999.

William H. Foege, M.D., M.P.H., is Emeritus Presidential Distinguished Professor of International Health, Rollins School of Public Health, Emory University, Gates Fellow, and former Senior Medical Advisor for the Bill and Melinda Gates Foundation. An epidemiologist who worked on the successful campaign to eradicate smallpox in the 1970s, Dr. Foege was appointed director of the U.S. Centers for Disease Control in 1977. He was a co-founder and later executive director of the Task Force for Child Survival. He was executive director and later Fellow of the Carter Center. Dr. Foege is the recipient of many awards, holds honorary degrees from numerous institutions, and was named a Fellow of the London School of Tropical Medicine and Hygiene in 1997. He is the author of more than 125 professional publications. Dr. Foege received his medical degree from the University of Washington and his Master's in Public Health from Harvard University.

James Thuo Gathii is Associate Professor of international law and business at Albany Law School, New York. He is the author of numerous articles on international law, including "The Legal Status of the Doha Declaration of TRIPS and Public Health Under the Vienna Convention on the Law of Treaties" (*Harvard Journal of Law and Technology*, 2002); "Markets, Rights and Patents and the Global Aids Pandemic" (*Florida Journal of International Law*, 2002), and "The Structural Power of Strong Pharmaceutical Patent Protection in U.S. Foreign Policy," in *Iowa Journal of Gender, Race and Justice*, 2003, on which his chapter in this volume is based. He graduated with his first law degree from the University of Nairobi, Kenya. He also holds two graduate law degrees from Harvard Law School.

Sara F. Goldkind, M.D., M.A., is the Bioethicist in the Office of Pediatric Therapeutics within the Office of the Commissioner of the Food and Drug Administration. She is a board certified internist. Dr. Goldkind completed a fellowship in clinical medical ethics at the University of South Florida School of Medicine, where she was on the faculty within the Department of Medicine. She also obtained a Master's Degree in religious studies focusing on comparative religious ethics and public policy.

Michael E. Gorman is Professor in the Department of Science, Technology & Society at the University of Virginia. His research interests include experimental simulations of science, described in his book *Simulating Science* (1992), and ethics, invention, and discovery, described in his book *Transforming Nature* (1998). With support from the National Science Foundation, he has created a graduate concentration in Systems Engineering in which students create case studies involving ethical and policy issues; these studies are described in *Ethical and Environmental Challenges to Engineering* (2000), which he coauthored with M. M. Mehalik and P. H. Werhane. He also has edited a volume, *New Directions in the Study of Scientific and Technological Thinking* (2004).

Joel W. Hay is Associate Professor in the Department of Pharmaceutical Economics and Policy in the School of Pharmacy and the Department of Economics at the University of Southern California. He is USC Project Coordinator for the Rand Evidence-Based Medicine Practice Centers of Southern California; Co-Investigator, USC Alzheimer Research Center; and Health Economics Research Scholar at the UCLA Center for Vaccine Research. Dr. Hay has served as a consultant to numerous agencies, including the U.S. Centers for Disease Control and Prevention, the U.S. Public Health Service, the U.S. FDA, the U.S. Health Care Financing Administration, the World Bank, and the California AIDS Commission. Dr. Hay is a founding member of the Board of Directors of the International Society for Pharmacoeconomics and Outcomes Research, founding Editor-in-Chief of its journal *Value in Health*, and founding Executive Board member of the American Society for Health Economics He recently completed a study of hospital and pharmaceutical costs for the national Blue Cross Blue Shield Association, which has been discussed in national media.

Representative *Rush Holt*, a physicist, represents the 12th district of New Jersey in the U.S. House of Representatives. Before arriving in Congress, Representative Holt held positions as a teacher, Congressional Science Fellow, and arms control expert at the U.S. State Department. From 1989 until he launched his 1998 congressional campaign, Holt was Assistant Director of the Princeton Plasma Physics Laboratory, the largest research facility of Princeton University and the largest center for research in alternative energy in New Jersey. Representative Holt serves on two committees, the Committee on Education and the Workforce and the House Permanent Select Committee on Intelligence.

Nien-hê Hsieh is Assistant Professor in the Legal Studies Department at the Wharton School, University of Pennsylvania. His research projects include study of the obligations of multinational corporations, the implications of distributive justice for corporate governance, and choice involving incommensurable values. He was a Postdoctoral Fellow at Harvard Business School and has held visiting fellowships at Oxford University and the Research School for Social Sciences at the Australian National University. Dr. Hsieh has published in *Utilitas*, *Social Theory and Practice*, *Business Ethics Quarterly*, and *The Journal of Political Philosophy*. He holds a B.A. in Economics from Swarthmore College, an M.Phil. in Politics from Oxford University, and a Ph.D. in Economics from Harvard University.

Juhana E. Idänpään-Heikkilä, M.D., is Secretary-General of the Council for International Organizations of Medical Sciences (CIOMS) at the World Health Organization (WHO) in Geneva. In 1990, he was appointed Deputy Director and in 1995, Director of the WHO Division of Drug Management and Policies in Geneva, Switzerland. He also acted as Secretary of the WHO ethics committee. Professor Idänpään-Heikkilä has held teaching positions at the University of Baylor in Houston, Texas, and the University of Oulu, Finland. He also has been Chief Medical Officer at the national medicines control agency in Finland (1971–90) and an adviser in drug regulations at the U.S. Food and Drug Administration in Rockville, Maryland (1982–83), and in the United Nations offices in Vienna, Austria. Professor Idänpään-Heikkilä has an M.D. and Ph.D. (in pharmacology) from the University of Helsinki in Finland.

Edward Greg Koski, M.D., Ph.D., is Senior Scientist at the Institute for Health Policy and Associate Professor of Anesthesia, Massachusetts General Hospital, Harvard Medical School. He was the first Director of the Office for Human Research Protections, U.S. Department of Health and Human Services (OHRP), established in 2000. Dr. Koski chaired the Human Subjects Research Subcommittee of the National Science and Technology Council's Committee on Science at the White House, and served as Executive Secretary of the National Human Research Protections Advisory Committee. As director of human research affairs at Partners Healthcare System, he was responsible for the ethical and regulatory oversight of human investigation, including protection of human participants in research studies. As a member of the Institute for Health Policy, Dr. Koski continues to advocate in the area of research ethics, responsible conduct and research integrity. Dr. Koski received his undergraduate education, Ph.D., and M.D. from Harvard.

M. Dianne Murphy, M.D., is Director of the Office of Pediatric Therapeutics in FDA's Office of the Commissioner. She is a board-certified pediatrician with subspecialty training in pediatric infectious diseases. In addition to her work at the FDA, she has had faculty appointments at the University of Florida, the University of Tennessee, and the University of Texas, where her work has focused on both primary care delivery and infectious disease research.

Robert M. Nelson, M.D., Ph.D., is Associate Professor of Anesthesiology and Critical Care at The Children's Hospital of Philadelphia (CHOP) and the University of Pennsylvania School of Medicine. He is a member of the Pediatric Advisory Committee (PAC) of the Food and Drug Administration, and Chair of the PAC Pediatric Ethics Subcommittee. Dr. Nelson also serves as a member of the Subcommittee on Research Involving Children of the Secretary's Advisory Committee on Human Research Protections Department of Health and Human Services (DHHS). He is Director of the Center for Research Integrity, established at CHOP to further the responsible conduct of pediatric research. Dr. Nelson received an M.D. degree from Yale University. He has received formal training in theology, religious and medical ethics, receiving a Master of Divinity degree from Yale Divinity School in 1980 and a Ph.D. in the Study of Religion from Harvard University in 1993.

Gary R. Noble, M.D. is a public health physician who has worked at the Centers for Disease Control and Prevention (CDC) for twenty-nine years and at Johnson & Johnson for ten years. Dr. Noble headed the WHO Collaborating Center for Influenza at CDC. In 1985, he chaired the Program Committee of the first International Conference on AIDS. He also served as AIDS Coordinator for the Department of Health and Human Services as well as CDC Deputy Director (AIDS). He retired from the Commissioned Corps of the U.S. Public Health Service in 1994 as an Assistant Surgeon General. Dr. Noble is former Vice President, Medical and Public Health Affairs, on the Corporate Staff of Johnson & Johnson. He has a B.A. from Albion College; an

M.A. from Oxford University, which he attended as a Rhodes Scholar; an M.D. from Harvard Medical School; and an M.P.H. in public health from the University of California at Berkeley.

Scott C. Ratzan, M.P.A., is Vice President, Government Affairs, Europe, for Johnson & Johnson. He is Editor-in-Chief of the *Journal of Health Communication: International Perspectives* and holds faculty appointments at Tufts University School of Medicine, George Washington University School of Public Health and Health Services, the College of Europe (Belgium), and the University of Cambridge. He recently led a project at the U.S. Agency for International Development to design strategic health communication implementation for more than 65 countries. Dr. Ratzan is principal author of *Attaining Global Health: Challenges and Opportunities* (2000), as well as *The Mad Cow Crisis: Health and the Public Good* (1998), and *AIDS: Effective Health Communication for the 1990s* (1993). He also has consulted with the World Health Organization, Institute of Medicine, and a number of U.S. Governmental agencies.

Meredith B. Rosenthal is Assistant Professor of Health Economics and Policy in the Department of Health Policy and Management at Harvard University. Dr. Rosenthal received her Ph.D. in health policy (economics track) at Harvard University in 1998. Her principal research interests revolve around economic incentives that influence consumer and provider healthcare decisions. Her other substantive interests include the pharmaceutical industry, mental health policy, and the economics of smoking. She is currently working on a series of related projects that examine evolving trends in the health insurance market, including consumer-directed health plans and financial incentives for improving healthcare quality and patient safety.

James E. Sabin, Clinical Professor of Psychiatry at Harvard Medical School, is the Director of Teaching at DACP, the Director of the Harvard Pilgrim Health Care Ethics Program, and the Director of the Center for Ethics in Managed Care, sponsored by Harvard Pilgrim Health Care and the Division of Medical Ethics at Harvard Medical School. Dr. Sabin is the author, with Norman Daniels, of *Setting Limits Fairly* (2002) and, with Steven Pearson and Ezekiel Emanuel, of *No Margin, No Mission: Health Care Organizations and the Quest for*

Ethical Excellence (2003). In 2002 the practical impact of this work was recognized by the American Association of Community Psychiatrists Moffic Award for Ethical Practice in Public Sector Managed Behavioral Healthcare.

Peter Singleton is a Senior Associate at the Judge Institute, University of Cambridge, a Principal Research Fellow at the Centre for Health Informatics and Multiprofessional Education (CHIME), University College London, and Founder and Director of Cambridge Health Informatics Limited (CHIL). For the past two years he has been leading the "Informed Patient" project, developing two reports on the benefits of informing the public and appropriate policy actions to improve practice in health information delivery across Europe. Mr. Singleton has worked extensively in the United Kingdom on consent and confidentiality issues, developing the U.K. NHS Confidentiality Code of Practice and their Information Governance Toolkit. He holds an M.A. in Mathematics (Corpus Christi, Cambridge, U.K.), and an M.B.A. (Judge Institute, Cambridge, U.K).

Sidney Taurel is chairman, president and chief executive officer for Eli Lilly and Company. Mr. Taurel is a member of the boards of IBM Corporation; McGraw-Hill Companies, Inc.; and the RCA Tennis Championships; and a member of the executive committee of the board of directors of Pharmaceutical Research and Manufacturers of America (PhRMA). Mr. Taurel was named to the President's Export Council, the United States's premier advisory committee on international trade. He graduated from École des Hautes Études Commerciales, in Paris, France, in 1969, and received a master of business administration degree from Columbia University in 1971.

J. Russell Teagarden is Vice President of Clinical Practices and Therapeutics at Medco Health Solutions, Inc. He holds academic appointments at Rutgers College of Pharmacy, Ohio Northern University College of Pharmacy, and the Philadelphia College of Pharmacy & Sciences at the University of the Sciences. He served for twelve years as a Drug Information Specialist and as a clinical pharmacist in the Chicago teaching hospital community. During this time, Mr. Teagarden was Assistant Professor at the University of Illinois College of Pharmacy. He was a visiting scholar in the Department of Clinical Bioethics at the National Institutes of Health from September 2001 to June 2002. Mr. Teagarden received a B.S. in pharmacy from the University of Illinois College of Pharmacy and an M.A. in research methodology from Loyala University of Chicago. He completed a residency in hospital pharmacy at Northwestern University Medical Center in Chicago.

William C. Weldon is Chairman of the Board and Chief Executive Officer of the global healthcare company, Johnson & Johnson. He has worked in various capacities for Johnson & Johnson, including as manager, ICOM Regional Development Center in Southeast Asia; executive vice president and managing director of Korea McNeil, Ltd.; managing director of Ortho-Cilag Pharmaceutical, Ltd., in the United Kingdom; vice president of sales and marketing at Janssen Pharmaceutica in the United States; and president of Ethicon Endo-Surgery. In 1998 Mr. Weldon was promoted to the Executive Committee and named Worldwide Chairman, Pharmaceuticals Group. He is an Executive Committee Member and Treasurer of the Pharmaceutical Research and Manufacturers of America (PhRMA). He is a member of The Business Council and The Sullivan Commission on Diversity in the Health Professions Workforce. He is a graduate of Quinnipiac University in Hamden, Connecticut.

Patricia H. Werhane is the Wicklander Chair of Business Ethics in the Department of Philosophy and Director of the Institute for Business and Professional Ethics at DePaul University, with a joint appointment as the Peter and Adeline Ruffin Chair of Business Ethics and Co-Director of the Olsson Center for Applied Ethics in the Darden School at the University of Virginia. She also has held faculty positions at Loyola University of Chicago and the American College of Switzerland. Professor Werhane is the author or editor of fifteen books, including *Organization Ethics for Health Care*, with E. Spencer, A. Mills, and M. Rorty (2000); and *Employment and Employee Rights*, with Tara J. Radin (2003). She is founder and former editor-in-chief of *Business Ethics Quarterly* and a founding member and past president of the Society of Business Ethics, and the American Society for Value Inquiry. She received a B.A. from Wellesley College and an M.A. and Ph.D. from Northwestern University.

Preface

The chapters in this book are written by authors with diverse experiences and perspectives. They come from government and industry, from advocacy organizations and academia, as well as from the scientific and medical communities. It is a notable sign of the force and maturity of globalization that most of the contributors, regardless of their nationality or backgrounds, quite naturally address these issues by considering different international perspectives. Although not every voice and every relevant issue appears in these pages, we believe we have made an unprecedented effort to gather a highly diverse and talented group of authors to address a broad spectrum of the issues that dominate the relationship between the pharmaceutical industry and society in a global context.

The diversity of viewpoints among the contributors is mirrored in the differing perspectives of the editors. Together, since the year 2000, we have taught a class at Rutgers Business School on the ethical and regulatory issues facing the pharmaceutical industry. Sometimes much to the unintended amusement of our students, and we hope occasionally to their enlightenment, we have sharply, though collegially, disagreed on many matters affecting the pharmaceutical industry. Our disagreements are perhaps rooted in two fundamentally different perspectives. First, Dr. Gorrie believes that healthcare is a commodity purchased by the individual or society, the provision of which is made through that most social of institutions, insurance. Government's role is to ensure that the economically disadvantaged have access to healthcare. By contrast, Prof. Santoro believes that healthcare is a fundamental human right that circumscribes the exercise of intellectual property rights, particularly in the case of life-saving drugs for diseases such as HIV/AIDS.

Second, although we both believe in the power of the free market to drive innovation and progress in healthcare, Prof. Santoro believes that stronger government regulation of the pharmaceutical industry is desirable and inevitable because he believes that the dictates of the market too often drive pharmaceutical companies to maximize their profits in a manner that fails to deploy social resources optimally to provide the best healthcare for citizens. Dr. Gorrie, by contrast, believes that marketplace forces can more effectively address issues in the system than can the controlling hand of government.

Our differing perspectives are, in part, based upon our different experiences – Dr. Gorrie has spent his career at Johnson & Johnson in a number of roles, most recently as the Corporate Vice President of Government Affairs; Prof. Santoro has devoted his academic career to bringing accountability to multinational corporations for global social issues such as human rights and the environment.

Our differences, philosophical and otherwise, are real and significant; however, we both believe that choice is the lynchpin of effective healthcare and that all people should have access to affordable products and services that will save, enhance, improve, and prolong their lives, a mandate that certainly extends to people suffering from global pandemics. Most importantly, we both believe that knowledge best emerges from dialogue and listening to diverse viewpoints. This book offers multiple perspectives about the highly charged ideological issues the industry faces today. Written by leading experts in their respective fields, the essays comprising this book are not biased toward one particular point of view (either pro-business or anti-corporate). We both highly value the opportunity to engage in public discourse about business and ethics, and, in particular, to talk about the complex ethical issues inherent in medicine and healthcare. We believe that reasoned discussion will open channels of communication, lead to better understanding, and ultimately result in progressive change.

Another area of agreement between the editors is that future healthcare innovations and solutions will arise from long-term partnerships. Too much of the debate thus far has focused on confrontation (e.g., advocates vs. industry). Although such conflicts are inevitable given the diversity of the material interests involved, in order for sustainable solutions to be achieved in the twenty-first century, we believe that parties on opposite ends of the debate must come together as global citizens, take responsibility, and be accountable for delivering results. There is work to be done. The public and private sectors, the advocacy organizations and academia, the medical and scientific communities, all need to work together on the development of technologies that add quality, value, and cost efficiency to healthcare systems. By doing so, we will provide citizens with the highest quality of healthcare and the continued hope that new technologies can bring a better future. It is to that end that we have brought together the extraordinary authors in this volume, and we hope that the debate and dialogue that follow will help point the way to a future when all people can enjoy the fruits of the global pharmaceutical industry.

Michael A. Santoro and Thomas M. Gorrie

Acknowledgments

We gratefully acknowledge the many and crucial contributions by our Book Project Director, Mary Child. The task of coordinating the submission and review of the various chapters in this book was a daunting one that Mary performed with professionalism and extraordinary equanimity. In the process, Mary became a partner in our work, offering many valuable suggestions in shaping the book.

Scott Parris, our editor at Cambridge University Press, was a strong and steady supporter of the idea of this book. He set the highest standards of quality and integrity and gently pushed us to make good on our promise of engaging diverse and outstanding authors to address a wide array of issues.

We are grateful to our students over the years at Rutgers Business School. They cheerfully endured the process by which we worked out many of our ideas and challenged us in an intelligent and knowledgeable manner. In addition, we were fortunate at various stages of this project to have a number of outstanding research assistants, including most notably the following: Caren Speizer, Mari Boggiano, Melanie Milhorat, Brian Moran, Jennifer Flynn-Uptegrove, Greg Adams, and Sharzad Moosavi. We are also grateful to Polly Chen for proofreading.

Reflecting the highest standards and aspirations of academic publishing, three anonymous reviewers carefully read the manuscript and offered many insightful and constructive criticisms and suggestions about the book as a whole and on particular chapters.

We especially want to thank the many outstanding authors who contributed chapters to this volume. They are an extraordinarily diverse group with one common denominator: each was far too busy to contribute a chapter. Nevertheless, they all came through in the end. We believe that ultimately all of the authors were driven by the same factor that motivated us to finish this book – the hope that by assembling such a talented and diverse group of thinkers some measure of insight and progress might be achieved in the goal of bringing the fruits of the pharmaceutical industry to the broadest possible spectrum of the world's citizens.

Michael Santoro gratefully acknowledges that at various stages of this project support has been provided by The Aspen Institute's Business and Society Program, The Rutgers Business School Research Resources Committee, The Prudential Business Ethics Center at Rutgers, and The Lerner Center for Pharmaceutical Management at Rutgers.

Tom Gorrie gratefully acknowledges the contributions of Patricia Molino and Michael Miller. He gives special thanks to Pat Gruber for her ongoing assistance. He also thanks his wife, Meg, for her support, friendship, and love, and his sons, Alex and Rob, for their daily enrichment of his life. Finally, he wants to remember his daughter, Kate, who will always be an inspiration.

Foreword

It is a privilege to help set the scene for the deliberations in this book on ethics and its applications to the pharmaceutical industry and health-care in the twenty-first century. In Classical Greek, the word "ethics" means the "beliefs of the people" – the study of what is right and good in human conduct and the justification of such claims. Applied to the complex and multifaceted world of healthcare, it is a formidable task to try and uncover the fundamental principles involved in "right and good conduct." Without a doubt, this task is not simply about setting up a list of rights and wrongs. Rather, it is a discussion, a process that helps to tease out the real issues and find ethical solutions to complex practical problems.

Herein lies the greatest success of this book. It brings together outstanding leaders and thinkers from all segments of global healthcare to engage in ethical debate. They are all highly knowledgeable and experienced and from their different perspectives they mold together a unique view on some of the burning questions of our time. These include the ethics of clinical research, the empowering of patients by providing access to quality information, and the critically important issues of equity and access to care, especially in the field of HIV/AIDS. You will notice that the contributing authors brilliantly succeed in sensitizing the conscience of the reader and the different stakeholders involved in the healthcare leadership. As we all know, a sensitized conscience is a prerequisite for sound ethical decision making.

Another highlight of the book is its focus on partnerships. For too long, decisions with major implications for global health have been made in a compartmentalized fashion. Often there is a very troubling divide in the thinking of public- and private-sector leaders, regulators and providers, and most important of all, the patients involved in the healthcare system and those working in it. Not only does this cause inefficiencies and high costs, but it can lead to ethically bad behavior. This divide can be overcome by constructive and synergistic partnerships, and fortunately this book, in itself, represents such a partnership. All of the authors believe in the value of promoting good ethics in healthcare. Surely this type of attitude and collaboration will help us address the global health issues we face.

Last, a word on the centrality of the patient in any discussion on the ethics of healthcare. Most professional healthcare associations acknowledge in their foundational policies that ethically, the health of the individual patient should be the first consideration in any decision on care. This book will definitely contribute greatly to this ideal. It calls for more effective communication and standards of health information and sets the informed, respected, and cared-for patient as the goal of all our collective efforts. Bravo!

My sincere wish is that after reading the book, you and your organization will have a greater understanding of the ethical complexities of healthcare in the twenty-first century. More importantly, I hope that you and your organization will be encouraged to participate in the ethics debate and the partnerships necessary to put patients first and make healthcare work. We owe it to them and to humanity.

> Delon Human, M.D.
> Secretary-General and CEO, The World Medical
>   Association (WMA)
> *The WMA is the global representative body for*
> *physicians worldwide.*

Introduction

Charting a Sustainable Path for the Twenty-First Century Pharmaceutical Industry

Michael A. Santoro

This industry delivered miracles, and now they're throwing it all away.
They just don't get it.[1]
    Dr. Roy Vagelos, former Chairman, Merck & Co.

THE UNRAVELING OF THE "GRAND BARGAIN"

Perhaps no business engages the worlds of science, medicine, economics, health, human rights, government, and social welfare as much as the pharmaceutical industry. As the twenty-first century begins, however, there is growing controversy and even hostility in the relationship between the pharmaceutical industry and the public. The millions of individuals, families, and communities throughout the world that have been stricken by the scourge of AIDS offer the most tragic human face to this controversy, but it is no overstatement to say that the pharmaceutical industry impacts the life of virtually every person in the world.

What we are witnessing is the unraveling of a "grand bargain" between the pharmaceutical industry and society. This grand bargain was a complex, implicit social contract that allowed the modern global pharmaceutical industry to emerge in the second half of the twentieth century. Although the industry prospered immensely, society also enjoyed a bountiful array of life-saving and life-enhancing drugs. As the twenty-first century begins, however, this grand bargain is in tatters and public mistrust and resentment of the industry run feverishly high. Many feel that the enormous industry profits are not sufficiently

1

matched by contributions to the common good. What factors are behind this growing tension between the pharmaceutical industry and society? Which of the criticisms of the industry are warranted and what reforms of the industry make sense? How can the fragile relationship between the pharmaceutical industry and society be repaired? Will a new social contract develop in the twenty-first century? These are the broad questions addressed in this book from a diverse array of perspectives.

While it is impossible to discuss all the controversies involving the modern pharmaceutical industry, the essays in this book attempt to address the most significant moral, scientific, and public policy issues that underpin the industry's complex relationship with society. Accordingly, the book is divided into four sections encompassing these broad themes. Section I is concerned with the research process by which drugs get discovered and developed. Section II casts an analytical and critical eye on the marketing of drugs directly to consumers and to physicians. Section III contains essays that critically assess the intellectual property rights protecting these discoveries and the related pricing policies this intellectual property regime allows both in developed economies and in third world countries. Finally, Section IV looks to the future and contains essays that reflect on a sustainable path for the pharmaceutical industry to thrive economically while serving the needs of society.

Many of the essays in this book address hot-button issues such as pricing for AIDS drugs and stem cell research. Indeed, several of the authors in this volume press these hot buttons quite deliberately because they believe passionately in the moral and scientific force of their positions. Such passion and commitment are only natural and understandable given the momentous human impact of these matters. When read together, however, the various essays in this book are intended to offer a fair, balanced, and insightful consideration of the troubled relationship between the pharmaceutical industry and society. Given the divergent ends of a for-profit industry and a product with immense public health implications, there will always be some tension in the relationship between the pharmaceutical industry and society. The hope is, however, that this book can help point to a more sustainable path where these divergent interests are better aligned and the inevitable residual tensions are better managed.

THE INDUSTRY'S DETERIORATING PUBLIC IMAGE

In recent years, drug companies have operated in the glare of the global court of public opinion. The verdict has been decisively negative. It is difficult to pick up a newspaper or a magazine these days without reading about some controversial issue presenting the pharmaceutical industry in an unflattering light: ever-rising drug prices in the United States and around the world; egregious overcharging for drugs sold to public health programs such as Medicaid; never-ending vitriolic trade negotiations over intellectual property and generic drug manufacturing in third world countries; sympathetic pleas by senior citizens and others to import drugs from Canada where government controls keep prices low; concerns about the rights of patients participating in clinical trials; troubling revelations that clinical trials are sometimes selectively published in scientific journals to overstate effectiveness and efficacy; the seemingly ubiquitous emergence of consumer advertising; revelations of shockingly large-scale bribes to physicians to prescribe particular drugs; and the international debate over the role of the industry in providing AIDS drugs to third world countries.

Among observers outside the industry, the greed and moral failings of the industry approach the status of a truism. Many observers, moreover, have come to question the industry's economic vigor and innovative vitality. Consider the following passing comment in a *New York Times* article: "[The pharmaceutical industry's] profits rely almost entirely on laws that protect the industry from cheap imports, delay home-grown knockoffs, give away government medical discoveries, allow steep tax breaks for research expenditure and forbid government officials from demanding discounts while requiring them to buy certain drugs."[2] What is remarkable about this quotation is that it comes from a *news* article, not an opinion piece. Moreover, the author did not even feel the need to cite a source for his damning conclusions!

Predictably, the barrage of negative media coverage has taken its toll on public perception. According to the Harris Poll, between 1997 and 2004 the percentage of adults believing that the pharmaceutical industry was adequately serving its customers declined from 79 percent to 44 percent.[3] Less than 14 percent described pharmaceutical companies as "generally honest and trustworthy." Fifty-six percent believed that drug prices were unreasonably high and that there should be more

government regulation of the industry. Indeed, public contempt in
the United States for the pharmaceutical industry sometimes reaches
startling heights of vitriol. A 2003 Gallup Poll revealed that Americans
rate the public image of the pharmaceutical industry among the bottom five.[4] Some critics even go so far as to compare the pharmaceutical
industry with the tobacco industry.[5]

For pharmaceutical executives, their declining public image is a bitter pill. Despite the fact that the industry has developed many life-
saving and life-enhancing products over the last half-century – including so-called "miracle" drugs for treating cancer, AIDS, and heart
disease – public trust and confidence are spiraling downward. Most
pharmaceutical executives are bewildered by the public's contempt.
Typical is the view of one executive who remarked, "We find it quite
incredible that we could be equated with an industry [tobacco] that
kills people as opposed to cures them." Others, however, are realizing
that the industry needs to change quickly and radically to adapt to a
fundamentally new political and social environment. Even an industry
stalwart such as Roy Vagelos, the former CEO of Merck, has begun
to complain about the high prices of drugs and to warn about the
inevitability of government price controls.[6]

TWO CORE ISSUES IN NEED OF RESOLUTION: PROFIT VERSUS
MEDICAL NEED AND THE NEED FOR COOPERATION

Although the essays in this volume are diverse and far-ranging, two
core themes emerge in charting a sustainable path for the pharmaceutical industry. One issue that cuts through virtually all the chapters
in this book is the imperfect alignment of private profit-maximizing
objectives with public health needs. The central paradox of the public
policy debate over the pharmaceutical industry stems from the fact
that private enterprise drives creativity and innovation, while simultaneously it restricts access and distorts medical priorities. Important
life-saving and life-enhancing drugs, such as protease inhibitors for
HIV patients, are invented, but many can't afford those drugs, especially in the third world. Some conditions, such as heart disease and
hypertension, which are prevalent in developed economies, offer doctors multiple options for treatment, whereas doctors in third world
countries have few options for treating the scourge of malaria. The

airways are filled with ads for erectile dysfunction drugs that make them seem curiously akin to a recreational drug, whereas working-class families wonder how they are going to afford life-saving asthma medication for their children. The disconnect between the profitability of drug companies and the public health manifests itself in a seemingly endless array of such ironies. What are the root causes of this misalignment? How big is the gap between profits and public health? What must be done to bridge this gap? In the process, how do we balance the intellectual property rights of pharmaceutical companies with the basic human right to healthcare? These questions are addressed by numerous thoughtful and knowledgeable authors in this volume.

A second theme that emerges in these pages is the pressing need for the pharmaceutical industry to increase dialogue and cooperation with various stakeholder groups. A number of authors in this volume, including those from within the industry, emphasize that to repair their relationship with society in a sustainable manner, drug companies must learn to think of diverse groups as active partners in the process of drug development and sales. If the pharmaceutical industry is able to adapt and change in this way, it will come to see advocacy groups, the medical and scientific community, governments, NGOs, and international institutions as essential partners in developing useful drugs to solve medical problems that often have social and transnational implications. If the industry is not able to make this transition, it will continue to be vilified and find itself increasingly isolated.

Inaction is not an option for the pharmaceutical industry. The void from the absence of cooperation and partnership with stakeholder groups will be filled ineluctably by increased government regulation, including the specter the industry probably fears most – price controls. The loser in this eventuality will not be just the pharmaceutical industry, which will inevitably be less profitable. Society, too, will lose because the heavy hand of government regulation and bureaucracy, although sometimes necessary, can rarely function as efficiently and creatively as coalitions of diverse groups, including government, working together. Therein lies the moral imperative for change in the pharmaceutical industry – the hope for a future where society continues to enjoy a steady stream of drugs to improve health and wellbeing and where these fruits are broadly distributed among rich and poor, and throughout the globe.

PROFITS, PATIENTS' RIGHTS, AND SCIENTIFIC PROGRESS

The Ethics of Clinical Research Conducted in Private Enterprises

Introduction to Part I

Michael A. Santoro

INTRODUCTION

Pharmaceutical research is a complex social enterprise. It involves persons, commerce, and the advancement of medical knowledge, and it raises a broad array of ethical, scientific, and public policy issues. The chapters in this section analyze and suggest reforms in a number of these areas, including (1) the conflicts that arise between the profit maximization objectives of pharmaceutical companies and the ethical requirements of scientific research and medicine, particularly in regard to safety concerns and the diseases that are targeted; (2) the ethical safeguards for conducting research involving human subjects, particularly vulnerable subjects such as children and citizens of third world countries; (3) the patient's right to be included in drug trials that offer hope for terminal medical conditions, as well as the public health implications of including minority populations in drug trials; and (4) the scientific and ethical issues underlying stem cell research.

MEDICINE, SCIENCE, AND PROFIT MAXIMIZATION: AN UNEASY MIX

The dictates of medical and scientific ethics are sometimes at odds in clinical research, as for example in the administration of placebos to patients in control groups.[1] Such conflicts arise because physicians are trained to cure and treat patients by administering therapeutic remedies, whereas scientists seek to establish facts and advance knowledge. For the most part, however, the advancement of knowledge and the betterment of patients ultimately are complementary goals.

9

It is the interjection of profit motivation into drug research that creates the greatest ethical challenges. In a sense, these challenges are endemic to the free market system. The power of the free market is that by appealing to self-interest it unleashes powerful incentives that spur creativity and productivity. Bolstered by the added incentive of patent protection – a subject discussed in Part III of this book – the pharmaceutical industry has attracted vast sums of private investment and it has employed these funds to invent and bring to market a wide array of life-saving and useful drugs. The problem with the market, however, is that it does not perfectly correspond to human medical needs. The market responds to consumer demand, which reflects wealth and ability to pay. Human medical needs, however, exist even where consumer markets don't. Conversely, as discussed in Part II of this book, the pharmaceutical industry sometimes attempts to create consumer markets for drugs that do not optimally serve medical needs.

When one considers the disjunction between medical needs and the dictates of capitalism in a global context, the gulf between commerce and medicine grows wider. On purely medical grounds, the needs of a poor child suffering malaria in sub-Saharan Africa should have priority over a middle-aged American man suffering from hair loss. Through the prism of capitalism, however, the balding man is a valued, potential customer and the African child barely exists. The numbers tell the story. Malaria research attracts 20 cents in research dollars for each infection, whereas ailments that are prevalent in developed countries attract hundreds of dollars per case.[2] As a result of such stark economic realities, many of the world's most pressing medical needs will remain unmet without resort to nonmarket solutions.[3]

Jürgen Drews, a physician who has been the research director of a major global pharmaceutical company, is uniquely qualified to examine the interrelationships among medical ethics, scientific ethics, and the profit motive. Drews argues that in recent years an obsessive, and ultimately self-defeating, focus on the bottom line, and the increasing costs of launching a new product, have led pharmaceutical companies to devote their research efforts increasingly to so-called "me too" remedies for conditions such as high cholesterol and hypertension for which useful therapies already exist.

To address the problem of malaria and other unmet medical needs in the third world, Drews suggests a number of nonmarket solutions, including a call for collaborative intergovernmental–nongovernmental–industry partnerships. One extraordinary example of this kind of effort has been launched by the Institute for OneWorld Health, led by Dr. G. Victoria Hale and funded by the Bill and Melinda Gates Foundation. The Institute accepts industry donations of patent rights and the volunteer services of industry scientists to develop drugs that could be useful in the third world. In return, companies can gain tax breaks and garner positive public relations.[4]

How great is the gap between global medical need and market forces? Is the only way to bridge this gap through resort to nonmarket solutions and charity? Or are opportunities to do good by doing well being missed by the pharmaceutical companies? Drews, who has viewed the pharmaceutical industry from within as a scientific director and from outside as an investment banker, tantalizingly suggests that scientific research is best served by a focus on medical research rather than the bottom line. Ironically, Drews observes, it is precisely the obsession with the bottom line that has led to a slowdown in the drug pipeline that in turn has hurt the bottom line. He regards this development as a fundamental departure from an earlier "golden age" when pharmaceutical research was more closely aligned with medical need and scientific purpose. As a scientist, Drews understands that important breakthroughs often come serendipitously in laboratories when the pursuit of knowledge is undertaken for its own sake, and not as a result of the best laid financial plans of MBAs in executive suites.

Doing Good by Doing Well: The Real Lessons of Merck's Cure for River Blindness

Drews's account of scientific creativity merits further study and debate. On an anecdotal level, however, Merck's development of a drug to cure river blindness offers powerful support for his view. River blindness, *onchoceriasis*, a terrible disease resulting in unbearable itching, swollen body tissue, and ultimately blindness, affects over 80 million people in poor settlements of Africa, the Middle East, and Latin America. In the late 1970s, Dr. William C. Campbell, a scientist at Merck, approached then-CEO Roy Vagelos with a proposal to test and develop a drug for river blindness. Merck justifiably won praise for devoting substantial resources to developing the drug even without any prospect of achieving a return on investment.

As an example of moral leadership in putting medical needs before profits, the Merck river blindness story is inspiring enough. However, the lessons of this story may run deeper. Invermectin, the drug Merck developed to combat river blindness, also had potency and effectiveness against a wide variety of animal parasites. Indeed, Merck made significant profits serving this market. It was no accident that this drug compound, which turned out to have applications in both profit-making and non-profit-making markets, was developed at Merck in a period when Roy Vagelos, a medical doctor, emphasized basic research and challenged Merck scientists to think of their work as a quest to alleviate human disease and suffering worldwide.

Is there a broader lesson here? Is scientific creativity, as Drews suggests, being choked off by the micromanagement of bottom-line-obsessed corporate executives without scientific backgrounds? It is hard to say, based on this one example, where profits and dedication to medical need seem to go hand in hand. But perhaps drug companies today might do well to heed the words of George W. Merck, the company's modern day founder, who in 1950 wisely said: "We try never to forget that medicine is for the people. It is not for the profits. The profits follow, and if we have remembered that, they have never failed to appear. The better we have remembered it, the larger they have been."[5] Some might argue that this sentiment is hopelessly quixotic and naïve at the turn of the twenty-first century, when drug development costs are ever rising. Perhaps, however, pharmaceutical executives need now more than ever to be reminded that sustainable profitability will result from addressing genuine medical needs.

DRUG SAFETY: PUBLIC POLICY, ETHICAL, AND REGULATORY CONSIDERATIONS

It is remarkable to reflect in retrospect that it was not until the second half of the twentieth century, with the passage of the 1962 Kefauver-Harris Amendments to the Food, Drug and Cosmetics act of 1938 (later followed by similar legislation in Western Europe and throughout the world), that pharmaceutical firms were required to demonstrate the safety and efficacy of new drugs through scientifically valid clinical trials utilizing human subjects.[6] (Interestingly, from China there is some evidence to suggest that the success rates of analgesic and therapeutic administrations of acupuncture and moxibustion by physicians were recorded in clinical records as early as the Han dynasty in the second century.[7]) In the modern era, a watershed event in determining public policy on the length and rigor of clinical trials was the thalidomide incident in the early 1960s, when a drug widely prescribed to pregnant women was brought to market in many countries despite data linking its use to severe birth defects such as missing limbs. In the aftermath of the thalidomide tragedy, a global social and governmental consensus emerged that would allow drugs to enter the market only after safety and efficacy have been demonstrated conclusively through increasingly large and rigorous clinical trials.

In recent years it has become apparent that the struggle to ensure the safety of drugs has not yet ended. Renewed concerns about safety can be traced to 1997 with the recall of the widely used diet pill Fen-Phen after it was discovered to be linked to a fatal lung condition.[8] In 2004, drug safety was once again thrust dramatically into the public debate when concerns arose over the safety and effectiveness of antidepressants. Of particular concern was the fact that the FDA had instructed companies to withhold information about studies suggesting that antidepressants were ineffective and that the use of antidepressants was linked to suicidal tendencies, especially among children and teenagers. When news of this data suppression came to light, members of Congress, medical journal editors, and even the pharmaceutical industry itself put forth various proposals to register all drug trials before they begin and to disclose the results regardless of the outcome.[9]

In September 2004, just as the furor over antidepressants subsided somewhat with the FDA's announcement that it would require a prominent "black box" warning label about the suicidal risks of antidepressants for children, came the astounding revelation that Merck was voluntarily withdrawing Vioxx – a "blockbuster" Cox-2 pain inhibitor used by over 20 million people worldwide – from the market because of studies tying the drug to heart attack and stroke risk. At the time of the withdrawal, Merck CEO Raymond Gilmartin claimed that the study results were "unexpected" and that the company was "really putting patient safety first." Within weeks, however, the company's commitment to patient safety was called into question. *The Wall Street Journal* reported that in internal company e-mails uncovered by a plaintiff's lawyer in a lawsuit, Merck's research director had alluded to the risks internally as early as 2000. The *Journal* also reported that training materials for salespersons visiting doctors' offices to sell Vioxx bore the title "Dodge Ball Vioxx" and that each of the first twelve pages listed various "obstacles" or statements that might be made by doctors, including "I am concerned about the cardiovascular effects of Vioxx." The final four pages each contained a single word in capital letters: "DODGE!"[10]

In its defense, Merck argued that company documents had been taken out of context by plaintiff's lawyers and did not paint an accurate picture of the company's conduct, although initially, citing litigation concerns, the company declined to release exculpatory documents and explanations. Two weeks later, however, under mounting pressure, the company's counsel asserted that "DODGE!" was the name of a sales training game that had nothing to do with avoiding physician inquiries about Vioxx's safety. He also explained that the e-mail from the company's research director seemingly acknowledging heart risks represented an "initial impression" and that, based on subsequent analysis of data, the company concluded that Vioxx only appeared to cause heart problems because it was being compared with naproxen, which benefited the heart. In February 2001, however, one member of a special FDA advisory panel reported that this explanation "was not very convincing to us."[11]

In May 2005, Merck's CEO, Raymond Gilmartin resigned and the company remained mired in what promised to be a long and protracted series of Vioxx-related lawsuits. In the wake of safety concerns about antidepressants and Vioxx, however, a number of long-term public policy, regulatory, and ethical concerns have emerged.

On a public policy and regulatory level, the antidepressant and Vioxx incidents resurrect a longstanding debate about the costs and benefits of the FDA's safety and efficacy requirements. Almost from the time that the 1962 Kefauver–Harris amendments were adopted, some have argued that the FDA's enforcement of safety and efficacy regulations needlessly increase drug costs and deny patients access to life-saving drugs.[12] This is a view that needs to be taken seriously in the public discourse because, as with most government regulation, drug safety and efficacy regulation results in both costs and benefits.

The benefits of safety regulation are difficult to assess accurately. They consist mostly of the number of lives saved and the side effects avoided as a result of the maintenance of a strong drug safety review process. The benefits of efficacy regulation, though real, are even more elusive. It is impossible to measure how many patients would take ineffective remedies instead of proven remedies if given the choice. In the 1970s, many desperate cancer patients traveled to Mexico to get Laetrile treatments instead of prolonging their lives with proven cancer therapies.[13] More recently, HIV/AIDS activists who lobbied for looser FDA regulation of efficacy have in retrospect come to realize that desperation led many AIDS patients to seek out ineffective treatments instead of proven therapies that promised less.[14]

The costs of drug regulation are somewhat more straightforward to quantify than the benefits. Drugs are more expensive because of long and large clinical trials. Patients suffer and may die as they wait for drugs to be approved. When drugs are kept off the market because of efficacy or safety concerns, patients are denied any hope for treating their conditions, as for example when one company discontinued trials of a drug to treat Parkinson's disease.[15]

As a result of the technical obstacles to conducting an accurate cost-benefit analysis of drug regulation, arguments for reducing the power of the FDA are sometimes pressed as a part of a blunderbuss ideological crusade. In 1994, for example, Congressman Newt Gingrich called the FDA the "No. 1 job-killer" in America and referred to FDA commissioner David Kessler as a "thug and a bully."[16] Wiser heads in the pharmaceutical industry greeted this idealogical posturing unenthusiastically, understanding full well that the confidence of doctors and patients depends crucially on the trust the public reposes in the FDA. As the overwhelming public outrage over the antidepressant and Vioxx incidents demonstrates, when it comes to drugs there is little political support for a *laissez-faire* regulatory approach. The American public wants drugs that work *and* are affordable *and* are safe.

Not surprisingly, the FDA was criticized harshly for failing to protect the public in the Vioxx and antidepressant incidents. Reflecting on the FDA's inaction in the face of evidence linking Vioxx with heart disease,

Republican Senator Charles Grassley, was moved to ask: "Did a cozy relationship between the FDA and a pharmaceutical company allow a drug with known safety risks to stay on the market longer than it should have?"[17] Senator Grassley's question became more poignant a few weeks later when the FDA itself released an internal study concluding that Vioxx might have contributed to 27,785 heart attacks and deaths from 1999 to 2003.[18] Then in November 2004, *The Lancet*, a highly respected British medical journal, published an editorial criticizing the FDA for acting out of "ruthless, shortsighted and irresponsible self-interest" for failing to remove Vioxx from the market.[19] Later that month the *Journal of the American Medical Association* called for the creation of a board independent of the FDA to track the safety of drugs after they were approved and in widespread use.[20] Responding to these criticisms, the FDA undertook a number of reforms, including seeking the advice of the Congressionally chartered Institute of Medicine in determining how well it was assessing the side effects of drugs and setting up a system for its employees to seek internal and external appeal of agency decisions.[21]

Although there is plenty of blame to be assigned to the FDA for the Vioxx debacle, at the end of the day safety remains fundamentally an issue of business ethics and the responsibility of the company manufacturing a drug. In the case of Merck and Vioxx, one has to ask whether this once highly esteemed company had remained true to the business principles articulated by its modern founder, George W. Merck. Ultimately, it was the shareholders who paid a steep price for management's missteps. The company's stock price tumbled as it faced the prospect of billions of dollars in product liability lawsuits. If the river blindness story illustrated how pharmaceutical companies can do well by doing good, the Vioxx story demonstrates how companies will do poorly when they pay insufficient attention to the medical well-being of the public.

PATIENTS' RIGHTS AND CLINICAL RESEARCH

The bizarre and cruel Nazi experiments forcibly conducted on Jewish participants served as a motivating force for protecting the rights of patients in clinical trials. Also contributing to these concerns were the outrageous facts about the Tuskegee syphilis study, which came to light in the 1960s. For a period of over four decades, the U.S. government monitored poor, unsuspecting African American men suffering from syphilis, but denied them treatment. As Dr. Valentine Burroughs notes in his chapter, the ensuing outrage over the Tuskegee study combined with years of racism and discrimination has built mistrust and hampered clinical trial recruitment efforts among African Americans.[22]

In 1964, the World Medical Association adopted the Helsinki Declaration of Ethical Principles for Medical Research Involving Human Subjects. Four decades after the Helsinki Declaration, however, many remain wary of experimental research.[23] In recent years, as clinical trials increasingly are conducted in third world countries with vulnerable and often illiterate populations, the issue of patient rights has taken on a new urgency.

In their chapter, Juhana E. Idänpään-Heikkilä, Secretary-General of the Council for the International Organizations of Medical Sciences (CIOMS) at the World Health Organization, and Sev Fluss, Senior Advisor at CIOMS, describe the various measures in effect worldwide designed to protect the rights of clinical trial patients, particularly those designed to protect vulnerable third world populations. They analyze a number of important ethical principles developed by leading world medical and scientific bodies such as the World Medical Association, the World Health Organization, and the Council for International Organizations of Medical Sciences. These principles are designed to traverse various cultural and gender gaps that can make it difficult to assure that participants in clinical trials freely consent to participate in clinical trials and fully understand the risks and benefits of participation.

Children: The "Sentinel Canaries" in the Mine of Drug Research

The rights of patients in clinical trials sometimes require delicate balancing against the rights of patients to safe and effective drugs. For example, administering placebos to a control group in a clinical trial is often the optimal way to determine the efficacy of a new drug, but patients receiving the placebo derive no benefit from participation in the study.[24] Often, as was the case with the Thalidomide tragedy, children bear the brunt of this delicate balance, which is why

Dr. Dianne Murphy and Dr. Sara Goldkind refer to them in their chapter as the "sentinel canaries in the mine of pharmaceutical therapeutics."

Murphy and Goldkind are physicians and scientists who, as FDA officers, are entrusted with protecting the interests of children in clinical research. As they note, the history of children in medical research has gravitated between concern for their role in drug research and concern about the therapies available to them as patients. Until the very end of the twentieth century, the predominating goal was to avoid the exploitation of children in clinical trials. As a result, as Murphy and Goldkind note, the medical community lacked information about the absorption, distribution, metabolism, and elimination of drug compounds in children. Doctors used a crude and risky methodology that was based on calculating children's dosages on the basis of weight-based comparisons with adult dosages.

Murphy and Goldkind analyze the effects of two developments occurring at the turn of the century. First, the FDA Modernization Act of 1997,[25] and the Best Pharmaceuticals for Children Act of 2002,[26] contained financial incentives – in the form of patent extensions – for companies that conduct specialized clinical trials to determine whether drugs are safe and effective in children. At the same time, a collaborative effort among governments, NGOs, patient advocates, and the medical and scientific community developed a series of ethical precepts for protecting the rights of children in clinical research. Murphy and Goldkind assess the lessons learned to date as these new incentives and safeguards have been put into action.

Dr. Robert Nelson is a pediatrician and medical school professor who works on a daily basis with children in critical care settings. In his chapter, Dr. Nelson compares and contrasts various ethical precepts to protect children in research that have been promulgated throughout the world. He then considers how these provisions apply to the use of control groups administering placebos to children. Finally, he considers the lessons learned from the controversy over the disclosure of safety issues uncovered in studies of antidepressants in children. He concludes by offering his thoughts on how we can enable children to participate in clinical trials without exploiting them.

Is There a Right to Participate in Clinical Trials?

Another trend at the turn of the millennium is that a better informed public is increasingly aware of the potential value of participating in clinical trials. Public attention was first drawn to this phenomenon in the 1980s and 1990s, when AIDS patients demanded access to experimental drugs that sadly came to market too late to help many. Today, for patients with a wide array of illnesses, particularly those that are life-threatening, clinical trials offer precious hope. Many patients endure long, expensive, and heart-wrenching campaigns to be included in clinical trials from which they might be excluded for scientific, geographic, or other reasons.[27]

In her chapter, Dr. Glenna Crooks, a health policy advisor in the Reagan administration and a former Worldwide Vice President of Merck's vaccine unit, considers whether patients have a right to participate in clinical trials. She notes that, ironically, although some clinical trials have too few slots for willing participants, others are not able to recruit enough patients.[28] Crooks makes the case that to increase participation, patients must be seen as active collaborators instead of simply human subjects. She envisions a new model for the future in which patients will take on a more active role in partnership with researchers regarding all aspects of clinical trials.

As in so many aspects of our society, there is no escaping the relevance of race and ethnicity in clinical drug research. In his chapter, Dr. Valentine Burroughs, a former president of the National Medical Association, which represents African American physicians, observes that African American and some other racial and ethnic minorities participate at a disproportionately lower rate in drug trials than do nonminorities. There are numerous reasons for this disparity, according to Dr. Burroughs. One is lingering mistrust in the African American community in the wake of the Tuskegee study controversy. Language and cultural barriers also play a role, as does the fact that minorities often receive healthcare in settings that are on the periphery of the research hospitals and institutions where drug companies are likely to sponsor clinical trials.

Burroughs foresees a future where genetic research will enable doctors to provide individualized therapies that go beyond crude markers such as race and ethnicity when prescribing drugs for patients.

Nevertheless, Burroughs argues, minority access to clinical trials will remain crucial for some time, because race and ethnicity sometimes offer physicians valuable guidance in assessing the efficacy and optimal dosage of a drug for a particular patient. This was dramatically illustrated in 2004 when a combination of drugs was found to dramatically reduce heart disease in African Americans.[29] As a consequence, Dr. Burroughs argues, the participation of ethnic and racial minorities in clinical studies becomes an important factor in moving toward more equal access to healthcare, and he calls on the pharmaceutical industry to increase the resources and commitment devoted to the inclusion of minorities in clinical trials.

STEM CELL RESEARCH: THE ROLE OF SCIENCE
AND PSEUDOSCIENCE IN PUBLIC POLICY

Medical researchers value stem cells because they develop into many kinds of human tissue. As a result, they offer the hope of treating diverse conditions, such as Alzheimer's disease and spinal injuries. Controversy arises, however, because the most useful stem cells for medical research are derived from human embryos. The proposed use of stem cells left over at fertility clinics for research has thrust the stem cell debate into the political minefield of abortion policy.

In his chapter, Congressman Rush Holt, one of the very few members of Congress with a scientific background, offers a thoughtful perspective on this debate. In the process, he provides a valuable template for how novel scientific issues can be meaningfully deliberated upon by legislatures and the general public. Unfortunately, what Congressman Holt reports is not very encouraging. He cites troubling examples of how meaningful ethical debate over the use of stem cells is thwarted by the glaring inability of many members of Congress to understand scientific facts and information. The ultimate lesson is a sobering one for our educational system and for our hopes of deliberative democracy. Public debate about scientific issues is destined to remain inadequate until citizens and their representatives become much more knowledgeable about science itself.

1

Drug Research

Between Ethical Demands and Economic Constraints

Jürgen Drews

Any list of our civilization's achievements in the past would have to include the advances made in medicine. Within the field of medicine, drugs have always played a key role, either directly in the treatment of diseases or indirectly by creating the conditions under which other forms of treatment could be applied. Drug research has been a particularly successful field of activity. However highly it may be regarded in general, this does not mean that there are no grounds for criticism. Some critical questions relating to the code of ethics of drug research will be discussed below.

MEDICAL AND SCIENTIFIC ETHICS

The intellectual and ethical mindsets that have shaped the direction taken by drug research are motivated in two contrasting, yet related, ways: the first one is directed at curing diseases or at least alleviating their symptoms; the second one is scientific in nature and aims at the reliability and reproducibility of the process by which drugs are discovered and developed.

Drug therapy, and hence also drug research, are perceived as part and parcel of the medical – or more specifically of the doctor's – vocation. The declared goal of all drug research has always been to satisfy therapeutic needs. This goal goes hand in hand with the need for effective and safe drugs and for the careful assessment of the risk/benefit relationship in the therapeutic use of drugs, particularly when the relevant side effects of the drugs in question are known. In the majority of industrialized countries these requirements are

safeguarded by detailed drug licensing provisions.[1] There are simple
professional rules for estimating the risk/benefit ratio. They require an
understanding of the risks associated with the condition to be treated,
a realistic assessment of other available therapeutic approaches, and
knowledge of the risks entailed in the proposed treatment. For
instance, prolonged pathologically high blood pressure is associated
with increased cardiovascular morbidity and mortality, however well
the patient may feel. Both the complications of this disease and their
life-shortening effects may be largely prevented by appropriate drug
treatment. Compared with its proven effectiveness, the risks entailed
by the treatment are generally so low as to be virtually negligible.

The situation is quite different in a patient with metastatic cancer
who, whatever happens, is going to die in a few months and must decide
whether a limited prolongation of life is worth the price of severe side
effects and a reduction in his or her quality of life. The principle that
patients should always receive the most effective therapy available
must be weighed against the personal situation of the patient. On the
one hand, the physician must be aware of the therapeutic possibilities
as they have evolved over time; on the other hand, he or she has to
understand his or her patients' individual needs. His or her actions
must reflect the optimal balance between these two perspectives.

Just as the Hippocratic oath enjoins physicians not to allow any
social differences – for example, political, economic, or class distinctions – to come between them and their patients, drug researchers,
too, are under a fundamental obligation to set their thematic priorities
according to the criteria of existing therapeutic needs and medical and
technical feasibility, leaving nonmedical and nonscientific considerations aside. Later we shall see that these principles are easily forgotten
when economic pressures are brought to bear. All goals that focus on
the safety and efficacy of drugs and their use in line with patients' needs
are rooted in – or at least related to – Hippocratic ethics, whether they
are expressed as laws and regulations or just present in the awareness
and skill of the medical practitioner.[2]

This approach contrasts with requirements inherent in the natural
sciences, that is, chemistry, physiology, pharmacology, and other disciplines, which are essential for drug research. Patients and doctors
expect modern drugs to obey strictly defined criteria of quality and
purity. Likewise, they expect that the discovery and development of

drugs follow established scientific standards. These requirements all focus on criteria of scientific accuracy and integrity that are not primarily treatment-related. They serve the need for objectivity and reproducibility of any intellectual or experimental procedures employed in the discovery and development of new drugs. These scientific criteria also include the complete and truthful disclosure of all data and observations, and the expectation that such data have been interpreted critically, within both the context of the problem investigated and the limits of the methods used (in a clinical trial, for instance). It is expected that the entire process of discovery and development will be described in scientific publications or patents with such openness that it can be understood and, if necessary, reproduced by a scientifically trained reader.[3]

Thus, like other therapeutically oriented types of research, drug research is driven by two distinct ethical approaches. The first is "non-scientific" and medical and sets out to maintain or restore human health and wellbeing. The second approach has to ensure the scientific correctness and reproducibility of experimental results and observations as well as the validity of conclusions drawn from such evidence.

The two ethical approaches are mutually complementary and, in large part, compatible. The symbiosis of the medical and scientific ethical frameworks is particularly apparent in the methodology of clinical research, where rigorous proof of the efficacy of a drug – often only possible in double-blind trials – has to be reconciled with the trial subject's right to the best possible treatment and to respect for his or her physical integrity. This is relatively simple if effective and well-tolerated medicines are already available for a specific disease, such as high blood pressure. In such cases, a new therapeutic approach claiming to offer advantages over known forms of treatment is compared with standard treatment. There is a good chance in such studies that all patients will be given effective treatment. What is more, the disease has been thoroughly investigated, and refractory cases are easily recognized and, if they become a problem, effectively treated.

In many situations, notably in diseases that are serious but not necessarily fatal per se and for which effective treatment already exists, the demands of medical ethics on the one hand and of scientific ethics on the other can easily be reconciled. In other cases, however, medical and scientific interests do conflict. Sometimes such conflicts can be to the disadvantage of patients. Examples can be found among certain diseases with a high percentage of fatal outcomes for which there is no broadly accepted mode of treatment. As an illustration, let us look at a double-blind, placebo-controlled trial in septic shock due to gram-negative bacteria. Despite intensive support measures, this condition is fatal in about 40 percent of patients.[4,5] The new drugs – for instance, a monoclonal antibody against tumor necrosis factor (TNFα) – would initially be used in a double-blind trial because the findings of pharmacological and animal studies suggest that it might reduce mortality in humans. If it is accepted that studies in animal models are of predictive value for the efficacy of a new treatment in human disease, the patients receiving the inactive control substance could be at a disadvantage compared with those receiving the active drug. About half of them would die as a result of the acute condition, while those treated with the new drug would at least have a chance to do better.

Medical ethics in this case would require that all patients be treated with a drug of proven tolerability that could reasonably be expected to have a curative effect. Because there is no such drug, the sponsors of this study would have to use historical controls. From the viewpoint of scientific ethics, however, the therapeutic value of a new drug has to be proven beyond any reasonable doubt before the drug can be used on a large scale. Clinical trials are, after all, conducted because doubt exists, and they can be justified only if they are structured in a way that will bring more clarity to an open therapeutic question. In the present case, therefore, different dosages of the active drug and placebo would be administered until analysis of the data revealed that one or more dosages of the test medication had the desired therapeutic effect. At this point, the placebo arm of the trial would be transformed into a treatment arm. This switch could not occur, however, before the differences between the various trial groups had reached levels of statistical significance, or in plain language, when more placebo-treated patients had died than those belonging to the treatment groups. In such cases we act on the premise that proof of the therapeutic effect of a new drug is of such fundamental importance that possible disadvantages for the individual patient have to be accepted.

The medically driven goal of helping and, if possible, curing patients and the scientifically driven goal of objectively determining the therapeutic value of certain treatment procedures come into conflict again and again, not only in individual cases such as those described above, but also on broader fronts.

There are cases in which the satisfaction of therapeutic needs is felt to be such an overriding imperative that – at the request of the patients concerned and with the support of the drug licensing authorities – scientific criteria are deliberately allowed to take a back seat or are even sacrificed in assessments of new drugs. An example of such conflicting goals is to be found in the use of nonapproved drugs against AIDS in so-called "expanded access" or "compassionate use" programs. In these treatment programs, drugs whose toxicological profile on the one hand and clinical efficacy on the other had not been fully studied were nevertheless made available to certain groups of patients suffering from advanced disease. (See Chapter 17, by Martin Delaney, for a more detailed discussion of AIDS drug development and treatment.) However justifiable the use of a test medication might seem under these circumstances, it is still possible that some patients were harmed in such "last resort treatments" and thereby had their lifespans shortened. In theory, at least, such patients could have been denied the chance to benefit from subsequent therapeutic advances.[6]

On the other hand, if formal scientific criteria are overemphasized, important drugs whose value already has been demonstrated may be launched only after a long delay or even not launched at all. There was a time when bureaucratic and defensive attitudes at the FDA delayed the introduction of important new drugs in the United States that had long been introduced in Europe. At the time, the FDA argued that certain formal safety and efficacy criteria had not yet been satisfied. Between 1977 and 1987, new drugs were launched on average 1.9 years earlier in the United Kingdom than in the United States. For certain therapeutic categories the difference was even greater, for example, five years for drugs to treat diseases of the airways, over three years for drugs to treat cardiovascular indications and diseases of the central nervous system, and almost three years for cytostatic agents. The assumption that such delays were offset by enhanced drug safety could never be verified. The figures for drug recalls in the two countries over an eleven-year investigation period were comparable. A total of thirteen drugs were recalled – eight in the United Kingdom and five in the United States. The slightly greater number of recalls in the United Kingdom was due to the fact that most of the drugs concerned were nonsteroidal anti-inflammatory compounds, a category of drugs launched in far greater numbers in the United Kingdom than in the United States during this period (nineteen introductions compared with eleven).[7]

ETHICAL GOALS AND ECONOMIC PRESSURES IN DRUG RESEARCH

Economic pressures constitute a considerable threat to drug research and, specifically, to its original therapeutic objectives. The growth of drug research in the industrial domain is as much the result of historical development as of functional necessity. The pharmaceutical industry was a product either of diversification in the dyestuffs sector or of the efforts of a small number of pharmacies toward the end of the nineteenth century to provide drugs of standardized form and consistently high quality. The diversification of the dyestuffs producers into pharmaceutical companies followed the advances made in chemotherapy, a field that owed its conceptual and experimental origins to the selective staining of host tissue and parasites with dyestuffs. This was the starting point for new therapeutic concepts that led to the identification and the development of many antiparasitic, antimicrobial, antiviral, and oncological medicines.[8] Technically, the "industrialization" of the pharmacies was initially driven by analytical and pharmaceutical methods. Whatever its roots, drug research – naturally – borrowed a large number of techniques from other disciplines. Chemistry, physics, pharmacology, biochemistry, and – later on – microbiology, molecular biology, toxicology, and clinical medicine became essential ingredients of successful drug research. The "innate" interdisciplinarity of drug research, the concentration of so many and such varied methods all focusing on one goal, virtually predestined its development in an industrial setting – and also made conflicts inevitable.

Unlike the practitioner or hospital physician or the scientist employed in a noncommercial organization, physicians or scientists in industry have a foot in two camps. They are members of the medical or scientific profession that formed them. Therefore, they continue to be bound by medical and scientific ethics. At the same time, however, they belong to industrial companies and have committed themselves to corporate goals, of which profitability is usually the most central. They must pay attention to three different codes of ethics: a medical one, a scientific one, and a corporate one. These obligations are not incompatible *a priori*. They may, however, conflict with each other in serious ways.

Up until the 1960s, drug manufacturers' research activities were largely shaped by scientific interests, by the success of the individual scientists involved, and by those therapeutic needs that were felt to be essential. With respect to the commercial exploitation of the research they were funding, the orientation of research-based pharmaceutical companies was opportunistic rather than strategic. For instance, the discovery and development of Prontosil® at Bayer was the result of a personal interest on the part of Gerhard Domagk and his colleagues rather than the outcome of a corporate strategy. The same can be said of many other drugs or classes of drugs. Penicillin, the early psychotropics, many antiparasitic agents, the benzodiazepines, calcium antagonists, beta blockers, ACE inhibitors, and HMG CoA reductase inhibitors, to name but a few, all owe their existence to the dynamics of science and to the personal interests of researchers within and outside of pharmaceutical companies. In many cases, it was the personal interest of one or a few scientists and/or clinicians that led to sudden, and often unexpected, insights and discoveries.[9,10] Surprise breakthroughs of this kind then generated developmental activities and, ultimately, commercial success.

Even though drug research is embedded in profit-oriented and profit-dependent companies, the development of drug treatment was driven primarily by scientific and medical impulses and not, or only secondarily, by strategic considerations, such as the targeting of specific markets. The coexistence of medically oriented motivation and intrinsic scientific interest, on the one hand, and economic exploitation, on the other, functioned efficiently as long as the cost of drug research remained within limits and therapeutic needs could be translated spontaneously and without delay into functioning markets.

In the early 1960s, however, all this changed. The cost of drug research and development spiralled dramatically. Whereas the development of a new substance cost 20 million dollars at the beginning of the 1960s, by the mid-1970s this sum had doubled and by the mid-1980s it had doubled again. In the mid-1990s, the much-cited average cost of identifying and developing a new drug was 231 million U.S. dollars.[11] Toward the end of the 1990s, this figure had grown to approximately

500 million dollars and as of today it has risen to 802 million dollars.[12] This development was accompanied by political upheavals, which isolated large parts of the world's population in economic and medical terms.

For a long time, tropical diseases were the most drastic case in point. In our days, the AIDS epidemics in Africa and more recently in Asia seem to have reached an even more frightening dimension.[13]

Though millions or even hundreds of millions of people suffer from malaria and other tropical diseases such as filariasis or schistosomiasis, there is no effective market mechanism by which their therapeutic needs can be satisfied. And even in areas in which effective drugs are available and functioning market segments exist, the resulting economic incentives and prospects for the research-based pharmaceutical companies are so limited that the large majority of companies have withdrawn from these areas in order to concentrate on lines of research that hold promise of greater commercial success.

The financial dimension in question shall be illustrated by an example: let us assume that the discovery and the development of a new antiparasitic drug would cost "only" 500 million dollars. At a relatively modest annual interest rate of 5 percent, this investment would have increased to 812 million in ten years, the minimal time period required for the discovery and development of a new drug. In order to recoup the costs for this drug, which would also have to be manufactured, registered, and distributed, the new drug would have to generate sales of at least 3.3 billion dollars. If a profit of 10 to 15 percent for the manufacturer is added (a reasonable sum in view of the risks involved), total sales of 4 to 4.3 billion U.S. dollars would have to be achieved during a product life of about twenty years to make the investment worthwhile. In practice, these figures mean that a drug has to achieve average sales of several hundred million dollars per year over its life span if it is to be economically viable. Understandably keen to achieve such returns on investments with as many drugs as possible, many companies prefer to address therapeutic needs of large numbers of people in financially strong countries. Relevant indications include cardiovascular diseases, certain cancers, mental disorders such as depression or schizophrenia, chronic inflammatory conditions or autoimmune diseases, infections, and several neurological diseases such as senile dementia and stroke. Many serious conditions such as rare metabolic diseases, hemoglobinopathies, cystic fibrosis, and other hereditary diseases do not satisfy these requirements and are, therefore, not specifically targeted in pharmaceutical research. And because of the long time and high costs involved in confirming the efficacy of new drugs, even chronic diseases such as multiple sclerosis or pulmonary fibrosis are not given the attention that their seriousness and the existence of theoretically feasible approaches to novel treatments would justify.

Exploratory research does not, in fact, take place within therapeutic categories but is conducted on a mechanistic and methodological basis. An intensive and multifaceted concentration on immunopharmacological questions with a view, for instance, to developing new treatment options for rheumatoid arthritis could quite conceivably result in effective agents for the treatment of some of the less common autoimmune diseases. Because of the economic pressures to which many companies are exposed, however, there is a danger that such drugs will not be developed. What we have here is an obvious conflict of goals between medical or Hippocratic ethics, on the one hand, and corporate interests, which focus on shareholder value, on the other. Medical ethics would require following scientific opportunity in addressing various medical indications. By contrast, corporate ethics call for maximizing profits without regard for special groups of patients who are in need. In fact, industrial research has been influenced by economic expectations to an extent, which is counterproductive. It is understandable that for the manager of a pharmaceutical company, diseases are not and never can be "equal."

For decision-making in the pharmaceutical industry, broad fields of medical indications that are endemic in the industrialized world will carry greater weight than diseases of the developing countries. It is a mistake, however, to let economic desirability have much influence on drug research. There is no scientifically sound way to find drugs that will generate big sales. To work on a single mechanism such as the inhibition of hydroxymethylglutarate CoA reductase because that mechanism has been shown to be operative in lowering blood cholesterol will most likely not lead to the generation of a *novel* drug, let alone a "blockbuster."[14] Like other scientific disciplines, pharmaceutical science unfolds in ways that are not predictable. Great successes will only come to those who are not afraid of uncertainty. The attempt to make drug research more successful by telling the research scientists what kind of results would be desirable from a marketing perspective reflects a fundamental misunderstanding of the scientific process – so fundamental indeed that one could speak of a transgression against scientific ethics. Obviously, such violation of the laws of science is doomed to failure. It therefore does not even serve the demands of corporate ethics.

The tendency of the pharmaceutical industry to concentrate on popular indications and traditional mechanisms has greatly intensified competition within these fields. By generating large clusters of drugs that cannot be differentiated on medical grounds, while neglecting mechanisms and indications that are seen as less likely to result in profitable drugs, the pharmaceutical industry has contributed to the "innovation deficit" that is threatening its economic wellbeing. The violation of scientific ethics does not serve the industry. It also does not help in bringing about an appreciable reduction in drug prices.

Government-imposed price restrictions, negative or positive lists, or cost-cutting programs of the type included in some healthcare legislation are not a solution to the problem, either. If anything, such measures tend to encourage industry to cut back on research activities and to develop alternative strategies that are not dependent on research, for instance, the manufacture of generics or entry into the over-the-counter (OTC) sector. But these strategies further diminish the potential for innovation, the scope for discovering new substances, and, in general, the therapeutic progress that results from the development of new drugs.

Above all, we need broad-based incentives to stimulate innovation and, specifically, to extend innovative activities to previously neglected fields. There is no lack of instruments for achieving these goals: they reach from price premiums for innovative products to tax relief for selected industrial programs and to the establishment of non-patent-related exclusive rights to the exploitation of "orphan" drugs. All these instruments are well represented in the United States's "Orphan Drug Law" and in parallel legislation that finally was accepted in the European Union in 1999. These laws contain specific incentives for the implementation of research and development programs that advance the treatment of rare diseases. The term "rare" is applied in the U.S. law to diseases affecting fewer than 200,000 persons. Given a population of about 300 million, this number represents a prevalence of less than one per thousand.[15,16]

ESTABLISHING A FOUNDATION FOR TROPICAL DISEASES?

The economic pressures to which the pharmaceutical industry is subjected mean that large segments of the world's population do not receive adequate healthcare with innovative medicines. This has applied to tropical diseases, for instance, malaria, leishmaniasis, schistosomiasis, filariasis, and trypanosomiasis, and – more recently – to AIDS. Hundreds of millions of people suffer from, or are threatened by, these conditions. In the mid-1990s, a proposal was made and discussed within the pharmaceutical industry to address this problem. It was suggested that a foundation be established for the study and treatment of tropical diseases, which would be founded in equal parts by the state or a group of states such as the European Union and by pharmaceutical companies. The annual contributions of the participating companies were suggested to be in the range of 1 or 2 million dollars per company. Thus, instead of conducting rudimentary research of their own in these fields, the member companies would be supporting an institute the explicit purpose of which would be to apply state-of-the-art knowledge of the epidemiology, immunology, and molecular biology of tropical diseases to the search for new medicines or vaccines for treating these diseases or protecting against them. Any promising substance emerging from such studies could be developed either by one of the participating companies or by WHO on its own or in collaboration with a member company.

The potential value of such an institute, which would combine under one roof all the disciplines necessary to contribute to the discovery and development of new treatment methods, would be considerable. With a starting annual budget of 20 to 30 million dollars it could have made important contributions and had a crucial influence on the prevention or treatment of tropical diseases. Annual contributions from ten to twenty major companies toward operating costs, together with the interest generated by an endowment capital of, say, 50 to 100 million dollars, were expected to provide sufficient funding for the operation of this research facility. Besides its humanitarian mission, the foundation would have filled an important scientific gap: institutes or even departments investigating these diseases on a broad methodological basis hardly exist either in Europe or in the United States. This is regrettable, given that the pathophysiology of tropical diseases, in particular its molecular and immunological aspects, is of great scientific importance. Moreover, an institute of this kind could have been a unique model of international collaboration to achieve therapeutic goals.

Unfortunately, the proposal to establish such an institute was eventually not accepted by the international companies, which were at the time participants in the so-called Dolder-Club Meetings. Although many individuals from single firms voiced their sympathy for the proposal, it did not find broad support.

What were the reasons for the refusal of the industry to embark on this course? Some companies insisted that they had programs in tropical diseases on their own, which they wanted to pursue individually in the usual competitive fashion. Others did not want to commit themselves to a project that would have political and societal ramifications they did not fully understand. Some shied away from the financial commitment that such a project would have entailed – even if it had been a modest one.

In retrospect, it appears that the main reason for the failure to establish an institute for tropical diseases within the industry resided in the fact that the pharmaceutical industry had not learnt to reconcile its individualistic profit-seeking culture with broader visions of common societal and political responsibility. This deficit persists to this very day. In the author's view, it corresponds deeply with the ethical dilemma addressed earlier: how can drug companies reconcile their dual membership in the medical and business worlds? Unfortunately, pharmaceutical companies tend more and more to act entirely as businesses, not as institutions whose commercial success depends on the successful completion of a medical mission.

In spite of this general picture, we should not see the industry as a monolithic block. There are companies, especially within the biotech sector but also among mid-sized companies with a more classical pharmaceutical profile, that would be interested in dedicating some of their intellectual and experimental resources to research into tuberculosis, AIDS, or malaria if they had partners to share with them the financial risks of such endeavors. These partners could be funds such as The Global Fund to fight AIDS, Tuberculosis and Malaria[17] or the

Bill and Melinda Gates Foundation.[18] The former entity represents a partnership between governments, civil society, the private sector, and affected communities. It sees itself as an innovative approach to international health financing. Since 2001, this fund has committed 3 billion U.S. dollars in 128 countries to support healthcare interventions against all three of these diseases. The fund works solely as a financial instrument and not as an organization of implementation. It must therefore find implementing organizations and program coordinators in the countries that are being targeted for certain medical interventions. The work of the fund is largely centered around disease prevention and to making "state of the art" therapeutics available to underprivileged populations.

Parts of the private sector have supported the fund's activity. Pharmaceutical companies such as Merck or Johnson & Johnson have made financial contributions. The Bill and Melinda Gates Foundation not only has provided donations to this fund in a major way, but also has set up a program of its own to fight tuberculosis, malaria, and AIDS. With an endowment of about 27 billion U.S. dollars, this foundation could play more than a charitable role in the fight against AIDS and tuberculosis. It could assume a commanding strategic position in dealing with diseases of the developing world. Although the thrust of the foundation has been community-centered – disease prevention, medical and epidemiological aspects, and healthcare for infected patients appear to be preferred areas of activity – it does also support some drug-related programs. More importantly, a foundation of such potential could finance original and promising drug or vaccine development programs in companies that are willing to make their products available to developing countries on a broad scale, once registration has been achieved. One could even go so far as to suggest that for sustained success in terms of disease prevention and containment, organizations such as the Bill and Melinda Gates Foundation must pay particular attention to the generation of novel drugs and vaccines against AIDS, tuberculosis, and malaria.

COLLABORATION WITHIN THE INDUSTRY ON AIDS MEDICINES

The founding of a research facility such as the one described above may appear utopian even at the present time. We should, however, not forget that limited cooperation between competing companies can function very well. In 1993, fifteen of the world's biggest drug manufacturers announced their intention of founding an international consortium in the field of AIDS research.[19] The idea behind this cooperative venture was very simple: like the chemotherapy of tumors, the treatment of AIDS depends on the combined use of several drugs. Therefore, the companies decided to exchange developmental drugs and data relating to these drugs as soon as proof of clinical efficacy had become available. It was expected that the exchange of such substances would help define useful drug combinations at the earliest possible stage of their development. Normally, such work is not done before at least one of the two drugs in a combination has been officially approved. It was, therefore, a rather bold step when a committee of specialists from the participating companies decided which of the substances produced by each individual research department were particularly suitable for use in combined therapy and which projects should be given priority. The member companies agreed that such decisions must be based primarily on clinical, scientific, and technical criteria rather than on financial considerations. At first, this may not appear as a momentous advance – it was, after all, no more than an exchange of data and substances at an early phase of clinical development. For the industry, however, such collaboration represented a fundamental departure from the rules of scientific and commercial competition.

The member companies entered into the agreement fully aware that it would set limits to the pursuit of their own interests. If, for instance, the consortium decided that a combination of company A's proteinase inhibitor with company B's reverse transcriptase inhibitor made better sense and held out better prospects than a combination with a similar substance produced by company A, it meant that the consortium was placing a higher value on the rapid, efficient development of a combined therapy regimen than on the interest of the individual companies in deriving maximum benefit from their own particular strengths.

Given the economic pressures constantly weighing on an industry that must aim to be profitable, greater "drug justice" can be obtained in only two ways. The first is that industry and government can work together on a case-by-case basis. They can try to find the best possible solution for a particular problem relating to the availability of effective drugs in a way that is acceptable for society as a whole but does not unfairly limit the industry's freedom to operate. Possibly, organizations like the Bill and Melinda Gates Foundation could function in such collaborations as financial facilitators as well as mental catalysts. Such solutions may not always be ideal but they are preferable to situations of the second type, in which government assumes total responsibility for pharmaceutical research and drug supply in certain critical areas, such as AIDS or tropical diseases. In the present economic climate, the first option would need the initiative or at least the support of the respective governments. Yet, as the example of an institute for tropical diseases shows, the influence of the state need not necessarily dominate the cooperative venture – management, research, and development may safely be left to the industry partners. Government bodies would catalyze the entry of several companies into such cooperative agreements and ensure conditions conducive to innovative work. They could then limit their involvement to certain supervisory functions. Initiative, imagination, and a cooperative spirit would be prerequisites besides, of course, a willingness on both sides, industry and government, to abandon the confrontational style that has at times characterized their relationship. The pharmaceutical industry possesses a unique range of instruments for discovering, developing, and marketing new drugs. The state could make proper and wise use of these instruments to create new therapeutic agents for rare conditions or for diseases affecting disadvantaged sectors of the population. Again, foundations or charitable funds could be helpful in reaching this goal.

One alternative to this cooperative model is complete state responsibility for specific sectors of drug research. Past experience of such state-directed endeavor does not, however, suggest that a model of this kind would work. The state-owned drug industries of the former Eastern bloc countries, for instance, were unsuccessful in all fields in which they were active. No doubt the industries of Hungary, former Czechoslovakia, or, for that matter, the former German Democratic Republic can look back upon a scientific tradition, and these nations do indeed possess notable professional skills. But not a single original drug emerged from these countries in a period of forty years. State enterprises in the industrialized countries of the West may not be comparable with the nationalized industries of the former Eastern bloc. Nevertheless, a model for partnership between state and industry combining free market principles and a sense of social responsibility offers better prospects for the future.

The process, which leads to the generation of new – and hopefully novel – drugs is extremely complex. A multitude of perspectives, medical, scientific, legal, and economic in nature, must be brought together in order to succeed in drug research and development. Each of these perspectives is governed by separate sets of ethical principles and rules.

Primarily, drug research and development are dominated by medical and scientific ethics. Although the two complement each other most of the time, there are situations in which they conflict. Medical, that is, Hippocratic ethics should have priority in these cases. But we must understand that scientific ethics may operate in the interest of the general patient population, whereas Hippocratic ethics always relate to the one human being who needs medical help. Reconciling medical and scientific ethics may, therefore, be a balancing act between the interests of the many and the needs of the few.

The innate interdisciplinary aspect of drug research requires an industrial setting. Inevitably, this fact leads to another conflict. Medical and scientific rules and values conflict with economic necessities. In order to solve these conflicts constructively, the drug industry must remind itself of its Hippocratic origins, which dictate that the wellbeing of patients has to come first and must rank even higher than the wellbeing of the staff and the shareholders of a company. Fortunately, the two coincide more often than not. Conversely, governments and the public at large must understand that companies are commercial entities. They must be profitable in order to survive and to grow. Difficult problems such as dealing with orphan diseases or with diseases of economically poor populations in developing countries, AIDS, tuberculosis, and malaria prominent among them, must therefore be solved within broader alliances that include governments, academic research institutions, afflicted communities, the drug industry, and foundations or charitable funds that are willing and able to provide financial support and, in some cases, to serve as intellectual facilitators.

2

Emerging International Norms for Clinical Testing

Good Clinical Trial Practice

Juhana E. Idänpään-Heikkilä and Sev Fluss

Advances in medicine depend on innovative and bold clinical research. Much of the progress we have seen in the effectiveness and safety of disease treatment, diagnosis, and prevention is the result of intensive research involving human subjects. The pharmaceutical industry has a leading role as a sponsor of clinical research and clinical trials aimed at development of new therapies. There is a consensus that clinical research conducted anywhere in the world should be ethically acceptable as well as scientifically sound.

A number of national, regional, interregional, and international ethical documents and norms have been developed during the last five to six years to guide investigators, ethical committees, the pharmaceutical industry, and other sponsors in the ethical conduct of clinical trials. Some of these documents, such as the World Medical Association's Declaration of Helsinki,[1] the World Health Organization's Guidelines for Good Clinical Practice (GCP) for Trials on Pharmaceutical Products,[2] and the International Ethical Guidelines for Biomedical Research Involving Human Subjects developed by the Council for International Organizations of Medical Sciences (CIOMS),[3] are sets of ethical principles and recommendations, but may become norms if they are included in national regulations and legislation. Others, such as the GCP Guideline of the International Conference on Harmonisation of Technical Requirements for Registration of Pharmaceuticals for Human Use (ICH)[4] and the EU (European Union) Directive on Clinical Trials,[5] are binding because they have been or will be implemented through national legislation. In fact, the EU Directive is legally binding for investigators and sponsors of clinical trials in the twenty-five

EU member states as of May 2004.[6] This article will review the current international ethical documents for clinical testing and clinical trials and consider how they guide the drug development research of the pharmaceutical industry.

WHY CLINICAL TRIALS ON NEW PHARMACEUTICAL PRODUCTS?

A pharmaceutical product can be authorized for marketing only if there is reliable and substantive documentation of its efficacy and safety. This principle has been agreed upon among drug regulatory authorities worldwide.[7] Comparative pharmacokinetic (bioavailability) studies in healthy volunteers or patients are normally required to document bioequivalence and to assure interchangeability of generic pharmaceutical products.[8]

Moreover, many pharmaceutical companies study new indications for use of their marketed products or develop new dosage forms or products for new administration routes. Public health systems and health insurance institutions are increasingly interested in cost-effectiveness and benefit-risk evaluations of long-term therapies and disease prevention, which require large, multicenter clinical trials. Fixed-dose combination products, containing two to four active ingredients, have become popular in the treatment of hypertension, malaria, tuberculosis, and HIV/AIDS and their development requires clinical trials. Although the pharmaceutical industry invests mainly in the development of innovative new pharmaceutical substances and products, an increasing number of research-based pharmaceutical companies have also developed and marketed generic products as a sideline.

EVOLUTION OF ETHICAL GUIDANCE AND NORMS
IN CLINICAL RESEARCH

Table 2.1 lists some major international ethical documents that guide the conduct of clinical trials. The Nuremberg Code of 1947 introduced, for the first time, the concept of informed consent. The Code, which consists of a series of ten principles, was applied in the final judgement in the Doctors' Trial (also known as "the Medical Case") held at Nuremberg, Germany, before a U.S. military tribunal in 1946–7. As a

Table 2.1. *Evolution of Essential International Documents that Guide the Ethical Conduct of Clinical Trials*

1947	The Nuremberg Code
1964	The World Medical Association's Declaration of Helsinki (the latest 2004 version available at www.wma.net)
1966	The United Nations International Covenant on Civil and Political Rights
1982	CIOMS: Proposed International Ethical Guidelines for Biomedical Research Involving Human Subjects
1991	CIOMS: International Guidelines for Ethical Review of Epidemiological Studies (available at www.cioms.ch)
1995	WHO: Guidelines for Good Clinical Practice (GCP) for Trials on Pharmaceutical Products (available at www.who.int/medicines)
1997	International Conference on Harmonisation of Technical Requirements for Registration of Pharmaceuticals for Human Use (ICH): Guideline for Good Clinical Practice (available at www.ich.org)
2000	Joint United Nations Programme on HIV/AIDS (UNAIDS): Ethical Considerations in HIV Preventive Vaccine Research (available at www.unaids.org/publications)
2001	The European Parliament and the Council: Directive 2001/20/EC (Directive on clinical trials) (available at www.europa.eu.int/eur-lex)
2002	CIOMS: International Ethical Guidelines for Biomedical Research Involving Human Subjects, Geneva, 2002 (available at www.cioms.ch)
2004	The Council of Europe: Protocol concerning Biomedical Research, Additional Protocol to the Council's 1997 Convention on Human Rights and Biomedicine (available at www.coe.int)

result seven physicians received the death sentence and nine received prison sentences because of unethical human experiments conducted in the concentration camps.[9]

The World Medical Association's Declaration of Helsinki in 1964 introduced, for the first time, ethical principles for physicians in the conduct of human research. The Declaration was revised in 1975, 1983, 1989, 1996, and 2000. The version of the Declaration of Helsinki that was adopted in October 2000 was further supplemented in 2002 and 2004 with "Notes of Clarification" designed further to protect research subjects from risk.[10]

The United Nations International Covenant on Civil and Political Rights in 1966 recognized, at the international level, the concept of free informed consent, as its Article 7 states that "no one shall be subjected without his free consent to medical or scientific experimentation." This UN document also gave legal and moral force to the Universal Declaration of Human Rights adopted by the United Nations General Assembly in 1948.[11]

CIOMS issued its Proposed International Ethical Guidelines for Biomedical Research Involving Human Subjects in 1982. A revised, updated version of the Guidelines was published in 1993, and in 1999 CIOMS again initiated a process for the revision of the Guidelines to deal with new emerging issues in medical research, such as those raised by HIV/AIDS.[12]

The revision process, which lasted some three years, involved hundreds of institutions and experts in research ethics worldwide and comprised consultative meetings, conferences, and the compilation of comments on draft versions placed on the CIOMS Web site.[13] As a result, the CIOMS Guidelines published in October 2002 include extensive guidance on the ethical conduct of human research and provide interpretations and practical solutions for implementation of the WMA Declaration of Helsinki.[14]

In 1995, WHO published Good Clinical Practice Guidelines (GCP) for Trials on Pharmaceutical Products[15] to set globally applicable standards for biomedical research. The International Conference on Harmonisation of Technical Requirements for Registration of Pharmaceuticals for Human Use (ICH) published, in 1996, a Guideline on Good Clinical Practice[16] for adoption by the drug regulatory authorities of the European Union countries, Japan, and the United States and for implementation by pharmaceutical companies and investigators. In an effort to elucidate and address ethical concerns related to HIV vaccine development activities, in 2000 the Joint United Nations Programme on HIV/AIDS (UNAIDS) published a Guidance Document entitled "Ethical Considerations in HIV Preventive Vaccine Research."[17]

In April 2001, the Council of Ministers of the European Union adopted a directive on clinical trials that is binding upon the twenty-five member states.[18] Finally, the Council of Europe, with forty-six member states, has adopted a Protocol concerning Biomedical Research, which is an Additional Protocol to the Council's 1997 Convention on Human Rights and Biomedicine.[19] The document will become legally binding in a member state once it ratifies the Convention. One more global document, a "Preliminary Draft Declaration on Universal Norms on Bioethics," has been prepared by the International Bioethics Committee of UNESCO. At the time of this writing, it is the subject of intergovernmental consultations. Provisions on the ethical aspects of research involving human subjects are included in the current draft.[20]

GENERAL ETHICAL GUIDANCE FOR CLINICAL RESEARCH

All international guiding principles for ethical conduct of clinical trials are in agreement that any clinical study involving human subjects must be scientifically sound and justified and ethically acceptable.[21] The CIOMS Guidelines (Guideline 1) outlines these prerequisites as follows:

The ethical justification of biomedical research involving human subjects is the prospect of discovering new ways of benefiting people's health. Such research can be ethically justifiable only if it is carried out in ways that respect and protect, and are fair to, the subjects of that research and are morally acceptable within the communities in which the research is carried out. Moreover, because scientifically invalid research is unethical in that it exposes research subjects to risks without possible benefit, investigators and sponsors must ensure that proposed studies involving human subjects conform to generally accepted scientific principles and are based on adequate knowledge of the pertinent scientific literature.[22]

Based on this and with reference to Paragraph 10 of the Declaration of Helsinki,[23] it is the primary duty of the investigator in medical research to protect the life, health, privacy, and dignity of the human subject and the study must be designed so that the risks involved have been adequately assessed and can be avoided or satisfactorily managed. Thus, one can conclude that a nonscientific clinical study is considered to be unethical and thus unacceptable, and that in order to be ethically acceptable the study must be scientifically sound. The statement also includes the principle that ethics and science are inseparable in research involving human subjects.

ETHICAL CONSIDERATION OF NONTHERAPEUTIC CLINICAL STUDIES

To receive a marketing authorization for a generic product, the manufacturer has to document the therapeutic equivalence and interchangeability of a generic product with an innovator's product or with any other selected reference product or comparator.[24] The aim of such studies is to demonstrate not therapeutic improvement or superiority but therapeutic similarity, in order to be able to market the product as an interchangeable alternative for commercial and economic reasons. Phase I studies in drug development research (in which a new candidate drug is administered for the first time to a human subject) similarly are classed as nontherapeutic clinical trials.

Phase I studies in healthy volunteers are normally considered ethically acceptable because the new drug candidate is thought to be potentially promising and may improve existing therapy. The volunteers need, however, to be informed about the nature of the nontherapeutic trial and their informed consent must be properly obtained, as described in more detail below.

But is clinical testing always considered ethically justified if its aim is simply to demonstrate, for commercial purposes, bioequivalence between a new generic product and an innovator's pharmaceutical product?

The Declaration of Helsinki (Paragraphs 5 and 6) and the CIOMS Guidelines (Guideline 1) state that the justification and primary purpose of medical research involving human subjects is to benefit people's health and to improve prophylactic, diagnostic, and therapeutic procedures. The documents also state that in medical research on human subjects, considerations related to the well-being of the human subject should take precedence over the interests of science and society. It is a known fact that any clinical trial, including nontherapeutic pharmacokinetic studies in healthy volunteers, may cause potential and unavoidable health risks. Taken literally, the documents cited above do not indisputably support the ethics of pharmacokinetic studies where the aim is only to demonstrate bioequivalence for commercial purposes.

In these circumstances, it is vital that prospective research subjects who are healthy volunteers in nontherapeutic trials be informed about the aim and nature of the study prior to giving their consent. Such information should explain the purpose of the study, for example, that it is being conducted for regulatory and commercial purposes and the subjects will not receive any therapeutic benefit. Any foreseeable risks, pain or discomfort, or inconveniences to the individual, and treatment

and compensation provided in case of injury or complications associated with the study, should also be explained.[25] If, after receiving proper
information, healthy volunteers have freely given consent, a nontherapeutic study may be considered ethically acceptable provided that it
has been endorsed by an independent ethics committee. If the products
to be tested are known to cause potentially severe adverse reactions,
healthy volunteers should not be used for bioequivalence studies.

NONTHERAPEUTIC STUDIES IN VULNERABLE GROUPS

If the subjects are not healthy volunteers but vulnerable subjects who
because of mental or behavioral disorders are incapable of giving
informed consent, the ethics of a nontherapeutic study may be questioned. In these circumstances, a nontherapeutic study raises fewer
ethical problems if it is conducted in patients who have a disease for
which the investigational drugs are in fact accepted and a recognized
therapy from which the patients benefit. Ethical justification for using
children in bioequivalence studies requires cautious consideration.

The WHO Guidelines for Good Clinical Practice[26] state categorically that "In a non-therapeutic study, i.e., when there is no direct clinical benefit to the subject, consent must always be given by the subject
and documented by his or her dated signature (see paragraph 3.3 (g),
Informed consent)." This excludes the use of healthy children in nontherapeutic trials. The ICH GCP[27] is more flexible, as it states that
"Nontherapeutic trials may be conducted in subjects with consent of
a legally acceptable representative provided the following conditions
are fulfilled." It then lists five conditions, and one of them is, "The
foreseeable risks to the subjects are low."[28]

It is a known fact in pharmacology that any pharmaceutical product administrated to a human being is potentially toxic and can cause
(although rarely but unexpectedly) untoward effects, such as anaphy-
lactic or other allergic reactions. These adverse effects can be caused
by the active pharmaceutical substance or inactive ingredients used
in the composition of the product. Thus, the reliable estimation of a
low foreseeable risk to the subject may be difficult to make, if not
impossible.

A parent or legal representative may give permission for a child's
participation in a clinical trial, but the purpose of the research must

then be to obtain knowledge relevant to the health needs of children.[29] It is therefore advisable to conduct comparative bioequivalence studies only in sick children who receive a therapeutic benefit from the pharmaceutical products. In fact, nontherapeutic study in healthy volunteers can thus be avoided, and as many diseases can modify the pharmacokinetic profile and metabolism of a drug, it may, in fact, be more useful even for scientific reasons to use sick children for such studies.

RIGHT TO INFORMED CONSENT – CULTURAL AND GENDER ASPECTS

Because the Nuremberg Code in 1947 stated that the voluntary consent of the human subject is absolutely essential, this concept has been accepted in all international ethical documents referred to in this article.[30] Operations of the pharmaceutical industry and its drug development research are increasing in the developing world and in particular in Asia, Africa, and South America.[31] In some cultures, an investigator may enter a community to conduct research or approach prospective subjects for their individual consent only after obtaining permission from a community leader, a council of elders, or another designated authority.[32] Some societies focus on the family rather than the individual.[33] For example, in China, family ties are still so strong that many decisions involving a family member are made by the family and not by the individual.[34] Although such customs must be respected, in no case may the permission of a community leader, a family, a relative, or other authority substitute for individual informed consent.[35] This is especially important in nontherapeutic trials such as vaccine trials or comparative bioequivalence studies.

In some cultures a wife-and-husband relationship may be regarded as inseparable, but a wife may be denied legal competence.[36] However, the CIOMS 2002 Guidelines[37] state that in research involving women, only the informed consent of the woman herself is required for her participation and in no case should the permission of a spouse or partner replace the requirement of individual informed consent. If women wish to consult with their husbands or partners or seek voluntarily to obtain their permission before deciding to enroll in research, this is not only ethically permissible but in some contexts highly desirable.[38]

Many people in all cultures are unfamiliar with scientific concepts such as those of placebo or randomization applied in clinical studies. This requires from the investigator and sponsor culturally appropriate ways to communicate comprehensible information in the informed consent process.[39]

ETHICAL REVIEW COMMITTEES AND CLINICAL STUDIES

All proposals to conduct research involving human subjects must be submitted for review of their scientific merit and ethical acceptability to one or more scientific and ethical review committees.[40] Clinical trials on pharmaceutical products and even the smallest Phase I clinical trials or comparative pharmacokinetic studies to demonstrate bioequivalence are not exempted from this principle. The ethical review committee must be independent of the research team, and any direct financial or other material benefit they may derive from the research should not be contingent on the outcome of their review.[41] The ethical review committee plays a particularly crucial role in situations where a study involves an investigational pharmaceutical product and the ethics of the study design is questionable.

The objectives of the research, the methods to be used, the qualifications of investigators and the research site, and essential information for prospective research subjects are some of the many items to be included in a protocol that investigator(s) and sponsor(s) should submit for the review of an ethical review committee.[42] A complete list of these items can be found, for example, in Appendix 1 of the CIOMS Guidelines.[43] All international ethical guidance documents emphasize that an investigator must obtain an approval, a favorable opinion or clearance for the protocol, from an ethical review committee before undertaking the research.[44]

OBLIGATIONS OF SPONSORS

The responsibilities of sponsors are outlined in detail in the ICH and WHO GCP guidelines and in the EU Directive.[45] The principles are applicable as such for any clinical trial, including investigational pharmaceutical products under development, marketed products, or vaccines.

The WHO GCP[46] is most specific in this respect and establishes that a sponsor is often a pharmaceutical company, but may also be an individual, the investigator, or an independent institution that initiates, funds, organizes, and oversees the conduct of a clinical trial.

One principle is that the available nonclinical and clinical information on an investigational product should be adequate to support the proposed clinical trial. In some cases, the active ingredient of a product has been in clinical use for years and the collected information is sufficient to support further studies, provided that the composition of the product is identical with that of the marketed product.[47] If the company aims to study extended or new indications, however, it may be necessary to perform some additional experimental studies prior to clinical trials and to conduct conventional Phase II and III developmental studies as if the product was a new drug.[48]

The sponsor is responsible for providing the investigator of the investigational and comparator products with all relevant information on their safe use. The sponsor has to ensure that the trial follows sound scientific principles and GCP by selecting qualified investigator(s) and a suitable research site, providing a protocol, and subsequently ensuring protocol compliance. Moreover, the sponsor has to comply with applicable legal, ethical, and regulatory requirements.[49]

In planning the trial, the sponsor is responsible for providing the investigator with chemical, pharmaceutical, toxicological, pharmacological, and clinical data on the investigational and comparator products.[50] The sponsor has an obligation to report adverse events and adverse drug reactions to investigators and drug regulatory authorities.[51] Additional responsibilities include monitoring and quality assurance of the trial, verification of data obtained and their statistical processing, and supporting the investigator in drawing up a final report or scientific publication.[52]

PUBLICATION OF CLINICAL STUDY RESULTS

Paragraph 27 of the WMA Declaration of Helsinki[53] provides advice on the principles to be followed in drawing up the report on, or publication of, a scientific study. Investigators, authors, and publishers have ethical obligations that are relevant to research on generic products.

In the publication of research results, the investigators are obliged to ensure the accuracy of the results. Negative as well as positive results should be published or otherwise made publicly available.[54] This aims to avoid the unnecessary exposure of human beings to experiments and to avoid duplication of clinical studies and the waste of research resources. There is abundant evidence that trials tending to produce poor results are quietly forgotten or stopped and that medical journals are loath to publish negative results. It remains to be seen how effectively this ethical principle of the Declaration of Helsinki will be implemented.

Sources of funding, institutional affiliations, and any possible conflicts of interest should be declared in the publication. Reports of experimentation not in accordance with the principles laid down in the Declaration of Helsinki should not be accepted for publication.[55]

CONCLUSIONS

The evolution in recent years of international guiding principles for the ethical conduct of clinical testing and clinical trials has resulted in comprehensive advice on the scientific and ethical conduct of research involving human subjects. It is advisable to consult these documents when any ethical or scientific questions arise in the planning or conduct of a clinical trial. The pharmaceutical industry as a sponsor and investigators conducting clinical development studies on pharmaceutical products should strictly follow these scientific and ethical principles, keeping in mind that, depending on the study design, research subjects, or study site, such studies may require special ethical considerations.

3

The Regulatory and Ethical Challenges of Pediatric Research

M. Dianne Murphy and Sara F. Goldkind*

By the 1970s, the American Academy of Pediatrics (AAP) and the Food and Drug Administration (FDA) had publicly stated that the same level of scientific investigation required before a product is marketed for adults should be required for pediatric therapies. We entered the twenty-first century with hundreds of exciting new therapies, studied and approved for use in adults, that were being used in pediatrics without even the most fundamental of studies. Studies of absorption, distribution, metabolism, and elimination (ADME) and clinical trials were not conducted in the pediatric population. Most pediatric dosing calculations were done on a weight-based metric derived from adult dosing recommendations. It is counterintuitive that a society would demand strict controls on product development for the more physiologically mature and stable organism – the adult – and simultaneously ignore the need for scientific data to guide therapeutic use in the more complex and physiologically evolving and developing pediatric population. This was the situation, however, toward the end of the twentieth century. This chapter describes (1) the regulatory changes that opened the gateway to pediatric trials; (2) parameters for the disclosure of trial results; (3) scientific information gleaned from pediatric trials; (4) pediatric safety concerns; and (5) ethical considerations in pediatric research.

* The views expressed are those of the authors. No official support or endorsements by the U.S. Food and Drug Administration is provided or should be inferred. No commercial or other conflict of interest exists between the authors and the pharmaceutical companies.

PEDIATRIC RESEARCH: THE CHALLENGE TO GOVERNMENTS

It is an unfortunate truth that children not only are the therapeutic orphans described by Dr. H. Shirkey in 1963, but also are often the "sentinel canaries" in the mine of pharmaceutical therapeutics.[1] Disasters involving therapies given to the pediatric population have influenced the regulatory framework of the United States. Tragedies in children associated with tetanus-contaminated diphtheria antitoxin led to the United States 1902 Biologics Control Act.[2] Efforts to develop a pediatric liquid formulation of sulfanilamide caused renal failure for those given this preparation and resulted in the 1938 Food, Drug, and Cosmetic Act (FD&C), which required demonstration of the safe use of a product.[3] Use of chloramphenicol, in a population without concomitant dosing studies, led to infant deaths and tragic discoveries concerning metabolic differences in infants and children. In the 1960s the thalidomide disaster revealed the profound teratogenic effects "safe" adult therapies could have, stimulating the 1962 Amendments to the FD&C Act. This act was responsible for a huge paradigm shift that still dictates the role and functions of the FDA today. Therapies are required to be not only safe, but also effective.[4]

Despite some evidence of significant differences between children and adults, publication of ethical breaches at well-reputed institutions[5] contributed to the societal ethos of protectiveness toward children, and hence the systematic exclusion of children from research. Children were left out of the rapidly evolving scientific progress in drug development that occurred in the latter half of the twentieth century. Recognition of the fact that children were repeatedly exposed to daily risks at the hands of their clinicians, in an effort to spare them potential research risks, ultimately resulted in corrective regulatory initiatives.

REGULATORY BACKGROUND: FAILURE OF THE BULLY PULPIT

In 1979, the FDA passed a labeling regulation that required statements regarding the pediatric use of a drug approved for adult indication(s) to be based on substantial evidence derived from adequate and well-controlled studies.[6] Throughout the 1980s, however, most pediatric therapies were used without safety, efficacy, and dosing studies in children. A review in 1999 presented data showing that from 1973 to

1994, between 71 to 80 percent of approved new molecular entities or products listed in the *Physician's Desk Reference* (PDR) did not have sufficient pediatric drug labeling.[7] In 1992, the agency (FDA) proposed regulations which, by codifying criteria, it hoped "...will make manufacturers more aware of how feasible it really is to get pediatric information in their labeling, show some that they may already have adequate information at their disposal to do so, show others that the evidentiary threshold is not so great as previously believed, and encourage all to pursue better pediatric labeling for their drugs."[8] The intent of this approach was multifaceted. It attempted to facilitate pediatric trials by introducing the concept of extrapolation and by requiring sponsors to submit previously conducted pediatric studies. The final 1994 pediatric labeling rule supported the concept of extrapolation of adult *efficacy* from adequate and well-controlled trials in adults into the pediatric population, provided certain criteria were fulfilled.[9] Despite the possibility of extrapolating efficacy from adults to children, or from older to younger children, additional *pharmacokinetic, safety*, and other focused studies might still be necessary.

At the end of the twentieth century, Congress and the agency enacted corrective efforts, legislation and regulations that finally propelled pediatric therapeutics onto a path of scientific and ethical development. This was dramatically realized by the 1997 FDA Modernization Act (FDAMA).[10] Section 111 of the Act provided a mechanism for powerful incentives if sponsors would develop pediatric studies defined by FDA, issued as written requests. Written requests require sponsors to obtain scientific data needed to make product safety and efficacy determinations for children. This incentive mechanism is a potent legislative "carrot," and was renewed in the 2002 Best Pharmaceuticals for Children Act (BPCA).[11] As of September 2004, sponsors have conducted and submitted pediatric studies on over 110 products in response to written requests. In addition, sponsors of over 100 other products have informed the agency that they either are or will be conducting the requested studies. All these studies have predetermined deadlines that must be met if the sponsor is to benefit from the exclusivity incentive provisions.

The 1998 Pediatric Rule (regulation)[12] and the 2003 Pediatric Research Equity Act (PREA legislation) function in parallel to the

FDAMA and BPCA, requiring sponsors to study certain drugs or biologics in the pediatric population. Unlike the incentive legislation, which is a voluntary participation program for sponsors, PREA requires sponsors to submit certain pediatric studies. This requirement is mostly restricted to cases where a sponsor has, or is planning to submit, an application for an adult indication (condition or disease) that also occurs in children, where there is substantial use in pediatrics, or where the development of pediatric studies of the product would result in a meaningful therapeutic benefit. The particularly effective part of this approach is the requirement that sponsors, researchers, and FDA reviewers assess and plan for pediatric needs in the early stages of product development.

Pediatric clinical studies of medical products will most likely continue to be fewer in number than studies conducted in adults. Once a sponsor has conducted the pediatric clinical studies of interest, no matter what legislative mechanism is used, it is unusual for additional clinical studies to be conducted. In adults, however, sponsors will often, in attempts to expand target market populations and to answer post-approval requirements, conduct new studies to gain additional indications or to demonstrate potential efficacy (sometimes despite previous negative studies). Because the pediatric market is often insignificant financially, additional pediatric clinical studies, once the sponsor has responded to FDA's WR or requirement for studies, have proven thus far to be unlikely.

Public availability of pediatric trial results not only might lead to better clinical decisions for children, but might also result in more informed future research. Hence, BPCA states that "Not later than 180 days after the date of submission of a report on a pediatric study under this section, the Commission shall make available to the public a summary of the medical and clinical pharmacology reviews of pediatric studies conducted...."[13] The legislative mandate for such public dissemination of clinical study information is blind to whether the data actually support the use of the product in children, and to whether the FDA approves the product for use in children. This is in contrast to the statutory limitations placed on the FDA with respect to its ability to disclose information from any other clinical studies. Short of a marketing approval, the FDA is usually prohibited from disclosing such clinical trials data.

Since July of 2002, FDA has been posting, as statutorily mandated, summaries of clinical studies conducted under the BPCA provisions. As of September 2004, forty-two medical and clinical pharmacology study summaries have been posted on the FDA's Web site: www.fda.gov/cder/pediatric/Summaryreview.htm.

WHAT HAVE WE LEARNED?

The pediatrics-oriented regulatory and legislative directives have been invaluable in stimulating pediatric trials, the results of which confirm that children have been the unwitting victims of societal protectiveness. The following five categories are examples of acquired pediatric knowledge clearly demonstrating the need for continued pediatric research to ensure that children will benefit from the drug development process:

1. ***Unnecessary Exposure to Ineffective Therapies.*** These are therapies that are effective in adults, but cannot be demonstrated to have the same predictable efficacy in the pediatric population. In this situation, the patient not only potentially remains untreated for the underlying condition but may be exposed to the adverse effects inherent to the therapy without any potential benefit. Examples:
   a. Many therapies for treatment of depression;
   b. Navelbine (vinorelbine) for recurrent, solid, malignant tumors;
   c. Detrol LA (tolterodine) in pediatric patients five to ten years of age;
   d. Buspar (buspirone) for general anxiety disorder;
   e. Camptosar (irinotecan) in previously untreated rhabdomyosarcoma.
2. ***Ineffective Dosing of an Effective Therapy.*** This is a variant of the first category. Here, the therapy is effective if the appropriate dose for the pediatric population is known. To base dosing solely on weight without confirming with adequate pharmacokinetic studies means that one is guessing at the therapeutic dose. When the substance is cleared or metabolized more rapidly or absorbed less effectively by the pediatric population, this functionally means the child is exposed to an ineffective dose. Once

again, the patient does not receive the expected benefit of the therapy while being exposed to the potential adverse effects of the therapy. Examples:

   a. Higher dosing required for adolescents taking Luvox (fluvoxamine) and children < five years of age taking Neurontin (gabapentin);

   b. Higher clearance of Lotensin (benazepril) in hypertensive children;

   c. Double the clearance rate of Ultiva (remifentanil) in neonates.

3. ***Overdosing of a Potentially Effective Therapy.*** The functional potential outcome here is that a child is unable to tolerate a therapy because of adverse effects secondary to inappropriately high dosing. Examples:

   a. Dosing of Luvox (fluvoxamine) in girls eight to eleven years of age;

   b. Reduced clearance of Arava (leflunomide) in pediatric patients < 40 kg;

   c. Decreased clearance of Pepcid (famotidine) in infants zero to three months of age and of Epivir (lamivudine) for HIV in one-week-old neonates.

4. ***Undefined Unique Pediatric Adverse Effects.*** This problem presents two difficulties. One is a variant of 3, above. If a product has not been specifically studied in the pediatric population, adverse effects (AEs) that may occur more frequently or uniquely in children will remain undefined. This also means there is no opportunity to manage the AE if such an approach is possible. Examples:

   a. Occurrence of rare seizures in patients without a prior history of seizures when exposed to Ultane (sevoflurane);

   b. Hypopituitary adrenal axis suppression with Diprolene (betamethasone);

   c. Increase of suicidal ideation with Rebetron (ribavirin/intron A).

5. ***Effects on Growth and Developmental Behavior.*** Because children are evolving and maturing organisms with rapid or chronic changes in physiology, effects on the evolving and maturing organ systems will not be defined without trials directed to

look for those effects. The following are examples of effects on growth, behavior, and learning:

a. Detrol LA (tolterodine): Hyperactive behavior and attention disorder occurred three times as frequently in treated versus placebo population;

b. Decreased growth rate described for Prozac (fluoxetine), Effexor (venlafaxine), and Rebetron (ribavirin/intron A);

c. Decreased bone density in patients twelve to seventeen years of age treated with Accutane (isotretinoin).

PHARMACOVIGILANCE

A critical part of drug regulation is monitoring safety after marketing. The concept of extending the science of pharmacotherapy to children includes issues of safety. The BPCA addresses this issue and requires a special additional assessment of all suspected adverse drug reactions that occur in both the adult and pediatric populations during the first year of general marketing in the pediatric population if the product has been granted pediatric exclusivity. This specific safety review is to be reported at a public meeting of pediatric experts. The FDA's Pediatric Advisory Committee has been reviewing these reports since 2003. This legislation was an effort to ensure that attention is focused on what happens after a product has been appropriately studied in, and then more widely marketed in, the pediatric population.

The current, passive pharmacovigilance as embodied by the FDA adverse event reporting system (AERS) generated by MEDWATCH reports[14] is effective at detecting rare events such as aplastic anemia or acute liver failure. It was not designed, however, to study relative risk or increases in risk quantitatively for more common events such as cardiovascular disease, common forms of cancer, or suicide.

One finds a contemporary example of the use of this kind of data in the recent review of the safety of the use of antidepressants in children. Zoloft was one of the first products eligible for discussion under the specific BPCA post-exclusivity safety requirements. By the time of the June 2003 Advisory Committee meeting, there were a few serious suspected adverse reactions and four deaths (two of these were suicides) reported in the pediatric population for the first year of reports. Within six months of the Zoloft review, the FDA completed the BPCA post-exclusivity safety review for Paxil. The number of reports of suspected serious adverse reactions (forty-three hospitalizations and thirteen deaths) was higher than what had been observed with two other recently reviewed antidepressants in the context of the BPCA mandate. Of particular concern were the seventeen suicide attempts, nine suicide deaths, new unexpected serious adverse reactions of aggression and violence, and an almost equal distribution of deaths between males and females. The results of these reviews were brought to two Pediatric Advisory Committee meetings in 2004.

One critical conclusion from these meetings was that the AERS system could not independently identify an increased rate of suicide in pediatric patients on a specific antidepressant therapy compared with the underlying risk of suicide associated with pediatric depression. The signal for treatment-related risk was generated by placebo-controlled trials. Safety is one area where placebo-controlled information is uniquely valuable. For example, a comparative study of Paxil versus Effexor in an efficacy trial would not have generated a signal for suicidality, as they both may entail this risk. (See section on placebo-controlled trials).

Discussion now is focusing on ways to improve the data for these post-exclusivity safety assessments further. In many cases, the need for prospective pediatric safety studies or data from *active* surveillance systems is clear. Because children's bodies are maturing, growing, and evolving over relatively short periods of time, one could postulate that identifying potential drug safety signals from such a population is even more difficult than identifying such signals from a physiologically stable adult population. From a regulatory perspective, historically neither drug approval nor granting of pediatric exclusivity is usually denied based upon the lack of longer-term follow-up studies. Many in the community now argue that additional longer-term follow-up in the form of prospective pediatric safety assessments or active surveillance systems would better inform us about true risks.

Summary of Scientific Lessons Learned

1. The current dearth of knowledge about many aspects of pediatric medicine has been a challenge in designing pediatric trials. As the FDA continues to issue written requests, and as more research is conducted on children, research designs should be informed by the knowledge gained in the conduct of pediatric trials and

become more confident in the use of pediatric-specific surrogate endpoints and assessment tools.

2. Extrapolations from adult studies and experiences are not always appropriate given differences in absorption, distribution, metabolism, elimination (ADME), growth, anatomy, physiology, hormonal factors, and neurobehavioral and sexual maturation. However, if a disease behaves similarly in adults and children, and if the expected response to therapy is also similar, then an efficacy trial involving children simply to "re-prove what is already known" is usually not necessary, and may require only pharmacokinetic and safety information to be obtained specifically from children to ensure that the correct dose in the pediatric population(s) is elucidated and to assess whether there are any unique pediatric safety concerns that need to be addressed when the product is used.

3. Extrapolations may not be applicable across all pediatric subpopulations because of the heterogeneity of the pediatric population. A premature infant may not share pharmaceutical responses with a full-term neonate, and neither is similar, despite the "pediatric" classification, to a 200-pound adolescent football player.

4. The pediatric population is even more variable than anticipated in response to therapies (both efficacy and adverse reactions) and pharmacokinetics/dynamics.

5. Effects on growth have been demonstrated in a number of therapies, including those for depression, hepatitis C, asthma, and attention deficit disorder. Assessment of effect on growth should be standard in most pediatric studies.

6. The need for adequate postapproval studies to assess potential adverse reactions that will not be identified in short clinical trials of limited numbers of patients continues to be of particular relevance to pediatrics.

ETHICAL CONSIDERATIONS

There is no longer any doubt that children need to be studied, to ensure that their medical treatment is science-based. Ethical pediatric drug development requires attention to whether specific study is needed as well as to how to conduct such study. Over the last decade the question in pediatric drug and therapeutics development has shifted dramatically from "whether children should be studied" to "how children should be studied."[15] The American Academy of Pediatrics Committee on Drugs said, "It is not only ethical, but also imperative that new drugs to be used in children be studied in children under controlled circumstances so that the benefits of therapeutic advances will become available to all who need them."[16]

There is a growing body of thoughtful literature to guide the ethical study of children. This includes international ethics documents, legislation, regulations, and agency-specific policies. Of particular note are the guidelines and commentaries of the Council for the International Organizations of Medicinal Sciences (CIOMS), the International Conference on Harmonisation Tripartate Guidelines (ICH), and the Code of Federal Regulations (CFR) Subpart D regulations, *Additional Safeguards for Children in Research* (see the Appendix). In Chapter 4, Robert M. Nelson analyzes these guidelines and regulations with reference to the inclusion of children in clinical trials. Dr. Juhana E. Idänpään-Heikkilä and Sev Fluss discuss the evolution of the international guidelines in Chapter 2. The first two international documents thoughtfully balance pediatrics-specific concerns with the clear necessity for the pediatric research. The Subpart D regulations limit the amount of risk that children can potentially incur in research endeavors. These regulations embody the ethical *prima facie* principles of beneficence,[17] nonmaleficence,[18] and distributive justice, leading to the understanding that benefits should be enhanced, harms should be reduced, and those who will reap the benefits of the research should, if possible, share the burdens of the research endeavor. Furthermore, Subpart D regulations underscore the importance of generalizable knowledge as one ethical component of the counterbalance to incurred research risk. The remainder of this chapter will discuss how these complex documents impact pediatric research and address the complex issue of randomized clinical trials, specifically placebo-controlled trials.

It would be catastrophic if the major advances enabling pediatric research resulted in the casual inclusion of children. As for all research, the scientific hypothesis-generated questions need to inform the selection of the study design and study population. The defined scientific research goals determine fair subject selection, that is, both inclusion and exclusion criteria.[19] Although this may seem elementary, the impulse to include children is sometimes handled in a less-than-thoughtful manner. Institutional Review Boards (IRBs) are a regulated component of ensuring ethical and scientific integrity to a research project. Yet not all IRBs that review pediatric trials have pediatric expertise or facility with the pertinent federal regulations. Shah surveyed 188 IRBs and found that there is much variability in risk assessments and the application of Subpart D, *Additional Safeguards for Children in Research.*[20]

Currently, there is profound confusion about pediatric research, reflected in the inconsistent application of Subpart D regulations, inappropriate inclusion of healthy children (when the research could easily have been completed in children with the disorder/condition), and unnecessary pediatric risk exposure. ICH E11, *Clinical Investigation of Medicinal Products in the Pediatric Population,* addresses the inclusion of children (see Nelson, Chapter 4, for a further detailed discussion of this aspect), focusing on a broad range of insightful parameters, including the prevalence and seriousness of the condition in the pediatric population, the availability and suitability of alternative treatments, and the age ranges of children likely to be treated with the product.[21]

Pediatric research needs to be deliberated in a hierarchical fashion, beginning with these basic yet invaluable queries:

- Do children need to be included at all?
- If so, can children with the disorder/condition be studied instead of children who are healthy or who do not have the pertinent disorder/condition?
- If so, can children who are less vulnerable be studied in lieu of others?
- How can research risks be minimized?
- How will the data be accrued to effect appropriate subset analysis?

Although these framing questions may seem obvious and elementary, they are not always considered. Coffey recently reviewed seventy clinical asthma trials involving children and identified several disturbing findings. Among those was the fact that of fifty-two studies involving both children and adults, only one study differentiated between children and adults. Subset analysis was thus largely unobtainable. This review concluded that "clinical asthma trials involving children and adults do not benefit children as a class because they rarely provide subset analysis."[22] It is imperative that if children are to be studied, then the design and method of data accrual must allow conclusions pertinent to children.

Once it is decided that children should be studied, then the next question is: Can research risk be minimized? This is addressed in ICH E-11, *Clinical Investigation of Medicinal Products in the Pediatric Population*, and ICH E6, *Good Clinical Practice: Consolidated Guidance*, the National Commission for the Protection of Human Subjects of Biomedical and Behavioral Research Report, and the Subpart D regulations *Additional Safeguards for Children in Research*. Available non-clinical and clinical information on an investigational product should be adequate to support the proposed clinical trial.[23] They also recommend reducing the number of participants and procedures, while still maintaining scientific rigor and establishing pediatrics-sensitive research environments.

Risk assessment is a major focus of the 1977 recommendations of the National Commission. These, in turn, are extensively reflected in the current Code of Federal Regulations. The Subpart D regulations stem directly from the National Commission's Report on Children,[24] and cap the amount of risk to which children can be exposed in research. Subpart D categorizes pediatric research by risk levels: minimal risk versus minor increase in minimal risk. Distinguishing these two risk levels may, on the surface, sound like a purely semantic exercise but it provides important clarity for addressing risk in pediatric research. At present these distinctions are made in public federal regulations and commission reports (to be discussed below) but remain very challenging in practice.

The ceiling on risk for healthy subjects, or subjects without the disorder/condition under investigation, is "minimal risk," which is defined as follows: *the probability and magnitude of harm or discomfort anticipated in the research are not greater in and of themselves than those ordinarily encountered in daily life or during the performance of routine physical or psychological examinations or tests.*[25] Although the regulations themselves do not tether the definition of "daily life" to a particular group of children, there is a consensus that "daily life" should be indexed to the lives of healthy children living in safe environments. This has been expressed over the years by the National Commission, by the National Human Research Protection Advisory Committee (NHRPAC), and most recently by the Institute of Medicine, which uses the description, "normal experiences of average, healthy, normal children."[26] It should be understood that this is a low level of risk. (See further discussion of "minimal risk" in Nelson, Chapter 4.)

The regulations state that an IRB can approve a protocol involving children with a disorder/condition under the following categories: (1) there is a prospect of direct benefit to individual subjects (21 CFR 50.52), or (2) the research is likely to yield generalizable knowledge about the subject's disorder or condition, even though there is no prospect of direct benefit to the individual subjects (21 CFR 50.53). For children who do have a condition relevant to the research project, there is still a limit on the amount of acceptable risk exposure (for example, "not involving greater than minimal risk, i.e., a minor increase over minimal risk"). Although this phrase is not defined in the regulations, the IOM Report explains it as "a slight increase in the potential for harms or discomfort beyond minimal risk." The IOM Report and the Secretary's Advisory Committee for Human Research Protection (SACHRP) guide risk analysis. For children who might derive direct benefit from the proposed research, research risks must be mitigated and balanced against the potential benefits.

There is growing agreement dating back to the National Commission Recommendations of 1977, and reiterated by the FDA Pediatric Advisory Subcommittee to the Anti-infective Drugs Advisory Committee in 1999, that "in general, pediatric studies should be conducted in subjects who may benefit from participation in the trial. Usually this implies that the subject has or is susceptible to the disease under study."[27] This is understood fairly broadly. Whenever possible, healthy subjects, or subjects without the disorder/condition in question, should be excluded from research unless (1) the study entails only minimal risk or (2) the study could not otherwise be done – either because unaffected children would be necessary as a comparison group, or because the research for some other compelling reason could not practicably be carried out in children with the disorder/condition;[28] and (3) the study offers the opportunity further to understand, prevent, or alleviate a serious problem affecting the health or welfare of children.

Under Subpart D regulations the latter two scenarios require referral to the appropriate federal agencies for sign-off by the Commissioner of the FDA and/or the Secretary of Health and Human Services (HHS) before the research could be initiated. The mechanism for federal review involves an opportunity for public comment, and consultation with an expert panel (see Chapter 3 Appendix). An example of this type of protocol referral is "Effects of a Single Dose of Dextroamphetamine in Attention Deficit Hyperactivity Disorder: A Functional Magnetic Resonance Study," which was reviewed by the Pediatric Ethics Subcommittee of the newly formed Pediatric Advisory Committee on September 10, 2004. The study involves administering a single 10-mg dose of dextroamphetamine to two groups of children – those with ADHD and those without – to be followed by functional magnetic resonance imaging (MRI) of all children. The goal of the trial – elucidation of the pathophysiology of ADHD – was found by both the principal investigator and the IRB of record to be meaningful and interpretable only if the non-ADHD children could be included as comparators, and that the study promises to increase understanding of a prevalent condition affecting the pediatric population. The Pediatric Advisory Committee, among its extensive deliberations, recommendations, and stipulations, concurred with this assessment. Final determinations from the FDA Commissioner are posted on the FDA Web site.[29]

Subpart D regulations place stringent protective boundaries around pediatric research, yet, as demonstrated by this referral mechanism, the regulations provide for flexibility, thereby simultaneously promoting pediatric research. The difficulty with the Subpart D regulations is the ambiguity associated with the risk definitions, and the consequent wide range of interpretation or misinterpretation of these classifications. As more pediatric research experience is accrued, the risk categories will need to be reevaluated.

After the appropriate study population has been defined, the next question is: Can the least vulnerable group of children be chosen for the research project and still arrive at the necessary data? Some guidance can be found in CIOMS Guidelines 13 and 14,[30] and in ICH Topic E8, *General Considerations for Clinical Trials*,[31] and in Recommendation 2 of the National Commission, which states: *Where appropriate, studies have been conducted first on animals and adult humans, then on older children, prior to involving infants.*[32] It is not always possible to make this type of hierarchical selection so that the most vulnerable groups of children are spared research burdens. This algorithm should be considered, however, each time pediatric subjects are to be selected.

There is a perpetual tension between the ethical requirement to minimize risk and the ethical/scientific requirement for adequately designed, robust trials capable of yielding reliable conclusions. In a noble effort to spare children research risks we should not short-change the validity of the results. As noted earlier, it is inherently unethical to base pediatric medical care on substandard science.

RANDOMIZED CLINICAL TRIALS

There are many protections for research subjects in randomized clinical trials that apply to pediatric subjects as well. Some of these are application of clinical equipoise, appropriate comparator groups, risk–benefit calculus for all study arms, thoughtfully derived inclusion/exclusion criteria, well-defined withdrawal criteria, data monitoring committee (DMC) oversight, IRB review, institutional ethics committee (IEC) input as appropriate, and a careful, informed consent process (parental permission, and assent as applicable). This section, however, will only address two topics: clinical equipoise, and the appropriate use of placebo-controlled trials.

Clinical Equipoise

Equipoise is uncertainty about the relative merits of two different interventions. If there is no consensus in the expert clinical community, even if the evidence is suggestive but not sufficient, then a state of clinical equipoise exists. Beauchamp and Childress emphasize that in multiarm trials, clinical equipoise must exist for each arm.[33] Thus, going into any clinical trial, there must be no *a priori* well-accepted superior treatment. The principle of clinical equipoise demands inherent ethical cohesion.

It is possible for an individual physician researcher to have a personal preference for one arm over another, and still to recommend the study to a patient. Clinical equipoise is referenced to the state of knowledge in the expert community. In practice it is very difficult to differentiate between the state of scientific knowledge and the eminence-based current standard of care.

It is also possible for a patient or a parent of a patient to have a preference for one arm over another. A careful verification of the subject's and/or parent's understanding of the randomization process is imperative. Subjects and parents need to be apprised fully of the nature of the randomized controlled trial; that is, is it nonbeneficial research or research that offers the prospect of direct benefit to the individual subjects? Therapeutic misconceptions can occur if the subjects and/or parents believe the research to be of direct benefit when it is not, or if the subjects and/or parents believe that the choice of treatment arm will be clinically selected for that subject's direct benefit. These misconceptions can sometimes occur despite careful information about the randomization process. Kodish conducted a multisite study of the informed consent process for randomized controlled trials for children with newly diagnosed leukemia. The informed consent processes were both observed and audiotaped. Randomization was explained to 83 percent of the parents, yet only 50 percent of the parents understood this process to be part of the study design.[34] Recognizing the power of hope, attempts (perhaps repeated) must be made to convey the nature of randomization and the meaning of equipoise in the informed consent process. There remains a need for further research in the area of informed consent and methods to maximize understanding.

Placebo-Controlled Trials

There is agreement that if no treatment exists, placebo-controlled trials are ethically acceptable. Conversely, there is agreement that if the subjects will suffer irreversible harm, placebos should not be used, even if there would be no other manner of conducting the study. Coffey found in his asthma trial review that despite IRB oversight, 69 percent of the studies included children who met the National Heart Blood Lung Institute guidelines for anti-inflammatory therapy but who were not treated accordingly. In approximately 13 percent of the studies, children who were clinically compensated were required to discontinue their medication regimen solely for the purposes of the trials.[35] Clearly, these children were in jeopardy of irreversible risk, when there were suitable therapies without excessive, associated adverse events.

There are many proposed trials, however, that fall within a gray zone not covered by these two dichotomous categories. Hence placebo-controlled trials remain a highly controversial area. One aspect of the controversy is the Declaration of Helsinki, Paragraph 29 (revised October 2000):

The benefits, risks, burdens, and effectiveness of a new method should be tested against those of *the best current prophylactic, diagnostic, and therapeutic methods.*[36]

This paragraph has engendered tremendous confusion. What constitutes the "best current therapy" is nebulous, frequently undefined, and subject to debate. It may not be based upon scientific evidence; it may be based on anecdotal experience, off-label use, or limited trials. Further research, including placebo-controlled trials, may lead to safer and more effective treatments that would ultimately be more beneficial. In response to these concerns the World Medical Association issued a note of clarification in 2002, which catalyzed further debates.[37]

The general ethical and scientific approaches to placebo-controlled trials also seem apropos to pediatric studies. Use of placebo-controlled trials may be ethically justified in the following circumstances, provided that risk is minimized:[38]

- High placebo rate in the disorder/condition (e.g., depression).
- Waxing and waning course of the disease/condition.
- Frequent spontaneous remissions.
- No known effective treatment.[39]
- Only partially effective existing treatments.
- Existing treatments with very serious side effects.
- Low frequency of the condition, making an equivalence trial impracticable.
- Demonstrating a new treatment having sufficient efficacy before large-scale equivalence trials are conducted. This type of efficacy testing could decrease the number of children exposed.
- Existing effective intervention as a comparator would diminish the interpretability and reliability of the results, and use of placebo would not add serious risk.

- Minimal risks to forgoing treatment that may be limited to symptoms only (e.g., allergic rhinitis).
- No harm done in delaying treatment temporarily (e.g., mild hypertension, mild hyperglycemia, mild hypercholesterolemia).

Minimizing risk involves excluding participants who are at increased risk of harm from a lack of therapeutic benefit, as well as drug risk. The ethical concerns and scientific merits of placebo-controlled trials need to be juxtaposed against the utility of alternative trial designs that may be more acceptable and still yield reliable results: superiority active control trials, add-on trials, dose-response studies, randomized withdrawal trials, and cross-over trials (in which the subject serves as his or her own control, with or without placebo). The fundamental principle is that proof of superiority is more robust and quantifiable than "proving" noninferiority. The pitfalls of noninferiority design trials are well discussed by Temple and Ellenberg.[40]

The experience with SSRIs is a good example of the inability to extrapolate efficacy from adult trials to children. Had efficacy in pediatrics been extrapolated from adult data for Paxil, for instance, we would have assumed efficacy and failed to conduct additional trials that were instrumental in identifying drug-associated risk for suicidality. In fact, the placebo-controlled trials provided the most robust signal for suicidality. Thus, although in many settings placebo control engenders risk, this trial design should not be marginalized based on ethical grounds.

CONCLUSION

In less than a decade we have transformed the landscape of pediatric research. In the past, pediatric drug research was avoided, based on ethically motivated protectiveness and market forces unfavorable to pediatric drug development. Time and experience have taught us that children are not only distinct from adults but heterogeneous as a population. Assumptions about adult efficacy, safety, and dosing extrapolations are not uniformly valid and can result in unwitting injury of children during the course of their regular treatments. Past lack of scientific data has left a void in development of pediatrics-specific endpoints and assessment tools. Unfortunately, pediatric studies may not be economically rewarding in the absence of special programs. Combination programs that include incentives and mandated requirements appear to provide an effective means of stimulating pediatric research.

Regulations and laws have been adopted that both encourage the inclusion of children in clinical trials and offer additional protections for pediatric subjects. Peer-reviewed literature and ethical international documents on ethics are also focusing attention on the delicate but necessary balance between careful inclusion and minimization of undue burdens, discomforts, and risks. Further work is needed to hone the definitions of risk, as well as other critical concepts embodied in the 21 CFR 50 Subpart D regulations. Advisory panels have begun to grapple with this, and federal guidance is in progress. The widespread dissemination of pediatrics-specific ethical analyses to sponsors, investigators, and IRBs remains essential, but extremely challenging. Future ethical studies will hinge on powerful educational approaches.

Both scientific and ethical considerations demand a secure infrastructure to ensure that pediatric drug development will continue. Robust, long-term clinical post-market safety studies must become more commonplace. Acceptable study designs will likely evolve in an iterative fashion as we gain more experience with pediatric research. Ethical challenges will likely continue to be highlighted in a similar fashion.

CHAPTER 3 APPENDIX

Subpart D Regulations

21 CFR 50.51/45 CFR 46.404
Clinical investigations/research not involving greater than minimal risk

21 CFR 50.52/45 CFR 46.405
Clinical investigations/research involving greater than minimal risk but presenting the prospect of direct benefit to individual subjects

21 CFR 50.53/45 CFR 46.406
Clinical investigations/research involving greater than minimal risk and no prospect of direct benefit to individual subjects, but likely to yield generalizable knowledge about the subjects' disorder or condition

21 CFR 50.54/45 CFR 46.407

Clinical investigations/research not otherwise approvable that present an opportunity to understand, prevent, or alleviate a serious problem affecting the health or welfare of children.

The Code of Federal Regulations 21 CFR 50 (applicable to the Food and Drug Administration) and Title 45 CFR 46 (applicable to seventeen federal agencies) contain Subpart D regulations *Additional Safeguards for Children in Clinical Investigations/Research*. While there are some noteworthy differences between the two sets of regulations, apropos to pediatric research, the above Subpart D categories are identical in both codes. The Subpart D regulations provide a guiding framework used by IRBs to classify pediatric protocols. IRBs may only approve protocols that fall within the first three categories. The fourth category provides a mechanism whereby a protocol, that is not otherwise approvable under the first three categories of Subpart D, can still be reviewed and approved if certain findings are made and certain conditions met. This involves a referral by an IRB to the appropriate federal agency(s) for review by an expert panel in an open public meeting. If the protocol involves FDA-regulated products it would need to be submitted to the Food and Drug Administration. If the protocol is to be federally funded or conducted it would need to be submitted to the Office of Human Research Protections. If the protocol is applicable to both agencies then a joint review would be conducted. It should be emphasizd that a federal referral by an IRB can only occur if the IRB itself finds that the research presents a reasonable opportunity to in some way affect the health or welfare of the pediatric population, regarding a serious problem.

4

Including Children in Research

Participation or Exploitation?

Robert M. Nelson

INTRODUCTION

The recent escalation in pediatric research, and thus the number of children exposed to research risks, raises concerns as to whether the ethical and regulatory framework for protecting children in research is adequate. What are the acceptable limits on the risks to which we should expose children for the benefit of others and society? To remain within these limits, the regulations and ethical guidelines on research involving children require careful interpretation and application. Are children truly research participants or are they merely being exploited for commercial gain? Research may be exploiting children if it does not result in publicly available knowledge regardless of the level of research risk exposure. We exploit children within research if we use them simply for the generation of profit or personal gain. The conduct of pediatric research is a privilege granted to us by the parents and children who willingly participate. The financial and professional benefits of performing this research reflect a social contract entrusting us with the future health and welfare of our children – a trust that requires transparency and full public disclosure of the research results.

This chapter (1) highlights important features of recent legislation to stimulate pediatric research; (2) reviews key elements of the U.S. pediatric research regulations,[1] compared to guidance from the International Conference on Harmonisation (ICH), the Council for International Organizations of Medical Sciences (CIOMS), and the 2001 EU Clinical Trial Directive;[2] (3) applies these guidelines to the choice of control group, illustrated by clinical trials of inhaled steroids in moderate asthma; and (4) briefly reviews the controversy over the use of antidepressants for major depressive disorder in adolescents.

The "off-label" use of medications for treating children is widespread, resulting in less effective and potentially harmful therapy.[3] The lack of reliable information on the use of medications for children has been addressed in the United States through two legislative initiatives – the Best Pharmaceuticals for Children Act (BPCA) of 2002[4] and the Pediatric Research Equity Act (PREA) of 2003[5] (discussed by M. Dianne Murphy and Sara Goldkind in Chapter 3). These two initiatives stimulated pediatric pharmaceutical research, resulting in valuable information to guide the appropriate use of many medications.[6] Noting the success of these initiatives, the European Commission is planning (2004) to establish a similar program.[7]

The BPCA renewed the reward of an additional six months of patent protection in exchange for conducting pediatric studies requested by the U.S. Food and Drug Administration (FDA). The BPCA established the FDA Office of Pediatric Therapeutics and mandated the hiring of at least one person with expertise in pediatric research ethics. The BPCA requires summaries of FDA reviews of pediatric studies to be posted on the public FDA Web site. This information was not available unless the drug label was changed. The BPCA also commissioned the Institute of Medicine (IOM) to review the adequacy of Subpart D, with a report issued in March 2004.[8]

The PREA gave the FDA legal authority to require pediatric studies for the labeled indications if a drug offers a meaningful therapeutic benefit and the absence of labeling poses a significant risk. The PREA allows extrapolation of pediatric effectiveness from adult studies if the disease and effects of the drug are sufficiently similar in adults and children. The PREA also established the Pediatric Advisory Committee (PAC) to advise on the ethics, design, and analysis of pediatric clinical trials. The PAC may review protocols referred under 21 CFR 50.54 and 45 CFR 46.407, establishing a process for public federal review of research that a local IRB cannot approve yet believes would further the understanding, prevention, or alleviation of a serious problem affecting the health or welfare of children.

The European Commission Proposal incorporates and modifies the major features of the U.S. approach. Similarly to the BPCA, sponsors would gain an added six months of patent protection for conducting requested pediatric studies. The Pediatric Committee (PC) of the European Medicines Agency (EMEA) would have an expanded role in requiring, deferring, or waiving pediatric studies. More importantly, there are stronger provisions for ensuring the availability of data from pediatric studies. The drug label would include pediatric study results, positive or negative. Sponsors would be required to submit the results of all pediatric studies whether or not they were conducted for added patent protection. All pediatric studies conducted in Europe and elsewhere would be incorporated into the database of clinical trials established by the 2001 EU Clinical Trial Directive. A long-term follow-up plan would be required to monitor the safety and efficacy of the pediatric use of the newly authorized drug.

THE ETHICAL AND REGULATORY FRAMEWORK FOR PEDIATRIC RESEARCH IN THE UNITED STATES

The National Commission issued a report in 1977 that served as the basis for Subpart D.[9] In reviewing Subpart D, the IOM concluded that "the federal regulations ... are, in general, appropriate" while acknowledging variability in interpretation and application of the criteria for approving research. The IOM felt that the regulations did not need to be revised, but that consistent and comprehensive guidance was necessary.[10] This section examines four key elements of Subpart D: (1) "fair" selection of subjects; (2) "minimal risk"; (3) "condition"; and (4) "direct benefit."

Justice and the "Fair" Selection of Children for Research

The National Commission appealed to beneficence, respect for persons, and distributive justice in arguing that "research risks should be allocated to adults rather than to children whenever feasible."[11] This principle is affirmed in paragraph 24 of the Declaration of Helsinki,[12] the 2001 EU Clinical Trial Directive, the ICH Good Clinical Practice (GCP) Guidelines,[13] and the ICH guidance on research involving children.[14] Children should not be included in research unless the question cannot be answered in any other way and answering the question would promote the health and welfare of children. Consistent with this principle, the FDA allows extrapolation of adult data to children, when appropriate.[15] By contrast, the National Institutes of Health policy on the inclusion of children is ethically problematic. Here the similarity of a disorder in children and adults supports including rather than excluding children, even when lacking sufficient numbers to perform a subgroup analysis.[16]

"Minimal Risk"

The concept of "minimal risk" sets the upper limit on research risks to which a healthy child may be exposed. Minimal risk is defined as the condition that "the probability and magnitude of harm or discomfort anticipated in the research are not greater in and of themselves than those ordinarily encountered in daily life or during the performance of routine physical or psychological examinations or tests."[17] The wide range of procedures and corresponding risks interpreted as minimal risk is well documented.[18] One source of variability is whether daily life or routine tests refers to healthy children or to the actual children in the research. The IOM recommended that minimal risk be interpreted "in relation to the normal experiences of average, healthy, normal children."[19] This recommendation is consistent with the National Commission's definition of "minimal risk," which was indexed to the daily life or routine examination "of healthy children"[20] (as discussed by Murphy and Goldkind in Chapter 3).

A second source of variability is the interpretation of risks of daily life. For example, a dose of dextroamphetamine was believed by some to present " . . . only minimal risks since the . . . effects of this medication were commensurate with risks ordinarily encountered in the daily lives of children (e.g., equivalent to . . . heavy caffeine consumption, etc.)."[21] The concept of minimal risk has been criticized, given the difficulty of interpreting and applying the criteria of the risks of everyday life.[22] This difficulty may stem from the observation that minimal risk includes both statistical and normative judgments. In effect, evaluating the risks of daily life involves two questions: Are children exposed to this level of risk in their daily lives? Should children be exposed to these risks? Given these interpretive difficulties, the 2002 CIOMS Guidelines omits the phrase "daily life" from the definition of "minimal risk."[23] The IOM acknowledged that assessments of risk are "more straightforward for comparisons to routine . . . examinations than for . . . the larger range of risks encountered in daily life."[24] However, the IOM did not remove the phrase "daily life" from the definition of minimal risk.

"Condition"

Subpart D allows children to be exposed to more than minimal risk during research not offering direct benefit provided that (a) the risk is only a minor increase over minimal risk and (b) the children have a "disorder or condition" about which the research would "yield generalizable knowledge of vital importance."[25] This category of research was most controversial, with two members of the National Commission dissenting. The disagreement was over whether it was fair to expose some children to more research risk than other children absent direct benefit. Others agree that there should be one risk category for nonbeneficial research involving children, reflecting, for example, the everyday parental decision to expose a child to the risks of a new situation.[26] Another approach redefines minimal risk as the appropriate level of risk to which a child may be exposed intentionally for educational purposes. The relevant difference justifying unequal treatment shifts from the presence or absence of a condition to the appropriateness of exposing children to "novel experiences compatible with their development."[27] Whether or not the children have a condition remains relevant to the research objectives, but not to the level of appropriate risk exposure.

Subpart D distinguishes between minimal risk and a minor increase over minimal risk. Thus, whether children have a condition remains essential to justifying greater than minimal research risk exposure. The IOM defined condition as "a specific (or a set of specific) . . . characteristic(s) that an established body of scientific evidence or clinical knowledge has shown to negatively affect children's health and wellbeing or to increase their risk of developing a health problem in the future."[28] The definition emphasizes the need for evidence linking an alleged condition with a negative impact on children's health and wellbeing. For example, the Maryland Court of Appeals viewed children enrolled in the Baltimore Lead Abatement Study as "healthy."[29] Yet exposure to environmental lead is a known risk factor for elevated blood lead levels and subsequent neurological injury.[30] Children enrolled in the Baltimore Lead Abatement Study had the "condition" of being at risk for neurological injury from exposure to environmental lead. Although framed using Subpart D, the controversy over the study involved the fairness of being exposed to higher environmental lead, and whether limited resources justified the study of less expensive forms of lead abatement.[31]

The 2002 CIOMS Guidelines distinguish between minimal risk and a minor increase over minimal risk, yet omit the phrase "daily life" from the definition of "minimal risk."[32] The ICH GCP Guidelines do not distinguish between healthy children and children with a condition based on acceptable risk exposure, but on scientific justification.[33] Unless Subpart D is modified, healthy children in the United States cannot be exposed to more than minimal research risk without review by a federal panel.

"Direct Benefit"

The prospect of "direct benefit" within Subpart D partially justifies exposure to more than minimal risk.[34] The National Commission explicitly linked direct benefit to the individual child enrolled in the research.[35] Also, the benefits that offset the risks of research should improve the individual child's health and wellbeing. The 2001 EU Clinical Trial Directive restricts "a clinical trial on minors" to cases in which "some direct benefit for the group of patients is obtained from the clinical trial."[36] This confusing language was adopted in response to arguments that nonbeneficial research should not be performed on persons unable to provide informed consent.[37] By contrast, the 1997 European Convention on Human Rights and Biomedicine allows research involving children under two conditions: the research (a) has "the potential to produce real and direct benefit to [the child's] health" or (b) promises "significant improvement in the scientific understanding of the individual's condition" and "entails only minimal risk."[38] Thus, the European Convention allows minimal risk research involving children absent direct individual benefit.

A research protocol may contain interventions offering possible direct benefit and others performed only to gather research data. The National Commission argued that the risks and benefits of each intervention must be evaluated separately – an approach now called the "component analysis of risk." The IOM agreed.[39] The separate analysis of risk limits the allowable risks of "research only" procedures that are bundled with therapeutic interventions. This approach can also be used to analyze the acceptable risk exposure for children enrolled as the control group in clinical trials.

The use of placebo controls in clinical trials is controversial. The 2000 Declaration of Helsinki restricted the use of placebo controls to cases where "no proven prophylactic, diagnostic or therapeutic method exists."[40] The 1999 ICH guidance on choice of control group allows placebo controls when withholding effective treatment would not result in "death or irreversible morbidity" or the treatment has severe toxicity.[41] The WMA then clarified the Declaration of Helsinki in 2002, adding that withholding effective treatment in a placebo-controlled trial may be ethically acceptable (1) if necessary for "compelling and scientifically sound methodological reasons" or (2) for "a minor condition" where there would not be "any additional risk of serious or irreversible harm."[42] Should the ICH standards on choice of control group apply to research involving children?

Under Subpart D, research presenting more than minimal risk and the prospect of direct benefit must satisfy at least two criteria: the risk must be justified by the anticipated benefit, and the relation of anticipated benefit to risk must be at least as favorable as in available alternative approaches.[43] The alternatives include assignment to any arm of the clinical trial, and also any effective treatments available outside of the research. By requiring this balance, the National Commission anticipated the concept of equipoise (also discussed by Murphy and Goldkind in Chapter 3), defined as "genuine uncertainty on the part of the expert medical community about the comparative therapeutic merits of each arm of a clinical trial."[44] With equipoise, the different arms of a clinical trial may be considered together as offering the prospect of direct benefit. Absent equipoise, the risks to children in each arm of the clinical trial should be evaluated separately. A clinical trial may proceed absent equipoise, but the risks to children in the less advantageous arm must be no more than a minor increase over minimal risk.

Placebo-controlled trials of inhaled steroids for moderate to persistent severe asthma often exceed this level of acceptable risk. For example, children receiving inhaled steroids for at least six months were randomized to one of three doses of the experimental drug (another inhaled steroid) or to a placebo control. As expected, a significant number of children withdrew from the placebo arm after an exacerbation of their asthma.[45] This study (and others) lack equipoise given the demonstrated superiority of inhaled steroids to placebo in moderate to severe asthma.[46] Withholding inhaled steroids from children with moderate to severe persistent asthma does not meet the ICH standard of no "additional risk of serious or irreversible harm,"[47] the WMA standard of a "minor condition,"[48] nor the Subpart D criteria of being no more than a minor increase over minimal risk.[49] A recent trial of an inhaled steroid in young children with asthma raises concern about the quality of data from pharmaceutical trials conducted for additional patent protection.[50] A placebo control arm was included although consensus treatment guidelines recommend daily anti-inflammatory medication for the enrolled children.[51] The study included 543 children from over seventy centers. Thirteen children in the placebo group had therapeutic blood levels of the study drug, and many children on active treatment did not have detectable levels, rendering the data meaningless.[52] The sponsor was granted added patent protection, as the FDA did not realize the data were useless until further analysis.[53] As a result, children were placed at inappropriate risk for useless data, yet the sponsor still benefited financially.

Are there compelling scientific reasons for withholding inhaled steroids from children with moderate to severe persistent asthma? The placebo group is unnecessary to establish efficacy given a clear dose-response relationship as "evidence of a drug effect."[54] The use of placebo controls in asthma trials of inhaled steroids for children with moderate to severe persistent asthma does not meet the regulatory and ethical standards of Subpart D, the clarified Declaration of Helsinki, the CIOMS Guidelines, or the ICH guidance on Choice of Control Groups. A remaining (and difficult) question is whether a placebo control group is necessary for determining the safety (rather than efficacy) of a drug.

PEDIATRIC RESEARCH AS "SOCIAL CONTRACT":
THE ANTIDEPRESSANT EXPERIENCE

The public disclosure of the results of research involving children is a moral requirement that follows from the privilege of performing such research. In the United States (as of 2004) there is no labeling requirement for negative studies, no marketing requirement of pediatric formulations used to obtain added patent protection, no legally required posting of clinical trial results in a public registry, and no requirement to submit the results of all pediatric studies to the FDA. However, the situation in the United States is changing rapidly, largely as a result of legal actions in response to the use of antidepressants in children and adolescents.

The studies on using newer antidepressants to treat adolescent major depressive disorder (MDD) were conducted to obtain added patent protection in response to FDA requests.[55] The FDA review of the pediatric studies for paroxetine found that "the most prominent adverse reactions not seen in corresponding adult trials... involve behavioral effects... such as hostility and emotional lability."[56] Because the "coding... was potentially confusing," the FDA asked that the data be reanalyzed using terms for suicidal thinking and behavior (i.e., suicidality). The resulting report (May 2003) suggested an increased risk of suicidality with paroxetine use, prompting the FDA to ask sponsors for similar data about pediatric suicidality with eight other antidepressant drugs.[57] When these data became available, the Medicines and Healthcare Products Regulatory Agency (MHRA) in the United Kingdom contraindicated all of the antidepressants in question except for fluoxetine.[58] The FDA, however, requested individual patient data, which were sent for outside review, reclassification, and analysis. In October 2004, the FDA directed manufacturers of all antidepressant drugs to include in the drug label a "black box" warning of "an increased risk of suicidality... in children and adolescents being treated with these agents."[59]

Some criticize the FDA for failing to act sooner; others are concerned that depressed children will go untreated. Even so, the antidepressant story is a success for the legislative changes stimulating pediatric research. Without this data, the increased risk of suicidality in children from antidepressants would not have been demonstrated. No one committed suicide in any of the pediatric antidepressant studies. The information generated may prove life-saving to other children who have or would have received these medications off-label. Critics of the recent increase in pediatric research often fail to appreciate that the choice is between research and unexamined "off-label" use, rather than not using drugs to treat children.

A clinical study is usually designed to determine whether a drug is effective, with the number of participants often insufficient to detect an uncommon serious adverse event. For example, only one of the 26 pediatric antidepressant studies reviewed by the FDA demonstrated an increase in suicidality due to a drug. Only two of the nine antidepressant medications demonstrated an increase in suicidality after combining data from the trials using that drug. The overall risk of a 2 to 3 percent increase in suicidality due to antidepressant medication was found only when data from all the trials were combined.[60] Thus, the safety of these drugs could only be evaluated when the adverse event coding was standardized to allow grouped analysis – an approach that should be standard for all future drug development. Also, the increase in suicidality due to a drug (and not disease) was found using a nondrug (or placebo) control group. An ethical analysis of the use of a placebo control must balance the acceptable risk of withholding known effective treatment against the scientific need to determine accurately the safety of a new drug.

The pediatric studies of antidepressants have had a major impact in the United States on the public disclosure of clinical trial results. The BPCA requires public disclosure of a summary of the FDA review. However, the summaries for seven of the antidepressants were insufficient and at times misleading. For example, the clinical review of venlafaxine focused on lack of efficacy with no mention of suicidality.[61] When pooled data were analyzed, venlafaxine had the highest overall relative risk of suicidality of all the antidepressant medications.[62]

The New York Attorney General sued GlaxoSmithKline (GSK) in June 2004 for concealing negative information on using paroxetine for treating major depressive disorder (MDD) in children and adolescents. The American Medical Association supported participation in a clinical trial registry as a requirement for IRB approval. In August, Eli Lilly announced "that it would disclose the results of all clinical trials...via a publicly available registry" by the end of 2004. GSK settled the New York lawsuit and established an online clinical trials registry. Shortly thereafter, Forest Labs agreed to publicly disclose clinical study results and Merck supported registering clinical trials.[63] The Pharmaceutical Research and Manufacturers of America (PhRMA) established a Web-accessible database to "contain the results of all controlled clinical trials . . . completed since October 2002 for PhRMA-member company drug products approved in the United States."[64] The International Committee of Medical Journal Editors will require public registration of clinical trials for articles to be considered for publication.[65] Finally, the Fair Access to Clinical Trials Act of 2004 was introduced in the U.S. Congress. If passed, this Act would (1) require public registration of all clinical trials as a condition for IRB approval, (2) require public disclosure of all study results, and (3) establish financial penalties for noncompliance.[66] In remarks introducing the Act, the antidepressant trials in children and adolescents figured prominently.[67]

CONCLUDING REMARKS: EXPLOITATION OR PARTICIPATION?

The increase in pediatric research over the past decade has benefited the health and wellbeing of children. Even so, this research must conform to at least three ethical principles. First, children should only be exposed to the risks of research if it is absolutely necessary to obtain knowledge applicable to the health and welfare of children. To meet this ethical standard, we must pay careful attention to our research designs, including extrapolation from adult studies, sufficient children for subgroup analysis, and standardized coding to permit combined analysis. Second, the research risks to which children are exposed for the benefit of others and society should reflect the ethical limits built into the pediatric research regulations. As stewards of the future wellbeing of children, we must carefully interpret and apply the guidelines for the ethical conduct of research involving children, while admitting (and making publicly accessible) the difficulties and challenges. Our interpretation and application of these standards should be consistent and open to public comment and criticism. Third, even within these limits, research may be exploiting children if the exposure to research risk does not result in publicly available knowledge. The results of all pediatric research, whether positive or negative, should be publicly disseminated in an understandable, consistent, and searchable format. By adhering to these three principles, we honor the commitment and sacrifice of children (and parents) who enroll in research as participants actively engaged in furthering the health and welfare of all children. The transparency of the process of review and approval of pediatric protocols and the public disclosure of research results establish the moral legitimacy of placing children at risk for the sake of others. Absent transparency and public disclosure, the participation of children in research is simply exploitation.

5

Racial and Ethnic Inclusiveness in Clinical Trials

Valentine J. Burroughs

INTRODUCTION

It is now well documented that substantial disparities exist in the quality and quantity of medical care received by minority Americans, especially those of African, Asian, and Hispanic heritage.[1] These disparities can be found across many aspects of healthcare, including the delivery of pharmaceutical services.

Implicit in this finding is the ultimate outcome of increased disease and mortality rates for African Americans and other minorities. This is mostly due to a diminished quality of medical care and health services. Studies in cancer patients demonstrate that chemotherapy[2] and analgesic therapy[3] are more likely to be given to nonminorities. In the area of cardiovascular care, there are clear differences, not related to clinical factors, in treatment regimens after coronary angiography.[4] Studies have shown that African Americans and Hispanics receive fewer antidepressants for clinical depression and are relatively undertreated with analgesics for pain from fractures or postoperative pain.[5] African American and Hispanic patients with severe pain are less likely to be able to obtain commonly prescribed pain medicine because pharmacies in predominately nonwhite communities do not normally carry adequate stocks of opiates.[6]

The disparity is also due, however, to a conscious or unconscious predilection to avoid using better quality but higher-cost pharmaceuticals in the treatment of African American and other minorities on the part of healthcare practitioners and institutions. This matters particularly with minorities because there is good evidence that the substitution of generic drugs places minority patients at greater risk. This is known because pharmacogenetic research shows that drug effectiveness and toxicity can vary substantially among racial and ethnic groups.

A greater effort must be undertaken by policymakers to hold publicly funded health plans accountable for providing beneficiaries with products and services equal in quality to those of privately funded health plans. At the same time, the healthcare research community must endeavor to expand on the current knowledge base about differences among subpopulations in health environments, attitudes, practices, disease progression, and drug responses. The physical dangers of overlooking differences in these factors, as well as the ethical and justice issues posed, demand that we move toward individualized pharmaceutical treatment that takes into account the advances in pharmacogenetic and pharmacogenomic research now available.

The pharmaceutical industry is but one in the line of institutions, groups, and individuals that play a role in patient health. But the roles it plays – in the early stages of drug research, design, and development, and in drug cost and marketing issues – are critical. Greater racial and ethnic inclusiveness in clinical trials is one important first step in a series necessary for delivering better and more equitable healthcare by means of individualized, rather than "one-size-fits-all," drug therapy. This chapter will discuss why physical (and in particular genetic) variations matter in drug therapy; the many compelling reasons for moving toward individualized therapy; the current inequities in the representation of minorities in clinical trials and the role of some drug companies in this inequity; and why the industry must continue to seek to correct this underrepresentation.

THE CASE FOR INDIVIDUALIZED THERAPY

Race, Ethnicity, Culture, and Drug Therapy

The demographic changes anticipated over the next decade magnify the importance of the disparities in drug therapy between white and nonwhite populations. According to the 2000 census, racial and ethnic groups other than "white" make up almost one-third of the U.S. population. African Americans and Hispanics represent a growing percentage of the urban population in the United States. These groups constitute the new urban majority in cities such as Washington, Detroit, and Los Angeles.

These groups bear a disproportionate burden of disease, and a high fraction of these urban Americans depend on Medicare or Medicaid as their sole healthcare payer. As drug coverage policies within these programs evolve, they must account for the special needs of this growing percentage of the most needy patient groups they are intended to serve. These groups may be further disadvantaged if they do not have access to individualized care with appropriate pharmaceuticals.

Race and ethnicity have been used as factors in assessing whether an individual will respond in the expected way to a given drug therapy. Race, however, is an imprecise substitute measure of genetic differences among populations. Genetic variations, or polymorphisms, are naturally occurring variants in the structure of genes and the products they encode. These genetic polymorphisms change gradually in prevalence across continents and do not separate populations into clearly demarcated groups that correspond to popular ideas of race. The most obvious manifestations of racial differences – skin color, cranial features, and so forth – are superficial characteristics that have little relevance to drug responses or to the progression of complex diseases such as diabetes mellitus and coronary heart disease.

In the United States, criteria used to identify "racialized" groups have not been based solely on biological markers, but also on the idea of ethnic or cultural indicators. Hispanics, for example, comprise a group of individuals who generally share a linguistic heritage, but who represent multiple nationalities and "racialized" groupings, including whites, blacks, and indigenous Indians.

The terms "ethnicity" and "culture" have also been subject to conceptual misunderstanding and thus require more precise and coherent definitions, if they are to be useful. Together, as S. Lee and coauthors have noted, they refer to combinations of "socioeconomic, religious, and political qualities of human groups, including language, diet, dress, customs, kinship systems, and historical or territorial identity."[7] Like "race," ethnicity and cultures are subject to social constructions whose borderlines are not easily mapped. Thus, we must resist any temptation to view these concepts as having material reality. We should speak not of "Hispanic culture," for example, but rather of cultural beliefs held by certain populations of persons from specific areas, say Puerto Rico or El Salvador.

Genetic Factors and the Need for Individualized Therapy

Although age and gender affect an individual's response to pharmacotherapy, the primary biological factor impacting the effectiveness of properly followed treatments is genetics.

The genetic makeup of an individual may change the action of a drug in a number of ways as it moves through the body. Genetic factors may influence a drug's action by altering its pharmacokinetic properties (absorption, distribution, metabolism, excretion) or pharmacodynamic properties (effect on the body). Clinically, there may be an increase in the intensity and duration of the expected typical effect of the drug.

Pharmacogenetics traditionally meant the study of polymorphisms in individual genes. With the national implementation of the Human Genome Project (the thirteen-year genomics research effort cosponsored by the Department of Energy and the National Institutes of Health), this field now has broadened into pharmacogenomics, which examines the effects of multiple genes on drug response. Large arrays of genes are studied in parallel, so that the entire spectrum of genes that determine the response to a particular drug can be examined at one time.

Common polymorphisms in drug metabolism genes have received the most attention because they affect the metabolism of many clinically important and commonly used drugs. These genetic variations most often affect drug metabolism by reducing it, sometimes by disrupting it, and occasionally by enhancing it. Those who metabolize drugs slowly, for example, because they are exposed to a given drug over a longer period of time and experience higher concentrations of the drug in the bloodstream, can experience the equivalent of an overdose.

Most pharmacogenetic studies have concentrated on several groups of drugs, including cardiovascular agents and central nervous system agents, and their activity in certain populations. Cross-racial variability in the action of these types of drugs is clinically significant and results from differences in inherited pharmacokinetic or pharmacodynamic factors. The pathophysiology and progression of diseases also have cross-racial variation; diabetes mellitus, for example, and other disorders have a higher prevalence and different outcomes in certain racial and ethnic groups.

Drugs used to treat conditions of the cardiovascular system and the central nervous system can be affected by polymorphisms. Within the black population, the cardiovascular effects are especially notable. High blood pressure is disproportionately prevalent in the black population and is associated with higher incidences of cerebrovascular and kidney complications and heart failure. The overall risk of coronary artery disease in the black male population, however, is lower than that in white males, particular in Europe and the Caribbean, and to a lesser extent in the United States.

There are general differences in the underlying causes of high blood pressure between the black and white populations. Black patients, for instance, retain more salt and therefore have a higher incidence of salt-sensitive high blood pressure. This may underlie some of the observed differences in the effectiveness of various high blood pressure drugs in black populations. Although there is long-standing discussion about the best type of drug for treating high blood pressure in black patients,[8] African Americans respond to drugs from all classes.[9] There is no specific class of high blood pressure drugs that categorically should not be used based on race. Ultimately, the choice of therapy must be tailored to the individual patient.

Within Asian groups, central nervous system agents show susceptibility to genetic polymorphisms. Asian groups, as compared to some whites, are likely to require lower dosages of a variety of different drugs used to treat mental illness, including lithium, antidepressants, and antipsychotics. Asians living in diverse areas of the world (Los Angeles, St. Louis, Hong Kong, and Beijing) have also shown consistently slower metabolism of tranquilizers, suggesting that genetic factors are more important than environmental factors in controlling metabolism of these agents.[10]

Hispanic patients also have been reported to require lower doses of antidepressants and to experience more side effects than white non-Hispanics. Likewise, for a given dose of an antidepressant, African Americans achieved higher blood levels and faster therapeutic response, but also more side effects compared with whites.[11]

Medicines used to treat pain, such as codeine, can be influenced by genetic polymorphisms. This may have important clinical implications, since codeine is often a drug of first choice for the treatment of chronic severe pain. Ten percent of codeine is metabolized in the body to morphine, from which it derives its pain-relieving effect. Poor metabolizers of codeine therefore receive no therapeutic effect from the drug even at higher doses.[12] Five to ten percent of white patients versus one percent of Asians lack an enzyme that converts codeine to morphine. But even the 99 percent of Asians who do convert codeine to morphine experience a weaker effect than do whites, because they clear morphine faster and more rapidly metabolize that portion of codeine that is not converted to morphine.[13]

Ethnic groups such as Ashkenazi Jews may also respond differently to antipsychotic agents, especially with regard to side effects. A drug used to treat schizophrenia was associated with the development of a potentially life-threatening blood disorder in 20 percent of this particular subset of Jewish patients, although this adverse reaction develops in only about one percent of chronic schizophrenic patients in the general population.[14]

Concepts of identity based on racial markers, ethnicity, or culture may be useful when discussing trends among populations, but they cannot predict individual responses. We cannot rely on a form of racial profiling – using visible or socially constructed markers, such as skin pigmentation, eye shaping, language use, or health beliefs, to accurately identify the presence or absence of polymorphisms in drug-metabolizing enzymes or drug receptors.[15]

The usefulness of these concepts lies in their ability to increase the clinician's awareness of differences and the threshold for considering alternative treatment modalities, but not for limiting options in diagnosis or treatment for an individual patient. Such stereotyping could, in turn, contribute to the inequities reflected in health disparities.

Nongenetic Factors and the Need for Individualized Drug Therapy

Effective, ethical drug therapy involves more than awareness of complex genetic variations. Drug makers and healthcare providers face the added challenge of delivering effective pharmaceutical care to patients within a psychosocial context appropriate to their living environments, level of health literacy, and cultural beliefs and practices. The great diversity in our patient population demands a framework in which the drug maker and practitioner can approach all patients as egalitarian partners in care, regardless of cultural background.

Environmental Factors. Environmental factors – diet, climate, smoking, alcohol, pollutants, and environmental toxins, for example – may cause wide variations in drug responses within an individual and even wider variations between groups of individuals.[16] Several of these factors can operate simultaneously in the same individual, thus affecting the process of drug absorption, distribution, metabolism, excretion, and receptor interaction in different ways and to different degrees.[17]

Differences in diet may significantly alter the rate of metabolism or the amount of a drug present in the blood among different ethnic populations. Studies comparing the metabolism of a specific drug (antipyrine) among Asian individuals in rural villages and Indian immigrants in England demonstrated that as immigrants adopted the lifestyle and dietary habits of the British, their drug metabolism accelerated. Similar findings have been observed among Sudanese and West Africans.[18]

Smoking can be an important factor in determining response to pharmaceuticals. This is particularly notable because cigarette smoking accelerates the metabolism of many prescription drugs commonly used to treat chronic diseases such as asthma and high blood pressure, thereby making them less effective. Some drugs used to treat these conditions, however, are not affected by smoking; prescribing can be individualized to use these agents in smokers.[19]

Smoking-related disease and mortality are disproportionately prevalent among African Americans. Up to 45 percent of urban African Americans reported that they were smokers, compared with 25 percent for the general population.[20] African Americans metabolize nicotine more slowly and have higher serum nicotine metabolite levels per cigarette smoked than whites.[21] They may also develop dependence at lower levels of smoking, making it more difficult for them to quit.[22] The success rate for blacks who try to quit smoking is 34 percent lower than for whites.[23] Sustained-release bupropion has been found to be particularly effective in helping African Americans quit smoking.[24]

The drug, in addition to its known effect as an antidepressant, seems to alter nicotine metabolism in blacks more than whites.

Given the preponderance of the information we have outlined, the pharmaceutical industry must include increasing numbers of ethnic minorities in all phases of new product development. This is especially true in the earliest phases of drug design and premarketing clinical trials. It is at this time that untoward or beneficial effects of the new product in minority users can be most usefully identified. Too often medical research has undervalued or ignored these growing populations' concerns, only to uncover belatedly adverse reactions to new products that have not been sufficiently tested in minority groups. Barbara Noah in "The Participation of Underrepresented Minorities in Clinical Research," covers this subject in greater detail.[25] The high concentration of minorities within the Medicaid and Medicare population and with "bare bones" health plans sets the stage for healthcare disparities in the statutory use of "therapeutically equivalent," but untested, less expensive, generic drugs within this group. This typifies what is referred to in a 2002 Institute of Medicine report as the "socioeconomic fragmentation" of health plans.[26] It has been suggested that such fragmentation leads to the development of "different clinical cultures, with different practice norms tied to varying per capita resource constraints." None of this favorably impacts outcomes in healthcare for racial and ethnic minorities.

Health Literacy and the Health Gap. Health literacy refers to the set of skills needed to read, understand, and act on basic healthcare information. Over 90 million adults in the United States have low health literacy skills, with limited ability to read and understand the instructions contained on prescriptions or medicine bottles, appointment slips, informed consent documents, insurance forms, and health education materials.[27]

Members of socioculturally disadvantaged groups, especially those for whom English is a second language, are more likely than socioeconomically advantaged adults to have limited literacy skills, impacting their ability to understand and follow prescribed healthcare regimens.[28] In one case, many patients receiving acute care at two urban hospitals were unable to read and understand basic medical instructions.[29] Forty-two percent did not understand directions for taking medication on an empty stomach, and 26 percent did not understand information on scheduling their next appointments. Thirty-five percent of the English-speaking patients had inadequate or marginal functional literacy; for the Spanish-speaking patients, the figure was even higher (62 percent).

For some serious chronic diseases, such as diabetes, low health literacy poses a compound threat to overall health. Because self-management relies heavily on printed instructions, literacy is a key factor. A study of low-income African American patients with non-insulin-dependent diabetes found that the functional health literacy level was adequate in only 25 to 47 percent of patients at diabetes clinics.[30] Another study found that patients with inadequate health literacy were more likely to have poor control of their blood sugar levels and to report eye problems (usually involving blood vessels of the retina), which may progress to blindness.[31]

Standard patient informational practices have been shown to be insufficient to overcome the barriers posed by low health literacy.[32] Often, health educational materials are written at an inappropriate reading level, especially for minority groups in which English may be a secondary language. Although much effort has been devoted to improving the quality of written information, improvement in oral and visual communication to convey necessary information has received inadequate attention.[33] Healthcare practitioners are therefore challenged to communicate clearly and concisely with patients and to take a patient-focused approach to care. This also involves perceiving and surmounting less visible barriers such as patient confidence, shame, or fear. Practitioners must be able to communicate effectively across cultural, socioeconomic, educational, and geographical differences.

This communication skill has been appropriately called "cultural competency." Cultural competency should be a curriculum requirement for all medical students and residents in training and for all responsible practitioners of medicine. The pharmaceutical industry should make every effort to enlist the involvement of more minority investigators who are culturally competent to conduct and to recruit minority participants to serve in clinical trials. As a minimum, there should be training of all investigators in the skills and techniques of cultural competency to assure the retention of minority patients in clinical trials.

Pharmaceutical companies must take their fair share of responsibility for educating their product end users. Health literacy campaigns and partnerships with advocacy groups, community-based organizations, faith-based organizations, and governmental educational agencies will certainly begin to help the problem.

Cultural Factors and Practices. Cultural or psychosocial factors, such as the attitudes and health beliefs held by various groups, may affect the effectiveness of, or adherence to a particular drug therapy. Attitudes toward diet, exercise, smoking, drinking, and body image, for example, are embedded in all cultural beliefs and practices, and these attitudes affect health and interactions with providers in important ways. Among some culturally based attitudes, for example, is the belief that people should keep their illnesses to themselves. Persons holding such beliefs may be likely to seek treatment at later stages of disease.

Patients' beliefs regarding the properties and effects of medications are of central importance in determining compliance. Variations in attitudes toward medicines tend to be driven by national characteristics, culture, and philosophy.[34] Some patients from non-Western backgrounds may have different expectations regarding the type of drug prescribed, tolerance of side effects, dosage form preference, or other aspects of drug therapy. This clash between patient and provider expectations may result in noncompliance with medications.

Some immigrants from countries with non-Western medical cultures are unfamiliar with the practice of taking long-term medication for chronic illness and with the notion of accepting unpleasant side effects as the price for effective treatment.[35] In some developing countries, medications are customarily prescribed for only a day or two,[36] and there is a general expectation that medicines will provide quick relief from symptoms and thus do not need to be taken long term. These beliefs may reflect experiences with indigenous herbal preparations, which generally cause fewer side effects, and with analgesics and antibiotics, which work rapidly.[37] Hispanics and Asians often expect rapid results and are cautious about the side effects of Western medicines.[38] These beliefs may interfere with the acceptance of drugs with a delayed onset of action (e.g., antidepressants).

Another cultural factor complicating drug treatment is the fact that immigrant minority groups may have access to controlled substances and other medications not generally available in the United States. For example, antibiotic, neuroleptic, antiemetic, and most other prescription drugs are easily obtained over the counter in Brazilian pharmacies. Many pain-relieving medicines are also available without a prescription. Once in the United States, it becomes difficult to obtain these drugs and persons requiring them on a regular basis often ask friends to bring a supply from Brazil. In Haiti, many medications can be purchased without a prescription, so Haitians are often accustomed to keeping numerous topical and oral medicines on hand to treat various symptoms. An individual who suspects a venereal disease might buy penicillin injections and have someone administer them without consulting a physician.[39]

The use of alternative remedies and supplements is common. Among a multiethnic population, 10.4 percent were regular users of alternative medicines; 7.4 percent regularly used nonprescribed vitamin supplements; and 5.3 percent used cod liver oil, primrose oil, or garlic preparations. People of African origin were more likely to use alternative medicines than either whites or South Asians, who were the least common users.[40]

The use of complementary and alternative medications, however, can result in drug interactions, disease interactions, adverse reactions, or toxic effects:

- A survey of Spanish-speaking Latino families visiting a pediatric clinic in Salt Lake City found that 39 percent of parents from Mexico and 21 percent from other countries reported using a nonsteroidal anti-inflammatory drug (metamizole) associated with a blood disorder side effect.[41] The drug is available over the counter in Latin American countries and in markets serving immigrant communities in the United States.
- Dozens of Chinese herbal remedies available in the United States contain the toxin aristolochic acid. The toxin was implicated in an outbreak of kidney trauma in Belgium, possibly causing cancers in more than thirty people, and is suspected of the same in several other countries.[42]
- Another study found clinically relevant liver enzyme elevations in about one of hundered patients treated with traditional Chinese drugs.

Given this information, the pharmaceutical industry is increasing its awareness of these herbal medications that are so widely used, particularly among minority populations, for all of the reasons that were cited above. Ideally, new products should be tested to allow for the possible interaction with many alternative medications that are ingested by unsuspecting patients. Product labeling should include warnings for possible interactions with other prescribed or alternative medications. There should be a concerted effort to develop medications that are more "literacy" friendly, requiring little disruption in activities of daily living, once-daily administration, and short courses of therapy (unless for chronic illnesses).

The Future of Genetic Research and Drug Therapy

Technological advances in the wake of the Human Genome Project (which sought to map all 30,000 human genes and the sequences of the 3 billion chemical base pairs that make up human DNA and make them available for further research) will eventually enable us to move beyond flawed concepts of race and to tailor drug therapy precisely to each patient. It is now possible to take a genetic "fingerprint" of an individual and precisely determine the presence of polymorphisms in the genes known to be involved in drug interaction. Instead of a person's racial category being a risk factor for the possession of polymorphisms involved in drug response, a genotypic profile can determine with certainty whether or not the individual possesses these polymorphisms.

In the future, drug treatment will be individually tailored rather than race-based. Genetic fingerprinting using DNA arrays is already practical, but the knowledge base relating genomic variations to drug response and disease progression has not been developed. Studies in which DNA fingerprints are correlated with data present in medical records about medical history and drug response will have a profound impact on the use and development of new drugs.

Continuing research in pharmacogenomics is likely to reveal significant and far-ranging information regarding interindividual and cross-racial differences in the actions of new and existing drugs. Projects such as the Howard University Genomic Research in the African Diaspora (GRAD) Biobank, which will collect the largest repository of DNA from blacks (25,000 samples), will help both to continue the discovery of causes of disease with high rates among African Americans, and advance the course of research on genetically informed drug therapy. These developments, along with the increasing prevalence and influence of patients from a variety of races and ethnicities and the continued pressure to manage healthcare costs, will require programs having the dual objectives of cost control and individualized therapy for a racially and ethnically diverse population of Americans. Balancing these objectives will challenge health policy makers in the coming decades.

As a result of advances in pharmacogenetics research, as well as political and social changes affecting racial and ethnic groups, more consideration is being given to the need for individualized drug therapy. The availability of a broader range of medicines enables physicians to treat patients with precision and provides options when the first agent used is ineffective, not tolerated, or proper compliance is not achievable due to side effects. Individualized prescribing takes into account a number of factors, among them environmental, genetic, and cultural factors that may affect a drug's effectiveness and compliance with prescribed treatment regiments.

CLINICAL TESTING AND THE MINORITIES GAP

Despite the growing recognition of and body of knowledge about variations in drug responses among minority populations, the representation of minorities in clinical studies has not become a given. Even after research institutions, such as the National Institutes of Health, and regulatory bodies, such as the Food and Drug Administration, have issued guidelines for increasing racial and ethnic diversity among test populations, the gap is far from closed.

The exclusion of racial and ethnic minorities from clinical trials until the mid-1990s has been well documented by Noah.[43] Recent data on clinical trials participation, corroborating Noah's findings, suggest that minorities remain underrepresented in other types of treatment trials, including those for asthma and lupus and for occupational cancer and cancer prevention studies, as well as those for heart failure therapies.[44] Noah herself cites several studies as evidence of these disparities. One found that among a number of heart failure research protocols, white participants predominated, reflecting a failure to represent the

30 percent of heart failure patients who belong to racial and ethnic minorities.[45] Another study undertaken in 1989 illustrated a broader pattern of discrimination among African American participants in particular. In an analysis of clinical trials for a variety of prescription drugs, African American participants were found to be underrepresented compared with their numbers relative to whites in the local community surrounding the research base and compared with the average nationwide population of African Americans.[46]

There are many reasons for this, some having to do with certain subgroups' lack of access to information about clinical testing opportunities (either through healthcare providers or other means); or their own reluctance, due to mistrust, to put themselves through medical experimentation; or low health literacy (which may prevent individuals from being able to participate in studies requiring following sets of instructions).[47]

In some part, however, pharmaceutical companies have played a negative role by designing studies excluding minority populations. Noah points, for example, to the example of HIV therapy clinical trials, in which sponsors have encouraged researchers to recruit white, homosexual males with higher education, whom they considered more likely to follow drug regimens and other accompanying health instructions (and thus demonstrate a therapy's success), rather than those in low-income or minority groups, whom they perceived to be riskier subjects.[48]

HOW POLICYMAKERS AND PHARMACEUTICAL COMPANIES CAN HELP PROMOTE INDIVIDUALIZED THERAPY

Noah suggests several potential policy levers to increase the participation of underrepresented minorities in clinical trials, including the carrot of increasing the patent life of clinical trials with inclusive policies and the stick of restricting publication in medical journals for trials that are not representative. She also suggests that HHS and the FDA should require institutional review boards to require, rather than simply recommend, racial and ethnic diversity. She even suggests that IRBs themselves should seek greater diversity in membership.[49] Even if such measures do not come to fruition, however, as a matter of basic procedural and substantive justice, pharmaceutical companies should voluntarily begin to include significant numbers of patients from varied racial and ethnic backgrounds in drug metabolism and clinical trials in cases where genetic polymorphisms for that drug class are relevant. The vast majority of drug manufacturers do some testing and evaluation of new pharmacological compounds on population subgroups, including racial and ethnic subgroups. This is likely to reveal drug actions and side effects specific to these groups, and may lead to the discovery of therapies of specific advantage to these populations. It may also reveal cultural barriers to use of a drug among particular groups.

Drug companies, in their pharmaceutical literature directed at healthcare providers, should acknowledge and encourage the practice of giving individualized treatment to each patient. For the practicing physician, each patient represents a unique and dynamic interaction among several determinants including environmental, genetic, and cultural. Although it may be impossible for a physician to anticipate how a particular patient will respond in every instance, it is imperative to individualize therapy with respect to the appropriate choice of both drug and dose, and to make sure that the patient both understands and is able and willing to comply with the prescribed treatment.

Drug researchers and manufacturers should help physicians stay alert for atypical drug responses or unexpected side effects when they treat patients from varied racial and ethnic backgrounds. Patients may not be taking the medications properly due to misunderstood instructions or to misperceptions of Western medicine or the severity of the disease. Dosage adjustments may need to be made for patients from different groups, as supported by pharmacological evidence. In some cases, substantial downward dosage adjustments may be necessary, since individuals in these groups may not be able to tolerate standard dosage levels. Alternatively, standard doses of some agents of a class may not be effective in certain racial and ethnic groups.

RACE-BASED THERAPEUTICS

In an interesting twist, some doctors expect the use of race-based therapy to increase, despite critics who question its validity and worry about the ethical implications of representing race as an easily distinguished biological trait. In one instance, a medication was approved specifically for one group of African American patients.[50] The pharmaceutical company NitroMed's medication BiDil was shown in clinical trials to reduce the risk of heart disease in African Americans. The study involved 1,050 African Americans with moderate to advanced heart failure. Half of the group was treated with isosorbide dinitrate and hydralazine, the other half received a placebo. After three years, thirty-two participants who took BiDil died, compared with fifty-four who took a placebo. In addition, it was shown that the number of first hospital admissions for heart failure among participants who took BiDil was 33 percent less than the number among those who took a placebo. It appears that the results of this recent study indicate almost certain Food and Drug Administration (FDA) approval for BiDil, which could be available in 2005. NitroMed would retain exclusive patent rights to the drug until 2022.

Earlier trials of BiDil suggested that African Americans might be prone to a nitric oxide deficiency that BiDil helps to correct and to be less responsive to ACE inhibitor therapy for hypertension and heart failure. NitroMed in the 1980s did not receive FDA approval to market the drug for all racial groups, leading researchers to conduct the most recent trial. Some opponents of race-based medicine say that approving a drug for only one group could prevent others who might have benefited from the medication from receiving it. Without testing in larger, more diverse groups of participants, FDA approval is not likely to be broadened, leaving doctors only the option of prescribing the drug off-label for use in patients of other races.

This situation is not unlike the testing of current medications for market approval in mostly white populations with few minorities included in the clinical trials to determine the efficacy of the medication on mixed populations. It might be said in these instances that doctors who are prescribing such a drug for minority patients are using it off-label relative to the FDA's approval for (*de facto*) exclusively white groups of clinical trial patients.

NitroMed plans to conduct additional trials to determine if other groups could benefit from their drug. Identifying such candidates for expanded testing, however, could be difficult because many people are from mixed racial backgrounds and are not fully aware of their heritage. It seems clear that because this study, done only in African Americans, showed a response dramatically different from that in the larger mixed group, African Americans are different genetically and this difference must be recognized in excluding or underrepresenting minorities in future clinical trials.[51]

Although race consciousness offers a faster way through the maze of FDA approval, there is a legitimate concern that emphasizing biological differences between social groups risks stigmatizing some groups in a more active way. This is in contrast to the passive overlooking of biological differences that is widespread in clinical trials today. Most trials do not include minorities in sufficient numbers to safely draw conclusions about their response to FDA approved medications. Both perspectives must be addressed if patients are to be treated with individualized pharmaceutical care.

It is incumbent upon pharmaceutical companies that have obtained regulatory approval and patent protection to sponsor further research aimed at clarifying any relevant genetic variations and their physiologic significance or manifestations. The ultimate answers lie just within our reach in the development of the science of pharmacogenomics. With this capability, we will be able to obtain genetic "thumbprints" of patients. This will obviate the need to use race as a weak surrogate for identifying genetic differences that might or might not exist between patients.

6

The Rights of Patients to Participate in Clinical Research

Glenna M. Crooks

RESEARCH: PROCESS AND PURPOSE

In the West, we trace the beginning of clinical research to Dr. James Lind, who in 1747 studied six treatments for scurvy on twelve sailors aboard the HMS Salisbury as it sailed from England to Plymouth Colony.[1] The study lacked the rigor of modern clinical trials, but it was the first recorded Western instance of a documented scientific approach comparing the effects of interventions in humans.

Modern clinical research is more sophisticated than this early example, but it has the same purpose – *prospective* studies comparing the effect and value of an intervention against a control in human beings,[2] requiring that an intervention be planned and applied *selectively* in humans to determine its impact. When properly planned and conducted, clinical trials assess the effectiveness of care and enhance treatment armamentaria.[3] By comparing alternatives, clinical research has great potential to save lives, improve the quality of life, reform healthcare, and control costs.[4] It is from these comparisons that conclusions are drawn about the value of an intervention.

PATIENT PARTICIPATION: IMPERATIVES AND DEMANDS

Patient participation is no small matter in today's healthcare systems, which treat both newly emerging communicable diseases and increasingly complex combinations of chronic and acute conditions afflicting young and old alike. Researchers need patients who are willing to participate in the studies that will generate answers to the questions of how to treat conditions effectively and efficiently, returning the patients to high-quality lives with good clinical outcomes at the lowest possible cost.

When clinical studies began in modern-era American healthcare, human research subjects were drawn from pools of patients within this country who were seeking access to the best medical care. Research endeavors were small at first and were funded privately by philanthropists supporting individual researchers. Beginning in the 1950s, increases in federal funding initiated the development of a larger, more complex infrastructure for conducting greater numbers of clinical studies, which thus created the need for even more research subjects. Researchers turned to institutions housing large numbers of accessible individuals: prisons, schools for the retarded, and the military. By the 1960s, the clinical research enterprise had developed even more and the demand for research subjects increased even further as Food, Drug and Cosmetic Act legislation required that drugs on the market be researched to ensure that they were safe and effective. Researchers not only improved the scientific methods of clinical research during this era, but also dramatically increased the number of research studies, creating even greater demand in the number of research subjects required for the development of new medicines.

The growth in both the number of research studies being conducted and the number of research subjects needed to fill them continues to accelerate. Pharmaceutical companies now predict a 65 percent increase in new compounds emerging from their labs.[5] Over 90,000 clinical trials are currently under way in the private and public sectors, 80 percent of which are not meeting enrollment deadlines for patients. Just over 25 percent of clinical development time is spent identifying and enrolling subjects, and though it spends an estimated $1 billion annually to recruit patients,[6] the pharmaceutical industry incurs losses of up to $1.3 million per day due to trials uncompleted because of enrollment difficulties in the United States alone. Even the U.S. government, for its own clinical research, has been required to develop Web-based communications to attract patients to research trials.[7] Researchers now also travel abroad for human subjects, searching particularly in developing nations. The number of foreign clinical investigations grew sixteenfold between 1990 and 2000, and the number of countries in which clinical trials were conducted grew from 28 to 79 during the same period.[8] Securing sufficient numbers of clinical trial subjects for this most basic participatory role is not a trivial concern.

PATIENT PARTICIPATION: MATURATION AND RECOGNITION

In the past, the goals, methods, mechanisms, and patient recruitment aspects of clinical research were the prerogative of scientists and regulators. Increasingly, however, patients are demanding the right to participate in all of these aspects of the clinical research process. Researchers, regulators, and policy officials should be asking and answering pertinent questions about this movement toward collaboration: Why would patients demand greater involvement in research? Should patients be granted this right? How will clinical investigations be impacted if patients have a right to participate not only in trials but in the determination of who will be studied, what will be studied, and how it will be studied? Will this result in a setback for research, or catalyze a giant leap forward? What changes will be required as patients become more knowledgeable about and active in the research process? Will patient participation help or hinder the development of new knowledge and innovative medicines? What are the dynamics at play in these new demands from patients and their advocates? What is the nature of the collaborations they seek? Is this an indication that we have failed them in some way?

Currently, it is patients, not researchers or regulators, who are leading the way in redefining patient roles by becoming more active in developing research agendas, determining research designs, and gaining access to trials themselves. This empowered "patient rights" movement comes late to the research ventures of healthcare. It trails behind the demand for rights to privacy, access, affordability, and quality, but it has come knocking at the research door nonetheless. In fact, the demands for collaborations in research should come as no surprise, as they are consistent with the evolving state of the physician-patient alliance. It is time for researchers to respond as clinicians have and welcome patients to a more mature partnership. Just as patients are becoming partners in the care they receive, now, too, they are also seeking similar partnerships in research.

In a very real way, however, it is not the *fact of participation* that is new, but the demand for *more comprehensive involvement* in the research enterprise and for *recognition of the influence* patients already have in research. It would be unwise to ignore these new patient demands and to fail to recognize the comprehensive contributions of patients. Patients have not only participated as human research subjects, but for many years they have been involved in clinical research in other ways as well. They have been active in private-sector fund-raising for research and have created organizations to support researchers in academia and the private laboratories. They have been active in public policy, lobbying for research training and clinical trial funding from governments. They have supported legislation promoting intellectual property protections and have argued successfully for access to new therapies. In recent years, they have contributed to our understanding of how to recruit human subjects into trials, increased our understanding of cultural sensitivities needed to conduct research among minority and certain disease groups, and argued successfully for expedited regulatory review of important products. It is not the *fact* of the participation that requires exploration, but the *nature* of that participation today. It is not the *reality* of participation, but the conscious *recognition* of participation that is a new imperative in the modern pursuit of innovation.

These matters are the subject of this chapter. I intend to address several of the critical issues that currently drive newly empowered patients to demand the right to participate in research in new ways, note the growing need for collaboration with those who are the subjects of research, and argue that patients can be effective partners in the development of new knowledge. This is not a new or radical idea – patients have long been partners. It is time we in biomedical research recognize their contributions and honor their willingness to assume more visible, integral roles. But how? What are the next steps we must take? I believe there are three fundamental tasks at the outset. If we fail to succeed in these, all of our efforts to engage in mature partnerships will likely fail. First, we must restore trust in researchers. Second, we must embrace those patients who are at the leading edge of patient demands. Third, we must return to our roots in medicine and recognize that a failure to accommodate patient demands is a failure to live within the oaths we have taken as healers.

RESTORING TRUST IN RESEARCHERS

Ensuring the ethical treatment of patients who participate in trials is neither trivial nor easy. Even the twentieth century – a time most people would have called "civilized" – produced examples of egregious behavior in clinical research, including dangerous and harmful experiments performed on nonconsenting patients.

In the worst cases, experiments were performed on institutionalized individuals, the poor, or groups regarded as "lesser humans," including Jews and others in Nazi concentration camps, the mentally retarded, prisoners, persons of African descent in America, and indigent patients. Often, these individuals were unable to decline to participate in the research study,[9] either because their consent was not sought or because a physician fraudulently described the experiment as a diagnostic procedure or treatment for the patient's condition.

In 1963, for example, American researchers injected live cancer cells into elderly debilitated patients in a Jewish chronic disease hospital.[10] In the same year, intellectually disabled children were injected with hepatitis in a New York State public institution.[11] For forty years, beginning in 1932, nearly 400 African American men in the Tuskegee study of syphilis were left untreated – and were actively discouraged from seeking appropriate care – as part of a study designed to observe the natural course of untreated syphilis. It was not until 1965 – nearly twenty years after penicillin was demonstrated to be effective against the disease – that clinicians objected to the experiment on ethical grounds and not until 1972 that the Associated Press (AP) was tipped off and released the story.[12]

In other studies, prisoners were subjected to malaria, typhoid, and cholera.[13] In an earlier example from the nineteenth century, a gynecological surgeon in the southern United States demonstrating a profound lack of compassion conducted surgical experiments on African American women without anesthesia, believing that they did not suffer and would "bear pain" better than white women.[14] Patients today may be unaware of the details of these atrocities, but they are not unfamiliar with the reality of major ethical breaches.

Modern research ethics came about largely because of these revelations. The global community responded, calling the Nazi experiments crimes and crafting the Nuremberg Code, the first international normative framework to regulate standards in clinical research trials.[15] This document was superseded by the Declaration of Helsinki, a code for research and experimentation that was endorsed by the World Medical Association (WMA) in 1964 (Juhana Idänpään-Heikkilä and Sev Fluss offer additional information on the history of international ethical codes in Chapter 2).

Nonetheless, ethical lapses have continued, even recently and in situations in which regulatory bodies exist to ensure patient protection. In New Zealand, for example, a hospital ethics committee and Institutional Review Board (IRB), both charged with protecting human research subjects, approved a study that denied treatment to women with cervical cancer, failing to tell them of the diagnosis or of the research study, though they were repeatedly brought back to the hospital for observation. Many died when timely knowledge and treatment could have saved their lives.[16]

Understandably, patients and advocates familiar with ethical misconduct are much less likely than others to be willing to participate in studies.[17] This should surprise no one in the research enterprise. Everyone involved – from researchers to regulators – should know that regardless of the good intentions of particular studies, or the high standards of adherence for most studies, all studies bear the burden of eroded trust created by these lapses in ethics. Today's empowered patients cannot be expected to willingly enter trials in the face of difficult-to-ignore ethical violations. There are many good reasons to offer patients a "seat at the table," but none is better than to initiate the transparency that will reassure them that researchers are doing their best, especially in situations where ethical issues are unclear and uncharted, to protect human research subjects. Opening the doors to previously closed discussions about clinical trial design and research methods will help to restore trust in the research process.

Unfortunately, past breaches of trust are only some of the barriers to earning the trust of today's patients. Other concerns include researchers' conflicts of interest, "finder's fees" paid to clinicians who refer patients to clinical trials, drug-pricing policies that put drugs out of reach of many who helped to develop them, and the lack of transparency of research results. These, too, are concerns that must be addressed if researchers expect trust from those who must willingly place themselves at risk as subjects of medical experiments.

Only by involving patients will it be possible to navigate these and other increasingly complex ethical waters that lie ahead in clinical research. Consider the evolving ethical and technical aspects of human subjects research. Some of the emerging ethical challenges into which patients can provide invaluable insight are cultural. In some countries, for example, individual consent on many matters important to life is not a commonly held value, and the notion of individual consent in research is quite foreign. In those countries, it is acceptable for consent to be granted by the community of the whole, by tribal leaders, or by some other person, such as the husband of a female subject.[18] The age of majority also varies around the world. In the United States, the legal age for consent is 18, but in many other countries it is much younger. Research conducted in those countries, and research on immigrants arriving from those nations, must be approached with sensitivity to these cultural practices, widely divergent as they may be from those in the United States.

Others of these ethical challenges are technical. Even though informed consent is legally viewed as a *process* rather than a *document*, the process is usually accompanied by a document that is signed by those involved. As Dr. Valentine Burroughs notes in Chapter 5, this can be problematic among those with low literacy[19] or in the case of immigrants from countries where citizens fear that signing a document may place them or their families at risk of reprisals from an oppressive government.[20] Informed consent is also problematic in countries where the language has no words for "research study."[21] In some cultures, research subjects' belief systems about science, health, and disease are so divergent from those of Western nations that the nature of the research intervention cannot be explained accurately.[22,23] Further complicating the technical challenges, requiring the name and telephone number of a research contact is impossible among poor or highly mobile groups where people do not have telephones or consistent contact information. At long last, these patient-centered research participation considerations – which go beyond those of informed consent – are being addressed by ethicists who are working to evolve ethical requirements for clinical research. They will be addressed successfully only if those from the affected communities are involved to ensure that their unique issues of importance are accommodated.

At the cutting edge of these new relationships, patient advocates are showing us the way to build and maintain their trust. Their demands go beyond informed consent and fair treatment as human subjects to the heart of research itself. They want, for example, studies to be conducted in scientifically valid ways in order to ensure that scarce financial and human resources are not allocated to projects that are unlikely to benefit humanity. They demand social justice in research, ensuring that subjects are selected in ways that are fair and do not stigmatize, or make vulnerable, someone who participates in a study. They want assurances that the poor and powerless should not be chosen for more risky (or less beneficial) research, whereas the rich and powerful are chosen for less risky (or more beneficial) studies. They suggest independent reviews of research to ensure public accountability and prevent potential conflicts of interest. Finally, in addition to informed consent, they believe that, out of respect for human subjects, all research subjects should be informed of the study results and of any negative outcomes of studies. To some in research, these might seem unreasonable intrusions. However, these are the steps that must be taken to ensure that patients have our trust and are willing, therefore, to continue to participate in the research ventures they have so long supported.

EMBRACING PATIENT DEMANDS

In Chapter 17 of this book, Martin Delaney includes a detailed discussion of the history of the AIDS patients' movement. There is no better, clearer contemporary example of patient leadership. The experience with AIDS patient advocates should inform all efforts to address patient needs today. It is precisely this type of leadership – at the cutting edge of patient demands – that we should embrace as the research enterprise grows and matures in the future. The appearance of empowered patients, triggered by HIV/AIDS in the 1980s, might seem to some to have been a threat to research. In fact, this new movement of patient involvement was an opportunity, and one we have not yet fully embraced within biomedical research, particularly with regard to other conditions.

As the virus took hold and the search for therapies progressed, the HIV/AIDS community influenced the nature of clinical study participation, creating a research-subject empowerment movement and the first highly successful patient-driven demand for research participation. AIDS patients became more influential in the conduct of research than any group before them. Facing social stigma, cultural bias, and certain death, they empowered themselves and forced change. They demanded that they be allowed to participate in the development of research priorities and the design of protocols and, as research subjects, even tested their experimental compounds in laboratories – a clear violation of research "blinding." Their activist demands to participate in research led to studies that accrued patients more quickly, addressed community-based concerns more successfully, and contributed to the development of current therapeutic regimens that have altered the life courses of those HIV-positive individuals.

The HIV/AIDS crisis also heightened awareness of the ethnic, gender and racial diversity of persons living with the disease. No longer was it acceptable to draw clinical trial subjects exclusively from groups of white, middle-class men. As it became increasingly clear that medicines had different effects on different groups of patients, the need for larger and substantially more diverse groups of patients in studies was recognized. As a result, investigators and regulators alike now seek a better balance of gender, racial, ethnic, and age groups in clinical trials to ensure that all groups of patients will be fairly represented and that the action of the medication in subpopulations of patients will be understood (this is also addressed in Chapter 5 by Dr. Burroughs). The recognition of patient diversity brings thrilling new ideas to medicinal innovations and increases the opportunities for better targeting of effective therapies. Unfortunately, it also brings the single greatest challenge to the researcher–subject relationship; that is, the need to develop new skills to reach out to increasingly diverse human subject populations. These skills are essential, given that the changes set in motion by HIV/AIDS activists have been adopted by women living with breast cancer, those living with hemophilia, and other vocal patient advocates addressing the unmet needs of their constituencies.

It was during the early AIDS research era that the most vocal patient advocates argued that participation is more than a *goal*. They argued that participation is a *right*. What type of right? The right to participate as a subject in a trial, the right to participate in the design of a clinical trial protocol, the right to participate in trials themselves, and the right

to have a voice in the research enterprise overall. I propose that patients
and their advocates have a right to participate in the planning, design,
and conduct of clinical research by virtue of their historical willingness
to participate as subjects and supporters of the research ventures I
have already described here. I also suggest, however, that they have
earned this right by virtue of their evolving skills within this arena. As
patients and their advocacy organizations today are more capable of
being mature partners with clinicians during the process of care, so,
too, are they capable of being more mature partners with researchers
during the process of knowledge development.

Once passionate but somewhat unprofessional, many patient groups
today are highly professional, organized, well-capitalized, competent
collaborators. They are knowledgeable about disease conditions, medications, and life-style issues and are trusted communicators within their
networks of patients and clinicians. They have sought, and heeded, the
advice of scientists and clinicians and are articulate spokespersons for
those they represent. They are effective in recruiting patients for clinical trials, particularly in situations where special disease, gender, racial,
or ethnic community concerns slow patient enrollment, and they are
sought out by regulators during the drug-approval process and in times
when crises arise in the use of medications.

Medical advances since the beginning of modern biomedical
research have extended the life span, reduced morbidity, and improved
the quality of life globally. This happened because patients were willing to participate. There is little doubt that the support of patients and
their advocates will continue to be required to design trials, to recruit
patients, to fund research, and to ensure that innovations are widely
available. Research will continue to require human subjects in order
to continue to make progress in addressing the prevalent and emerging diseases of the world. We owe a great debt to those professionals
who advance medical technology and science. However, any progress
in acquiring new knowledge depends on the willingness of those individuals who risk pain, disability, and even death as research subjects.
We owe a great debt to them as well.

It would be unfortunate to ignore the even greater contributions that
patients and their advocates can now make to the progress of science.
The time has come to accept and acknowledge their role and potential
by granting them access to participation not only as subjects, but as true

partners in mature, comprehensive relationships in research. We'll all be the better for it. But is that enough?

Epidemiology and population-based studies, computer simulations, and *in vitro* studies yield insights about health and disease. Eventually, however, human studies are necessary to tease the mysteries from the body. It may well be a messy business to deal with empowered patients who hold divergent views about research. Some will fear the motives (including the profit motives) of investigators, or may distrust institutional review boards. Others will have access to medical care close to home and be unwilling to travel to research centers. Still others will hold diverse cultural notions of disease or ethnic biases about research. Nonetheless, cooperation with patients is necessary and will both improve the nature of the investigative process and ultimately hasten the development of the knowledge we all seek. Failure to cooperate will hamper the progress we all envision.

In fact, those involved in the healing enterprise have little choice in the matter. The solemn oaths they take as healers require not only that they care for patients, but also that they seek new knowledge about the human body, health, and disease. The Oath of Hippocrates included research by implication in this commitment to learning and teaching, swearing:

To consider dear to me as my parents him who taught me this art...to look upon his children as my own brothers, to teach them this art if they so desire....[24]

The oath developed by the twelfth-century Jewish sage Maimonides was considerably more explicit:

Thou hast granted man the wisdom to unravel the secrets of his body, to recognize order and disorder; to draw the substances from their sources, to seek out their forces and to prepare and apply them according to their respective diseases.... Permit not the thought to awaken in me: You know enough....[25]

The oaths align the roles of caregiver and researcher. There is no conflict or discord between the roles. The healer and the researcher are at one in their work.

That healers would also be researchers and develop new knowledge was clear. *How* they would do that, however, was not prescribed. Just as, in 1747, Ship's Surgeon Dr. James Lind could never have envisioned double-blind, randomized clinical trials approved by IRBs, today's clinical researchers may not yet be able to envision a full partnership with empowered patients, capable of contributing more than their physical bodies to the process of research. It is time they do, as patients have earned this right. They have demonstrated their ability to participate in a myriad of ways. It remains for us now, in the research enterprise, to reciprocate by acquiring the skills to work with patients who are prepared to participate with us in mature ways.

To accomplish this, I suggest we now engage in a comprehensive review of our own practices within the public and private sector research enterprise. We should examine every aspect of resource allocation, research design, clinical trial recruitment, and the regulatory interface to determine how we can improve the productivity of research by collaborating with patient groups. This assessment should not be confined to our own soul-searching, but should ask patient groups for their critical review of our historical performance and request constructive comments about how to improve our efforts. On the basis of that review, we should determine what new skills, tools, and research processes we should acquire in order to be better research, regulatory, and policy partners with patients, and we should organize our research ventures accordingly. Next, we should practice these new skills, monitoring the impact on our relationships with patients and on research productivity. Finally, we should recognize that this is a new era of patient participation, that patients' rights to participate, though unrecognized when they first became research subjects long ago, are not new, but merely maturing. It is appropriate that we recognize that now, and mature in our own management of this most critical of relationships in research.

It is not simply by showing that researchers understand these issues that we will rebuild trust, benefit from those patient advocates on the leading edge of leadership, or meet the terms of the oaths we take as healers. Rather, we will do so by proving it through our actions as researchers, regulators, and policy makers.

7

How Should Government Regulate Stem-Cell Research? Views from a Scientist-Legislator

Rush Holt

THE GOVERNMENT AND MORAL ISSUES

All governments are faced with the difficult task of grappling with ethical issues upon which many scientific, philosophical, and religious leaders are unable to reach consensus. Government sponsorship of stem cell research is clearly such an issue.

Legislative issues are often heavy with ethical considerations. War and peace, for example, and crime and punishment are clearly predicated on ethical judgments, but so too are less obvious decisions on the relative allocation of resources to highway safety, school lunches for poor children, space research, AIDS in Africa, military equipment, and park preservation. These ethically based deliberations are made much more difficult when the legislators do not understand the scientific or technical issues involved.

Stem cell research is a subject that involves both ethical decision-making and science. It is generally believed that the political difficulties of stem cell research come from the ethical differences of debating parties. I suggest that they come more from a fundamental misunderstanding of the science. If so, there is a possibility of reaching consensus on regulations that would also be widely accepted by the public.

Most members arrive in the U.S. Congress with clear moral and ethical beliefs regarding human life. Generally, these convictions are based on personal and religious beliefs developed outside the public policy arena. Some are elected to office in part because of these beliefs and are unlikely to change their convictions based on Congressional debate. Because they view stem cell research as an ethical issue, members feel prepared to confront it. This is despite the fact that most members of Congress have no more than a high school education in the sciences. The sheer volume of information, the range of issues, and the variety of demands on a member's time means that members have detailed understanding of at most a few subjects. Yet most are quite skillful at using a few key concepts upon which to base decisions that are consistent with the wishes of their constituents and the member's own record – except in subjects with large scientific components.

STEM CELL RESEARCH

Stem cells have two very important traits. They are unspecialized cells that can renew themselves for long periods through cell division. More important, under certain conditions, they can be induced to differentiate into specialized cells such as heart, kidney, or insulin-producing cells. Hence, stem cell research has been described as holding the promise of cures for a wide range of diseases. Any disease involving cell damage or cell malfunction may be receptive to treatment using stem cells to replace the faulty cells in the patient. This promise is far from realization. To achieve practicality will require extensive stem cell research. Currently, there is research on embryonic stem cells, somatic cell nuclear transfer cells, and postnatal, or "adult," stem cells.

Stem cells are found in fertilized embryos (actually blastocysts, which are embryos several days old and undergoing cell division but not yet cell differentiation) and have a full, normal complement of chromosomes. Because such cells have the capacity to differentiate into each of the 200 or so cell types that make up the body, they are known as pluripotent embryonic stem (ES) cells. They give rise to differentiated cell types, capable of integrating into all fetal tissues during development. ES cells can be isolated and grown outside the uterus, where they continue to replicate through an unlimited number of symmetrical divisions without differentiating. A single ES cell can give rise to a colony of genetically identical cells, or clones, which have the same properties as the original cell.[1] This process might be used to create cells almost indistinguishable from those of a receiving patient who is a candidate for some kind of cellular repair.

In a process called somatic cell nuclear transfer (SCNT), the nucleus of an unfertilized egg cell is removed and replaced with the material from the nucleus of a "somatic cell" such as a skin, heart, or nerve cell, for example, from the recipient patient and then stimulated to begin dividing. The nucleus of the somatic cell, having a full, normal complement of chromosomes, provides the genetic information. The remaining part of the cell or oocyte provides the nutrients and other energy-producing material. Once the cell begins dividing, stem cells can be extracted five to six days later for use.

One of the exciting possibilities of this technique is that it could generate stem cells using SCNT from a person's somatic cells and then create tissues or organs for grafting in that same person. Because the graft is autologous (the genetic control of the composition and behavior of the replicating stem cells is the same as in the receiving individual), the immune system would not reject the graft, relieving the recipient from troublesome immunosuppressive drugs. This is called therapeutic cloning.

A clarification that is very important to make is that SCNT is not reproductive cloning, because it generates differentiated tissue but not a complete new individual. Reproductive cloning involves duplication of an individual by implantation of a cloned embryo into a uterus. The scientific community generally agrees that cloning to produce humans should be illegal, but therapeutic cloning and SCNT should be allowed. Many lay people and their representatives in Congress erroneously believe that any and all uses of SCNT can and will result in the creation of an exact copy of a human.[2]

Finally, adult stem cells are undifferentiated cells found among differentiated cells in a tissue or organ.[3] Unfortunately, adult stem cells are generally limited to differentiating into different cell types of their tissue of origin. In other words, they are not pluripotent. Some evidence suggests that the adult stem cells may exhibit some plasticity, which may increase the number of cell types they can become. ES cells can proliferate for a year or more in the laboratory without differentiating, whereas adult stem cells cannot.[4]

U.S. LAW AND STEM CELL RESEARCH

Because ES cells are taken from a blastocyst, opponents of ES stem cell research contend that life is destroyed. This position is the basis of the Dickey Amendment, in which the U.S. Congress attached language to the 1996 Department of Labor, Health and Human Services, and Education, and Related Agencies Appropriations Act prohibiting the use of any federal funds for research that destroys or seriously endangers human embryos, or creates them for research. Research in SCNT or therapeutic cloning is also prohibited, and the Act bars the Patent and Trademark Office from spending money "to issue patents on claims directed to or encompassing a human organism." This restriction could potentially deter human stem cell research because researchers might not be able to claim ownership of their work.[5,6] On August 9, 2001, President George W. Bush announced that federal funds would be awarded for research using human embryonic stem cells if the following criteria were met:

- The derivation process (which begins with the destruction of the embryo) was initiated prior to 9:00 p.m. EDT on August 9, 2001. It was announced subsequently that investigators from ten laboratories in the United States, Australia, India, Israel, and Sweden have derived stem cells from seventy-one individual, genetically diverse blastocysts.[7]
- The stem cells must have been derived from an embryo that was created for reproductive purposes and was no longer needed.
- Informed consent must have been obtained for the donation of the embryo and that donation must not have involved financial inducements.

This decision was touted as a Solomonic one, but it produced outcries from both sides of the issue. Pro-research advocates countered that there were not enough ES cell lines available for research, and that existing lines were unsustainable. Pro-life supporters were equally critical in that federal funds would support research on cell lines created by the destruction of embryos, even though the destruction had already occurred and could not be reversed. An imbroglio occurred in Congress. Comments on the societal consequences of using SCNT cells to produce a stem cell line produced a myriad of peculiar arguments, such as the following:

- "Women of low economic means will be paid anywhere from $3,500 to $4,000 to donate eggs, leading to the establishment of human embryo farms."

- "It will lead to the exploitation of women: namely poor women and women of color."
- "It will lead to increased depression in women and cause suicide."
- "It will compromise women's health."
- "It will result in the horror of unscrupulous doctors performing cloning on unwary women."

Congressional opponents also contended that:

- "The FDA cannot stop human cloning, it can only regulate it, and so Congress must prevent it. Since we cannot enforce regeneration research on SCNT, we must ban it all."
- "If cloned embryos are made, introduction into the womb and then conception will take place."
- "It will usher in reproductive cloning. It will encourage genetic manipulation and enhancement. They want to create human models of diseases; they want to create human beings that are engineered to manifest these diseases. Cloning must be totally banned."
- "On a technical level, cloned human embryos are not likely to yield cures for major illnesses. Therapeutic cloning is going nowhere. Other lines of stem cell research are more favorable: placental cord blood and adult stem cells."

On February 27, 2003, the U.S. House of Representatives passed H.R. 534, the Human Cloning Prohibition Act of 2003, sponsored by Rep. Dave Weldon (R-FL), by a vote of 241-155. H.R. 534 amends Title 18 of the United States Code to ban the process of human cloning and the importation of any product derived from an embryo created via cloning. Under this measure, cloning could not be used for reproductive purposes or for research on therapeutic purposes, which would have implications for stem cell research. H.R. 534 includes a criminal penalty of imprisonment of not more than ten years and a civil penalty of not less than $1 million. H.R. 534 is essentially identical to the measure that passed the House in the 107th Congress (H.R. 2505). A companion bill, S. 245, introduced by Sen. Brownback, similar to H.R. 534, never made it out of committee for a Senate vote. No bill has yet become law.[8]

I believe much of the emotion and rancor in the debate was based in confusion about the facts. Most of this confusion could have been averted by proper access to scientific and technical advice. Congress has been without a good, local source of such advice for almost ten years.

The Congressional Office of Technology Assessment (OTA), established by an act of Congress and signed into law by President Nixon in October 1972, existed to provide the Congress with an objective, thorough analysis of many of the critical technical issues of the day. For example, it examined science relevant to policy in medicine, telecommunications, agriculture, materials, transportation, defense – indeed, in every discipline and sector important to the United States. OTA took on a variety of subjects, including some controversial ones, examining them objectively and comprehensively for legislators' benefit.

OTA brought science into the center of many congressional discussions. At times, OTA took part in high-profile debates on major pieces of legislation such as the 1980 Energy Security Act, Superfund, the Clean Air Act, and the Foreign Assistance Act. Also, the agency contributed to specific technical issues that puzzled nontechnical congressional staff, such as risk reform, long-term African development, acid rain, dismantling nuclear weapons, the Strategic Defense Initiative, and police body armor.[9] As part of the larger aims outlined in the *Contract With America*, Republican leaders eliminated the OTA in 1995.[10] Since the demise of OTA, Congress has struggled with the scientific underpinnings of many issues including cloning and stem cell research.

CLONING: WHAT DOES IT MEAN?

Scientists rely on a dialect of specialized terminology to communicate precise descriptions of scientific phenomena to each other. In general, that practice has served the community well; novel terms are created when needed to document new findings, behavior, structures, or principles. The lexicon of science is constantly evolving. Scientists who are fluent in the language of any specific discipline can speak to one another using shorthand expressions from this dialect and can convey an exact understanding of their intended meanings. However, when the scientific shorthand makes its way to the lay public, there is potential for such meaning to be lost or, worse, misunderstood, and for the terminology to become associated with research or applications for which it is inappropriate.

This is exactly what has occurred in the public interpretation of ES cell research. The major stumbling block is a lack of understanding of the word "cloning." The word is widely used in lay society and has been given various meanings. In scientific terms, cloning means making a copy of an object, whether it is a stretch of DNA, a virus, or a cell. In today's lay vernacular, cloning is often interpreted as making an exact copy of a living animal such as the sheep Dolly or a human. This misinterpretation is the basis for the subsequent evil associated with the words "clone" and "cloning." Scientists generally agree that cloning a human being, aside from the moral or ethical issues, is unsafe under present conditions and should and must be prohibited. The scientific distinction between "therapeutic cloning" and "reproductive cloning" to a layperson is not apparent. These two processes with radically different purposes and outcomes are interpreted as the same thing. More careful use of terminology would help the public and lawmakers sort out the substantial differences between SCNT and human cloning. Something like the OTA would help the situation.

I believe that because stem cell research has not produced practical applications for ordinary people, few people have bothered to learn about stem cells. As long as it remains the province of researchers and not the general patient, it is easy for the public to resist an examination of the subject. Legal and moral comparison with assisted reproductive technology (ART) and *in vitro* fertilization (IVF) can be instructive.[11] The first IVF baby was born in England in 1978, and IVF was introduced in the United States more than two decades ago. When first presented to the public, IVF was technically complex and forbidding. It was promptly dubbed a process for making "test tube babies," invoking the dehumanizing image from Aldus Huxley's novel *Brave New World*. Many religious people and others deemed it ethically objectionable. As the IVF research yielded practical results with safe births and the public began to learn about the procedure, objections subsided and IVF came to be seen as a comprehensible and acceptable procedure that could help infertile couples conceive. Indeed, many called the procedure a blessing for infertile couples. There is no federal legislation prohibiting IVF. An existing law, the Fertility Clinic Success Rate and Certification Act of 1992, provides consumers with reliable and useful information about the efficacy of ART and the services provided by fertility clinics.[12] It also provides states with a model certification process for embryo laboratories.

IVF was introduced in the United States in 1981, and from 1985 through 1998 the American Society for Reproductive Medicine and its affiliate, the Society for Assisted Reproductive Technology, counted more than 91,000 babies conceived through IVF. Through the end of 2000, more than 212,000 babies have been born in the United States as a result of reported ART procedures.[13] IVF has become a standard medical technique used for the treatment of infertility. In each of these successful IVF births, a number of oocytes were obtained. Practitioners estimate that between eight and fifteen oocytes are retrieved from a patient undergoing an ART procedure, and two to five embryos are transferred to the uterus, resulting in three to thirteen embryos being left over, which are either discarded or frozen for later use.[14] It has been estimated that more than 400,000 embryos are in cryostorage as of April 2002.[15] There are no federal regulations on storage or destruction of IVF embryos.

Across the nation IVF creates thousands of fertilized eggs that will not ever be brought to term in a pregnant woman, yet IVF is fully accepted and regulated only with regard to safety and is subject only to normal ethical concerns involving treatment of patients.[16] The practice is so common today that since the 1980s, fourteen states have passed laws requiring insurers to either cover or offer coverage for infertility diagnosis and treatment. (Nine states have laws that require insurance companies to cover infertility treatment and five require insurance companies to offer coverage for infertility treatment.) While most states with laws requiring insurance companies to offer or provide coverage for infertility treatment include coverage for IVF, California and New York have laws that specifically exclude coverage for the procedure.[17,18]

If it is not considered immoral or illegal to sacrifice embryos from IVF clinics for treating infertility, then will it be considered immoral to utilize IVF embryos scheduled for destruction in order to cure or treat devastating diseases?[19]

U.S. RULES AND REGULATIONS

The process by which the government establishes rules and regulations can be arcane. The Administrative Procedure Act (APA)[20] establishes the general procedures that an agency must follow when promulgating a rule.[21] Rulemaking is referred to as "informal," or "notice and comment" rulemaking. For example, when an executive agency, such as the National Institute of Health (NIH) within the Department of Health and Human Services (HHS), promulgates a substantive regulation pursuant to the APA, it must:

1. Publish notice of proposed rulemaking in the *Federal Register*;
2. Provide an opportunity for the submission of written comments by the public; and
3. Publish any subsequent final rule and a general statement of basis and purpose in the *Federal Register* "not less than thirty days before its effective date."[22]

These requirements constitute a procedural minimum for rulemaking, with the drafters of the APA contemplating that "[m]atters of great import, or those where the public submission of facts will either be useful to the agency or the protection to the public, should naturally be accorded more elaborate public procedures."[23] Accordingly, the NIH may choose to include additional steps in certain rulemakings to increase public participation, including, but not limited to, the conduct of a second round of notice and comment proceedings, as well as by holding public conferences.[24,25]

In January 1999, HHS determined that the Dickey amendment ban on federal funding of human embryo research did not prohibit funding human ES cell research using already existing embryos from IVF clinics. NIH published guidelines in the *Federal Register* for support of such research in August 2000. In addition, entities and individuals that conduct research on humans are both federally and institutionally regulated. *Ex vivo* embryos are not considered "human subjects" for these purposes. By this interpretation, the Dickey amendment regulates research on *ex vivo* embryos but not on stem cells per se.

Two agencies are primarily responsible for oversight of ES cell research. The mission of the Food and Drug Administration (FDA) is to ensure the safety and efficacy of food, drugs, medical devices, and cosmetics. It regulates stem cell research that is aimed at the development of any product subject to FDA approval. The NIH is the medical and behavioral research agency: it regulates NIH-funded research on stem cell research in compliance with President Bush's 2001 policy banning embryonic cloning, both reproductive and therapeutic. NIH established the human ES cell lines that meet the President's eligibility criteria and assigned each an official registration number.

U.S. STATE RULES AND REGULATIONS

The Dickey amendment restricts federal funding for embryo research. States are the principal sources of direct regulation of non-federally-funded embryo research. State laws vary widely in their application and content. The combinations and variations of restrictions have created a complicated legal landscape, and include permission to do research on embryos and fetuses.

New Jersey and California encourage stem cell research involving the derivation of human embryonic stem cells and cloned embryos, and permit state funding for it.[26] Their laws provide assurances to researchers and sponsors, do not contradict President Bush's 2001 policy, and expressly permit and encourage research. In 2004, California voters approved $3 billion in state-bond funding for embryonic stem cell research, although as of 2005 the funding faces legal hurdles. In New Jersey, a bill was signed by the governor to create the first state-funded embryonic stem cell research center, a $25 million endeavor. Both laws have the potential to entice researchers and medical industries to relocate from other states.

As of 2005, seventeen states have restrictions on research using tissue derived from processes other than abortion, such as in IVF or cloning,[27] and sixteen states restrict research on aborted fetuses and embryos, both of which possibly preclude some forms of stem cell research. The restrictions on aborted fetal and embryonic tissue vary in scope among the states, with some prohibiting research on living and nonliving fetuses or embryos.[28] At the other extreme, Nebraska prohibits the use of state funds for embryonic stem cell research.[29]

FOREIGN RULES AND REGULATIONS[30]

The international community has taken a variety of actions regarding stem cell research. In 2004, the United Nations abandoned its effort to develop a restrictive human cloning treaty.[31] The European Union (EU) clarified its stem cell rules in November 2003, smoothing the path for EU funding and support for human embryonic stem cell research.[32]

Under the terms of its sixth research framework program (FP6), the EU may fund embryonic stem cell research regardless of the date on which the stem cells were procured from embryos. A cut-off date, which would have created a restriction similar to President Bush's 2001 policy, was under consideration, but was summarily rejected. FP6 allows funding for research on tissue derived from spontaneous or therapeutic abortion, but not for the creation of human embryos for the purpose of stem cell procurement. According to members of the European Parliament, FP6 funding decisions should depend "both upon the contents of the scientific proposal and the legal framework of the Member States involved."[33,34]

EU member states are considering a range of legislative options. Sweden's parliamentary committee on genetic integrity proposed no prohibition on the production of fertilized eggs for research. In Italy, a proposal would prohibit any experiments on human embryos, the production of embryos for research purposes, and any destruction of human embryos. By contrast, a proposal before the Spanish Parliament would allow research using surplus frozen embryos that can no longer be used for reproductive purposes, provided that the consent of the donor is given. Stem cell research is still illegal in Ireland, Portugal, and Austria. Recently, the French parliament gave final approval to a bioethics law that will allow human embryonic stem cell research.[35] The legislation, which was passed after nearly three years of debate, updates a 1994 bioethics law and will allow stem cell research on human embryos for five years. The French parliament also passed a measure that bans human reproductive cloning as a "crime against the human race" punishable by twenty years in prison. Germany allows stem cell research only on imported cells and cells existing before January 1, 2002.[36]

The United Kingdom is the only European country that allows therapeutic cloning research. The British Parliament amended the 1990 Human Fertilization and Embryology (HFE) Act in 2001 to allow the creation of embryos for harvesting of stem cells provided they were less than fourteen days old. The Blair government has provided more than U.S. $60 million in public funding to ensure that British-based companies can exploit the new technology. The United Kingdom Stem Cell Bank in Potters Bar, outside of London, received its first donation of two stem cell lines developed by researchers in Newcastle and London in May 2004. British scientists are licensed by the HFE Authority to derive new embryonic stem cells from human embryos. The scientists must agree to donate samples to the UK Stem Cell Bank, which will serve as a global repository of stem cells for scientists, maintaining active cell lines and distributing them to laboratories around the globe for a fee.[37,38] Because these cells were derived after August 2001, U.S. researchers are banned from using them.

In March 2004, the Canadian government enacted legislation allowing stem cell and other research to be conducted on donated embryos created, but no longer needed, for reproductive purposes.[39,40] Singapore, Australia, Israel, and England have made stem cell research a national priority and are providing large amounts of funding for its advancement.

In Asia, the South Korean government adopted a law barring cloning for reproduction in late 2003. Experiments that use embryonic stem cells have to receive reviews and authorizations from a government ethics panel. Further regulations are to take effect next year. A South Korean research team reported success in cloning human embryos.[41] Thirty embryos were created and kept alive in test tubes for five days. Although the South Korean government has helped finance animal cloning research, the human embryos were cloned without government funding or corporate sponsors. The idea is to make embryos that are clones of patients suffering from spinal injuries, diabetes, and other illnesses, take the precious stem cells from those embryos and grow tissues from the stem cells. This tissue would be genetically identical to the patients' and would not be rejected by their immune systems. The new tissue could be used to repair the defective organs. Since no sperm was used, it has been argued that the embryos cloned by the team do not qualify as human lives. The team has agreed not to transfer the cloning technology overseas without government permission, and as a result, work on the human embryo project after the publication of their findings is halted while the South Korean government drafts specific ethical guidelines on human embryo cloning.

Japan recently approved its first medical research project using domestically created human embryo stem cells.[42] Another Australian company, Stem Cell Sciences, established Japan's first stem cell company in June 2002 with U.S. $150 million worth of Japanese government credits. Regulations are less restrictive in China. The director of a large fertility clinic simply asked some of the dozens of women who walked through the door each day to donate their leftover eggs. The director claims that 5 percent of the cloned embryos develop to blastocysts.[43,44]

CONCLUSIONS

The economic and psychological tolls of chronic, degenerative, and acute diseases in the United States are enormous. It has been estimated that up to 128 million people suffer from such diseases; thus, virtually every citizen is affected directly or indirectly. The total cost of treating diabetes, for example, is approaching $100 billion in the United States alone. As more research takes place, the developmental potential of different kinds of stem cells will become better understood. As the research begins to yield some results benefiting patients, we can expect greater recognition and acceptance of the work.

As the science is understood now, adult stem cells are limited in their potential to differentiate. Embryonic germ (EG) cells, which are isolated from the primordial germ tissues of aborted fetuses, have a great capacity to differentiate, and embryonic stem (ES) cells are thought to be able to differentiate into almost any tissue. Thus, different types of stem cells could have different applications. In the United States, much of the basic research on animal stem cells and human adult stem cells has been publicly funded. Under the fully applied Dickey amendment, research in the United States using human ES cells could only be done in the private sector.[45]

Private sector organizations have pursued and been awarded patents on the stem cells themselves and methods for producing and using them to treat disease. Even as federal funding continues to be debated, it seems likely that private sector companies will continue to play large roles in the future development of stem cell based therapies. Indeed, all research is now global. The United States has no monopoly on intelligence and innovation; other countries will fill in the science and applications gap created by a legislative body unwilling to permit such research.

The present U.S. guidelines for ES research were predicated on the immediate and widespread availability of more than seventy-eight embryonic stem cell lines established by the NIH's Human Embryonic Stem Cell Registry. However, the latest registry lists just twenty-one available cell lines.[46] Furthermore, these lines suffer from limited genetic diversity and, because they were developed from mouse feeder cells, viruses contaminate some of the lines.[47] Because of the federal political uncertainty in stem cell research, private investors and potential pharmaceutical partners are hesitant. In addition, the NIH is prohibited from studying privately derived stem cell lines derived after August 2001. What are the implications when private companies take cell lines into the clinic? What role will the NIH then assume?[48]

When stem cell research gains acceptance, regulations should be developed. These guidelines for using human pluripotent stem cells eligible for federal funding are a modification of existing NIH guidelines:[49,50]

- Cells are created for the purposes of fertility treatment and are in excess of the clinical needs of the individual seeking such treatment.
- No inducements, monetary or otherwise, have been offered.
- There is a clear division between the decision to donate and the influence of researchers; the attending physician responsible for the fertility treatment and the researcher cannot be one and the same person.
- Blastocysts older than fourteen days may not be used. This would also include those made by SCNT technology.[51,52]
- Informed consent is obtained with proper documentation.
- An Institutional Review Board approves any derivation protocol.

Research agencies should establish

- Specifying metrics for each stem cell line, including sterility, karotype, and other characteristics.
- An electronically accessible national registry of human embryonic stem cell lines.[53]
- Training programs for interested investigators, including proficiency testing and certification.
- A centralized agency responsible for maintaining a stem cell bank and guidance on clinical trials.

The difficulties arriving at a legislative consensus on stem cell research does not come primarily from the ethical considerations. Congress is not usually reticent to deal with ethical problems. In fact, it frequently deals with issues having significant ethical components. The problem with stem cell debate is a poor understanding of the science and the terminology involved. As a result, the issue is mistaken for an ethical debate only. As *in vitro* fertilization has gained a level of scientific understanding and ethical acceptance, so too will stem cell research. Stem cell therapy, assuming it proves feasible, will be subject to the same degree of regulation as IVF. The process of developing a legislative consensus for regulation of stem cell research would be hastened and improved if Congress were once again aided by an Office of Technology Assessment.

MARKETING AND THE EFFICIENT UTILIZATION OF HEALTHCARE RESOURCES

Ethical and Public Policy Challenges

Introduction to Part II

Michael A. Santoro

It would seem logically impossible to be both exquisitely subtle and affrontingly obvious at the same time. However, a widely viewed television commercial managed to do just that. The ad displayed the name of the product as a smiling, middle-aged man threw a football through the center of a car tire. We are not told what kind of product is being promoted. Subtle, it would seem, until one learns that the product being advertised is a drug – for erectile dysfunction. In retrospect, knowing what the product purports to do, the ad seems appallingly suggestive. Indeed, one feels pretty dumb for not getting it in the first place. Another recent ad eschews subtlety and goes right for the jugular. An impossibly thin, glamorous woman suddenly falls to the floor. Her cholesterol level is flashed on the screen along with the name of the drug.

With clever and hard-hitting ads peddling drugs as one might sell soap or beer, it is no wonder that many are concerned about the effects of direct-to-consumer advertising.[1] Such suspicions are further fueled by the fact that this seemingly ubiquitous advertising is coming at a time when overall drug spending is rising and new drug prices climb ever higher.[2] That much of direct-to-consumer advertising (DTCA) is for so-called "lifestyle" drugs – for erectile dysfunction or hair loss, for example – only serves to add to the tawdry image of the drug companies.

It is virtually impossible to watch the evening news or read a magazine without being exposed to DTCA. Remarkably, however, DTCA is only the tip of the iceberg when it comes to drug marketing. It has been estimated that of the $25.6 billion spent in 2003 on prescription drug promotion, $22.4 billion (87.5 percent) went to free samples and sales representative visits (referred to as "detailing" in the industry) to physicians, whereas only $3.2 billion (12.5 percent) was spent on DTCA.[3]

As we saw in the chapters about pharmaceutical research, the authors in this section are also concerned about the potential conflict arising from the profit-maximizing objectives of pharmaceutical companies and the social goal of optimizing public health outcomes. The principal objectives of drug promotion are to increase market share and to increase the size of the market for the class of product. In the cases of DTCA and physician detailing, the central concern is that these marketing tactics inevitably will lead to inappropriate and wasteful usage. Moreover, a corollary concern is that drug promotion undermines the special relationship of trust between the physician and the patient.

Part II addresses three sets of issues at the intersection of drug marketing, commerce, and public health: (1) Does DTCA encourage patients to use unnecessary drugs or switch from adequate cheaper drugs that are not part of an advertising campaign? Is there a significant disconnect between the profit-maximization objectives of private pharmaceutical companies and the public good? Or might there actually be some good to come from the awareness such ads garner for healthcare issues? (2) Can we really trust physicians to be unbiased gatekeepers for the medical needs of their patients? Or are physicians unduly under the sway of the powerful marketing machines run by pharmaceutical companies? (3) With public monies increasingly accounting for more of what is spent on drugs, how can drug expenditures be more closely aligned with medical needs and cost-effective therapeutic outcomes?

DTCA AND PUBLIC HEALTH

The watershed event in DTCA was a 1997 ruling by the FDA clarifying the disclosure of risk required in broadcast advertisement. Previously, in printed DTCA ads, drug companies were required to provide a brief summary of side effects, contraindications, and effectiveness. The 1997 FDA ruling, however, permitted these factors to be communicated through a toll-free number, a Web site, a print advertisement, or a consultation with a physician.[4] After the FDA ruling, the floodgates of television drug ads were opened.

From a public policy perspective the key issue is how the most valuable benefit of DTCA – encouraging consumers with undertreated conditions to seek out medical care – can be achieved while minimizing the wasteful and inappropriate drug utilization stemming from the simplistic and incomplete information that is currently found in DTCA. Here again, as we saw earlier in the case of clinical research, the profit-maximizing objectives of pharmaceutical companies diverge from public health objectives. Without a doubt, the purpose of drug promotion is to increase profits not to advance public health. But how wide is this divergence between private and public goals and what can be done to minimize it? A number of chapters in this section help us to answer this question.

As Director of the FDA's Division of Drug Marketing, Advertising, and Communication, Thomas Abrams deals first-hand with DTCA regulations and works to promote higher industry standards. In his chapter, Abrams reviews recent FDA disciplinary actions against pharmaceutical companies for improper direct-to-consumer and physician advertising. He emphasizes the FDA's crucial role in monitoring DTCA content, as recent research indicates that patients are becoming increasingly independent in their search for prescription drug information, particularly in their utilization of the Internet. Pharmaceutical companies, Abrams notes, have caught on to this trend and have responded with a blitz campaign of DTCA. Abrams presents several examples of commonly seen violations of regulations relating to the promotion of prescription drugs, and recent FDA enforcement actions. He explains the basis for the agency's actions and describes some general principles for future review of pharmaceutical advertising.

In their chapter, Professors Meredith Rosenthal and Julie Donohue, two scholars with expertise in economics and health policy analysis, assess what existing research tells us about whether DTCA serves a positive function or whether it encourages patients to use drugs that are either unnecessary or not cost-effective when compared to other, less expensive drugs that are not subjects of ad campaigns. Rosenthal and Donohue acknowledge positive benefits from the increasing involvement of patients in medical decision-making, made possible in part by the rise of the Internet, DTCA, and other information technologies. Nevertheless, they advocate stronger regulation of the content of drug advertisements to both physicians and patients so that better information about the risks and benefits will become available. Rosenthal and Donohue call for increasing the public resources devoted to supplying physicians with independent information about cost-effectiveness, efficacy, and side effects. They also recommend tying physician reimbursement more closely to cost-effective prescribing and cost-sharing by patients.

Professor Donald Detmer, a physician and healthcare educator, Peter Singleton, an academic researcher who has consulted in industry, and Scott Ratzan, a pharmaceutical industry executive working on European healthcare issues, also place the rise of DTCA within a broader context of rising consumer awareness. In their chapter, they introduce the concept of the "informed patient" to suggest that people with illnesses (as well as healthy individuals) need appropriate information to be involved effectively in their own healthcare. Detmer, Singleton, and Ratzan describe the results of the Informed Patient Project, a study at the Judge Institute of Management of the University of Cambridge aimed at guiding future policy on the provision of information to patients in Europe. They describe various methods of correcting what they regard as the patient "information gap," and offer a model for doing so ethically and effectively.

DTCA is a relatively new phenomenon the effects of which we are just beginning to understand. As Rosenthal and Donohue demonstrate, existing regulations do not enable optimal alignment between public health goals and the profit-maximization goals of industry. Moreover, as Tom Abrams illustrates, many companies are trying to stretch even what is allowed under existing regulations. While regulators and analysts grapple with finding and enforcing the regulatory mix that best serves public needs, the pharmaceutical industry has been nimble and opportunistic in exploiting the novel and uncertain regulatory environment. Clever advertising firms are designing sophisticated and appealing broadcast commercials employing jingles, humor, sex appeal, and all the other tricks of the trade. Whatever the merits of an informed patient might be, the actual DTCA practices too often are less about presenting information and more about manipulation.

As a number of the authors in this section demonstrate, the regulatory environment is playing catch-up with the fast-moving wizards of Madison Avenue. Sensing that public backlash might lead to legislative curtailment of DTCA, the industry in 2005 developed a voluntary code of conduct for DTCA. Such efforts are long overdue as the industry's public reputation has already been significantly eroded by the more tawdry publicity campaigns. It remains to be seen, moreover, whether self-regulatory efforts will work or whether further government regulation is required.

QUIS CUSTODIET IPSOS CUSTODES? THE PHYSICIAN AS GATEKEEPER OF PATIENT HEALTH

The physician, of course, is at the heart of the medical system. The patient reposes an uncommon trust in the physician's integrity and in her uncompromising loyalty and devotion to the patient's health. Inroads into physician independence and loyalty are especially troubling because doctors are gatekeepers for the medical system as a whole.

On their graduation from medical school, many physicians recite a modern version of the Hippocratic Oath that provides that "I will apply, for the benefit of the sick, all measures which are required, avoiding those twin traps of overtreatment and therapeutic nihilism."[5] The marketing practices of pharmaceutical companies pose a significant threat to the essential integrity and trust expressed in this oath.[6] Drug companies spend many times more than they do for DTCA on "detailing" visits by sales representatives to doctors' offices. These sales reps give out free samples in an effort to induce doctors to prescribe these pills. Doctors are regularly wined and dined and paid "honoraria" to attend "informational seminars" about drugs. Often these informational seminars are in exotic locales, trips to which are paid for by the pharmaceutical companies.[7] And this just describes the legally permissible activities!

As a dean of a prestigious medical school and a practicing clinician, Dr. Charles Bardes offers us a unique and honest picture of a world few of us can experience – the physician's perspective on treating patients with drugs. The modern patient, often influenced by DTCA, as described by Dr. Bardes, comes to the examining room with a host of expectations about the kind of treatment she will receive. For the physician, these expectations create ethical dilemmas as she tries to match the patient's expectations with her assessment of medical need. Dr. Bardes's account leaves one with awe for the physician's complex task of sorting through the various medical, scientific, financial, and social dimensions of deciding whether or not to prescribe a medication; which medication to prescribe; and whether to prescribe a generic or brand name drug, a prescription or over-the-counter drug, or a new or time-tested drug. Add to these complex choices the ever-present reality of a litigious society and questions about how to communicate side effects and how to comply with formulary lists, and one can begin to appreciate how difficult and complex it is for even the most knowledgeable and caring physician to fulfill her ethical commitment to the patient's health.

The fact that physicians have the legal right to prescribe drugs for off-label or nonconforming uses not approved by the FDA offers yet another challenge to maintaining physician independence and loyalty. In some areas of practice such as cancer care over 50 percent of drugs administered are off-label.[8] Scott Danzis, a specialist in food and drug law with the distinguished Washington firm of Covington & Burling, surveys the legal backdrop behind such nonconforming uses by physicians and describes a legal environment that is far from clear and well-settled. Danzis discusses at length one particularly egregious example of the ethical dangers of off-label use. In 2001, Parke-Davis, the maker of the epilepsy drug Neurontin, was accused of intentionally directing its sales force and medical liaisons to promote the drug for numerous unapproved uses.[9] Doctors were encouraged to prescribe Neurontin for everything from pain control to attention deficit disorder. Physicians also were allegedly rewarded with kickbacks. Patients were unwittingly induced to submit false claims to Medicare to pay for the off-label usage of the drug. This last factor ultimately led, as Danzis recounts, to the company's prosecution under the federal False Claims Act.

Danzis offers recommendations on how the confusion and lack of clarity in the current law might be transformed into a more predictable legal regime that protects patients and doctors but at the same time honors the First Amendment right of pharmaceutical companies to inform doctors about scientifically valid information concerning off-label usage.

In recent years, prosecutors have uncovered a host of unsavory and illegal marketing practices, including kickbacks, employed by pharmaceutical companies to market their drugs. Since 2001, the industry has paid over \$2 billion in fines to settle such claims.[10] The American Medical Association was so concerned about physician integrity and loyalty that in 1998 it updated a code of ethics governing gifts from drug companies to doctors.[11] In 2002, the Pharmaceutical Manufacturer's Association of America followed with its own code of ethics for interactions with doctors and other healthcare professionals.[12] As illustrated in the Neurontin case, it is as important to hold the pharmaceutical companies liable for exaggerating or falsifying off-label medical indications as it is to preserve a physician's freedom to collect information and prescribe drugs as she sees fit. Time will tell whether self-regulation by the medical profession and the pharmaceutical industry will be enough to stem the tide of abuses. If not, more government regulation is sure to follow because, as Dr. Bardes so eloquently reminds us, physician professionalism, integrity, and independence will always be the ethical lynchpins of our medical system.[13]

PUBLIC HEALTH AND PUBLIC FUNDING

Another distinctive aspect of the pharmaceutical industry raising ethical and public policy concerns is the third-party payer system. The cost of drugs, like many other healthcare product and services, is often borne by third parties – insurance companies, health maintenance organizations, and, increasingly, governments. The expenditure of third-party, and especially public, resources on drugs inevitably leads one to question whether those resources are being expended in the most cost-effective matter.

In recent years, pharmacoeconomic studies have sought to establish answers to questions about the relationship of drug costs and healthcare benefits, to wit: Do the healthcare benefits of drug expenditures outweigh the costs? Are the drugs that are being purchased more cost-effective than alternative medications for treating the same conditions? The answers to these questions are sure to have profound implications for how the federal government will implement the Medicare drug benefit enacted in 2003 by the U.S. Congress. In his chapter, Professor Joel Hay, who holds a joint appointment in the economics department and pharmacy school at USC, offers a comprehensive analysis of what we have learned thus far (and what we have yet to understand) from such cost-benefit and cost-effectiveness studies.

Hay begins his analysis by observing that some pharmaceuticals, for example, childhood vaccines for smallpox, polio, measles, mumps, and so forth, are highly cost-effective, while others are not. Among those he considers "decidedly not" cost-effective are the Cox-2 inhibitors, such as Vioxx, in their use as pain relievers, because studies have shown that various over-the-counter medicines (OTCs) are both comparable in efficacy and significantly cheaper.

Overall drug expenditures have come under tremendous scrutiny in recent years because they represent the fastest growing segment of a fast growing healthcare sector. In 2002 U.S. healthcare expenditures reached $1.6 trillion, 15 percent of that year's gross domestic product, and $5,440 per capita.[14] As Hay observes, in recent years pharmaceuticals have for the first time reached 10 percent of total healthcare costs, a trend he also observes in virtually all the world's advanced economies, particularly in Europe, Japan, and Canada. These trends raise an obvious question. Are prescription drugs cost-effective in comparison to other healthcare expenditures? Hay offers a detailed and subtle answer to this question based on research conducted with cross-national data.

Hay concludes by observing that the increasing precision of cost-benefit and cost-effectiveness studies, combined with the trend of public funding for drug therapies, will herald an era of rational cost controls for drug expenditures in Europe and the United States. He even goes so far as to envision a time when pharmacoeconomic analysis will make it feasible to encourage additional drug innovation and development through a publicly funded reward system that complements rather than replaces the existing patent system.

Underlying public policy questions addressed by Hay are some very deep moral issues. From a public perspective it is critical that government expenditures make cost-effective use of limited resources. Simply put, if government is footing the bill for drugs, the public has a right to know that drug expenditures achieve the intended public health benefits by means of the lowest cost alternative. However, the particular health needs and priorities to which those limited resources are directed by insurers, HMOs, and governments also raise important moral questions. Such decisions will have significant impacts on the health and welfare of individual citizens. Which drugs should be covered and which should not? What dollar limits should be placed on drug expenditures for given conditions? These and related questions are addressed in the final chapter in this section, a unique collaboration among a moral philosopher, Norman Daniels, a medical doctor, James Sabin, and a pharmaceutical benefits coordinator, Russell Teagarden. They propose an ethical template for pharmacy benefits and a fair process for applying it. The template delineates various levels of decisions about pharmacy coverage, connecting ethically acceptable types of rationales for limits with decisions made at each level. The authors argue that such a template and process will facilitate public learning about fair limit-setting regarding drugs, and more broadly, other healthcare.

8

Ethics and Prescribing

The Clinician's Perspective

Charles L. Bardes

Pharmacology, our word for the science of therapeutic drugs, derives from the ancient Greek. Yet the Hippocratic physicians were mistrustful of drugs. Their word, *pharmakon*, referred originally to magical potions, evil spells, and poisons. When Circe turns the men of Odysseus into pigs, she does so by giving them a *pharmakon*.

Herein lies the paradox: joined to the potential to do great good is the potential to do great harm.

Practicing physicians make dozens of decisions regarding pharmacological therapy each day. A decision becomes *ethical* insofar as it must select among *conflicting* values, especially if these reflect divergent interests of different stakeholders. That is, ethics is invoked not when the clear-cut choice is *A*, but when the choices are *A* or *B*, each with its pros and cons.

What kinds of ethical decisions must a physician make? What goes into the choice? What are the criteria, implicit or explicit, according to which one chooses? Reflection on the daily practice of medicine reveals a nuanced set of questions.

DO I TREAT THIS PATIENT WITH A MEDICATION?

Visitors to doctors' offices will frequently, perhaps usually, leave with a prescription for medication. This is a complex transaction that has become deeply imbedded in the expectations and behavior of both the patient and the physician. It must be understood as a phenomenon of contemporary Western biomedicine, our present healthcare construct, defined in large part by mechanistic concepts of health and disease.

Table 8.1. *Risk–Benefit Analysis of Prescribing Antibiotics in Viral Upper Respiratory Infections*

Pros	Cons
Meets patient's expectations	Violates "good practice"
Low cost to patient	High cumulative cost to society
Low risk of toxicity	Some risk of toxicity
Treats bacteria "just in case"	Low likelihood of bacteria
Less blame if patient gets worse	More blame if patient has side effect
Gratitude if patient feels better	Resistant organisms in the community
	Resistant organisms in the patient
	Opportunistic infections (yeast, etc.)

Other cultures and other eras have behaved differently, sometimes mistrusting drug therapy (the Hippocratic tradition), sometimes relying on it heavily (the Ayurvedic tradition).

One ramification is that a patient who is *not* given a prescription may be disappointed at the unmet expectation. The physician has a lot of explaining to do. How much easier to prescribe an antibiotic for what is likely a common cold (a viral illness for which antibiotics are ineffective) than to explain to the patient about viruses, the self-limited nature of the illness, the body's capacity to heal itself, issues of probability in diagnosis, and so on. Calculating the risk–benefit balance of antibiotics in viral upper respiratory infections, the physician might reason as shown in Table 8.1.

In sum, the net risk seems to outweigh the net benefit – in *most* instances. What of the patient with pre-existing lung disease, for whom an untreated bacterial infection, even if unlikely, could prove disastrous? What of the patient who demands an antibiotic especially emphatically? What if he or she seems likely to litigate? And does the physician decide unilaterally, or should the choice be negotiated?

The physician must decide if a given problem is severe enough to warrant medication. This decision also depends on cultural influences as well as a patient's personal idiosyncrasies. Experiencing pain, we sometimes "brush it off" and sometimes demand relief. Who decides? This is usually negotiated between the physician and the patient, but dissonance can occur. Patients who request more analgesic than the doctor thinks the problem should require may find their motivation doubted, or their fortitude. Conversely, the doctor may be more eager to treat than the patient to receive, thinking that to prescribe is to vanquish the symptom.

New, stringent practice guidelines have lowered the threshold for drug therapy. These implore the physician to prescribe drugs for persons with less severe manifestations of a condition than in the past. For example, when should cholesterol-lowering medication be prescribed? Take the example of a fifty-five-year-old man who takes medication for high blood pressure. In 1994, the National Cholesterol Education Program (NCEP) recommended drug therapy for such a person when the LDL cholesterol was 160 mg/dl or higher.[1] In the 2004 version, the NCEP cut-off for such a person was 130.[2] This lowering of the threshold means that many millions of persons will newly require drug therapy. But the benefit of medication is lower for persons with mild cholesterol elevation than for persons with severe cholesterol elevation. Thus, the millions of new patients taking drugs are likely to receive only modest benefit.

Are there data to support the decision to prescribe? This is a more complex question than may at first appear. Doctors are taught to base their clinical decisions on published scientific studies. However, a physician is more likely to invoke or recall clinical studies that are widely disseminated or publicized, usually those with dramatic findings or those that are vigorously promoted. Studies that do not show benefit often remained unpublished, although the advent of public drug trial registries may provide greater access to the full spectrum of research. A further complication is the crucial distinction between relative risk and absolute risk. To examine a hypothetical situation, imagine that the success rate is 98 percent for treatment A and 99 percent for treatment B. This means that the failure rate is 2 percent for A and 1 percent for B. An enthusiast (or advertiser) proclaims that B improves the success rate by 50 percent. Fifty percent better! The skeptic rejoins that the reduction in absolute risk is only 1 percent. Stated in other terms, a physician who prescribed B for 100 patients would help only one of them. Is this worth it, if B is more expensive, more toxic, or less time-tested?

Have nonpharmacologic strategies been sufficiently explored? Persons with hypertension can successfully lower their blood pressure by means of exercise, weight loss, salt reduction, and alcohol reduction.

Table 8.2. *Four Classes of Drugs for Treating Hypertension*

Class	Effectiveness	Side Effects	Price
Thiazide diuretics	Low	Low to medium	Very low
Beta blockers	Medium to high	Medium	Low to high
ACE inhibitors	Low to high	Low	High
ARBs*	Medium to high	Very low	High

* Angiotensin receptor blockers

How many clinicians take the time to discuss these options in any depth with patients before reaching for the prescription pad?

Doctors who advise against a drug treatment face an additional challenge in the modern era of health-maintenance organizations and similar insurance formats. The patient may believe – sometimes with justification – that the physician withholds treatment to save costs as an agent or employee of the insurer. That is, the physician appears to act in the best interests not of the patient, but of the insurer. This mistrust of the physician's motives drives a wedge between the patient and physician.

WHICH MEDICATIONS SHOULD I PRESCRIBE?

Once the decision has been made to treat with a drug, the next choice is *which* drug. Many conditions are amenable to treatment with a variety of medications, which vary in cost, convenience, potency, toxicity, cachet, and allure.

For example, first-line drug treatment of hypertension consists of four classes of medications, each with advantages and disadvantages. See Table 8.2. For my patient, otherwise well, who must start antihypertensive medication, which class do I choose? Practice guidelines call for thiazides or beta blockers, both cheap, effective, and time-tested.[3] But both can have significant side effects: electrolyte abnormalities, diabetes, and gout for thiazides; fatigue, impotence, and nightmares for beta blockers. Should I start one of these medications, monitor for side effects, and switch if one occurs? Or should I start with a medication from one of the newer classes, ACE inhibitors or ARBs? This question looks different from the vantage points of the different stakeholders. For a planner of public health policy, the low cost of the older medications is appealing. For an individual patient, the low

side-effect rate of the newer medications is attractive – provided that
someone else, a third-party payer, is covering their high price. And
there is yet another point: perhaps we only think that ARBs have
few side effects because they are new, and unanticipated effects of
long-term or widespread use have not yet been recognized. A 2004
editorial raised this question, arguing that ARBs used to treat hypertension might increase the risk of heart attack.[4] Further, do I prioritize
the relative importance of side effects and price differently in different patients? Is the low cost–high side effect option acceptable for low
income patients, but not for their wealthier neighbors? Which would I
choose for myself? (Answer: ARB.)

GENERIC OR BRAND-NAME?

Patent law in the United States results in a peculiarity in drug pricing:
new drugs, under patent, are expensive, whereas older drugs are cheap.
Compared with prices in Europe, a drug is more expensive in the
United States when new, and less expensive when old. As soon as a
patent expires, competing manufacturers immediately market generic
equivalents at low prices.

Should a physician prescribe the brand name version, or its generic
equivalent? Well, how equivalent is equivalent? The Food and Drug
Administration (FDA) has certified that the generic version is "identical, or bioequivalent to a brand name drug in dosage form, safety,
strength, route of administration, quality, performance characteristics
and intended use."[5] The other constituents of a pill, such as binders,
fillers, dyes, coatings, buffers, and dissolving agents, may be different.
Normally, these differences are inconsequential – we think. This interpretation has led the states to legislate that a pharmacist must fill a prescription with its generic equivalent, unless explicitly countermanded
by the physician.

For most medications, there is likely to be little biologic difference
between one version and another. For a small number of drugs, such
as the thyroid medication levothyroxine, small changes in blood level
can have significant effects, so that consistency from one month to
the next is desirable. Consistency could be achieved by insisting on the
brand-name version – or just as easily by sticking with the same generic
version. (This latter step is harder to specify in a prescription.)

Some argue that equivalent $\neq$ equal. An individual patient might react adversely to one of the "inactive" ingredients of a pill. Others insinuate that a pill made overseas might be contaminated by industrial pollutants – cadmium or lead in the sacred Ganges. A pharmacology professor in medical school taught us that we should prescribe brand-name versions to compensate the inventor for costs of research and development; nowadays, most would counter that these costs have already been compensated during the years of patent protection.

Brand-name names are typically easier to remember (and to pronounce!) than generic names. Compare: Reopro versus abciximab, Lexapro versus escitalopram, Allegra versus fexofenadine.

Patients frequently ask the physician to specify brand-name versions. Why? If they have had an adverse reaction to one version of a drug but not another, the request seems legitimate. But more likely, one suspects, they are reasoning by analogy. In one's usual consumer experience with paper towels, packaged foods, and so on, generics are perceived as low-quality, cheap, flimsy substitutes for the authentic products. One avoids "store brand" toilet paper and "no-name" gasoline. This degraded quality probably does not apply for most medications. But does the physician take the time for this discussion with the patient, or just write "Dispense as written" on the prescription and satisfy the patient, at no cost to himself/herself?

PRESCRIPTION OR OVER-THE-COUNTER?

The FDA specifies which medications must be prescribed by a physician, and which can be purchased without a prescription (over the counter, "OTC"). The typical pattern is that a medication is originally prescription-only, then found to be safe after years of experience, then licensed for OTC sale. Leading examples are certain anti-inflammatory medications, such as Motrin (ibuprofen); antihistamines, such as Claritin (loratadine); histamine-2 antagonists, such as Zantac (ranitidine); and the proton-pump inhibitor Prilosec (omeprazole).

The price is usually substantially lower for an OTC medication than for a prescription medication. But the cost *to the patient* might be substantially higher. The reason is that third-party payers in the United States rarely pay for OTC medications. (A notable exception is

Medicaid, at least in some states.) Thus, the physician faces a dilemma. For my patient with reflux esophagitis, an inflammation of the esophagus, do I prescribe Prilosec OTC or Nexium (esomeprazole)? The two are made by the same manufacturer and are virtually identical in every respect. The price for a twenty-eight-day supply is $19.68 for Prilosec OTC and $125.40 for Nexium.[6] The physician who is most mindful of the individual patient's best interests will recommend Nexium if the patient's insurance plan covers prescriptions, but Prilosec OTC if not. (This comparison sets aside the possibility that the insurer has negotiated a better price with the manufacturer.) And what of the cost to the physician? Prescribing Nexium often means a phone call from the pharmacist, or a fax from the insurer, asking the physician to justify the decision.

A new twist on the prescription or OTC decision involves a new practice among pharmaceutical companies. Just as a patent is about to expire on a popular drug, they release a new, slightly modified drug for the same indication. The new release is advertised as "new and improved" and is linked to the older medication via such means as naming, appearance, or packaging. For example, just as Claritin (loratadine) was released in OTC and generic forms, the manufacturer marketed Clarinex (desloratadine). While these two medications are nearly identical, the physician might prescribe the more expensive Clarinex in the misperception that it is better, in response to advertising, in reaction to a patient request, or to circumvent the cost issue.

An assumption that underlies the prescription or OTC decision relates to power and safety. (See the afterword to this chapter on aspirin.) If OTC medications are safer than prescription medications, are they less powerful? Is the physician who recommends an OTC medication offering a weak intervention? Failing to do what doctors do (write prescriptions)? Trivializing the patient's concerns?

TRIED AND TRUE OR NEW AND SNAZZY?

A new medication will almost always be promoted vigorously, usually under the banner "new and improved." Consumers seem especially attracted to this approach – witness the reiterating generations of "new and improved" toothpastes.

In pharmacology, newer medications sometimes represent real improvements. The first beta blocker was propranolol, a breakthrough innovation. Subsequent beta blockers improved on one or more features of the original; they were longer-acting and could be taken once daily, and they had fewer side effects. The cephalosporin class of antibiotics has produced successive generations, each one expanding the number of susceptible bacteria.

But there are downsides to new medications. They are almost always more expensive than the drugs they mean to replace. Further, they carry the possibility of side effects that have not yet been recognized. By the time a new drug is released, it has typically been tested in a few thousand persons. But once the drug is released, it may be prescribed for millions of people. Thus, if a side effect occurs at a rate of 1:10,000, it may not be recognized until a year or more after release. A salient example is the antibiotic Trovan (trovafloxacin). By the late 1990s, many hospitals recommended this drug as the treatment of choice for most patients with pneumonia. After a few years, it became apparent that the drug caused liver damage and even liver failure in a number of patients, and it was removed from the market. The physician who prescribed the "new and improved" drug would have exposed the patient to unnecessary danger.

Aging drugs may lose their luster. The once-daily beta blocker Tenormin (atenolol) was widely prescribed for many years, with good results. Around the time its patent expired, the newer Toprol XL (extended-release metoprolol) appeared and became extensively adopted, capturing the market niche from Tenormin. Toprol XL is newer and more expensive than the generic forms of atenolol – it must be better, no? (Answer: probably not.)

Should the physician adopt a new medication early or late after its release? There are tremendous pressures for early adoption: advertising, "expert" opinion, patient demands, the desire to be up to date and à la mode. Late adopters withhold benefits from their patients. A middle course seems best for most conditions – perhaps a year or two after release. But earlier adoption is preferred for potentially fatal conditions, such as cancer. When the anti-cancer drug Gleevec (imatinib) was first released, demand was so great that the manufacturer had to ration it.

HOW DO I RESPOND TO A PATIENT'S REQUEST FOR MEDICATION?

The customary therapeutic paradigm is that the patient presents a symptom, for which the physician renders a diagnosis and recommends a treatment. Increasingly, however, a new pattern has emerged in which the first step is the patient's request for a medication. This reverses the order of operations and causes the physician to work backward to the symptom and the diagnosis. Each party may feel its judgment challenged.

Direct-to-consumer advertising plays a major role. Patients call to request the "purple pill" for their stomach aches, when a few dimes worth of antacid might do just as well. How much easier for the physician to write the prescription than to explain the antacid. But advertising confers subtle advantages as well. Advertising creates awareness. How easy it is now to prescribe cholesterol-lowering medications – all the patients have heard of them, and many have been wondering why they aren't taking one yet.

If I say yes to a request, the patient is happy – at least in the short term. If I say no, the patient may be unhappy, may suspect my motives, may mistrust my concern. How should I respond? If treatment is clearly wrong, it's easy to say no. But what if the treatment is not wrong but merely questionable, or borderline?

HERBAL, ALTERNATIVE, AND COMPLEMENTARY MEDICINE

A huge number of persons worldwide take herbal, alternative, and complementary medicines. These range from traditional remedies with a thousand years' experience, such as cinnamon, to very recent arrivals, such as coenzyme Q-10.

On face value, the physician's approach to these medications is the same as for conventional ones: weigh the potential benefits and risks. But this is more problematic than may first appear. First, the benefits and risks are not always clear. Second, doctors are very susceptible to fads in this area. How many cardiologists prescribed beta-carotene a few years ago, only to learn later that it was associated with increased incidence of certain cancers? Third, a reluctant physician may appear pig-headed, antiholistic, narrow-minded, and hidebound.

Fortunately, data are available regarding many of the most popular remedies: glucosamine-chondroitin, saw palmetto, ginseng, garlic, and fish oils. Unfortunately, these rarely translate into specific formulations and dosages that a physician can prescribe. In addition, few reliable data are available for most products. Although many persons *feel* that they are safe, recent experience with *ma huang* (ephedra) illustrates their potential danger. Although this herb has been used in China for centuries, widespread use in the United States led to several cases of severe side effects and even death. Thus, the physician who wants to be fair-minded must make the extra effort to look critically at the data and render an informed opinion – outside the usual learning channels, and with the personal expenditure of time.

AM I FOLLOWING PRACTICE GUIDELINES?

Many pharmacologic decisions are made easier by the increasing use of practice guidelines. Generated by a consensus process among experts, under the mantle of international professional societies, these now cover a wide variety of conditions such as heart disease, hypertension, hyperlipidemia, congestive heart failure, pneumonia, asthma, and diabetes.

But practice guidelines can be formidable. For example, the American College of Physicians recently (2004) published guidelines for the treatment of chronic stable angina, recommending that every patient receive four medications: aspirin, a beta blocker, a "statin" cholesterol-lowering medication, and (newly) an ACE inhibitor.[7] These are proposed as a minimum; others may be necessary. This is a lot of medication, more than many people want to take. Each additional medication increases cost, likelihood of side effects, possibility of drug-drug interaction, and chance for patient error or omission. Some of these eventualities are obscured in the highly controlled clinical trials on which the experts base their recommendations. Moreover, guidelines call for higher doses than have previously been used, aiming to achieve still lower cholesterol values, still lower blood pressure measurements.

If I follow practice guidelines, I am blameless in the public eye but potentially heavy-handed for individual patients, loading them down, encumbering them with cost, side effects, and a weighty belief that they must be really sick, to need all these pills.

AM I DOING WHAT SUBSPECIALISTS DO?

Subspecialty care is different from generalist primary care. The subspecialists often deal with sicker patients, for whom simpler treatments have failed. The generalists are often better versed in evidence-based medicine, which casts a shadow of cautious skepticism over therapeutic decisions.

But the patients are paying attention. "I went to the subspecialist, who prescribed Fantastica – that must be a better medication." So the generalist who wants to be smart or to appear smart the next time will prescribe Fantastica off the bat.

CONTROLLED SUBSTANCES

In the United States, the Drug Enforcement Agency (DEA) places special controls on the prescription and sale of certain medications with potential for recreational abuse. Typical examples include opiates (for pain), benzodiazepines (for anxiety and insomnia), and amphetamines (for narcolepsy and attention deficit disorder.) The DEA monitors prescriptions for these medications and investigates physicians who prescribe more than the usual amount. If the physician is a cancer specialist, no problem. If not, red flags go up. Physicians who prescribe opiates legitimately for patients with chronic, severe pain may find themselves prosecuted and occasionally imprisoned. Prescriber beware! One might have to choose between relieving the patient's pain effectively and protecting oneself against investigation.

DISCUSSION OF SIDE EFFECTS

In principle, physicians should fully discuss all the potential side effects of all medications. In practice, this is nearly impossible. A conscientious physician will discuss the most frequent or most important side effects, to be sure. But how far should I go? In prescribing an antidepressant, I will tell the patient about possible fatigue, sleep disturbance, and gastrointestinal upset. What about the risk of suicide? In prescribing penicillin, do I tell the patient that there is a chance of anaphylaxis and death?

Written lists of possible side effects, usually provided as a package insert or as a print-out from the pharmacy, only help a little. These are typically so inclusive that they make it difficult to distinguish common from rare side effects, and nuisances from catastrophes.

FORMULARIES

Third-party payers typically maintain formularies, lists of medications that they prefer. Formulary selections are based on analyses of safety, efficacy, and cost. Cost, in turn, reflects negotiations between the insurer and the manufacturer, bidding one product against another.

How much should the prescribing physician pay attention to the formularies? For any given class of medications, such as ACE inhibitors, a practicing physician will typically use one or two on a regular basis, and have only passing familiarity with the others. But every insurer's formulary is different. If my patients have different insurers, my usual prescriptions will be on-formulary for some insurers, and off-formulary for others. In the latter instance, I will receive a fax or phone call from the insurer, the medication management company, the pharmacist, or the patient, to which I must respond. This not only takes my time and annoys me, but may push me to use a medication with which I am unfamiliar. I know of one case in which such a sequence led a physician to prescribe an unfamiliar medication and dose it incorrectly, initiating a series of mishaps that led to the patient's death.

HOW DO I INFORM MYSELF ABOUT MEDICATIONS?

The sources of information are innumerable: direct-to-physician advertising, direct-to-consumer advertising, drug detail representatives, professional meetings, practice guidelines, journal articles, the popular press, word of mouth, subspecialist consultation, and on and on. Few of these sources are completely impartial. The ethical dilemma is that learning more, always desirable in itself, conflicts with other time commitments to patients, institution, family, and self.

The conscientious choice is to distance oneself as much as possible from the hurly-burly of promoters and advocates in favor of unbiased judges. My personal favorite is *The Medical Letter on Drugs and*

Therapeutics, an independent, nonprofit newsletter published twice monthly, that evaluates treatments based on available evidence. A healthy skepticism pervades its pages.

HOW DO I RESPOND TO PHARMACEUTICAL COMPANY
REPRESENTATIVES?

Sales representatives from pharmaceutical manufacturers are eager to visit physicians. Typically amiable and attractive, they usually offer something. What?

- Information for physicians. Sales representatives from pharmaceutical companies, like their counterparts in other fields, generally tout the advantages of their products over those of other manufacturers. They often substantiate their assertions with scientific facts – though of variable relevance. The representatives are naturally one-sided.
- Information for patients. Sales representatives often leave pamphlets and brochures for distribution to patients. These are sometimes neutral but often contain a subtle "pitch" in favor of a drug.
- Teaching materials. Teachers at medical schools and hospitals sometimes accept slides or other teaching materials. Although some are quite impartial, such as depictions of physiology, these can be followed by subtle arguments in favor of specific pharmacologic approaches, which in turn can be favorable to the manufacturer.
- Gifts to physicians, and staff. These range from cheap pens to large consultation fees, major travel stipends, or honoraria. The latter may be appropriate if the compensation is commensurate with the educational service provided – but the risk is that an expensive junket may serve more to curry favor than to support learning.
- Free medications for patients, physicians, and staff. The "samples closet" found in many physicians' offices is stocked with free drugs dropped off by drug representatives. They can provide a significant service to the indigent, and a pleasant convenience to the rest of us. To receive these drugs, the physician must sign a document brought by the representative, who generally slips in a few words supporting the company's product line.

Physician responses to pharmaceutical representatives vary tremendously. Many make it a practice not to see the representatives, nor to accept their gifts. This is the ethical high road but is not completely unambiguous, as it forestalls accepting free medications for the indigent and accepting stipends for legitimate educational activities. Nonetheless, there are other sources of free medications for the truly indigent, other ways to support education, and much better sources of impartial information for physicians and patients.

DISEASIFICATION?

If drugs are treatments for diseases, the corollary is that every prescription implies a disease. A middle-aged woman who is a little overweight might easily be taking medication to reduce blood pressure, cholesterol, glucose, and bone loss. Though she feels perfectly well, each morning she takes four or five pills. If any of the conditions becomes complex, we add another one or two or three. Although each of these medications may prove salutary in its own right, the net effect is that she has been *diseasified*, made to feel ill, labeled with diseases. For the physician, the ethical dilemma is that prescribing medications, even when "indicated" may transform a person's self-perception from well to sick.

Prescribing medications casts the patient into a field of metaphor. Antibiotic? – the body has been invaded, the invader must be killed. Anti-inflammatory? – the body is inflamed and set afire and must be cooled. Morphine? – not just pain relief, but a subtext of severity and finality and a tinge of illicit pleasure.

FIDDLING WITH BIOCHEMISTRY

It is easy to practice pharmacology naively. A particular antidepressant is said to work by increasing levels of norepinephrine. Where, one might ask? In the brain, of course, in the mood centers. And where else? And what else does it do? The honest answer is that norepinephrine is distributed throughout the brain and throughout the entire body. What are the complete effects of modifying its levels? We don't know.

In an era in which there seems to be a pill for everything, the ethical practitioner will exercise a healthy skepticism in prescribing medications. Biochemistry is complex. Simple explanations are oversimplifications. If there is a nonpharmacologic solution to a particular problem, that is probably the best place to start – though it cuts against substantial pressures to prescribe a pill.

Reflecting on these notes, it is striking how often questions of ethics in pharmaceuticals devolve to matters of cost. The physician must negotiate a difficult transaction in which the patient perceives one course as best for himself or herself, *as an individual*, which the physician must weigh against the net benefit and cost to the *community*. The third stakeholder is the *physician*. Many issues in therapeutic ethics also pose an expense to the physician in terms of *time* – time to explain, time to discuss, time to wrangle with insurers, time to defend against litigation – and in what might be called psychological energy. Far from being an abstract concern to be left to philosophers, healthcare administrators, and policy-makers, the ethics of prescribing engages the physician nearly every hour of every day.

AFTERWORD: ASPIRIN

"Take two aspirin and call me in the morning" – so goes the old joke. The cartoon scenario is a concerned patient who feels unwell, telephones the doctor, and receives the little advice. The text is concise and small.

What is the subtext? First, that the ailment is minor and self-correcting. There is nothing special that medicine, as opposed to common sense, has to offer for this sort of ailment. It would get better by itself. There is no specific cure, only a tactic for feeling less uncomfortable while the body heals itself – or gets worse, which would then warrant a more substantial medical intervention.

The second implicit message is that the physician has dismissed the illness. The patient was concerned, but the doctor is not. This medical unconcern, depending on how it is expressed and perceived, will be either reassuring ("it's nothing serious") or offensive (uncaring, haughty.) The doctor, meanwhile, has intended to forestall the offensive interpretation by the "call me in the morning" clause. The physician has expressed interest by requesting an update. If the "call me" clause is delivered in too offhand a manner, however, the patient will perceive a dismissive tone all the same.

"He only told me to take aspirin." "Only aspirin." The premise is that aspirin is a trivial medication. This triviality is reinforced by the legal distinction between prescription and over-the-counter medications. Prescription medications must be powerful and perhaps risky. Over-the-counter medications must be less powerful and harmless.

The Bayer pharmaceutical concern has waged an earnest, prolonged campaign to rehabilitate the status of its star product. The bark of the willow tree was a traditional remedy for fever and pain for many centuries. Bayer, a German company, isolated a compound from willow (Latin *salix*), named it acetylsalicylic acid, and marketed the product under the name "Aspirin," beginning in 1899. Over the ensuing decades, both the patent and the trademark lapsed, and the word entered the general international vocabulary. Anyone could make acetylsalicylic acid, and anyone could call it aspirin. Furthermore, anyone could buy it, and cheaply. Aspirin must be a big nothing.

Not so, say the ads of Bayer. "Aspirin – the miracle drug" reads the copy. And surely, aspirin is potent. It not only relieves pain and inflammation and fever, but also retards atherosclerosis and blocks steps in blood clotting. These latter actions account for its effectiveness in preventing and treating heart attack and stroke. They are also the basis for the Bayer advertising of the past decade. But listen to what is being implied here. It is not "only aspirin," a little remedy for little problems: aspirin strikes at the core of our concerns, it fights heart attack and stroke, saves heart and mind, could save my life.

What has Bayer to gain by the ad campaign? Even if the public is persuaded to buy more aspirin, one would not expect it to buy much Bayer aspirin, which is much more expensive and no more effective than its generic competitors. (There are admittedly sidetracks: Bayer is said to be "pure aspirin," implying that the competitors are impure or otherwise suspect.) Rather, the effect is to uplift the public appreciation of aspirin in general – and of its proud papa, Bayer. Aspirin is good, and important; Bayer is good, and important; pills are good and important.

Bayer began as a dye manufacturer in the 1860s. Aspirin led it into pharmaceuticals. By 1925, Bayer was a mainstay of the consolidation of the German chemical industry into the I. G. Farbe cartel, at its peak the dominant chemical concern in the world. During World War II,

I. G. Farbe built a synthetic oil and rubber plant at Auschwitz to avail itself of slave labor from the concentration camp there. This became a symbol of the collaboration of German industry in Nazism in general and the Holocaust in particular. (Witness *Gravity's Rainbow.*) The cartel was dissolved by the Allies in 1945, and several of its leaders were convicted of war crimes at Nuremberg. But Bayer reappeared in 1951. Thus, the Bayer advertisements participate in the rehabilitation not only of the drug but of the entire company, and (by extension) of German industry, even of Germany itself. It resembles the corporate sponsorship of an art exhibit or a concert series – the Texaco Metropolitan Opera, the Mobil Masterpiece Theater – a sort of "feel good" policy. And, by the way, aspirin *does* make you feel good – or stops you from feeling quite so bad.

9

The Regulation of Prescription Drug Promotion

Thomas Abrams*

INTRODUCTION

You are in the reception room of your physician's office with other patients waiting for your turn with the doctor. You are looking around the room – doing a little people watching – and you notice a well-dressed young woman carrying a brown bag that looks like a book bag from your elementary school days. You then observe that the young woman is called into the physician's office but is told by the receptionist that "the doctor only has a few minutes, so you need to be quick." When you are later escorted into an examination room by one of the nurses, you pass the young woman, who is taking cartons out of her book bag briefcase and talking to the doctor. What you have witnessed is one of the many ways that pharmaceutical companies promote their prescription drug products. This chapter will describe the various ways in which companies promote prescription drugs and how the government regulates this promotion.

The marketing of prescription drugs is a significant business. Prescription drug sales in the United States alone were \$228.8 billion in 2003.[1] So even small shifts in sales from one product to another can result in millions of dollars of added or reduced revenue for a company. Companies are therefore aggressive in their promotion of prescription drugs. In addition, there does not appear to be any slowing

* Thomas Abrams is the Director of the Division of Drug Marketing, Advertising, and Communications of the Food and Drug Administration. This chapter was written by Thomas Abrams in his private capacity. No official support or endorsement by the Food and Drug Administration is intended or should be inferred.

down or leveling off of drug company expenditures on promotion. In fact, expenditures on promotion more than doubled from 1998 to 2003, increasing from $12.7 billion to $25.6 billion.[2] The number of vehicles that companies use to promote prescription drug products has also increased dramatically and includes sales representatives, television ads, direct-to-consumer print ads, the Internet, exhibit booths at medical conferences, and dinner meetings for physicians.

BACKGROUND

Pharmaceutical companies have long sent sales representatives to visit healthcare practitioners to promote their prescription drug products. During a typical sales call a representative gives a brief presentation, often referred to as a "detail," on the promoted product and generally uses a sales brochure or "detail aid" to illustrate the points that the company wishes to emphasize. A discussion period normally follows the representative's presentation and the representative then answers the healthcare practitioner's questions and tries to "close" the sales call by getting a commitment from the healthcare practitioner to prescribe the drug more often, or to try the drug, if the healthcare practitioner has never prescribed it. The representative's job is to emphasize the benefits of the product for healthcare practitioners and for their patients.

Prior to the 1980s, the pharmaceutical industry directed most of its promotional attention toward healthcare practitioners in the form of promotion by sales representatives with supportive detail aids. Things began to change in the 1980s, however, as consumers became increasingly involved in discussions and decisions about their health and industry became interested in the concept of advertising directly to the consumer. This time period marked the beginning of direct-to-consumer advertising (DTCA, also the subject of the next Chapter (10) by Meredith Rosenthal and Julie Donohue).

When we look at the evolution of DTCA, it is important to note the ways in which society was changing and the impact that these changes may have had on DTCA. Prior to the early 1980s, many pharmacies did not even put the name of the drug a consumer was taking on the label of the prescription bottle, a circumstance that made it difficult for consumers to even know what medication they were taking, let alone seek out additional information about prescription drug products. In fact, many earlier references indicate that pharmaceutical manufacturers and healthcare practitioners were instructed to keep consumers in the dark about their medications. For instance, there is a passage in a 1938 Federal Register that states that drug labeling is to be written "only in such medical terms as are not likely to be understood by the ordinary individual."[3]

Consumers today are in a much different position. Now, prescriptions are clearly labeled as to their contents and consumers increasingly seek out additional information about their drug products. As this trend toward information-seeking on the part of consumers has increased since the early 1980s, companies have responded in a variety of ways, including the development of special information sheets about some of their prescription drug products for consumers, commonly called "Patient Package Inserts." The Internet has also come into wide use and many consumers are using this medium to seek out information about their health and prescription drug products. According to data from research conducted by the Food and Drug Administration (FDA), the percentage of consumers surveyed that sought information about prescription drugs from the Internet increased from 18 percent in 1999 to 38 percent in 2002.[4]

This growing trend toward information-seeking on the part of consumers is not unrelated to the growth in DTCA. As consumers sought more and more information about prescription drugs, industry found it beneficial to promote directly to consumers. The early 1980s saw the first two advertisements that were directed to the consumer. One was for a generic version of a prescription arthritic drug and the other was for a vaccine for pneumonia. Many people were surprised at this new direction in promotion and concerns were raised that DTCA could adversely affect public health. Most agreed that not enough was known about this new means of promotion to make it possible to determine clearly whether DTCA would be harmful or beneficial for consumers. As a result of these concerns, Arthur Hull Hayes, then Commissioner of the FDA, asked industry for a "voluntary moratorium" on DTCA to allow the agency time to assess the situation. The voluntary moratorium was in essence an appeal from the FDA for deliberate restraint on the part of the pharmaceutical industry in moving forward with DTCA until the agency was able to assess DTCA's potential impact on consumers. After meetings, discussion, and research were conducted over a multiyear period, the FDA lifted its request for this voluntary moratorium in 1985, based upon its stated determination that the regulations that were already in effect for prescription drug advertising provided sufficient safeguards to protect consumers. The lifting of the voluntary moratorium was a significant event in the development of prescription drug promotion, as companies began running direct-to-consumer (DTC) print advertisements in consumer magazines for the first time. DTCA started off slowly, but by the beginning of the 1990s, it was common to see many DTC ads in consumer magazines.

Following the advent of DTCA in the 1980s, three types of advertisements have been commonly used: full product advertisements; reminder advertisements; and help-seeking advertisements. Full product advertisements state the indication of the drug, generally make claims about its beneficial properties, and discuss risks associated with the use of the drug. Reminder advertisements state the name of the drug but do not make any representations or suggestions about the drug. Help-seeking advertisements do not discuss or identify specific drug products but instead present information about a medical condition such as diabetes and encourage consumers to seek medical care if they have symptoms of or may be at risk for the condition.

Throughout the 1990s, print DTC advertisements proliferated. Although the number of full product advertisements in consumer magazines increased significantly in this time period, full product ads were not placed on television to any large extent. Instead, reminder ads were being used on television. These ads, which state the name of the drug and little else, can be a useful way of increasing brand awareness when directed toward an audience, such as healthcare practitioners, who already have background knowledge about the drug. However, they caused confusion among consumers, as many did not have any clear idea what the drugs being advertised were for. The FDA received complaints from healthcare practitioners and consumers indicating that reminder ads were counterproductive – consumers would go to their healthcare professionals to talk about a drug thinking it was for something very different from the use for which the product was actually indicated. The reason that reminder ads were used instead of full product ads on television was that reminder ads did not have to contain the "brief summary." The brief summary is a detailed listing of essentially all of the adverse information about a drug that is contained in the approved product labeling (also called the physician package insert (PI)). In the print context the requirement to provide the brief summary is generally fulfilled by including all the risk information from the PI, usually in small type on the page adjacent to the DTC ad. It was not clear to industry how they could fulfill, in a television ad, the requirement for a brief summary, as it is impractical to present all this information in a broadcast context. Attempting to "scroll" it on television could require several minutes and realistically it could not be read in its entirety.

The regulations provide an alternative to the presentation of the brief summary in broadcast ads (television, radio, and telephone ads) known as "adequate provision." Essentially, to fulfill the "adequate provision" requirement, an advertisement must provide the audience viewing the television ad with access to the physician package insert for additional product information. In providing this access, it is important that the company advertising its product take into account the wide range of potential viewers and the differences among these viewers with respect to privacy concerns, information-seeking behavior (e.g., active versus passive), and levels of technological sophistication. In August of 1997, the FDA issued the draft *Consumer-Directed Broadcast Advertisements* guidance, which provided for the first time guidance on how to fulfill the existing regulatory requirement for adequate provision. This guidance described a multicomponent approach, consisting of four factors that, if present in a broadcast DTC ad, would provide adequate access to the PI for the wide range of viewers of that advertisement. These four factors are (1) a reference to a toll-free phone number where viewers could obtain the PI; (2) a reference to a Web site where viewers could obtain the PI; (3) a reference to a currently running print ad for the drug where viewers could obtain the brief summary information; and (4) a reference to a healthcare professional as an additional source of information about the product. This guidance was finalized in 1999.

Since 1999, FDA has conducted research in the DTCA area, held public meetings to discuss its research as well as other research that has been conducted in this area, and reviewed numerous comments about DTCA to ensure that its policy on regulating DTCA is optimal.

Although there is much attention to and discussion about DTCA, it is important to note that the overwhelming majority of money spent by industry for promotion of prescription drugs is still for promotion directed to healthcare professionals. Of the $25.6 billion spent in 2003 on promotion of prescription drugs, $22.4 billion, or 87.5 percent, was spent on promotion to healthcare professionals, whereas $3.2 billion, or 12.5 percent, was spent on DTC promotion.[5]

Although the amount spent on DTC is still much less than the amount spent on promotion directed to healthcare professionals, the *growth* in spending on DTC promotion has been greater. DTC expenditures have increased 246 percent from 1998 to 2003, while promotion directed to healthcare professionals increased 196 percent during the same period.[6]

On the healthcare professional side, visits to physicians by pharmaceutical sales representatives, such as the hypothetical woman with the brown "book bag" described at the beginning of this chapter, remain a major component of promotion. Companies have consistently increased the number of sales representatives they employ during recent years. These representatives discuss claims about their drugs in an effort to persuade doctors to prescribe the drug, and they must also discuss the risks associated with the use of their drugs. Sales representatives usually make sales calls to the same healthcare professional with regular frequency, generally falling within a four- to eight-week cycle, but this differs from company to company and from product to product.

The cartons that the hypothetical representative was taking out of her briefcase were samples of prescription drugs. Sales representatives commonly leave samples for healthcare practitioners to give to their patients so that patients can try a prescription drug before filling a prescription for the drug. Distribution of drug samples represents an important part of promotion to industry, which spent $14.8 billion on this in 2003.[7]

Companies also have increased the different types of promotional vehicles they used to deliver their promotional messages to healthcare professionals, particularly as advances in technology paved the way for different promotional formats. In addition to sales brochures and advertisements in medical journals, companies also promote through computer programs, animated CD-ROMs, and the Internet. They also use promotional booths in commercial exhibit halls at medical meetings, dinner meetings for healthcare professionals, promotional conferences and audioconferences, and direct mailers. The large volume of promotion and promotional vehicles is reflected by the number of promotional pieces submitted to the FDA at the time of their initial use. Companies submitted more than 38,000 promotional pieces to FDA in 2003.

REGULATION OF THE PROMOTION OF PRESCRIPTION DRUGS

Once one realizes the extent to which prescription drugs are promoted, one may ask how this promotion is regulated and by whom. Under the Federal Food, Drug and Cosmetic Act (FDCA), Congress has given the FDA the authority and responsibility for regulating the promotion of prescription drugs. "Promotion" consists of advertisements and other promotional material (called "promotional labeling") disseminated by or on behalf of the promoted product's manufacturer, packer, or distributor. Mostly, this means materials that the product's company issues or directly influences. The materials that the FDA has authority to regulate under the FDCA include promotional pieces

- Printed in magazines, journals or newspapers;
- Broadcast over the television, radio, or telephone;
- Presented on the Internet;
- Produced to promote to healthcare professionals, such as detail aids used by sales representatives, convention displays, file cards, booklets, and videotapes; and
- Produced to promote to consumers and patients, such as brochures, letters and flyers sent through the mail, videotapes, pharmacy counter displays, billboards, and patient compliance program materials.

All prescription drugs have risks associated with their use. The seriousness and frequency of these risks will vary from product to product. The American public, whether they are consumers or healthcare professionals, is entitled to receive a fair and balanced picture of the drug in promotion; thus, promotional pieces are required to present the risks of a drug as well as its benefits. The FDA regulates prescription drug promotion with the goal of protecting and promoting the public health by ensuring that prescription drug information is truthful, balanced, and accurately communicated. This is accomplished through a comprehensive surveillance, enforcement, and education program. The FDA's actions and efforts are based on the authority given to the FDA by the FDCA and its implementing regulations. The regulations relating to the promotion of prescription drugs can be found in Title 21 of the Code of Federal Regulations.

For prescription drug advertisements sponsored by a product's manufacturer, these regulations require that the advertisement

- Not be false or misleading;
- Not recommend or suggest any use that is not in the approved product labeling;
- Present a fair balance between the risks and benefits of a drug product;
- Reveal "facts material" in light of representations made by an ad, or in light of the consequences of using the product as advertised; and
- Disclose all the risks in an advertised product's PI, or, for broadcast advertisements, either disclose all the risks or disclose information relating to "major side effects and contraindications" and make "adequate provision" for disseminating the PI to the advertisement's audience.

These regulations also require that advertisements not overstate the effectiveness or minimize the risks of the prescription drug being promoted. In addition, all claims made in an advertisement must be supported by substantial evidence (that is, evidence from adequate and well-controlled studies by experts qualified by scientific training and experience to evaluate the safety and effectiveness of the drug involved) or substantial clinical experience. For example, if a company wishes to make a claim that its product is more effective than another product, it must have supporting data from adequate and well-controlled, head-to-head clinical studies. The information presented in promotion must also be consistent with the drug's PI. For example, a company could not claim that its product reduces total cholesterol by 40 percent if the information in the PI states that it has only been shown to reduce it by 20 percent.

Promotional labeling for prescription drugs is subject to similar requirements. However, such materials are required to be accompanied by the promoted product's full PI, rather than a "brief summary" of risk information from the PI.

Under the FDCA, promotional materials that do not comply with the requirements of the Act and regulations discussed above, whether they are promotional labeling or advertising pieces, "misbrand" the drug product. Misbranding a drug is a prohibited act under the FDCA, and when this occurs, the FDA is empowered to address the violation in a variety of ways, which are discussed in the section on "Regulatory Tools."

Monitoring and Enforcement

Title 21 of the Code of Federal Regulations[8] requires that advertisements and other promotional materials be submitted to FDA at the time they are first disseminated publicly; this is commonly known as the postmarketing submission requirement. The FDCA generally does not permit the FDA to require that the content of advertisements be approved prior to their use,[9] except in certain narrow circumstances. Thus, the FDA's review of promotional materials is designed to occur primarily after the materials have appeared in public, and any enforcement action is taken after the materials in question have been used publicly. Thus, the FDA's enforcement actions are aimed at stopping the violative promotion. In some cases, the agency asks companies to run corrective advertisements or issue corrective letters to remedy misimpressions created by false, misleading, or unbalanced promotional materials.

The FDA receives more than 38,000 promotional pieces annually in fulfillment of companies' obligations under the postmarketing submission requirement. With limited staffing, it is virtually impossible to review every single piece thoroughly. However, the FDA does flag certain materials for expedited review. These include the promotional materials that introduce newly approved products or products with new indications ("launch materials"), the materials for products with significant risks, and TV or radio advertisements. Similarly, if these materials are found to be in violation of the FDCA and its implementing regulations, enforcement action is expedited.

In addition to the above materials, FDA also routinely reviews promotional materials that are the subject of complaints received from

competing companies, healthcare practitioners, or consumers. FDA
also monitors commercial exhibit halls at medical meetings as well as
promotional audioconferences, Internet Web sites, and other evolving
technology.

Regulatory Tools

When a promotional piece that has been used publicly is found to be
in violation of the FDCA and its implementing regulations, the FDA
has a variety of enforcement options it can use to address the violation,
including the following:

- Untitled letters – these are essentially notices of violations issued to
  companies by the FDA in letter form that inform the company that
  it has violated the FDCA and request that the company discontinue
  the violative materials and all materials with the same or similar
  violations.
- Warning letters – these are letters issued to companies for more
  serious violations, such as those posing serious health risks to the
  public or those that represent repeated violations by the company.
  In addition to requesting that the violative materials be discontinued, the FDA generally asks companies to disseminate corrective
  messages to the audience that received the violative message.
- Injunctions and consent decrees.
- Referrals for criminal investigation.
- Seizure of the drug product.

Recent Actions by the FDA

The most common violations that the FDA observes in promotional
pieces include minimization or omission of risk information, overstatement of effectiveness or safety, misleading comparative claims, and
promotion for uses that are not in the product labeling. Below are
examples of these commonly seen violations from three recent warning letters issued by the DDMAC.[10]

OxyContin (Oxycodone HCl Controlled Release) Tablets. This drug is
an extended release form of an opioid used for the treatment of moderate to severe pain when a continuous around-the-clock analgesic is

needed for an extended period of time. OxyContin is a Schedule II controlled substance (heavily regulated by the Drug Enforcement Agency) because it has an abuse liability similar to that of morphine and other opioids, both legal and illicit. There are serious risks associated with the use of OxyContin, including potentially fatal respiratory depression. Therefore, there are important limitations on its indicated uses. In the warning letter, the FDA objected to advertisements in medical journals for the drug that minimized or omitted risks associated with OxyContin and also suggested uses that were not in the PI. For example, the body of the advertisements contained prominent claims of effectiveness but omitted serious and potentially fatal risks associated with the use of the drug. Following the issuance of the warning letter, the company discontinued the misleading promotion and, as requested by the FDA, ran remedial ads to correct the misleading messages in subsequent issues of the same journals that ran the violative ads.

MUSE (Alprostadil) Urethral Suppository. This drug is indicated for the treatment of erectile dysfunction. MUSE is associated with risks of low blood pressure and fainting. The product's labeling also states that MUSE should not be used in men for whom sexual activity is inadvisable due to heart problems. In the warning letter, the FDA objected to promotional information on the company's Web site and a DTC television advertisement that omitted or minimized these important risks of the product and made unsupported effectiveness claims. For example, the television ad did not disclose the fact that MUSE is not to be used in men for whom sexual activity is inadvisable due to heart problems, and failed to convey the warning associated with the drug regarding low blood pressure and fainting. The television ad also made unsupported claims that implied that MUSE is superior to other products used to treat erectile dysfunction. For example, the spokesman in the ad claimed, "Just like you, I've tried many products. Nothing worked for me until I tried MUSE." The warning letter resulted in the discontinuation of the television ad and the promotional material on the Web site. The company also ran a remedial advertisement on television and remedial messages on its Web site to correct the misleading promotional messages.

Prograf (Tacrolimus Capsules and Injections). This drug is indicated for the prophylaxis of organ rejection in patients receiving certain liver and kidney transplants. Patients on Prograf have an increased susceptibility to infection and use of the drug may result in the development of lymphoma. These serious risk concepts are conveyed in a boxed warning in the drug's PI. The product's PI also contains warnings about the risk of diabetes in patients given the drug. In the warning letter, the FDA objected to a medical journal advertisement as lacking sufficient information about the serious risks of the drug in the body of the advertisement, such as the seriousness of the increased susceptibility to infection, possible development of lymphoma, and risk of diabetes. The warning letter resulted in the discontinuation of the misleading promotion. The company ran remedial advertisements in medical journals to correct the messages from this misleading promotion.

Comments on Proposed Promotional Materials

In addition to monitoring promotional materials that are in the public domain, the FDA also provides comments on proposed materials before the materials go into use, when requested to do so by companies and in certain other circumstances.

Accelerated Approval Products. Promotional materials for drugs approved under subparts H and I of Part 314 of Title 21 of the Code of Federal Regulations[11] and subpart E of Part 601 of Title 21 of the Federal Regulations[12] have special submission requirements. For these products, companies must submit to the FDA for consideration during the preapproval review period copies of all the promotional materials that they intend to disseminate or publish within the first four months following marketing approval of the drug.[13] After the first four months, companies must submit all materials they intend to use at least thirty days prior to the intended time of public use. The FDA reviews all materials submitted pursuant to these regulatory requirements. The FDA's review of these promotional materials is especially important because drugs approved pursuant to subpart E and subparts H and I have been approved on the basis of a different standard of evidence than that typically applied to new drug applications, are for especially serious illnesses, or may pose significant risks to patients. It is particularly important that their promotional materials communicate the sensitive balance between the risks and benefits of these drugs.

Introductory Campaigns. Companies typically design extensive promotional campaigns to introduce newly approved drugs into the marketplace. With the exception of drugs approved under subpart E and subparts H and I (see above) and other limited circumstances, companies are not required to submit their promotional materials to the FDA prior to using them. Nonetheless, many companies ask the FDA to review their introductory materials before these materials are used to introduce (launch) their newly approved drugs into the marketplace. The FDA's promotional regulations provide that any advertisement may be submitted to the FDA prior to publication for comment.[14] The FDA carefully reviews these proposed materials to ensure that the first impressions that healthcare practitioners and consumers get about the new product are accurate and balanced.

Direct-to-Consumer Promotion. As discussed above, in recent years, companies have substantially increased the amount of DTC promotion of prescription drugs. The FDA is responsible for ensuring that the regulations requiring accurate and balanced promotion are applied to consumer-directed pieces as well as to those directed to healthcare professionals.

As discussed earlier, DTC promotion encompasses a variety of materials, including broadcast and print ads, direct-mail letters and flyers, pharmacy counter displays, and other materials. The impact of television and radio ads can be especially significant because of the large number of people who can be exposed to such campaigns. At least partly because of the potential cost to sponsors should they be asked to "pull" television ads that are deemed violative, companies often voluntarily seek comment from the FDA prior to running broadcast ads for many of their planned broadcast campaigns. This reduces the likelihood that they will be subject to an enforcement action. Because of the potential impact of broadcast campaigns on public health, the FDA reviews proposed broadcast ads promptly and ensures that they are compliant with the FDCA and its implementing regulations.

Guidance Development

In addition to providing comments on proposed promotional materials and its monitoring and enforcement program, the FDA also acts to fulfill its obligations under the FDCA by articulating its positions on important issues in the area of prescription drug promotion in guidance documents. Guidance documents do not create new rules or obligations, but rather articulate the FDA's current thinking on and interpretations of compliance with existing rules, facilitating voluntarily compliance by industry with the FDCA and regulations. When the FDA initially issues guidances, it issues them in draft form to provide an opportunity for industry and the public to comment on them. The FDA then reviews the comments that are submitted about draft guidances and carefully considers them when finalizing the guidance. This process often results in revisions to the draft before the guidance is finalized.

Recent FDA Guidances

Two draft guidances issued in 2004 are entitled *Brief Summary: Disclosing Risk Information in Consumer-Directed Print Advertisements* ("brief summary" draft guidance)[15] and *"Help-Seeking" and Other Disease Awareness Communications by or on Behalf of Drug and Device Firms* ("help-seeking" draft guidance).[16]

The brief summary draft guidance addresses the presentation of risk information on the "brief summary" page that typically appears adjacent to the DTC ad. Data from research conducted by the FDA illustrates the importance of this information to consumers, indicating that a large percentage of consumers read most or all of the brief summary when they are interested in the drug. Unfortunately, the information is usually presented in small type size, clustered in large paragraphs that make it difficult to read, and is generally presented in medical terminology that is difficult for readers without a medical background to understand. There have been many comments about the difficulty that consumers encounter when reading the brief summaries in print DTC ads and suggestions that this information should be presented in a manner that would make it more consumer-friendly. This draft guidance offers alternative ways in which the FDA believes companies can more usefully present this information for consumers. The

FDA is optimistic that this guidance will result in a shift toward more useful presentations of the brief summary information.

There are many serious medical conditions that are underdiagnosed and undertreated in the United States. Medical conditions such as hypertension, diabetes, hyperlipidemia, and osteoporosis can have devastating health consequences if they go untreated, yet many individuals do not get timely medical attention for these conditions. The help-seeking draft guidance encourages efforts to educate consumers and healthcare practitioners about medical conditions, particularly conditions that are serious and undertreated. Help-seeking or disease awareness communications do not discuss or identify specific drug products but instead present information about a medical condition and either encourage consumers to seek medical care if they have symptoms of the condition or encourage healthcare professionals to be aware of and treat the condition. These materials are not branded, in that they do not name a drug or make representations or suggestions about a drug, and therefore are not considered to be promotional materials for a particular drug. Thus, the FDA typically does not regulate this form of communication. In its draft guidance, the FDA describes the criteria it applies in determining whether a communication is a help-seeking or disease awareness communication and also describes the circumstances under which it would regulate company communications that contain information about medical conditions as branded promotional materials. The guidance also contains recommendations for the content of these communications that are aimed at making them as informative as possible.

CONCLUSION

Prescription drug promotion comes in a wide range of forms and reaches a wide range of audiences, as discussed throughout this chapter. The importance of promotional communications to the prescription drug industry is illustrated by the amount of and escalation in expenditures on this form of communication and by the continuous evolution of new promotional vehicles to reach broader audiences.

As part of its overall mission to protect the public health, the FDA uses the powers allocated to it by Congress to regulate prescription drug promotion. As this form of promotion has developed, the FDA has made use of the variety of tools available to it – including its monitoring and surveillance programs, enforcement actions, advisory comments, and guidance documents – to communicate with industry and the public and to enforce the applicable statutory and regulatory provisions. As this field continues to evolve, the FDA will work to fulfill its public health mission by keeping abreast of new developments and working to ensure that prescription drug promotion provides accurate and balanced information to the American public.

10

Direct-to-Consumer Advertising of Prescription Drugs

A Policy Dilemma

Meredith B. Rosenthal and Julie M. Donohue

INTRODUCTION

In the United States, the rapid rise of prescription drug spending, coupled with exorbitant prices for new drugs have generated concern over the value and sustainability of the level of pharmaceutical spending. In the midst of this period of rapid spending growth, in which prescription drugs outpaced all other components of personal health spending, another highly visible trend has emerged: prescription drug advertising (see Figure 10.1). Many believe that the simultaneous burgeoning of prescription drug advertising and sales of high-priced drugs is more than coincidence and is cause for alarm.[1]

Proponents of direct-to-consumer advertising (DTCA) claim that it may increase awareness and/or reduce the stigma associated with seeking care (in the case of mental health problems and sexually transmitted diseases, in particular), both of which may yield substantial gains in health.[2] Further, advocates of DTCA argue that advertising may improve adherence to medication therapy for chronic conditions. Opponents of DTCA argue that the informational content of advertisements and the types of drugs that are advertised make it highly unlikely that public health has benefited, whereas spending has surely increased.[3] This perception is no doubt influenced by the high visibility of national broadcast advertising campaigns and the prevalence of lifestyle drugs such as Viagra and Levitra among the advertised drugs.[4]

From a public health perspective, concerns about DTCA have focused on three potential types of negative effects. First, DTCA may lead to inappropriate treatment of patients. That is, patients will receive

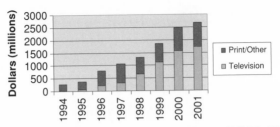

Figure 10.1. U.S. Pharmaceutical Industry Spending on DTCA 1994–2001 by Media Type. *Source*: IMS Health.

prescription drugs that pose more adverse risks than expected health benefits. Second, patients will receive therapies valued at less than the total cost of the treatment. The third concern is that direct marketing of prescription drugs will have a negative effect on physician–patient relations, which in turn will have a negative effect on health. In this chapter, we briefly discuss some of the important factors driving the increase in spending on DTCA. We then review the evidence on the effects of DTCA and draw inferences about the empirical realities as they relate to the concerns outlined above. Based on our conclusions we suggest several directions for policy in the era of consumer marketing of prescription drugs. Our recommendations seek a balance between efforts to inform consumers about health conditions and treatment on the one hand with the need to reduce inappropriate use and spending on the other.

FACTORS BEHIND THE RISE IN DTCA

A confluence of events in the 1990s, including the clarification of FDA rules regarding broadcast advertising of prescription drugs, the introduction of more consumer-oriented pharmaceutical products, and the trend toward consumerism in healthcare led pharmaceutical manufacturers to invest in consumer-directed marketing strategies.

In 1997, the U.S. Food and Drug Administration (FDA) clarified its policy regarding risk disclosure in broadcast advertisements for prescription drugs. This policy change made advertising prescription drugs on television more feasible and almost certainly contributed to the significant increase in spending on DTCA. Unlike advertisements for other products, prescription drug ads that provide the name of the product and its therapeutic indication are required to disclose information on the major risks associated with use of the drug. The regulations promulgated in the 1960s for physician-directed advertising and later applied to DTCA required "information in brief summary relating to side effects, contraindications, and effectiveness" or "adequate provision" of the full product label. These rules served as a *de facto* barrier to broadcast advertisements that mentioned the name of the drug and the condition it was meant to treat because it was costly to air the entire brief summary on television. Moreover, the meaning of "adequate provision" of the product label was unclear.[5] In August 1997, the FDA clarified that manufacturers could make adequate provision for the dissemination of the approved product label, and all of the information on a drug's use, risks, and benefits contained therein, by referring consumers to a toll-free number, a Web site, a print advertisement, and their physician in the context of the broadcast ad (21 C.F.R. 202.1 (2000)).

The increased use of DTCA was also related to changes in the types of pharmaceutical products being introduced. Several pharmaceutical products introduced in the 1990s were focused more on quality-of-life issues than on reducing morbidity or mortality. For instance, DTCA was used to create a market for Rogaine in the late 1980s. Male pattern baldness was not considered a "disease" and it would have been difficult for Rogaine's manufacturer, Upjohn, to convince physicians to initiate a discussion with their male patients about a cosmetic product through traditional forms of promotion such as detailing (one-on-one visits from a pharmaceutical sales representative to a physician).[6] Consumer-directed advertising campaigns have been used to create markets for new products and to expand existing markets as in the case of treatments for undertreated illnesses such as hyperlipidemia (high cholesterol) and depression.

In launching DTCA campaigns, pharmaceutical firms also capitalized on a significant cultural change in the healthcare system that accumulated momentum in the 1990s, one that emphasized the consumer's role in medical decision-making. Consumer involvement in healthcare – critical to the financial success of pharmaceutical advertising campaigns – was on the rise. The consumer movement in healthcare has been characterized by efforts to expand the legal rights of patients[7] and to make physician practice styles more "patient-centered."[8]

Dramatic advances in information technology, specifically the wide availability of health information on the Internet, have contributed to more consumer involvement in medical decision-making. DTCA of prescription drugs is a highly visible symbol of the trend toward consumer-oriented medicine. The very existence of pharmaceutical products that are designed to improve the quality of life rather than to treat disease, and that require patients to self-diagnose, signals the consumer's increasing importance in medical care.

EFFECTS OF DTCA

The forces that led to the rise of DTCA are complex and intertwined. They include both underlying changes in consumer demand and efforts by the industry to create new markets and increase profits. Not surprisingly in this context, the pattern of effects generated by DTCA is also difficult to disentangle. A range of research designs have been employed to study the effects of DTCA, including surveys of consumers and physicians and economic analyses of pharmaceutical advertising and sales. Little experimental evidence exists on the effects of DTCA. We rely instead on a review of the quasi-experimental and survey literature to get a handle on the economic and clinical effects of DTCA. Consumer surveys have asked respondents to report on their exposure to advertising as well as visits to physicians, requests for prescription drugs, adherence to medication therapy, and other outcomes. Other analytical approaches have sought to link spending on DTCA with trends in aggregate pharmaceutical sales or treatment patterns observed at the individual level in insurance claims or in large national survey databases. In some areas of the literature, a consistent picture emerges of the effects of DTCA, whereas in other areas the evidence is either absent or mixed. Because of the difficulties in drawing causal inferences from the available studies, many of the findings discussed below are merely suggestive.

To shed light on the concerns about DTCA mentioned earlier – that DTCA may lead to overuse of prescription drugs resulting either in unnecessary harm or spending or both, and that DTCA negatively impacts the physician–patient relationship – we review studies that seek to answer the following questions. First, does DTCA expand treatment for certain conditions? Second, does DTCA affect appropriateness of treatment received? Third, does DTCA influence treatment choice? And fourth, does DTCA have educational value for consumers?

Does DTCA Expand Treatment?

DTCA and Prescription Drug Sales. Understanding the relationship between DTCA and prescription drug sales is an important preliminary step in understanding the effects of advertising on public health. For instance, studies showing that advertising resulted primarily in "business stealing," an increase in one brand's market share over its competitors, would challenge the argument that DTCA expands treatment for underdiagnosed conditions. Several studies have examined the relationship between DTCA and pharmaceutical sales. The weight of evidence to date suggests that DTCA has a significant impact on total class sales but little influence over individual product market share. A recent study of the impact of DTCA on aggregate sales of prescription drugs in five therapeutic classes with high DTCA expenditures found that although DTCA was associated with an increase in sales to the therapeutic class as a whole, it had no impact on market share.[9] Studies of marketing in the H2-antagonist and nonsedating antihistamine classes suggest that DTCA has a very small impact on market share relative to the effect of physician-directed marketing efforts.[10] These studies used aggregate data on sales and marketing and thus did not take into account the effects of individual characteristics on demand for prescription drugs. These studies also relied on aggregate measures of price and therefore did not account for the enormous variation in prices of prescription drugs across different types of consumers or for the presence of insurance.[11]

Consumer Surveys. Findings from consumer surveys are consistent with those of the economic analyses. Surveys suggest that DTCA motivates people to discuss previously untreated conditions with their physicians. According to several national consumer surveys, awareness of prescription drug ads is high and a substantial number of consumers have talked with their physicians about a condition as a result of seeing

DTCA and Consumer Choices

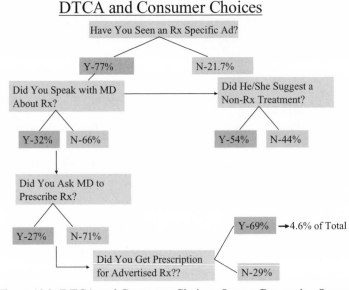

Figure 10.2. DTCA and Consumer Choices. *Source*: Prevention Survey.

an ad. The percentage of consumers who reported seeing any ad for a prescription drug increased from 63 percent in 1997 to 85 percent in 2002. And when consumers are provided a list of drugs that have been advertised, 98 percent say they have seen an ad for at least one of the products mentioned.[12]

In 2002, 32 percent of consumers who had seen an ad for a prescription drug talked to their physician about the medicine (see Figure 10.2).[13] Roughly half of consumers who talk to their physicians about a drug they have seen advertised are seeking treatment for the condition for the first time.[14] The proportion of consumers who talk to their doctors about a drug they have seen advertised has remained remarkably stable since 1997 in spite of the fact that spending on DTCA more than doubled over the same time period.[15] Of consumers who saw an ad and talked to their doctors, 27 percent (or about 8 percent of the total) asked their doctors for a prescription.[16] The proportion of consumers who have asked for a prescription has also remained virtually unchanged since 1997 when the first national consumer survey was conducted on DTCA. Of those consumers who specifically asked their physicians for a prescription as a result of seeing an ad, 69 percent (or about 5 percent of the total) had their requests honored.

DTCA and Visits to Physician. Another way to measure the impact of DTCA is to examine whether there has been an increase in physician visits and diagnoses for conditions for which prescription drugs are advertised. Zachry et al. found that DTCA was associated with an increase in diagnoses of some conditions but not others.[17] The time period for this analysis ended in 1997, before the upsurge in spending on DTCA. Using data from 1994 through 2000 and controlling for trends in the treatment of high cholesterol, Iizuka and Jin found that DTCA for antilipemics increased the number of outpatient visits for hyperlipidemia.[18] Taken together, these studies suggest that DTCA increases the proportion of individuals treated for some conditions. The important question is whether the new treatment represents appropriate use or overuse of these medications.

Does DTCA Affect Appropriateness of Medication Use?

The effect of advertising on appropriate use of medications is among the most difficult to measure. One of the primary concerns about DTCA is that it will lead to overuse of the advertised drugs relative to less expensive therapies or lifestyle changes. A recent national survey of physicians indicates that roughly four out of five physicians think DTCA encourages patients to seek treatments they do not need.[19] Three methodological challenges exist to understanding the relationship between DTCA and the appropriate use of medicines. First, some conditions for which drugs are advertised lack clear guidelines for appropriate use versus overuse or misuse. Second, the extent to which practice guidelines or other quality-of-care benchmarks are met cannot always be measured with existing data. Third, it is often difficult to isolate the effect of advertising on quality of care among many competing factors.

A few studies have sought to overcome these methodological challenges. A 2002 study by Teleki examined the relationship between exposure to DTCA and inappropriate prescriptions for Cox-2 inhibitors.[20] She found that those who had seen an ad and talked to their doctors were eleven times more likely to meet her definition of inappropriate use than those who had seen an ad and not talked to their doctors. Other studies have linked temporal variation in spending on DTCA with appropriate use of advertised medications. Dubois examined whether the relative proportion of appropriate use and misuse of lipid-lowering therapies changed between 1997 and 1999, a period with high spending on DTCA for these medications.[21] The authors found that despite the 60 percent increase in the number of individuals treated with lipid-lowering medications, there was no change in the rate of appropriate use over the time period. This study was not, however, directly able to relate changes in advertising spending with the distribution of individuals treated for high cholesterol across risks groups. Donohue et al. examined the effect of DTCA spending for antidepressants on the likelihood that someone diagnosed with depression received medication therapy.[22] The authors found that individuals diagnosed following periods of high advertising spending were more likely to fill a prescription for an antidepressant than those diagnosed following periods of low advertising spending. Further research is needed on the impact of DTCA on appropriate use of medicines. Because of the methodological challenges outlined above, these findings are merely suggestive.

Does DTCA Affect Treatment Choice?

One of the concerns about DTCA is its effect on the doctor–patient relationship, specifically, that physicians feel pressured to prescribe treatments they would not otherwise recommend to accommodate the wishes of patients who have seen DTC advertisements. According to a survey conducted by the FDA, 22 percent of general practitioners and 13 percent of specialists surveyed indicated that they felt "somewhat" or "very" pressured to prescribe drugs to their patients who had seen DTC advertisements.[23] Consumer surveys indicate that over 70 percent of consumers who request a specific brand of medication as a result of seeing an ad have their requests honored.[24] Due to the lack of a control group, these surveys cannot, however, tell us what would have happened in the absence of advertising.

Another way to shed light on the effect of advertising on the doctor–patient relationship and on physician prescribing behavior is to examine the impact of DTCA on treatment choice. The available studies show that DTCA has a very small effect on treatment choice. Wosinska found that advertising for cholesterol-lowering drugs had a small positive impact on drug choice, but only for drugs with a preferred status in the health plan's formulary.[25] In addition, the 2002 study found that detailing has a much more significant effect on drug choice than does DTCA. Similarly, using aggregate data on pharmaceutical promotional spending and individual-level insurance claims data from Medstat's MarketScan database, Donohue and Berndt found that DTCA had little effect on choice of medication in the antidepressant market.[26] On the other hand, detailing for antidepressants had a substantial impact on medication choice even several years after the introduction of some of the drugs in the class. In addition, using data from the National Ambulatory Medical Care Survey and Competitive Media Reporting data on DTCA spending, Iizuka and Jin found that DTCA had no effect on physician's choice of medication.[27]

Does DTCA Improve Adherence to Medication Therapy?

Proponents of DTCA often claim that advertising has the potential to improve adherence to medication therapy, which for chronic conditions such as diabetes, depression, and hyperlipidemia is a significant public health problem. Consumer surveys suggest that advertising makes people more compliant with medication therapy.[28] Similarly, many physicians, when surveyed, agree that DTCA encourages patients to follow the treatments recommended by their physicians.[29]

The few studies that examined the relationship between DTCA and adherence directly pointed to a statistically significant but clinically insignificant positive effect of advertising on adherence to medication therapy. Wosinska found that advertising for medications used to treat hyperlipidemia reduced gaps between prescriptions by about one day.[30] Donohue et al. found that DTCA for antidepressants at the class level slightly increased the probability that an individual with depression received medication treatment for an appropriate duration of time.[31] DTCA could be related to improved adherence by way of selecting a more adherent patient population or reminding patients to take their medication and/or refill their prescriptions. Patients who initiate conversations with physicians about a medicine they have seen advertised may also be more likely to adhere to the treatment regimen if they are better informed about a drug's use, benefits, and risks.

Does DTCA Improve Consumers' Understanding of Conditions and Treatments?

The educational value of DTC ads has been evaluated by a number of studies. Expert review of the content of DTC ads has found that related health information about risk factors, prevention, and alternative therapies is mostly lacking.[32]

Both physicians and consumers report that the informational content of advertising is insufficient and that the benefit/risk ratio of a drug is not accurately portrayed in DTC ads. Weissman and colleagues find that although 73.5 percent of physicians agree that DTCA helps to educate and inform patients about treatments available to them, an even greater proportion (82 percent) agree that prescription drug advertising does not provide information on medications in a balanced manner.[33] Similarly, in a survey conducted by the FDA, 75 percent of general practitioners reported that prescription drug ads exaggerate the benefits of the medications advertised.[34]

Consumer surveys have also been used to gauge consumer understanding of the health conditions described in the ads, risks and benefits of the advertised product, and perceptions about the nature and value of advertising itself. Findings from these studies suggest that DTCA is not an important source of detailed public health information. Experimental evidence suggests that although prescription drug ads are good at communicating the name of a drug and its indication, they do not communicate risk information in a way that aids consumers.[35] Information about a drug's benefits is seldom quantified in DTC ads, leaving consumers to believe that the advertised drug is effective in all cases. One experiment showed that when consumers are given more detailed information about a drug's benefits than is typically provided in DTC ads, they are less likely to rate the drug as highly effective.[36] In addition, consumers appear to misunderstand the extent to which advertising is regulated by the FDA. For example, one study reported that 22 percent of consumers agreed that advertising of drugs with serious side effects had been banned.[37] Moreover, surveys indicate that the brief summary, the chief mechanism for communicating information about a drug's use and risks, is seldom read by consumers.[38]

LESSONS FROM THE LITERATURE

Thus far, the scientific literature has yielded only indirect evidence on the positive or negative effects of DTCA on public health and welfare. Evidence suggests that DTCA increases demand for prescription drugs, resulting in an increase in the total size of the market. To date, no published analysis has established whether DTCA stimulates new use that is primarily appropriate and cost-effective or the opposite. It is important to shed light on whether advertising affects the appropriate use of medicines given the evidence that DTC ads are not effective at providing risk information to consumers. The methodological challenges to conducting a study on the impact of DTCA on appropriateness are substantial. Thus, any policy or regulatory approach related to DTCA must account for the uncertainty that exists about the extent of both positive and negative effects.

COULD DTCA IMPROVE PUBLIC HEALTH UNDER ANY CIRCUMSTANCES?

Given the lack of definitive data on the net effect of DTCA, it seems important to ask whether we can rule out the possibility that DTCA, in conjunction with some set of regulatory policies, might have a positive effect on public health. Some groups have called for stricter limits or a ban on DTC advertising. Yet a ban might either raise or lower consumer welfare, depending upon the relative magnitudes of the public health benefits and the costs generated by advertising.

The first point to make is that pharmaceutical companies are concerned primarily with maximizing profits, and undertake advertising as part of a strategy to do so. Thus, advertising is intended to increase profits, not public health. The literature on the value of advertising content as public health education also confirms that advertising should not be confused with complete and unbiased health information.

Nonetheless, in considering the potential impact of DTCA, it is important to bear in mind that prescription drugs are different from other goods. The key difference of course is that a doctor or other licensed prescriber must participate in the purchasing decision. Thus, to conclude that because advertisements do not contain full or accurate information, DTCA can only induce the inappropriate use of drugs is to suggest that physician act as poor agents for their patients. Whereas studies have indicated that physicians sometimes prescribe unnecessary medications in response to patient requests, and in other cases are themselves misinformed by pharmaceutical company promotional activity,[39] neither situation is likely to occur in the majority of instances. Doctors thus stand at least a modest chance of helping consumers to process the information or misinformation they receive through advertising and ensuring that prescriptions are made appropriately. Moreover, surveys have shown that doctors view as constructive the discussions that result from patients mentioning advertisements they have seen.[40] It does not seem unrealistic to believe then that, however accidentally, DTCA could have a salutary effect even if advertisements are misleading and factually incorrect, simply by creating an opportunity for discourse with a physician. Examples that are often cited in this type of argument are advertisements for antidepressants and cholesterol-lowering drugs, which treat conditions that are believed to be "undertreated" relative to the social optimum. It would be naïve to suggest that only appropriate treatment results from DTCA; however, physicians can and likely do improve the outcome that is implied by a model in which consumers use only the information they receive from advertisements to make a decision about what drug to take.

In addition to physicians, health plans influence the drugs that consumers actually receive after asking doctors about an advertised drug. In particular, the empirical literature suggests that the formulary status of an advertised drug is an important determinant of the responsiveness of demand to advertising.[41] These findings suggest that gains from getting consumers to talk to their doctors about the conditions described in drug advertisements may be decoupled from the negative effects of advertising in terms of low-value or inappropriate treatments.

POLICY ALTERNATIVES

Given that DTCA may have positive effects through engaging consumers in appropriate help-seeking behavior, it is worth considering policies that are less blunt than an all-out ban. Policy alternatives should be targeted at retaining the benefits from DTCA that relate to getting consumers to talk to their physicians about serious, under-treated conditions, while better matching patients to the most cost-effective interventions. Inappropriate or low-value prescription drug treatments may result from DTCA for one or both of the following reasons. First, physicians may acquiesce to the demands of misinformed patients or be misinformed themselves about the true net benefits of the drug, and second, consumers and/or their physicians may be shielded from the social costs of drugs by financing arrangements. Thus, three possible routes to limiting the negative impacts of DTCA are to (1) make physicians better agents for their patients and the public health, (2) improve the information that patients receive about both advertised and unadvertised treatments and the related health conditions, and (3) alter financing arrangements to reduce consumer and physician moral hazard.

Regulating Physician Promotion and Academic Detailing

Pharmaceutical marketing to physicians is still the principal way that the pharmaceutical industry promotes its products.[42] Physician detailing and the distribution of free samples, in particular, constitute a large part of the marketing budget for pharmaceutical firms. Unfortunately, physicians appear to rely too much on the information and advice offered by representatives of individual firms in forming opinions about the relative effectiveness of alternative drugs.[43] This influence is of particular concern in light of recent court cases relating to inappropriate financial inducements offered by particular companies to physicians in return for market share. Tighter regulation of physician promotion should thus be a high priority for FDA policy in this area. In addition, private actors such as hospitals and physician group practice associations could take a more assertive role in controlling physicians' contact with pharmaceutical sales representatives.

Studies have shown that "academic detailing" of physicians can be an effective means of improving evidence-based prescribing.[44] Academic detailing uses the same face-to-face methods as the industry to educate physicians about cost-effective treatment alternatives. The Centers for Medicare and Medicaid Services are considering a substantial investment in academic detailing to improve quality prescribing in conjunction with the implementation of the Medicare prescription drug benefit. Similarly, some delivery systems have undertaken sampling of generics with the goal of encouraging the use of low-cost alternatives.

Improving Available Information on Treatment Risks and Benefits

The first way to improve the information that patients receive about prescription drug therapy would be to allow DTCA, but improve upon the regulatory system currently in place to monitor prescription drug promotion. This would require more extensive review of the content of advertisements (ideally both those aimed at consumers and physicians) and more serious consequences for noncompliance (i.e., substantial fines or corrective letters to physicians). Such a regulatory system would require substantial public monies and may not be politically feasible in some countries.[45]

Alternatively, a public information campaign could be aimed at consumers, physicians, or both. Such a campaign could provide consumers and their providers with information on the comparative effectiveness and costs of medications to facilitate better purchasing decisions. One way in which such a policy might be economically feasible would be to use DTCA to finance a parallel public health campaign using the model of the Fairness Doctrine. The Fairness Doctrine, which was in place in the United States from 1967 until 1971, mandated tobacco counteradvertising in proportion to cigarette advertising on television, thus essentially requiring that the industry support the public health counteradvertising. Notably, some have claimed that the net impact of the subsequent ban on television advertising of cigarettes was to raise consumption, because it also eliminated the counteradvertising.[46]

Altering Financing Arrangements for Advertised Drugs

Another way to mitigate the potential for DTCA to lead to inappropriate medication use is to alter financing arrangements for consumers and physicians. For example, advertised brands of low value could be subject to additional cost-sharing (as in a tiered formulary or reference pricing scheme) or not covered if indeed they provide little benefit relative to alternatives. In the United States, many private health plans have taken this tack, with some evidence of success.[47] Similarly, physician reimbursement might be tied in part to cost-effective prescribing or controlling spending on pharmaceuticals.

DTCA of prescription drugs has generated a great deal of controversy, in part because of its contemporaneous rise with national spending trends. Some policy makers and consumer advocates are concerned that wasteful and inappropriate utilization may occur if consumers respond to the simplistic and incomplete health messages that these advertisements deliver. The empirical evidence suggests, however, that the demand response to DTCA can be moderated by consumer cost-sharing and the formulary status of drugs as well as by physician preferences. In addition, there appears to be a potentially substantial benefit from DTCA in encouraging consumers with undertreated conditions to self-identify and play a more active role in decision making with their doctors. Further research is needed to understand better the patterns of both inappropriate and beneficial prescribing that result from DTCA, as well as their relative magnitudes in different therapeutic classes. Given the likelihood that research will find both substantial costs and benefits to DTCA of prescription drugs, policy strategies should be sufficiently nuanced to target wasteful demand creation while preserving public health benefits.

11

Off-Label Communications and Prescription Drugs

Scott D. Danzis*

The Federal Food, Drug, and Cosmetic Act (FDCA) prohibits pharmaceutical manufacturers from promoting their products for uses that have not been approved by the federal Food and Drug Administration (FDA). Manufacturers must prove, by a rigorous evidentiary standard, that drugs are safe and effective for each use for which a drug is promoted. If a manufacturer promotes a product for a use that is not approved by FDA, and thus inconsistent with a product's approved label, the promotion is referred to as "off-label" promotion.

Policing off-label promotion is one of the key facets of the FDA's regulation of prescription drug marketing. The agency requires, moreover, that all promotional messages contain "fair balance," including safety information and relevant warnings about the drug product. In this way, the FDA encourages the dissemination of accurate and complete information about approved uses for prescription drugs.

But over the past several years, two developments have emerged with respect to off-label communications about prescription drugs. First, there has been a burgeoning recognition that the FDA's authority to regulate communications about prescription drugs is not just limited by the authority granted by Congress in the FDCA, but restricted by the free speech principles of the First Amendment. A series of judicial decisions have held that the free speech protections afforded by the First Amendment apply to communications about products regulated

* Mr. Danzis is an attorney at the law firm of Covington & Burling in Washington, D.C. The views expressed in this chapter are the author's alone and do not represent the views of Covington & Burling or its clients.

by the FDA. These decisions have signaled that manufacturers may have greater opportunities to communicate limited off-label information than the traditional FDA policies allow.

The second development – which is more recent and less defined – cuts in the opposite direction. Over the past several years, courts have endorsed the use of the False Claims Act to police promotional activities by manufacturers. Typically, these cases are brought by private parties, often company insiders, and allege that promotional activity by pharmaceutical manufacturers causes the submission of false or fraudulent claims to federal healthcare programs. Recently, in a controversial and closely watched case, a federal judge accepted an argument that off-label communications, including truthful communications about drugs, can cause the submission of false claims. The outcome of this case and the language used by the judge suggest that off-label communications may subject manufacturers to new and potentially far-reaching penalties.

This chapter proceeds in four parts. The first describes the statutory background relating to off-label communications and the FDA's interpretations of these restrictions. The second discusses the commercial speech doctrine of the First Amendment and how courts have applied that doctrine to communications about prescription drugs and related products. This is followed by an examination of the role of private lawsuits targeting off-label communications under the False Claims Act. The final section offers observations about these competing developments, including the many unanswered questions that they raise.

THE STATUTORY FRAMEWORK OF PRESCRIPTION DRUG PROMOTION

New Drug and Misbranding Provisions

The FDCA provides the substantive requirements that govern prescription drug advertising and promotion, including the primary restrictions on off-label promotions. The FDCA, however, does not directly proscribe off-label promotion. Instead, the FDCA prohibits manufacturers from introducing a new drug into interstate commerce unless that drug and its labeling have been approved by the FDA. In addition, the FDCA prohibits the introduction into interstate commerce of a drug that is "misbranded."

Section 505 of the FDCA prohibits the introduction of a "new drug" into interstate commerce.[1] A "new drug" is a statutory term of art that refers not just to a novel drug substance, but to any divergence from the FDA approval for the drug.[2] A common misperception is that the FDA approves drug substances. In reality, the FDA approves drug products in specific dosage forms, for specific populations, for specific medical indications, under conditions set forth in FDA-approved labeling. If a manufacturer introduces a drug into interstate commerce that is different from the product or its labeling as approved by the FDA, the drug will be considered an unapproved "new drug."

The FDCA also requires that all drugs bear adequate directions for use. This requires that the accompanying label of a drug describe how a drug may be safely administered, including all indications for which the drug is approved and all the other elements of the FDA approval. If a drug fails to bear adequate directions for use, the drug is "misbranded." Both the new drug and misbranding provisions of the FDCA carry significant administrative and criminal penalties.

"Labeling" under the FDCA

The specific elements of the FDA's approval for a drug, along with the "adequate directions for use," are incorporated into the FDA-approved "labeling" for a drug product. Labeling is a term of art that encompasses all written, printed, or graphic material "(1) upon any [drug or device] or any of its containers or wrappers, or (2) accompanying such [drug or device]."[3] The most self-evident form of labeling is the package insert that accompanies the drug, which is referred to as the product's "approved labeling." The approved labeling sets forth all of the elements of the FDA approval.[4]

But the term "labeling" has also been construed to encompass more than just the approved package insert that physically accompanies the drug product. In *Kordel* v. *United States*,[5] the Supreme Court held that circulars and pamphlets distributed to consumers were "labeling" under the FDCA, despite the fact that these materials did not physically accompany the product when it was shipped in commerce:

One article or thing is accompanied by another when it supplements or explains it.... No physical attachment one to the other is necessary. It is the textual relationship that is significant.[6]

Under *Kordel* and its progeny, printed materials are "labeling" when the product and the materials are distributed by a manufacturer to promote the sale of a product as part of an integrated commercial transaction. If there is a relationship between the text of the materials and the product – primarily that the materials explain or discuss the use of the drug – the material is labeling. Therefore, according to the FDA, "labeling" includes nearly every form of drug company promotional activity, including booklets, pamphlets, mailing pieces, bulletins, and all literature that supplements, explains, or is otherwise textually related to the product.[7] Labeling other than the approved package insert is referred to as "promotional labeling."

Off-Label Promotion

The FDCA, in implementing the misbranding and new drug provisions, restricts the permitted bounds of prescription drug promotion to on-label indications. The FDCA and the FDA's implementing regulations require that manufacturers have an FDA approval for every "intended use" of a drug.[8] The "intended use" for a drug is determined, in part, by the claims made by the manufacturer for the drug. Certainly, the approved indications set forth in a drug's approved labeling are intended uses for the drug. But if promotional labeling suggests a use for a drug that is not consistent with its FDA approval, the promotional labeling may create a new intended use.[9] Shipment of the drug for this intended use may introduce an unapproved new drug into interstate commerce. Moreover, the drug may be misbranded because the approved labeling will not bear adequate directions for use for the unapproved indication.

Therefore, if a manufacturer wishes to promote a product for a use that is not within its approved labeling, it must resubmit the drug for another series of clinical trials similar to those for the initial approval. Until this subsequent approval has been granted, the unapproved use is considered to be off-label. Accordingly, manufacturer promotion may not suggest any off-label use and must conform to the FDA-approved prescribing information in all respects.[10]

Importantly, however, the FDCA's restrictions on off-label promotion do not restrict how physicians may use pharmaceuticals. The FDA has repeatedly stated that it does not regulate the practice of medicine.

Once a drug has been approved by the FDA for marketing for *any* use, the actual prescription choices regarding those drugs are left to the discretion of the physician.[11] In fact, for many medical conditions, off-label use of drugs has become the accepted standard of medical care.

THE FIRST AMENDMENT AND OFF-LABEL COMMUNICATIONS

Although the FDCA and FDA policy generally prohibit off-label communications by drug manufacturers, in recent years several courts have held that speech regarding products regulated by the FDA is protected by the First Amendment. These decisions suggest that manufacturers may have more flexibility to discuss off-label topics than traditional FDA policy allowed.

The Commercial Speech Doctrine

The First Amendment to the United States Constitution guarantees the right to free speech. This protection also applies when the speaker is a corporation, rather than a real person.[12] In *Central Hudson Gas & Electric Corp.* v. *Public Service Commission of New York*, the Supreme Court established a four-part test for evaluating restrictions on commercial speech[13] under the First Amendment.[14] This test remains the operative doctrine for commercial speech today.

Under the first prong of that test, a court reviewing a restriction on commercial speech must initially consider whether the commercial speech is entitled to First Amendment protection at all. Commercial speech that proposes an unlawful transaction, and speech that is false or misleading, is not entitled to First Amendment protection. If the speech is deemed to be entitled to First Amendment protection, however, the second prong of the test requires the court to consider whether the government has advanced a "substantial interest" to justify the restriction. If the court concludes that the government has identified a substantial interest, the third prong of the test requires the court to consider whether the restriction "directly advances" that interest. The fourth and final prong of the test requires the court to consider whether the restriction is "more extensive than is necessary" to advance that interest. If the government's interest may be satisfied by less restrictive means, the government must use the less invasive method of regulation (e.g., requiring a disclaimer rather than an outright ban on speech).[15]

Washington Legal Foundation Litigation

The application of the modern commercial speech doctrine to speech by pharmaceutical manufacturers was put to the test in litigation brought by the Washington Legal Foundation (WLF).[16] The WLF initially challenged guidance documents issued by the FDA concerning manufacturer distribution of reprints of medical textbooks and peer-reviewed journal articles ("enduring materials") and manufacturer involvement in continuing medical education seminars and symposia (CME).[17]

With regard to enduring materials, the FDA's Guidance Document prohibited a manufacturer from proactively distributing publications that addressed off-label uses for the company's previously approved products, except in very narrow circumstances. This policy included articles written by independent researchers and published only after the articles underwent an independent peer-review process. With regard to industry support for CME programs, FDA policy prohibited the industry from suggesting or directing the content of any CME program that dealt with off-label topics, although manufacturers were permitted to provide financial support for such programs. Only truly independent CME providers could design and conduct such programs.

The district court applied the *Central Hudson* commercial speech doctrine and concluded that the FDA's policies were unduly restrictive of manufacturers' speech rights. First, although noting that it was a close question, the court characterized the speech at issue as commercial speech, rather than core political speech. Second, the court concluded that scientific information published in peer-reviewed journals or textbooks or provided at CME programs was not unlawful, or inherently false or misleading. The court concluded that the FDA's interest in encouraging manufacturers to seek supplemental approvals for new indications was substantial, and that the Guidance Documents furthered that interest. However, because the FDA could use less restrictive means to further its interests, the FDA's policies unconstitutionally restricted speech.

The court found that the FDA could require prominent disclaimers and other types of information disclosures, rather than banning manufacturers from engaging in these types of speech altogether. Accordingly, the court issued an injunction prohibiting the FDA from enforcing the Guidance Documents at issue. However, the court held that the FDA could constitutionally require manufacturers to include disclaimers noting that information in the enduring materials or in a CME program is not approved, as well as other disclosures.

Although a number of procedural complexities followed the court's decision,[18] *WLF* is still regarded as a landmark decision establishing that dissemination of scientific information by pharmaceutical manufacturers is protected speech under the First Amendment. In response to a citizen's petition submitted to the FDA by the WLF following the litigation, the FDA stated that it was unlikely to initiate any enforcement action based only on distribution of truthful and nonmisleading enduring materials that contain off-label information.[19] Accordingly, some pharmaceutical companies have made a decision to follow the injunction issued in *WLF*, by proactively distributing peer-reviewed journal reprints that discuss off-label uses for their products, but also including the disclaimers and other information proposed by the district court in *WLF*.

First Amendment Case Law Surrounding *WLF*

The *WLF* court was not alone in reaching the conclusion that certain statutes and FDA policies were unduly restrictive of speech. For example, in *Pearson* v. *Shalala*, which pre-dated *WLF*, the D.C. Court of Appeals struck down an FDA policy that prohibited manufacturers of dietary supplements from making health claims for their products.[20] The court held that a complete ban on speech was inappropriate because the FDA's concerns "could be accommodated ... by adding a prominent disclaimer to the label."[21]

In *Thompson* v. *Western States Medical Center*,[22] the Supreme Court reached a similar conclusion. In *Western States*, the Court struck down provisions of the Food and Drug Administration Modernization Act ("FDAMA") that prohibited licensed pharmacists from advertising drug compounding services. In *Western States*, the Court concluded that "the Government has failed to demonstrate that the speech restrictions are 'not more extensive than is necessary to serve'" the stated interest of preventing large-scale manufacturing of compounded drugs in circumvention of FDA's drug approval process.[23] The Court emphasized that "we have made it clear that if the Government could achieve its interests in a manner that does not restrict speech, or that restricts less speech, the Government must do so."[24] Accordingly, the Court held that such advertising must be permitted.

In sum, *WLF*, as well as other recent commercial speech cases involving the FDA, suggests that entities regulated by the FDA may have more flexibility to communicate information about off-label topics than traditional FDA policy allowed.

THE FALSE CLAIMS ACT AND OFF-LABEL COMMUNICATIONS

The False Claims Act

The Federal False Claims Act ("FCA") prohibits any person from submitting, or causing to be submitted, any false or fraudulent claim for payment to the federal government.[25] The statute empowers private parties to bring suit on behalf of the United States for false claims that were submitted to the federal government.[26] If, for example, a person learns that a healthcare provider has submitted fraudulent claims for payment to a federal healthcare program, such as Medicare or Medicaid, the person can sue the provider to recover the damages incurred by the government. Although the suit is brought by a private party – called a "relator" – the actual party to the suit is the United States. If successful, the damages that are awarded are paid to the United States, although the relator gets to keep a substantial portion.[27] In addition, the United States has the option to intervene in the suit and take over the suit, or decline to intervene, which permits the relator to continue the suit.[28] FCA cases that are brought by private parties are known as "*qui tam*" suits.[29] Most *qui tams* are brought by so-called "whistleblowers," usually employees of the allegedly violating company.

Franklin v. Parke-Davis

Franklin v. *Parke-Davis* is one of the most important developments involving the intersection of the FCA and off-label communications. *Franklin* was brought by a relator who was employed by the pharmaceutical company Parke-Davis. According to Franklin's complaint, Parke-Davis directed its sales force to promote their drug Neurontin for a number of off-label uses.[30] Not only were these uses not

FDA-approved, but, according to the relator, they were not covered by federal healthcare programs such as Medicaid.[31] Franklin alleged that because these uses were not covered by Medicaid, Parke-Davis "caused" the submission of uncovered, false claims to the federal government through off-label promotion.[32]

The theory employed by the relator in *Franklin* was a novel application of the FCA. The court itself acknowledged this fact. "To be sure, Relator's theory of liability takes the parties into territory that is not well charted by the existing decisional law."[33] Nevertheless, the court accepted Franklin's argument that the FCA could be used by private litigants to police off-label communications.

The court rejected Parke-Davis's argument that it was physicians who prescribed the drug for off-label indications and thus "caused" the submission of a claim, rather than the manufacturer. The court held that the chain of causation was not broken by the intervening actions of the physician. Because the submission of a claim to the Medicaid program was a foreseeable result of the company's actions, the company was legally responsible for the claims submitted to federal programs.[34]

In addition, Parke-Davis argued that it could be held liable under the FCA only if it intentionally made material false statements that led to the filing of false claims. Parke-Davis argued that the FCA contains a "double falsehood" requirement – an FCA plaintiff must prove a false statement that led to a false claim. The court disagreed, holding that the "[r]elator is not required to present evidence that Parke-Davis lied to physicians about Neurontin's off-label efficacy or safety to induce them to prescribe Neurontin for uses ineligible under Medicaid." Instead, an FCA case could be based on "truthful off-label marketing and financial incentives like kickbacks."[35]

The court held, therefore, that no false statements by the manufacturer were needed to sustain an FCA suit based on off-label communications. Perhaps more than any other, this holding has caused significant concern in the pharmaceutical industry. If an FCA suit can be based on truthful off-label communications, this holding could lead to lawsuits based on the dissemination of scientific information. Furthermore, if a future court extends the *Franklin* holding, it is possible for FCA suits to target the limited off-label communications traditionally accepted by the FCA.

Although *Franklin* is currently the only case to endorse such an expansive interpretation of the FCA against pharmaceutical manufacturers, there are indications that the plaintiff's bar is targeting the pharmaceutical industry using just such theories. Indications from federal authorities are more ambiguous. Although several prosecutors have stated that the United States is unlikely to bring or intervene in an FCA suit based only on dissemination of scientific information, other statements by federal authorities have been more ambiguous.[36] Moreover, even without support from the government, private litigants are unlikely to be deterred from suits targeting the dissemination of off-label information.

THE FUTURE OF OFF-LABEL COMMUNICATIONS

These two developments – one suggesting that manufacturers have greater flexibility with respect to off-label communications, and one suggesting that off-label communications could subject manufacturers to harsh new penalties – have led to a considerable amount of uncertainty. To date, courts have extended the protections of the First Amendment only to the dissemination of peer-reviewed, scientific material and industry support for CME programs. No court has held that other types of communications – such as company-created promotional labeling – are protected speech under the First Amendment. On the other side of the coin, use of the FCA as a vehicle to police off-label communications has, to date, only been applied to allegations of extensive off-label promotion coupled with alleged kickbacks. No court has held that the FCA can be violated when the defendant does no more than disseminate truthful, accurate off-label information.

This situation thus leaves the vast majority of possible communications by manufacturers in a gray area. Take, for example, company created promotional materials that present scientific information about an off-label use for an approved drug. There is at least a colorable argument that this material would receive protection under the First Amendment. If the material does no more than present truthful and accurate scientific data, it would be difficult to argue that the material is false or misleading. Moreover, although the FDA has substantial interests in regulating such promotion, prominent disclaimers could suffice as the least invasive means of achieving those interests. At the same time, if a court does not accept a First Amendment defense, there is a chance that this same promotional piece could be subject not only to enforcement under the FDCA, but also to lawsuit under the FCA. The *Franklin* court refused to rule out the possibility of an FCA case based on truthful communications about off-label uses for a drug. If such promotional labeling leads to claims to federal programs for an uncovered, off-label use, there is the danger of FCA suits and enormous monetary damages.

Public policy arguments can be marshaled on both sides of this issue. On one hand, there is no question that physicians prescribe drugs for a wide variety of uses, including uses not approved by the FDA. When doing so, the public health demands that physicians receive as much information as possible about safety and effectiveness for these conditions. And more often than not, manufacturers of prescription drugs possess a great deal of scientific information about off-label uses of their products. The proponents of allowing manufacturers to disseminate truthful and accurate information concerning these uses argue that broader free speech rights further this important public policy goal. On the other hand, the opponents of manufacturer off-label speech point out that manufacturers have an inherent conflict of interest. Manufacturers have an interest in having their drugs used for the widest possible uses, including off-label uses. This conflict of interest may result in manufacturers disseminating only information that supports the effectiveness of their drugs and discounting information that questions efficacy. Opponents argue, therefore, that the FDA is a necessary gatekeeper and restricting manufacturer speech ensures that information is accurate and balanced. Thus, it is argued, using the FCA to police manufacturer speech is not only appropriate, but is a positive development in ensuring that truthful and complete information is disseminated.

How these developments evolve, therefore, is an important and complex issue. Certainly, if courts interpret the First Amendment as applying to additional categories of speech, FCA suits targeting such speech will be mitigated. But if courts retreat from the *WLF* holding, or extend *Franklin* to allegations involving only truthful communications that fall outside established areas of First Amendment protection, use of the FCA by private litigants will likely become even more widespread. One thing, however, is certain – the law surrounding off-label communications is still evolving and in coming years the courts and lawmakers will further shape and define these issues. Accordingly, where these developments will lead, as well as the resulting consequences for the public health, are still open and controversial questions.

12

The Need for Better Health Information

Advancing the Informed Patient in Europe

Don E. Detmer, Peter Singleton, and Scott C. Ratzan*

INTRODUCTION

The relationship between patients and physicians or other health professionals has steadily changed over time from an authoritarian, paternal relationship to one in which the patient is more empowered and involved in treatment choices. As the public has become more "consumerist," people are less accepting of a passive role in their healthcare. This change allows healthcare decisions to reflect the patient's own values and priorities rather than those presumed by clinicians.

As the dynamics between doctors and patients change, the relationships among professionals are also shifting toward a "team-based" model of healthcare delivery that draws upon the range of skills and expertise needed to address health problems, particularly chronic illness. The team-based delivery model, although it brings certain benefits, can also create tensions among different parties to a patient's care program, and poses the risk that important health information for the patient may somehow get lost in the process.

The term "informed patient" presumes that people with illnesses (and healthy people) both deserve and need appropriate health information. An informed patient is enabled to become involved in his or her own healthcare, to seek out the best care, to decide on the best courses

* The principal materials in this document are from a research effort of a Cambridge University Health (the health policy and management research center at Cambridge University) team led by Don Detmer and Peter Singleton. The study was supported by Johnson & Johnson.

of action, and to follow the agreed-upon course of treatment. The informed patient concept, as used in this chapter, also includes non–professionally trained caregivers (often family members), because they may serve as proxies for an incapacitated patient and are often part of the social unit making decisions for the future.

This chapter discusses the problem and implications of the current patient information gap and the compelling reasons to address it, as well as the role of direct-to-consumer advertising in patient information. We describe findings from The Informed Patient project, a study initiated by the authors at the Judge Institute of Management of the University of Cambridge in 2002.[1] This project was designed to guide future policy on the provision of information to patients in Europe; the conclusions of this study, however, have ramifications for all patients.

WHY INFORM PATIENTS?

One of the basic ethical requirements for medical research is informed consent, as supported by the 1964 Helsinki Declaration. This forms part of a continuum, from potentially risky interventions for medical research, through accepted procedures (which still include some element of risk), to organ and tissue retention and use of medical records for epidemiological research with negligible risk.

At the latter end, it may be argued that aggregate anonymized records pose little threat to patients or their privacy, so consent is not required. This may be acceptable, but does not prevent the ethical requirement for transparency to engender trust, as well as meeting the strictures of data protection laws.

Economists would also argue that free availability of information is necessary to create efficient markets and appropriate allocation of resources. In Europe, with state-controlled healthcare systems, there has often been little capacity for choice by patients, but things are changing, both within and between member states. For example, the United Kingdom has patient choice as a major plank of its current health strategy. In Europe patient mobility, whereby patients can be treated in other member states but paid for by their country of residence, has been established in principle at the European Court of Justice and is currently being developed and clarified by the European Commission.

The Informed Patient study brought together evidence showing that, on balance, better-informed patients:

- are more involved and follow advice better;
- are less anxious – though some may be more so;
- select fewer or lower risk interventions;
- start treatment earlier;
- are more satisfied and less likely to litigate;
- have lower healthcare costs through more self-management and a more efficient use of resources.[2]

IS THE PUBLIC WELL-INFORMED?

A study by Coulter et al. showed that information provision in the United Kingdom was generally poor:

- many materials contain inaccurate and out-of-date information;
- few provide adequate information about treatment risks and side effects;
- topics of relevance to patients are omitted;
- technical terms are not explained;
- coverage of treatment options is incomplete;
- uncertainties are ignored or glossed over;
- information about treatment effectiveness is often missing or unreliable;
- few materials actively promote shared decision-making.[3]

Often the content of health literature is not targeted to patients' real needs. Patients seeking information about living with a disease or condition, for example, often find that most professionally produced materials focus on clinical details rather than the impact on lifestyle and family. Even materials compiled by patient advocacy groups can be forbiddingly technical for newcomers unfamiliar with the terminology of a disease.

The challenges, of course, are not limited to print media. With increasing Internet usage, few patients may be able to grasp the range of material available online or know which sites provide reliable, high-quality information. However, there is some evidence that the public may be better at handling uncertainty and discerning quality than they are generally given credit for.[4]

The accessibility, comprehensiveness, and clarity of health information are as important as availability. Studies have shown that the readability level of patient materials often exceeds the reading skills of the general public. In a large U.S. study, one-third of English-speaking patients were unable to read "basic" health materials.[5] This reflects both that the disadvantaged, often most in need of good information, tend to have poor reading skills, and that clinicians, who often write these materials, tend to write assuming a graduate-level audience.

Drug information leaflets are often poorly presented, which can lead to a patient taking medication improperly. Steps are being taken in Europe to try to improve the relevance of drug information leaflets to patients. The priority, however, seems to be on legal exactitude rather than on protecting patients' lives by helping them understand their medicines and how to take them.

Many patients are unable to decipher the risk factors, either because they lack the requisite numeracy skills or because the facts are poorly and inconsistently presented. Often the risks are presented without balancing materials on the benefits. Patients need the capacity to assess risk among a proposed set of interventions, and require accessible materials to help them weigh alternatives and make informed decisions.

These factors have contributed to a patient information gap that undermines the interests of both patients and healthcare providers in the effective delivery of healthcare. In addition to medical considerations, there are compelling ethical, economic, and health management reasons to develop policies to help close this gap.

HOW WELL-INFORMED SHOULD PATIENTS BE?

The preamble of the WHO Constitution states that "Informed opinion and active cooperation on the part of the public are of the utmost importance in the improvement of health of the people." Informing is a necessary precursor to consent. Physicians and healthcare providers, in properly informing patients about their treatment, show respect for patient rights to autonomy and choice.

Exactly how much information is sufficient for a patient to feel fully informed is a complex calculus; depending on the nature of the message, emotional reactions, for example, can interfere with and limit a patient's understanding of health and treatment information. Evidence from research shows that up to 35 percent of patients do not recall what clinicians tell them and patients are nervous about raising concerns.[6]

Too often patients being "informed" prior to surgery are given a list of possible adverse outcomes, often overwhelming the positive reasons for undertaking the intervention – not to ensure that patients are fully aware of their options and the consequences of their choice, but primarily as a legal protection for doctors. Informing should be a process driven by a patient's needs and preferences, so that the patient can properly give consent. Some patients may prefer the "ignorance is bliss," approach and it may be just as important for their wellbeing not to be frightened by too much doom and gloom. Many are happy to trust their clinicians' judgment, though that trust should not be taken for granted.

THE ECONOMIC IMPACT OF THE INFORMED PATIENT

Although there is much to justify a greater emphasis on improving information to patients from an ethical standpoint of openness and increased patient autonomy, there are payoffs to be considered between the possible individual benefits and the wider effects on society, particularly healthcare costs.

Better informed patients not only may have a improved chance of achieving better health status, but also may make more efficient use of healthcare resources, through more appropriate treatment decisions, better adherence to the agreed-upon treatment, and better understanding of the ramifications of clinical decisions.

Effective gains may require changes in working practices as well as better information. For example, in the Netherlands, the provision of aids for disabled patients (the adaptation of cars and installation of handrails, for example) was replaced with a "personal budget" allowing patients to choose the care that best suited their lifestyles. While the direct cost was much the same, there were significant savings in administration and transactions costs as well as the provision of far better and faster service to the public. This is a classic example of "empowering" patients to good effect.

Better health status, although a valuable social good in its own right, may also lead to higher productivity and better economic performance for individuals, employers, and countries. Constraints on funding in most healthcare systems may limit the levels of information provision below the ideal, since providing information takes time and, at some level, impacts upon budgets.

There is concern that increasing information will increase pressures on health resources without corresponding improvements in cost-effectiveness. Withholding information is an effective way to constrain demand and ration services – the basis for the current ban on the promotion of prescription-only medicines in Europe.

There is insufficient evidence as of now to decide whether better information would be good or bad for health budgets. Some studies show that a better informed patient may choose less risky or less invasive intervention.[7] A better informed patient, who is more engaged in the decision-making, may prefer a wait-and-see attitude rather than adopting a more assertive regimen suggested by a clinician. This suggests lower healthcare costs as a possible result of better informed patients, though there could be correspondingly higher social care costs from supporting the patient through the wait-and-see period.

MANAGING DEMAND FOR HEALTHCARE

Providing more information may reduce demand on the healthcare system by encouraging self-care, a more appropriate use of resources, and/or more prudent lifestyles. Controlled trials have found that patient information leaflets caused no significant change in the use of health services, though one leaflet did reduce consultation rates, suggesting that some unnecessary consultations were avoided.[8]

Information campaigns can be effective, as we have seen in the United States, where the provision of a healthcare manual to households has had compelling results.[9] This experience might not carry through to Europe because people in the United States must pay for such consultations – a clear incentive on the part of the consumer to restrict consultations. Only a few major public health campaigns in Europe have sought to inform the public about how best to use the system and there may be difficulties in changing public behavior in accessing the healthcare system. In the United Kingdom, NHS Direct (a telephone triage system) is promoted to increase patient satisfaction by giving more prompt information and diverting callers from using more expensive primary-care or emergency resources. Reports suggest that it has increased patient satisfaction, but also created a greater demand for services (presumably from unmet needs), rather than having reduced operational costs overall.[10]

DIRECT-TO-CONSUMER INFORMATION

In some developed economies, notably the United States, consumers are increasingly exposed to detailed advertisements encouraging them to become proactive and request specific medications and procedures. Direct-to-consumer advertising (DTCA) remains permitted in the United States and New Zealand, but is presently forbidden in the EU. Debate continues over the interpretation of studies in the United States on the effects of DTCA on consumer behavior and other outcomes, and whether the overall outcome from DTCA is positive or negative. (Drs. Meredith Rosenthal and Julie Donohue discuss the American debate and research findings on DTCA in Chapter 10.)

There has been much debate recently in Europe on the provision of information on prescription-only medicines by industry directly to the public. This is currently tightly controlled and restricted to official information (technical sheets and patient information leaflets).

There are concerns that promotional activities, including direct-to-consumer advertising, may be used to promote new prescription drugs at the expense of equally effective older drugs, especially generic alternatives, thereby increasing the overall healthcare budget.

In 2001 the European Commission offered some proposals to relax regulation in three key areas: diabetes, AIDS, and asthma. This was challenged successfully by consumer rights groups, who believed that industry could not be trusted, but also by excluded patient groups who wanted the same privilege of access to information.

There is little evidence of the effects of DTCA from the European scene, as advertising is banned, and it is not clear to what degree U.S. experience would translate to Europe, given the differences in the healthcare systems.

There is sufficient evidence, however, that direct-to-consumer *information* can be effective, though interpretations vary as to whether this is beneficial. Public campaigns are permitted as long as they do not promote a specific product or its effects. Novartis ran a campaign in the Netherlands promoting the issue of "nail fungus" and encouraging patients to see their doctors. This led to a surge of enquiries and a significant increase in sales of Lamisil®, Novartis' product for this condition (and presumably for other potential treatments). However, Dutch physicians have pilloried Novartis for raising public concerns unnecessarily through its campaign. To our knowledge the view of the public is not known and such information would be useful.

SHOULD INDUSTRY USE DTCA EVEN IF PERMITTED?

Advertising costs will be passed on to the consumer through higher prices, unless sales volumes are raised sufficiently to compensate – either way, government drug budgets will increase. This may be off-set by reductions in costs elsewhere (e.g., by reducing hospital stays or improving the productivity of the workforce) if drug treatment is actually more effective. Advertising may have ancillary effects such as improving brand image, reputation, or trust, which may have benefits for the company in other areas or products.

Although promotion will be targeted at newer or more profitable drugs in order to gain or maintain market share, there are ultimately limitations to this strategy, because drugs will normally only be adopted into formularies if there is increased effectiveness or reduction in adverse side effects.

Should the pharmaceutical industry use DTCA, or lobby to be allowed to promote its products in Europe in the same way that any other industry can (apart from arms, drugs, and tobacco)? Provided promotions are legal, decent, honest, and truthful, there should be no further ethical issues. It is important, however, that the industry realize that people's health and lives are at stake, and any exploitation or even a serious perception of exploitation is likely to have significant adverse long-term consequences in terms of lost trust and poor reputation. Breaches of research codes have already tarnished the image of the pharmaceutical industry, and could take many years to repair.

The most successful approach would be collaboration with governments and professional bodies to promote campaigns whereby all players are prepared and committed to a project to improve public health. The Novartis promotion clearly benefited the public, as there was unmet need through ignorance of the condition or of its curability – the problem appears to be that the professionals were unprepared, and reacted negatively because of how the campaign affected them. It is possible that they considered the condition relatively benign and not deserving of more aggressive treatment.

THE INFORMED PATIENT AND THE FUTURE

In 2003, the Informed Patient project found enough evidence of the benefits of enhanced health and healthcare-related education to recommend that a coherent plan be developed to improve the current status of patient information to engage government, industry, patient groups, the health professions, and the media. The information and knowledge support must be available at the government level and also at regional/local levels to assure sufficient education and support.

The Informed Patient study concluded that an appropriate strategy and implementation effort for health information for patients/citizens and their caregivers will:

- deliver impartial, sound (evidence-based), and accessible information and knowledge support;
- ensure that such support will mitigate some of the burden of the growing numbers of elderly people with chronic illnesses on the already constrained healthcare systems;
- help patients and healthcare professionals better evaluate treatment choices as medical science and healthcare become increasingly complex;
- increase transparency and accountability of the healthcare system so that choice and cost-effectiveness are evident; and
- continually adopt new information and communications technologies so that healthcare operations will promote best practices, adopt new effective treatments, and discard ineffective and/or unsafe old treatments.

In February 2004, a further conference was held in Dublin to produce a policy action plan, "An EU Framework for Action." The framework was published in August 2004 and launched at the European Health Forum Gastein 2004 conference.[11]

Closing the patient information gap will require the commitment of government to support the creation and distribution of sound information in the near term, and more timely and rigorous research on the effectiveness and costs of direct-to-consumer advertising and other methods of patient information delivery. This is not a short-term matter, particularly as consumers eventually interact directly with their doctors and nurses over the Internet; entire models of care will emerge, and long-held assumptions from the past may not hold sway. The future just won't be what it used to be.

13

Who Should Get Access to Which Drugs? An Ethical Template for Pharmacy Benefits

Norman Daniels, James E. Sabin, and J. Russell Teagarden*

SOCIAL LEARNING ABOUT FAIR LIMITS

Pharmacy benefits have become the problem child of healthcare coverage. Rising demand, increased utilization, and surging costs terrified large purchasers even when the economy was good. Limiting access to some drugs, whether through restrictive coverage policies or tiered co-pays, has often been met with patient and clinician resentment and distrust. Placing this problem child in a properly equipped classroom, with appropriate educational tools and processes, can school us all in how to develop, understand, and accept fair limits.

Most public encounters with limit setting in healthcare, both in the United States and abroad, have been episodic and involved big-ticket items. Often, these have featured denials of "last chance" treatments, creating life-and-death dramas. In 2002 in Boston, for example, Belynda Dunn, an HIV-positive patient, was denied a liver transplant by a managed care organization (MCO) on the grounds that it was "experimental" for patients whose immune systems might be compromised. The MCO then contributed to a charity set up to "rescue" Ms. Dunn and others like her from the consequences of reasonable limit setting.

From episodes like this one, the public is likely to draw confused lessons about the necessity and reasonableness of limits to care. From the Dunn case, it would be easy to conclude that there is always a

* This chapter was first published as an article in the journal *Health Affairs* (2003, *22(1)*: 123–35). The authors and editors gratefully acknowledge Health Affairs for permission to include it here.

way around denials if one advocates vigorously enough, can point an accusing finger at the "evildoer" who is denying care, and can attract public sympathy. The public furor following denial of funding for Child B in England, like similar cases in Norway, Australia, and New Zealand, shows the great difficulty of accepting limits even when public officials replace private insurers as the "evildoers" in question.[1]

In contrast, pharmacy benefit management lacks such high drama. This mundane dullness may provide a distinct advantage in helping society to move along a learning curve about setting limits fairly. We are more prepared to learn about limits when we are not in extremis.

In addition, pharmaceuticals potentially touch everyone, especially the chronically ill, for whom they are often the main treatments. What is generally seen as the problem – growing patient demand for higher cost drugs, fed by direct-to-consumer advertising – actually offers an opportunity to teach large numbers of us about the need to find ways of setting limits we can accept as reasonable and fair. Pharmacy benefits may provide a last chance to come to grips with the broader issue of health cost management. If this is not accomplished with proper public learning, it is an area that could bog the health system down in incessant conflict, escalating distrust, litigation, and ever-increasing costs.

A TOOL FOR LEARNING, A PROCESS FOR USING IT

We take up this challenge by viewing the management and implementation of pharmacy benefits as a school in which patients, clinicians, and the public as a whole can learn how to share valuable medical resources fairly. We equip that classroom with a tool for learning, specifically an ethical template for pharmacy benefits, and we describe a process for using that template. The template delineates four levels of decisions about pharmacy coverage and connects ethically acceptable types of rationales for limits with decisions made at each level. The template is useful for evaluating the basis for "tiered" co-pays and not just explicit exclusions from coverage. In short, the template provides a framework for organizing reasons for coverage or noncoverage that people can accept as *relevant* to meeting healthcare needs fairly under resource constraints.

The process for using the template should ensure the transparency or *publicity* and the *relevance* of the rationales underlying limit-setting decisions. People affected by decisions will accept limits only if they see the rationales for those limits as relevant to meeting drug needs fairly under reasonable resource constraints. The ethical template makes it easier to understand and evaluate rationales – in this sense it gives us a graspable framework for delineating relevant reasons. (It goes without saying that we presuppose an honest, nondeceptive representation of rationales throughout.) The process also allows for the *revisability* of decisions in light of new evidence and arguments, including the learning that comes from a fair appeals process.

Together, these three elements of the process – publicity, relevance, and revisability – assure what we elsewhere have termed "account-ability for reasonableness."[2] Making pharmacy benefit management accountable for reasonable limits helps to establish its moral legitimacy. Nevertheless, acceptance of the reasonableness of limits also depends on social learning about fair limit setting. A public that has no grasp of the need for fair limits is unlikely to accept even reasonable limits. In that spirit, the ethical template is an important tool for societal learn-ing because it provides a framework for constructing relevant reasons for pharmacy coverage decisions and clarifying policy alternatives.

The ethical template, appropriately used, offers a disciplined ap-proach to the process of seeking ethical justification. It thus embodies the type of approach to decision-making called for by some others writ-ing on the ethics of pharmacy benefits.[3] From a consumer and market perspective, it carries out an informative and educative role regard-ing the value and cost of pharmaceutical care.[4] We also agree with Uwe Reinhardt's recent comment that "Whatever means employers and government ultimately adopt to shift more of the rising cost of prescription drugs onto patients, one can expect much rancor over the practice – and possibly much litigation – unless the underlying formu-laries or therapeutic grouping can be explained to physicians, patients and juries with appeal to scientifically sound cost benefit analyses."[5] The ethical template provides a framework for understanding what kinds of explanations are required and how they need to be structured.

THE CONTEXT OF DRUG BENEFIT ALLOCATION

Every system making resource allocation decisions about prescription drug benefits must take into account a set of general considerations, each one involving important values about which there is some disagreement. Is the system primarily concerned to treat significant illnesses and conditions with a defined pathophysiological basis, or will it also provide for drugs that enhance otherwise normal health, function, and appearance?[6] Is the system willing to pay for unproven, experimental interventions, and, if so, under what conditions, or is it primarily obliged to provide proven or medically accepted treatments?[7] What requirements for effectiveness and/or cost effectiveness will it impose? How will it make trade-offs when there are competing needs among more or less seriously ill people?[8] Even a universal coverage system that aims to deliver what is judged to be fair from a societal perspective would have to address these questions. The answers given to them serve as priority-setting or resource allocation principles. An important factor complicating the situation is that the details of answers to some of them may have to be worked out and judged acceptable only through practice and not a priori or ahead of time.[9]

A second set of considerations arise because of specific political, market, or regulatory situations. Specific political constraints may affect a particular public program, such as Medicare or Medicaid, that does not serve the whole population at once. One large private purchaser of prescription drug benefits may have to compete to attract highly mobile workers; another may be primarily concerned about keeping its relatively stable workforce productive. Some large purchasers will be constrained by contractual obligations (for example, a unionized workforce); others will not.

These more specific motivations and constraints can produce limits on prescription drug benefits that are not ideal from the societal perspective of a universal coverage system. They may push purchasers to provide more or less than a societal perspective would require.[10] Some criticisms of allocation decisions will arise because of these conflicts between a societal perspective and that of particular purchasers of benefits in a mixed and nonintegrated system. Whether or not the limits (or excesses) that result from these specific considerations ultimately prove ethically defensible, we believe they should be made explicit so that they can be evaluated.

THE ETHICAL TEMPLATE

The ethical template (see Table 13.1 for an overview of its elements) maps decisions about drug coverage limitations onto generic rationales.

Table 13.1. *Elements of the Ethical Template*

Allocation Decision Level	Coverage Policy Question	Central Ethical Issues	Relevant Rationales
Level 1: Drug categories included	Which categories of drugs to include? Example: triptans	Giving priority to important health needs	1. Appeal to acceptable general priority principles 2. Facts about effectiveness risks, cost-worthiness
Level 2: Drug selection within category	Which drugs from the category to include? Example: Imitrex but not Zomig	Gaining cost advantage without undue burden or risk to patients	1. Facts about interchangeability 2. Facts about costs 3. Fair exceptions process
Level 3: Drug indication	Which uses of the drug are covered? Example: for migraine treatment, not prevention	Giving priority to important health needs	1. Appeal to acceptable, general priority principles 2. Facts about effectiveness, risks, cost-worthiness
Level 4: Drug use coverage limitations	How many can be covered? Where and how can they be purchased? Example: dosage sufficient for several episodes per month	Gaining cost advantage without undue burden or risk to patients	1. Reasonableness of coverage limitations 2. Facts about cost savings 3. Fair exceptions process

Source: Authors' own analysis.

We call this mapping a "generic template" because it serves as a pattern or guide for constructing and evaluating pharmacy benefits. Unlike true templates, however, the benefits patterned on it are not replicas or duplicates of the template. Rather, the pattern is a guide to the overall structure but not its fine details. As the details of specific coverage decisions and the rationales underlying them are worked out, the fine structure of various reasonable benefit plans emerge from the same basic pattern or template. When a plan is fully specified, the generic template is converted into a detailed "blueprint" that shows the pattern of values that governs the actual plan.

A Hierarchy of Coverage Decisions

The template we describe reflects a hierarchy of four levels of decision making about drug coverage. Specifically, in designing a pharmacy benefit, decisions must be made about (1) the categories and subcategories of drugs to be covered, (2) the selection of drugs within categories, (3) the indications or uses for which selected drugs may be used, and (4) further "use" limitations on the amounts (for example, on quantity/unit time or dosage form) or source (retail or mail order) of drugs that may be covered.[11] Many people encounter these decisions not as strict limits on what drugs they can obtain within their pharmacy benefit, but as different tiers of co-pay for different drugs or as limits on prescription size or on the source (pharmacy or mail order) they must use.

To illustrate these levels of coverage decisions, consider how a hypothetical pharmacy benefit might view Imitrex (sumatriptan), a common treatment for migraines. Because migraine headaches are a significant form of pathology for many people, it would be important to include in the benefit the category (or subcategory) of triptans, a large family of drugs that significantly reduce the seriousness and consequences of migraine attacks (Level 1). Ideally, the identification of needs and the specification of drug categories at Level 1 would be based on evidence about the disease profile of the covered population and evidence about effective ways of managing these diseases.

Several of the triptans are generally interchangeable, having similar effectiveness and similar side effects for most people. Because of discounts and rebates, pharmacy benefit managers (or other administrators and purchasers) can usually secure some of these interchangeable drugs at lower costs than others. The lower cost is potentially an advantage for all stakeholders in the plan, depending on how the savings are distributed or used. Since, in our hypothetical example, Imitrex offers such a cost advantage, it will be selected for coverage over others not offering such an advantage. Alternatively, Imitrex may be available with little or no co-pay, whereas the drugs with less cost advantage are available, if at all, only with higher co-pays (Level 2).

Imitrex has proven efficacy, however, only for treatment, and not for prevention, of migraines. Accordingly, at the drug indication level (Level 3), Imitrex is covered for treating migraines but not for preventing them. Finally, because there is evidence that most people with migraine problems do not experience more than a few episodes a month,[12] a benefit plan can avoid wasteful expenditures on drugs if it limits drug coverage to a quantity sufficient to treat only a few episodes of migraine (Level 4), provided, as we emphasize later, there is an easy way for patients who need more treatments to get them.

A Pattern of Ethical Concerns and Rationales

At each level within the hierarchy, as the illustration and the table suggest, there are management issues, central ethical concerns, and rationales for decisions that take those issues and concerns into account. One important feature revealed by the template is that different types of ethical issues are raised at different levels in the hierarchy. At the Drug Category and Drug Indication levels (Levels 1 and 3), the ethical issues focus on meeting important health needs. At the Drug Selection and Drug Use levels (Levels 2 and 4) the central ethical issue is how to gain a cost advantage without placing undue burden or risk on certain patients – either the burden of noncoverage itself or the burden of too much hassle obtaining an exception to the policy.

The generic rationales that emerge at the different levels reflect this pattern. We shall focus on three such generic rationales, two that are prominent at Levels 1 and 3 and one that is prominent at Levels 2 and 4. These rationales are not intended to be exhaustive, though they are central. Each is widely accepted at a general or abstract level, but all raise controversy in their application. This very controversy is an opportunity for social learning.

Generic Rationales and Priority Principles: Treatment versus Enhancement

Each of the generic rationales involves what may be thought of as a rationing principle.[13] More euphemistically, we can think of each rationale as appealing to a priority that reflects a collective goal in providing the benefit. One such priority, evident at Levels 1 and 3, is to give weight or importance to providing drug treatments (including some forms of prevention) for significant medical problems, that is, significant pathology, and to give little or no weight to interventions that involve the enhancement or improved control of otherwise normal conditions. This priority principle is widely invoked, both in the United States and abroad, and has an important influence in shaping medical insurance coverage.[14] For example, consider a typical drug indication (Level 3) coverage limit: the topical tretinoin Retin-A is to be covered for treatment of acne but not for control of wrinkles that result from aging. The relevant generic rationale for this restriction would then appeal to the priority principle that values treatment of pathology more than cosmetic enhancements.

This priority principle is not always as uncontroversial in its application. Consider the Level 1 exclusion made by many health plans that do not cover oral contraceptives (occasionally this will be a Level 3 exclusion, allowing their use for medical purposes but not for family planning). Even if preventing normal pregnancy cannot count as treatment of pathology, many would argue that support for reproductive planning is itself an important social goal, and we ought to share the burdens of financing it through drug coverage. Indeed vasectomy and tubal ligation are generally covered as medical procedures, even when they are also aimed at reproductive planning. Making rationales for limits explicit means that there is greater pressure to develop consistent, justifiable patterns of coverage based on a coherent set of priorities.

This point is given special relevance by the outcry about gender bias that arose several years ago when Viagra (sildenafil) was covered by many health plans that denied coverage for oral contraceptives. If both were "lifestyle" drugs, and not simply treatments of illness, then why one and not the other? Another controversial exclusion by some plans concerns costly treatments for infertility. Although infertility often involves clear pathology, so that treatment would ordinarily be covered, the exclusion is justified in the minds of some by the (unpersuasive) claim that treating infertility is just a "lifestyle" choice. Similarly, confusion often surrounds the rationales underlying Level 1 decisions to exclude coverage for smoking deterrents and treatments or weight loss agents. A real debate and deliberation about coverage policy at Level 1 would be furthered by the practice of making rationales for limits explicit.

Proven versus Unproven Effectiveness. A second priority principle that is prominent in decisions at Levels 1 and 3 is to provide coverage for interventions known to be effective and to exclude those that have been shown to be ineffective or whose effectiveness is not yet proven. The restriction of Imitrex to the treatment of migraines depends on this principle, for it is effective for their treatment but unproven for their prevention. This priority principle can sometimes be controversial in its application, as when an unproven use of a drug may offer some patients a last chance at treatment. Here too, making the rationale explicit – including evidence for the argument of the rationale – promotes clearer grounds for debate and deliberation.

Cost-Worthiness. A third rationing principle requires that we aim for more, rather than less, cost-effective or cost-worthy modes of treatment. The justification for this priority is that we meet more needs by following this principle than not, given resource limits. Though this principle could also be invoked at Level 1 or 3, we have found few examples in the United States of that happening (but see the discussion of Viagra in the next section).[15] At the Drug Selection and Drug Use levels (2 and 4), however, some version of the third rationing or priority principle plays a dominant role, because cost advantage is a crucial driver of these decisions.

Nevertheless, the appeal to cost advantage should not operate alone. Further ethical considerations should qualify or constrain this priority principle. Specifically, the cost advantage to the purchaser or collective in these cases should not impose significant risks or burdens on individuals affected by the limitations.

Constraints on Seeking Cost Advantage. To illustrate this additional ethical constraint, suppose that two drugs are considered to be generally interchangeable; that is, that they are expected to have the same clinical effects for most people most of the time in the same situations. Then using the less expensive one will generally not impose a significant burden on patients. If there are reasons that particular patients will not do well on the selected drug, there should be quick and easy ways for those patients to secure a more appropriate drug. We therefore have two important constraints on appeals to cost-advantage: not only must the selected drug be generally interchangeable with those that are excluded (or require a larger co-pay), but there must be in place a quick and efficient way to remedy the situation for patients for whom interchangeability does not hold. The generic rationale for limits at Level 2 (and 4) would refer not only to the principle requiring cost-worthy treatment, but also to the evidence about general interchangeability. There should also be publicly accessible evidence about the effectiveness of the process that is implemented for obtaining exceptions for patients who truly need the drugs that are not selected.

One further ethical constraint on cost advantage is also important to note, because it has a bearing on complaints made by some purchasers and consumers against pharmacy benefit managers. The complaint is that the cost advantages obtained by benefit managers have not worked to the collective advantage of purchasers or enrollees, and sometimes have disadvantaged them. The further ethical constraint identified in the template is the requirement that the benefits that derive from seeking cost advantage be distributed in a way that serves shared interests of the various stakeholders – employers, enrollees, benefit managers. Minimally, this constraint means that there should be an accounting of how the saving from limits at Levels 2 and 4 are used to sustain the benefit, to stretch it further, or to reduce costs to various stakeholders. In short, the cost advantage must be explained so that all can see whether and how collective cost-lowering mechanisms, including discounts or rebates, work to help meet healthcare needs fairly, that is, how they meet the relevance requirement.

Because drug coverage limitations at Level 4 (for example, quantity of drug per unit time, dose format, or drug distribution channel for procurement) also depend on cost-advantage claims, a structure for generic rationales applies at this level very similar to that at the drug selection level (Level 2). For example, the evidentiary basis for claiming that most patients only need so many migraine treatments per month should be supplied in a rationale for such a limit. In addition, a clear process that is quick and efficient for patients who need more treatments in a month should be specified. There must be a reduction in the risk to them when the collective scheme takes advantage of the cost advantage of paying for fewer treatments that may go unused. Finally, the savings that result must be used in a way that serves the varied but shared interests of different stakeholders in the plan.

Disagreement and Deliberation

Developing and using the template does not resolve all the disputes that will arise in designing and implementing pharmacy benefits. Rather, it focuses those disputes on the underlying rationales – the evidence and argument and principles, the underlying reasoning – for decisions. The template thus leaves room for the kind of variation among principles and rationales that may arise in diverse health plans. Whatever the rationales, however, accountability for reasonableness requires that they be public, be viewed as relevant by those affected by them, and be revisable in light of further evidence or argument. The template facilitates but does not substitute for scrutiny by various stakeholders of the adequacy or appropriateness of rationales.

USING THE TEMPLATE

We have developed the ethical template for two practical purposes – as a tool for design and management of pharmacy benefit plans and as an educational tool or heuristic device to foster public deliberation and societal learning about setting limits fairly. Given these objectives, the template must be judged by real world relevance, not simply theoretical appeal. Is it useable and useful for questions about drug coverage? Can it foster deliberation and learning? We are convinced that it can, though it is not a panacea for the many forces – the emotionality of many treatment settings, the vested interests pushing for business as usual, the time and resources needed for rational deliberation, and the absence of institutional structures insisting on deliberation – that create the gap between what we call for and standard practice.

The best way to show that the template can be useful would be for us to report on its actual use in practice and demonstrated results. We cannot do that yet since the template is too new. An alternative would be for us to argue hypothetically: to describe just how the template might be used in a hypothetical case. Because that would leave the template open to the objection that it is part of an unrealistic, even utopian project, we adopt here a third approach. We suggest how the template may prove useful by describing some examples of actual practice where key elements of our approach are employed, and we then suggest how the outcomes would be even better if the full approach were deployed.

This extrapolation from real cases of coverage decisions provides an antidote to the charge that what we propose is not realistic.

Specifically, in this section we use vignettes about Viagra coverage at a not-for-profit insurer (Harvard Pilgrim Health Care) and selective serotonin reuptake inhibitor (SSRI) coverage at a prepaid group practice (Kaiser Permanente) and an example from one of the authors' clinical practice to show how the template could be used to improve coverage decisions and education. In our view, these instances stand as exemplary practices just because the organizations and clinicians acted in ways that anticipate and are in accord with the template's requirements. We also describe how actual use of the template in these cases would have resulted in further improvements. To us, this suggests that the template and the process for deploying it have practical value and should be more widely used.

Viagra

In 1998, Harvard Pilgrim Health Care had to decide about coverage for Viagra, which had received FDA approval in February. The team charged with recommending a policy decision elected to consult with the Harvard Pilgrim Ethics Advisory Group (EAG). The EAG includes consumers insured by HPHC, physicians who provide care under the insurance, employers who purchase Harvard Pilgrim insurance for their employees, and staff. It deliberates about cases brought for consultation and offers nonbinding advice about the ethical dimensions of the situation. We note that the EAG's involvement of a broad group of stakeholders facilitates accountability for reasonable decisions by increasing the likelihood that rationales that are adopted will be seen as relevant and acceptable to those who are affected by them.

At the meeting several participants applied terms such as "enhancement" and "lifestyle drug" to Viagra and questioned whether it should be covered. At this point a woman EAG member from a purchaser group spoke with great force. "I can't believe that at the end of the twentieth century – after all that Freud taught us – that we are talking as if sexuality were an optional matter of 'lifestyle.' Sex is an essential aspect of our being. To reduce the ability to have intercourse to the status of a 'life-enhancing' activity is to belittle a patient's valid desire to restore a basic function."

These comments led the EAG to see Viagra as an innovation offering important value. It should not be dismissed as "mere enhancement" or a "lifestyle choice." As a result, it answered the Level 1 question about whether the drug should be eligible for coverage positively. But it advised Harvard Pilgrim's management that although Viagra should be allowed to compete for coverage within the overall insurance pool, its use should be compared to the value provided by alternative uses of the funds. It advised that if the organization made a decision to limit coverage (a Level 4 decision, according to the template), it should explain the cost factor to members of the health plan and the public. This recommendation is exactly what the template proposes.

The fact that the Ethics Advisory Group followed the steps suggested by the template suggests that the kind of reasoning the template asks for is not pie in the sky. Had the template actually been available, however, it would have reassured participants in this EAG decision, as well as within HPHC, that the kind of reasoning they were using fits well with the overall requirements of Level 1 decisions. The template leaves explicit room for airing disagreements about how to interpret basic concepts, such as treatment and enhancement. The structure it incorporates, however, assures that use of the template will foster coherence among decisions over time. The one-time consultation in this case would have been connected to a structure that embodies broader experience over many similar decisions.

In the aftermath of the Ethics Advisory Group discussion, Harvard Pilgrim decided to cover four Viagra tablets a month at the discretion of the prescribing physician, thus imposing a Level 4 restriction. In announcing the policy, the Medical Director tried to educate members and the public about limits:

I don't want to be in the position of saying how often people should have intercourse. We are not telling physicians they can write prescriptions for only four pills. They can write for 30 or 90 or whatever. What we are saying is that we will pay for only four a month.... As to why Harvard Pilgrim settled on four pills as opposed to, say, eight, Dorsey [the Medical Director] admits there is no scientific logic to that number. It demonstrates a commitment to using the resource pool to help make it possible for people to use the medication . . . but it also reflects the fact that Viagra is too expensive for us to pay for unlimited use.[16]

Managed care and HMOs are typically vilified in the U.S. press, so the response of Boston's major newspaper was not at all typical. In an editorial titled "A Sensible Compromise on Viagra," the Boston Globe wrote that "Massachusetts HMOs have devised a policy that reasonably balances medical and cost considerations."[17]

This narrative about Harvard Pilgrim Health Care and Viagra policy suggests that the clarity of the rationale for limits on drug coverage and the lucid public explanation called for by the template promote improved decision making about a pharmacy benefit and foster public understanding of the need to make difficult Level 1 and Level 4 choices and readiness to accept limits as disappointing but fair. Had the template itself been available, it would have added assurance that the type of decisions made in this case were not idiosyncratic or ad hoc, but fit a pattern that had coherence and justification.

Selective Serotonin Reuptake Inhibitors

Our second example of how the template could be used effectively for management and education is based on a recent article that describes how Kaiser Permanente manages coverage for SSRIs.[18] SSRIs are more expensive than the tricyclic antidepressants that predominated when Prozac first came onto the market. Because the SSRIs do not produce a higher cure rate than the older medications, many drug coverage programs initially tried to exclude them as a category, except when tricyclics did not work (Level 1). Over time, however, from a combination of consumer demand, physician acceptance, favorable side effect profiles, reduced risk of death in overdose situations, and studies that suggested cost effectiveness,[19] SSRIs have become the most widely used antidepressants. Not surprisingly, the discussion of how Kaiser Permanente handles SSRIs within its drug benefit simply assumes the Level 1 decision to include them as a category of antidepressant.

As called for by the second level of the template, the physician-governed Permanente practices used the research pharmacists in its Drug Information Service to compare the four extant competing SSRIs (Celexa, Paxil, Prozac, and Zoloft) for clinical effectiveness. Though the details of this examination are not clear from the article, it is likely that the comparison also examined side effects and other risks, providing a basis for what the template calls a judgment about general therapeutic interchangeability. They concluded that none of the four was a clear "winner." Given comparable efficacy – or, more explicitly, general interchangeability – for treating depression, cost advantage, as the template proposes, became the appropriate determinant for choosing a drug of preference. At this point, Kaiser, which serves eight million members, used its substantial bargaining power to seek discounts from the manufacturers.

Although the article does not tell us which medication(s) were chosen or what members are told about the rationale, it reports in detail on how the organization interacts with physician prescribers. Drug education coordinators (trained clinical pharmacists) present the clinical and economic rationale behind the formulary choices. Had the template been available, the specific case here could have been shown to be consistent with a more general approach, and the template might have allowed comparisons to further cases.

Because no general rule can apply reasonably to all members of a large population, Kaiser builds in a simple, hassle-free approach to the exception process. If a Kaiser member is expected to be unresponsive to, intolerant of, or allergic to the formulary choice, the physician prescribes a nonformulary drug and indicates the reason on a special prescription form. This ease of application of the exceptions process is the only way to undercut the most common quality-oriented criticism of this kind of limit, namely that it exposes individual patients who do not fit the general rule to medically burdensome outcomes.

Internationally, similar cost-conserving measures have been shown to impose no undue medical burdens on patients, provided there are an appropriate exemption policy and careful selection of interchangeable drugs. A study of reference pricing for angiotensin-converting-enzyme (ACE) inhibitors for older patients in British Columbia, Canada, showed no significant health outcome differences for patients who switched to fully covered ACE inhibitors as compared to those who continued with their previous drugs despite co-pays.[20] The British Columbian practice was noteworthy because it also included the two patient-protection provisions the template requires: evidence of general interchangeability and a hassle-free exception policy. In the Canadian case, physicians could simply declare some patients frail and exempt them from the need to switch or bear co-pays.

The Kaiser approach to choosing a preferred SSRI, explaining the rationale to prescribing physicians, and making clinically based exceptions is precisely what the template calls for, again confirming that the template does not make unrealistic demands. Had the template itself actually been available to the physician prescribers, it could have been used in their discussions with patients, a point we clarify in the next vignette.

A Clinician Encounter about Drug Dosage

A clinically trivial example illustrates how clarity about the rationale for limits can support communication and education in the doctor-patient relationship. Some years back one of us (JES) spoke as follows with an elderly street smart man who was benefiting from Paxil: "You are taking 10 mg of Paxil each day. If I prescribe 20 mg and ask you to break the pill in half, it will cost the pharmacy less than if I prescribe the 10 mg pill size. The pharmacy can use the savings for other medications. Is it fair for me to ask you to break the pill in half?" After a few moments of thought the patient emphatically agreed it was fair – "Doc, if anyone fights you on that one, they're just out to break your [expletive]!"

This exchange represents the essence of Level 4 coverage decisions, but here it takes place as an isolated decision in a physician's practice. The physician proposed a way of prescribing that saved money for the pharmacy budget in a prepaid program (Level 4). Savings would benefit other patients. The rationale was made clear to the patient, who endorsed it in his own vivid language.

Had the template been available, the clinician here not only would have been able to show the good common sense of the dosage regimen, but also would have been able to demonstrate that it was part of a broader plan to use resources wisely within the plan. The template encourages stakeholders to exchange pertinent information, and if the patient expressed concern about whether pill splitting was safe, a well-prepared clinician would be able to cite pertinent literature.[21] More to the point, the role the physician played here on his own could become part of a more general educational strategy if proper technology made tools available to clinicians. We have in mind something not beyond the reach of technological feasibility today – say handheld devices with access to plan rules and rationales organized in the way the template suggests. Armed in this way, physicians could educate themselves and could extend that schooling to their patients. The same point can be made for pharmacists at the point of service, who could similarly educate themselves and their patients in the pharmacy.

SOCIAL LEARNING ABOUT PHARMACEUTICAL VALUE FOR MONEY

Though not a panacea for the many forces in medicine that stand in the way of the kind of deliberation we call for, the template can facilitate some positive steps already in practice. We conclude, however, by pointing to some features of the American situation that make it harder to learn about the true value, or true value for money, of pharmaceuticals. In most countries, purchasers of drug benefits are the populations covered by them – either through national health systems or social insurance schemes. The interests of the societal agents who manage the insurance are similar to the interests of the insured populations.[22]

In the United States, however, employers, the largest purchasers of private insurance, have various motivations and interests that may diverge from the health interests of their employees and their insured dependents. Kleinke argues, for example, that the high turnover rates in health plans – some 22 percent annually, he claims – means that employers and health plans may not have an economic interest in the long-term savings that many drug regimens offer.[23] Further, he cites Bryan Luce's point that "the separation of pharmacy budgets from other entities . . . dictates that simple acquisition costs often determine coverage decisions,"[24] where these acquisition costs may have no real relationship to the value of the drugs – or their value for money spent – to the covered population. Neither incentives nor regulation properly aligns the interests of purchasers with the interests of the populations for which they buy insurance. This misalignment reflects how the United States structures insurance pools, not the intrinsic ethical orientation of employers who purchase pharmacy coverage.

In countries where the interests of purchasers and managers are more closely aligned with those of the public they insure, social learning about limits to coverage is facilitated. Were an ethical template to be used in that context, there would likely be more agreement about how to achieve societal value for money through drug coverage. What counts as a "relevant rationale" is less likely to be controversial than in the United States.

We see the ethical template as a way to address the American mismatch between purchaser and covered population interests. If it is used as we have suggested, the template will facilitate discussion about the relationship between acquisition costs and more scientifically based calculations of cost-effectiveness (or cost-value)[25] of certain drugs. With transparency, with a focus on relevant reasons to which stakeholders can agree, and with the opportunity to revise decisions, the discussion will generate understanding about the proper basis for limits to care. The social learning curve that results then not only will inform drug coverage decisions, but also will contribute to broader democratic understanding of how to improve the regulation and design of the insurance system as a whole.

This role points us to another key context in which the template and its use are important: in the education of regulators and legislators who aim to improve the ways in which the insurance system, including pharmacy benefits, meets public needs. Rather than encouraging piecemeal mandating and regulatory intrusions in specific decisions, the template and the lessons it teaches puts the focus on improving the transparency and elements of fair process that surrounds such decisions. This result would work to the advantage of all parties.

With the exception of Oregon a decade ago, America has resisted any effort to discuss limit setting in a public way that could help the population learn about setting limits fairly. We have not had the national commissions set up in a number of other countries with universal coverage to propose principles for setting limits or priorities. Whatever their limitations,[26] these commissions at least begin a public effort at education about the need for limits and a fair way of establishing them. Although "cost containment" is widely talked about in the United States, the pretense is always that this effort concerns only the elimination of waste or unnecessary services and never anything more. This pretense is maintained at the federal and state levels, as well as in the language of private insurance plans. Far from reassuring the public, the pretense builds suspicion and distrust.

Our policy proposal for public education is to encourage private and public corporations and agencies in the United States and abroad that make decisions about pharmacy benefits to use the ethical template in the context of procedures that are accountable for reasonableness.[27] Perhaps, as many observers claim, Americans are "different" and lack the concern about solidarity or sharing that people in other countries have. Without a serious effort at education, using proper tools, the claim is untested and possibly self-fulfilling.

ACKNOWLEDGMENT

This work was supported, in part, by grants from the Merck Company Foundation and the Open Society Institute.

14

The Application of Cost-Effectiveness and Cost–Benefit Analysis to Pharmaceuticals

Joel W. Hay

WHY ECONOMIC ANALYSIS OF PHARMACEUTICALS IS IMPORTANT

Healthcare costs are continuing to escalate rapidly around the globe, reflecting aging populations, greater access to medical services, and improved medical technologies. In 2002 U.S. healthcare expenditures reached $1.6 trillion, 15 percent of that year's gross domestic product, and $5,440 per capita.[1] As shown in Figure 14.1, pharmaceutical expenditures have been escalating even more rapidly than overall healthcare expenditures over the past decade, reaching 10 percent of overall healthcare spending for the first time in forty years.

In 1970, early in Medicare and Medicaid implementation, prescription drug spending was $43 per capita, and the lack of Medicare drug coverage was not a major political concern.[2] By 2002, as political momentum for a Medicare prescription drug coverage program neared its peak, prescription drug expenditures reached $569 per capita, with the Medicare population spending nearly quadruple this amount.[3] Drug spending and drug insurance coverage have become prominent U.S. economic and political issues.

Similar concerns about drug spending are surfacing globally. Per capita drug expenditures vary widely internationally, reflecting differences in economic circumstances, pricing policies, government programs, and population characteristics.[4] Nevertheless, drug expenditures are increasing rapidly in all industrialized countries (see Figure 14.2).

Health economists vigorously debate whether healthcare costs generally and pharmaceutical costs specifically are rising too rapidly.

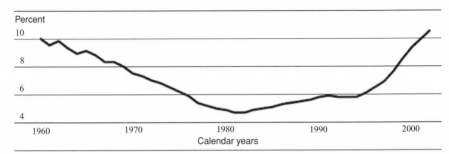

Figure 14.1. Prescription Drug Spending as a Share of U.S. Health Spending, 1960–2002. *Source:* Centers for Medicare and Medicaid Services, Office of the Actuary, National Health Statistics Group.

Many say that healthcare is precisely the kind of superior good[5] that people consume more of as their income and wealth rise.[6,7] After all, "you can't take it with you!" On the other hand, if healthcare growth rates continue to outpace workforce productivity indefinitely, per capita resources available for nonmedical spending will eventually decline.[8]

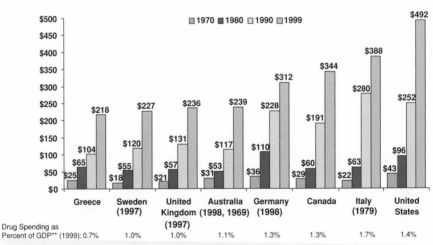

Figure 14.2. Per Capita Spending on Pharmaceuticals and Other Nondurables by OECD Country, 1970–99. *Note:* Data are arrayed by spending levels for 1999. *Source:* OECD Health Data 2002.

Healthcare is consumed primarily by patients who face heavily subsidized prices, because of either government programs or third-party insurance coverage. Access to healthcare is also tightly controlled by physicians and other providers. Most healthcare providers operate in financial environments that reward them for supplying more medical care. Furthermore, healthcare markets are heavily regulated, licensed, credentialed, and restricted. In every country, healthcare satisfies few of the Economics 101 criteria for free market competition. Under these circumstances, the "invisible hand" ensuring that scarce medical resources are being produced or consumed efficiently is severely atrophied and arthritic.

The politics of drug spending is even more contentious than that of any other healthcare component. Enormous profits are made by the manufacturers of brand-name patented medications with legally protected monopolies over their product pricing and sales. Patents do such an outstanding job of encouraging and rewarding R&D and investment in intellectual property that the Founding Fathers established patent protection in Article 1 of the U.S. Constitution. But despite the logic of rewarding innovation through patents, it is difficult to make the case that a life-saving medication should only be sold for many times its marginal cost of production when economically less fortunate patients who could pay that production cost die or suffer because they cannot afford the monopoly price established by the manufacturer to recoup its R&D investments and provide its shareholders with a competitive earnings per share. Economic theory shows that everyone is better off if manufacturers can provide drugs at lower prices for poorer patients or in less developed countries, just as airlines and computer manufacturers segment markets by income classes. But when drug manufacturers attempt to charge higher prices in richer countries, the citizens of those richer countries demand re-importation laws so that they can receive the same drug price bargains found elsewhere in an increasingly global marketplace.

The United States accounts for 63 percent of the global sales of the top twenty-five pharmaceuticals,[9] and substantially more than that share of global drug industry profits. If the United States imposes Canadian- or European-style drug price controls on a major portion of its population, for example, through the Medicare program, the incentives to invest in R&D for innovative medications will shrink and the future health of the United States and global populations will be jeopardized.[10] As discussed below, global investment in pharmaceutical R&D should be encouraged to improve global health and wealth, not discouraged to reduce healthcare costs. A strong case can be made that even the United States, much less other countries, is underinvesting in new drugs. But balancing adequate incentives for investment in risky pharmaceutical R&D against fair and equitable prices for current medications is a crucial global concern.

HEALTHCARE COST-EFFECTIVENESS AND COST–BENEFIT ANALYSES

Cost-effectiveness and cost–benefit analysis are methodologies for evaluating healthcare spending efficiency. In the severely distorted healthcare marketplace, they are designed to simulate the invisible hand of competitive markets with a "virtual reality glove" to guide healthcare decision makers toward medical decisions that improve efficiency and increase social welfare. They are used to address the question, "Does each healthcare intervention achieve equivalent *bang for the buck*?" If the answer to this question is negative, then society can reallocate resources either to produce just as much health with less spending, or to produce more health with existing spending. With healthcare absorbing an increasingly larger share of GDP, ensuring that every healthcare dollar is spent wisely becomes imperative.

Both cost-effectiveness and cost–benefit analysis compare the costs of medical or drug interventions against the value of intervention outcomes. The primary distinction is that cost-effectiveness measures intervention outcomes in clinical units or in some index of health-related quality of life, whereas cost–benefit analysis measures all intervention outcomes, as well as intervention costs, in monetary terms.[11] Cost-effectiveness predominates in economic evaluations of drug therapy because many clinicians and policy makers resist assigning monetary values to changes in patient survival, pain, suffering, or quality of life resulting from drug interventions.[12]

The United States Public Health Service cost-effectiveness "reference case" evaluates drug or medical intervention outcomes in terms of quality-adjusted life years (QALYs), with each additional year of life gained through intervention weighted by the fraction of perfect health achieved (0 percent – death, 100 percent – perfect health).[13] Thus, if a patient's migraine headaches are cured with drug therapy, and migraine headaches reduce the typical patient's quality of life by 50 percent, then the therapeutic QALY gain would be 50 percent times the number of days of migraine headaches avoided. On the other hand, for cardio-vascular drugs, the QALYs gained from avoiding heart attacks would reflect not only the improved quality of life for avoiding nonfatal heart attacks, but the life expectancy gains from avoiding fatal heart attacks. Cost-effectiveness analysis based on cost per QALY ratio predomi-nates in healthcare resource allocation.

Weinstein showed that rather than having to plan the entire menu of medical decisions simultaneously, healthcare decision makers merely follow a simple rule of authorizing all medical interventions with cost per QALY below the threshold value and denying all medical interventions with cost per QALY above the threshold in order to ensure that resources are used optimally.[14] Thus, each medical deci-sion maker will have a threshold cost per QALY revealed by the cost per QALY of the most expensive drug or medical intervention that it authorizes, under the important caveat that all medical interven-tions are consistently subjected to cost-effectiveness analysis. If any medical interventions are observed with costs per QALY above the threshold value, this indicates that resources are not being efficiently allocated.

In private markets people can pay as much per QALY as they want, but when third party insurance plans or government programs foot the bill, public consensus on the threshold value of a year of healthy life is needed to implement cost-effectiveness analysis. In the U.S. context, the health economics literature generally considers the societal cut-off threshold for cost per QALY to be in the range from $50,000 to $160,000. The lower bound values are motivated from a human capital framework, assuming that people are worth at least as much as they can earn, on average, in the labor market, and recognizing that the average U.S. worker is employed for approximately 2,000 hours per year at an average hourly compensation cost of U.S.$25.[15] The higher range estimates are motivated by attaching the average hourly compensation rate to all available hours, rather than just those that are compensated by employers, assuming that people value leisure time at the margin at least as much as they value labor, or else they would readjust their work hours (both in the short term and over the life cycle). They can also be motivated by empirical research on willingness to pay to avoid fatal risks.[16]

Since cost-effectiveness analysis values all quality-adjusted life years equally, irrespective of patient sociodemographic characteristics, social status, or fortune, the cost per QALY metric has a built-in egalitarian bias.[17] This is consistent with the view that communal resources from an insurance or government program should not be allocated to favor one eligible beneficiary over another. It is also consistent with egalitarian principles. As Gold et al. put it:

> Imagine individual citizens in a state prior to their birth, uncertain of which of many prospects, including possible health scenarios await them. Then rational individuals seeking to make themselves as well-off as possible but blinded to the specifics of their futures, would opt for societal decision rules based on maximizing aggregate (or average) utility across the "population" of possible lives; they would choose a pure utilitarian distribution.... If (1) deliberators behind such a veil of ignorance would choose to maximize expected utility across possible life scenarios, and (2) we assume that individual preferences for health outcomes are expressed by quality-adjusted life years, then we are led to a societal effectiveness measure equal to the sum of quality-adjusted life years gained.[18]

Because only a fraction of all possible drug and medical interventions have been subject to rigorous cost-effectiveness analysis, it is useful to benchmark the cost-effectiveness of specific interventions under consideration against others reported in the literature for the same disease or therapeutic category. Such rankings are referred to as "pharmacoeconomic league tables" after the professional soccer league tables followed avidly by European sports fans.[19] Although imperfect, this gives decision makers some perspective on the relative worth of any specific intervention in the context of what is currently known.[20]

Cost–benefit analysis, or more precisely net benefit analysis (benefits – costs), requires the analyst to convert all drug intervention impacts into monetary values, determining how much patients or other parties impacted by the intervention would be willing to pay, or need to be compensated, to be indifferent between the pre- and post-implementation states. For drugs and medical interventions, where markets are often distorted, this is usually done by asking representative subjects to reveal their preferences in a series of hypothetical experiments where drug alternatives with different prices, efficacies, and side effects are compared.[21,22] Cost–benefit analysis has long been preferred by economists to cost-effectiveness analysis, because it is easier to ground in traditional economic utility theory and social welfare analysis. There are many limitations in using QALYs as a measure of individual well-being or societal measure of welfare.[23–26] It is plausible that different people under different circumstances would prefer shorter periods of greater expected pleasure to longer periods of greater health – or in economics lingo, the marginal utility of a QALY is not constant and invariant to consumption opportunities or budget constraints. How else to explain sky diving, skiing, or eating Japanese blowfish?

Because willingness to pay is a function of ability to pay, cost–benefit analysis is dependent on the prevailing income and wealth distribution. It gives greater weight to the preferences of those with greater financial means. QALYs or other outcome measures that are based on a person's underlying life expectancy don't reflect wealth or income differences, but they have a definite bias favoring patient groups with longer normal life expectancies, including Asians, whites, younger patients, females, and those without chronic disease.

Cost–benefit analysis has a stronger theoretical foundation, but cost-effectiveness is more transparent and acceptable to clinicians and medical decision makers, because the outcomes are measured in units that are closer to health than money. For these reasons, and to hasten the practical application and dissemination of economic evaluations in healthcare, it is better that a theoretically imperfect evaluation methodology such as cost-effectiveness be used if it is more transparent, and can gain wider acceptance and real-world application, than a theoretically superior methodology such as cost–benefit analysis.

ARE PHARMACEUTICALS COST-EFFECTIVE?

Pharmaceuticals are highly cost-effective in some situations and not in others. Childhood vaccines such as those to prevent smallpox, polio, measles, mumps, rubella, diphtheria, pertussis, and tetanus are some of the best bargains in healthcare, because vaccine doses costing a few hundred dollars over a lifetime can prevent serious, permanent, or fatal disease consequences.[27] Vaccines save lives, quality-adjusted life years, and overall medical expenditures. They are particularly economically favorable because the benefits accrue not only to vaccinated individuals but to all of those nonvaccinated individuals who avoided disease because transmission risks were reduced by the vaccine.

Some drug interventions are decidedly not cost-effective. For example, use of Cox-2 inhibitors for pain relief, such as celecoxib and rofecoxib, has expanded rapidly in the past decade into a multibillion-dollar global market. Yet for the majority of patients without elevated risk of gastric bleeding or ulcer from use of nonsteroidal anti-inflammatory drugs (NSAIDs), Cox-2 inhibitors are no better than cheap, over-the-counter medications such as naproxen or ibuprofen, while being many times more expensive per pill, and at least in the case of Vioxx being much less safe.[28] It has been estimated that the use of Cox-2 inhibitors as a substitute for NSAIDs costs more than \$275,000 per quality-adjusted life year, even without consideration of their potential cardiovascular risks.[29] As mentioned earlier, pharmacoeconomic league tables show wide variation in the cost-effectiveness of different medications and for the same medications in different therapeutic contexts.[30]

Before addressing whether pharmaceuticals are cost-effective in the aggregate, it is useful to consider the broader role of costly medical technology in improving population longevity, quality of life, and functional abilities. There are two themes that emerge from the healthcare literature. The first theme, dating back to the pioneering studies of Wennberg and Gittelsohn, suggests that much of the variation in medical practice and in the use of medical technology cannot be explained by underlying differences in patient or disease characteristics, and reflects ignorance, excessive cost, and inefficiencies in the delivery of healthcare.[31,32] Along these lines, the Rand Healthcare Appropriateness Methodology Research Program has documented substantial levels of inappropriate care being delivered in the United States, despite or possibly related to the fact that the U.S. healthcare system is the most technologically advanced and most expensive in the world.[33–35] This body of research suggests that advanced healthcare technology is often either overutilized or underutilized. Twenty to thirty percent of U.S. healthcare may provide more harm than good, and 50 percent of patients may not receive recommended preventive care.[36] It is frequently pointed out that the United States uses expensive and advanced medical technologies such as MRI and CT scans, organ transplants, invasive coronary procedures, and kidney

Table 14.1. *Summary of Research on the Value of Medical Technology Changes*

Condition	Years	Change in Treatment Costs	Outcome		
			Change	Value	Net Benefit
Heart attack	1984–98	$10,000	One-year increase in life expectancy	$70,000	$60,000
Low-birth-weight infants	1950–90	$40,000	Twelve-year increase in life expectancy	$240,000	$200,000
Depression	1991–96	$0	Higher remission probability at some cost for those already treated		
		<$0	More people treated, with benefits exceeding costs		
Cataracts	1969–98	$0	Substantial improvements in quality at no cost increase for those already treated		
		<$0	More people treated, with benefits exceeding costs		
Breast cancer	1985–96	$20,000	Four-month increase in life expectancy	$20,000	$0

Source: Cutler DM, and McClellan M, "Is Technological Change in Medicine Worth It?" *Health Affairs*, 2001, *20* (5):11–29.

dialysis at rates substantially greater than in Canada and Western Europe, with no discernable relative improvements for aggregate U.S. population life expectancy, disease survival, or overall quality of life.[37]

The second healthcare literature theme suggests that improvements in pharmaceutical and medical technology result in substantial positive health status gains in the United States and elsewhere. This view has prevailed among health economists for many years.[38,39] Cutler and McClellan recently examined five major disease categories and found that the returns on investment in medical technology substantially outweigh the costs for four of these diseases (see Table 14.1). They concluded that "...medical care as a whole is clearly worth the cost increase, although we cannot present a specific rate-of-return evaluation."[40]

Murphy and Topel estimate the returns on investment for medical research at greater than 100:1.[41] They show that the increase in U.S. population longevity between just 1970 and 2000 was worth an additional $75 *trillion* to the U.S. economy, and that further reducing heart disease mortality by just 10 percent would be worth an additional $5 trillion to Americans. These estimates are based on multiplying the average American increase in life expectancy during the time period by economic estimates of the value of additional life years.

Most medical researchers believe that it is quite feasible to find new drugs and technologies that can reduce mortality rates for cancer, cardiovascular disease, and other major chronic diseases. Murphy and Topel point out that even if it cost $30 billion to reduce cancer or cardiovascular mortality rates by 1 percent through drug R&D, the social return on investment would exceed 13:1. The entire NIH annual research budget was $28 billion in 2004,[42] and the U.S. pharmaceutical industry spent $33 billion on R&D in 2003,[43] suggesting that current medical and pharmaceutical R&D may fall substantially below levels that could be socially or privately justified in the United States All other countries invest substantially less in biomedical R&D than the United States, both absolutely and on a per capita basis, so there is a global problem of underfunded biomedical research.

It is possible that both literature themes are correct. Higher levels of healthcare technology adaptation may exhibit greater inefficiency at the individual patient level, but also be highly cost-effective and socially beneficial in the aggregate. Everyone would prefer to reduce inefficiencies in healthcare delivery while protecting the rapid development of new drugs and other medical technologies, but as Cutler and McClellan point out in the context of managed care, efforts to reduce healthcare costs per capita may simultaneously slow the adoption of valuable healthcare technologies.[44]

International comparisons suggest that other countries have been able to achieve improvements in life expectancy and disease reduction similar to those in the United States, although spending much less per capita on healthcare and without investing as much in medical and pharmaceutical R&D, but this merely raises the question of whether these other countries are "free-riding" on American technological

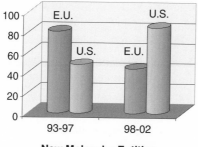

New Molecular Entities

Figure 14.3. Invention of New Pharmaceuticals. *Source: The Economist* 2004.

innovation. Being the first to adopt any new technology will always be more expensive and inefficient than adoption after the technology has matured. It has been observed that since 1992 the United States has spent an additional $1 trillion on pharmaceuticals relative to Europe because of newer drugs and higher drug prices.[45]

In a dramatic reversal from just a decade ago, Europe currently spends less than 60 percent as much as the United States on pharmaceutical R&D per capita and invents only about half as many new drugs (see Figure 14.3). The Economist, citing a Bain Consultants study, stated that:

In 2002, Germany saved $19 billion because it spent much less per head than America on drugs. On the other hand, says Bain, in the same year, Germany lost out on $4 billion from R&D, patents and related benefits that went elsewhere. It lost $8 billion because high-value jobs went somewhere else – plus the benefits of those jobs from the "multiplier effect." German drug firms would have made $3 billion more profit if they had kept pace with rivals elsewhere. A further $2 billion was lost as the country shed corporate headquarters and the benefits they bring. The cost of poorer-than-necessary health was $5 billion. . . . In sum, it reckons that Germany's $19 billion saving is in fact a $3 billion net loss. "When you add up all of the costs, the free rider model is actually quite expensive," argues (co-author) Mr. Rosenburg.[46]

If anything, the Bain estimates of the losses to the German economy are too low, because the job multiplier effect was estimated conservatively, and the value of reduced health did not include the full cost of reduced longevity and quality of life.

Frank Lichtenberg has carried out the most extensive research on the aggregate cost-effectiveness of pharmaceuticals. Using the U.S.

1996 Medical Expenditure Panel Survey data, he found that each additional dollar spent on new prescription medications was associated with approximately a $4 reduction in total healthcare spending per capita.[47] In a recent analysis of mortality and drug use using World Health Organization data for fifty-two countries, Lichtenberg estimates that new drugs accounted for 0.8 years (40 percent) of the 1986–2000 global increase in population longevity. The average annual increase in life expectancy across these fifty-two countries resulting from new drug launches was 0.056 years, or 2.93 weeks per person.[48] He calculates that the average cost per QALY gained for a new drug launch over this time period is substantially below $4,500, affordable in all but the least developed countries of the world. Moreover, in North America and Europe, where the societal threshold cost per QALY is many times greater than this level, this implies that new drugs are highly cost-effective and that pharmaceutical R&D should be substantially expanded.

APPLYING COST-EFFECTIVENESS AND COST–BENEFIT ANALYSIS IN THE PHARMACEUTICAL MARKETPLACE

Drug and healthcare cost containment is an increasingly important goal as costs continue to escalate globally. It is often argued that drug utilization and cost containment programs have failed because they have been too simplistic or too narrowly focused on reducing drug expenditures without regard to their impact on total healthcare costs or patient outcomes. Clearly many pharmaceutical benefits managers have a "silo mentality."[49] They are rewarded for saving money in their drug budgets, even if other healthcare costs increase and patient outcomes worsen. These broader health consequences are more difficult to measure and are usually ignored.

Restricting access to drugs through excessive co-payments or quantity controls or through inflexible therapeutic substitution policies without regard to specific circumstances cannot be expected to produce good results for patients or budgets, and is often "penny wise and pound foolish." Most studies find that traditional drug formulary management and drug utilization policies designed to curb drug expenditures boomerang.[50] Inappropriate drug cost-sharing and utilization reviews designed to control drug expenditures result in unintended consequences, including suboptimal use of medication; health status declines; or increased use of more costly ambulatory or institutional care.[51–54]

Standard drug and healthcare cost containment efforts are referred to as "input management" tools, because they dwell exclusively with the inputs side of the equation. A more comprehensive approach to healthcare cost containment involves looking at healthcare "outcomes" as well as healthcare inputs, but very little research has been directed at the outcomes of healthcare until the past two decades. The concepts of "patient-reported outcomes" and "evidence-based medicine" are very recent innovations in healthcare research. During the past decade, the evolving view that the focus of healthcare should be to provide outcomes that are meaningful and valuable to patients, and that patient-reported outcomes can and should be measured in a scientifically valid and reliable fashion, has created a paradigm shift, the "outcomes revolution" in healthcare management.[55]

Cost–benefit analysis and cost-effectiveness analysis fit perfectly into the "outcomes management" paradigm, because they specifically address the issues of how much patients, their families, their employers, and society are willing to pay for drug or other healthcare "outcomes." They measure inputs and outcomes comprehensively, using scientifically rigorous methods. They provide a framework for balancing the costs of drugs and other healthcare inputs against the value of the resulting health outcomes.

Australia was the first country to establish formal cost-effectiveness guidelines for new pharmaceuticals in 1992.[56] Starting then, manufacturers were required to submit evidence that new medications were cost-effective in order to obtain reimbursement under the Australian national healthcare program. Australia is a relatively small pharmaceutical market, and drug manufacturers were not strongly motivated to do rigorous studies to prove cost-effectiveness for the Australian market.[57,58] Nevertheless, this began a movement of "pharmacoeconomic" assessment of medications that has spread rapidly and globally.[59–62]

The International Society for Pharmacoeconomics and Outcomes Research now lists twenty-four countries with explicit pharmacoeconomic guidelines in place.[63] Many of these countries do not have mandatory pharmacoeconomic requirements for reimbursement, but all of them are actively expanding the importance of satisfying guidelines to enhance the efficiency of their healthcare delivery systems. In the United States, the Academy of Managed Care Pharmacy (AMCP) has established a formulary submission format that is used to help guide drug formulary decisions for more than 130 million beneficiaries.[64] The AMCP pharmacoeconomic dossier submission process creates a dialogue between manufacturers and managed care decision makers to improve the application of evidence-based medicine and cost-effectiveness analysis in the drug formulary evaluation process. Making the rationale for these decisions transparent and rigorous gives managed care enrollees confidence that their healthcare outcomes are being managed effectively and efficiently, along with the healthcare inputs.[65] Managed care is under great pressure to implement these approaches, since there has been substantial consumer and physician backlash against perceived arbitrary restrictions in access to drugs and medical procedures in order to save money or increase profits.[66]

In the United Kingdom, the National Institute for Clinical Excellence (NICE) evaluates the cost-effectiveness of new drugs and other medical technologies, in large part because the United Kingdom has been relatively slow to adopt newer medications. It was felt that an independent expert scientific advisory body rating new technologies could help speed the adoption of truly valuable innovations while weeding out the wasteful or ineffective approaches.[67] NICE contracts with academic experts to synthesize available literature and evaluate technology issues that they consider to be of particular importance because of their clinical and economic implications. Although NICE is only advisory to the British National Health Service, its recommendations carry much weight in determining how quickly newer technologies are adopted and reimbursed. By providing favorable evaluations of many drugs and technologies, NICE has probably hastened the adoption of several cost-effective but cost-increasing medical interventions relative to the pre-NICE era.[68]

Other country-specific pharmacoeconomic guidelines follow a variety of formats and levels of scientific rigor.[69] Although there is substantial expert consensus regarding the components of pharmacoeconomic studies that ensure quality,[70,71] pharmacoeconomic analysis still has a long way to go before it can be used consistently and rigorously.[72] Even Kaiser Permanente, the largest managed care organization in the United States, does not currently use formal pharmacoeconomic decision criteria in its drug formulary management.[73] Nevertheless, the logic of applying these pharmacoeconomic tools to drug decision making is quite compelling. The alternatives to using these transparent, scientifically rigorous methods for assessing drug value and for recommending drug usage are less scientific, more unfair, inefficient, hidden, and arbitrary.

The U.S. Medicare Modernization Act (MMA) of 2003 provides a clear example of why cost–benefit analysis and cost-effectiveness analysis will become increasingly relevant to drug decision-making. By implementing a comprehensive Part D drug benefit for Medicare recipients, this law recognized the obvious: pharmaceuticals are increasingly vital to healthcare treatments and patient outcomes. Failing to provide an ambulatory drug benefit under the flagship healthcare program for America's elderly was creating substantial financial burdens for middle class retirees, causing many to forgo needed medicines, and often leading Medicare providers to substitute expensive inpatient and recuperative care for inexpensive medications.

The Medicare Modernization Act barely squeaked through Congress in 2003, pleased no one, and will devote less than half of its projected $500 billion additional spending over the first decade to new drug coverage. Most of the new MMA spending will actually replace existing drug and healthcare coverage already provided to poor retirees by states under Medicaid, and persuade corporations not to eliminate their existing retiree drug coverage programs. Of greatest concern, the MMA has no real cost containment or efficiency provisions.

A key controversial element of the MMA is that Medicare cannot use its enormous bargaining power as a future purchaser of drugs for all American retirees to negotiate below-market prices for drugs, as is routinely done in other countries.[74] This aspect of the legislation was an essential compromise to placate the pharmaceutical industry's fears that European- or Canadian-level prices for patented pharmaceuticals would drastically cut not only industry profits, but also industry R&D. Using similar arguments, thus far the U.S. pharmaceutical industry has successfully fought off several Congressional attempts to lower drug prices by loosening restrictions on the re-importation of cheaper drugs from Canada and elsewhere.[75]

The MMA also provides some incentives to expand managed care alternatives to the standard Medicare fee-for-service benefit, but few beneficiaries are expected to take advantage of this option. Even if such competition has potential beneficial effects, the numbers will be too low to impact overall Medicare cost trends. Because the traditional Medicare program lacks any meaningful cost containment incentives, the MMA drug coverage expansion is projected by Medicare's own actuaries to add an additional $162 billion in annual costs within the first five years of implementation, and an additional $8.1 trillion to Medicare's unfunded liabilities through 2078.[76]

These federal deficit projections do not even contemplate other major healthcare program expansions, such as universal health insurance or other new coverage benefits. Should some really important new drugs be discovered over the next several years, such as cures for cancer, heart disease, Alzheimer's disease, or diabetes,[77] these deficit projections are likely to be exceedingly optimistic. Moreover, this deficit drug spending is just icing on top of the already-projected $40–$60 trillion unfunded liabilities for federal Social Security and Medicare promises to future American retirees.[78] To paraphrase Senator Everett Dirksen, "... a few tens of trillion dollars of debt here, and a few tens of trillion dollars of debt there, and pretty soon you're talking real money!"

Other than papering over deficits with smoke and mirrors, as Democrat and Republican politicians continue to do, there are only three ways to bring projected deficits for U.S. federal healthcare entitlements into manageable proportions: increase taxes, reduce benefits, or use healthcare resources more efficiently. It is likely that some combination of all of these methods will be implemented. The least painful approach is to use healthcare resources more efficiently, and if the Rand Medical Care Appropriateness estimates are in the right ballpark, this approach could reduce healthcare spending by roughly 30 percent without harming healthcare outcomes. Thirty percent of $8.1 trillion is real money!

Determining how to use drugs more efficiently is precisely the pharmacoeconomic agenda of cost–benefit and cost-effectiveness analysis. It is inevitable that the Medicare program will substantially increase its research and implementation of programs that encourage the

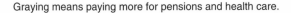

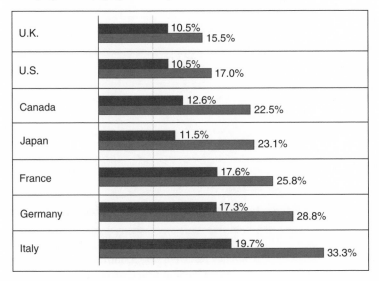

1995

2030 (Official Projection)

By comparison, total G-7 public spending on defense, education and R&D was 8.1% of GDP in 1995.

Figure 14.4. G7 Public Spending on Pensions and Health Benefits as a Percent of GDP by Country. *Source:* OECD (1996, 1997) and Census (1997) and "Global Aging – The Challenge of the New Millenium," Watson Wyatt/CSIS Report.

cost-effective use of drugs and other medical interventions. Even if only 5 percent of the Medicare drug budget were allocated toward this goal, this would mean Medicare spending of $8 billion annually on pharmacoeconomics and outcomes research by 2012. Medicare and other federal programs currently spend only a few tens of million dollars on these issues today.

Lest non-Americans think that the Medicare deficit projections and unfunded U.S. federal liabilities are a uniquely American problem, it is sobering to realize that the U.S. concern over unfunded government entitlement programs pales in comparison to the projected parallel burdens in Japan, Europe, and Canada. As shown in Figures 14.4

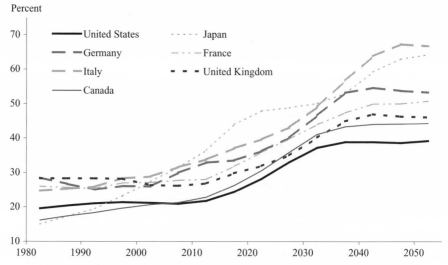

Figure 14.5. Old Age Dependency Ratios in G7 Countries. *Source:* Eurostat; United Nations (1998); and "Ageing Populations: Economic Issues and Policy Challenges," Ignazio Visco, OECD, Economic Policy for Ageing Societies," Kiel Week Conference, June 2001.

and 14.5, aging populations and generous levels of retiree entitlements will cause all other G7 countries to experience similar government funding problems, and in most cases the problems will be much larger (on a per capita basis) and will occur sooner than in the United States. The need to employ pharmacoeconomics and other methods to utilize healthcare resources efficiently will be as crucial in the rest of the world as here.

Another important potential application of pharmacoeconomics relates to future trends in global reimbursement for pharmaceuticals. As mentioned earlier, patent protection policies have done an excellent job of ensuring new drug R&D. This has occurred even while the FDA and foreign drug regulators have continuously strengthened requirements for demonstrating drug safety and efficacy. Patents solve the simultaneous problem of ensuring that innovators are rewarded for developing intellectual property, while allowing the private market to determine how large these innovation rewards should be, rather than having government bureaucrats or politicians make what could easily become biased and favored decisions regarding who deserves what size prize for what innovation.

Patents are antithetical to market competition. They reward innovation by having the government patent office grant time-limited monopolies to the patent holders. It is well known to first-year economics students that monopolies create inefficiencies, including the dead-weight loss associated with monopolistic supply restrictions below levels that unambiguously improve social welfare. As the music, software, and motion picture industries can attest, protecting the rewards to innovation and intellectual property is increasingly difficult in a globalized electronic marketplace. But the problems associated with the patent system are particularly acute in an area such as pharmaceuticals, where lives are needlessly lost, and patients needlessly suffer not because the patient or payer can't afford the medication cost, but because the patient (or his or her insurer, government program, or international aid agency) cannot afford the marginal cost of the medication plus the monopoly markup established to reward innovation.

Patients in Africa, Asia, and many less developed countries simply ignore patents by purchasing generic knock-offs of patented drugs, whereas patients in countries that honor patents in Europe, Canada, and even the U.S., federal and state governments (through purchases for Medicaid and VA patients) use their financial clout to negotiate substantial discounts below "market" prices for drugs. It is left to the well-insured American consumer (and after the 2006 implementation of the Medicare drug benefit, the U.S. taxpayer) to carry most of the global weight of rewarding innovation in the pharmaceutical industry.

The problem is further compounded in the pharmaceutical case, because some of the most important medical innovations are not easily patentable, and some are not patentable at all, because the product has already passed into generic or nonprescription status. Aspirin to treat or prevent heart attacks and cheap antibiotics such as clarithromycin to treat or prevent gastric ulcers are two of the most important drug advances of the twentieth century. Had they been developed and marketed as quickly as statins or H2 receptor antagonists, millions of lives and billions of dollars could have been saved; but in both cases knowledge and use of these therapies lagged for decades precisely because there was no potential patent reward for pharmaceutical companies to establish and market a new use of a product that any company in the world could already sell generically.[79,80]

A potential solution to the problem of rewarding drug innovation, while eliminating the inefficiencies and price distortions created by the monopoly patent system, would be to have the government establish cash prizes, rewards, patent buy-outs, or guaranteed government drug purchases payable to successful innovators in return for putting drug patent rights into the public domain. The government could purchase these patents immediately after the FDA approval process, or if prior to approval, the government would undertake the necessary safety and efficacy studies for FDA approval. Once the government acquired the patent rights, it would allow any and all drug manufacturers to produce the new drug competitively, subject to standard FDA requirements.

Financial rewards for placing patents in the public domain are not a new idea, going back at least to the French government reward for the invention of daguerreotype photography in 1839. Michael Kremer and others have advocated the reward approach, particularly in the context of pharmaceuticals for less developed countries, to stimulate development of new medications and vaccines for malaria, dengue, diarrhea, sleeping sickness, and other tropical diseases where patents do not create adequate rewards for private sector innovation, even though the global societal costs of these diseases would clearly justify the R&D investments.[81-83] For these cases, the per capita income of patients is too low to recoup the R&D costs that a pharmaceutical company would risk for a patentable medicine or vaccine, even though the global disease costs are in the hundreds of billions of dollars and would easily cover the risky R&D investments if, say, the World Health Organization offered adequate multibillion-dollar financial rewards for effective interventions that would then be placed in the public domain.

The reward system would not replace the patent system, nor would it necessarily focus only on patentable innovations. Patent holders would not be forced to sell their patents to the government. They could take their chances in the marketplace if they felt that the government offer was too low. The reward system would be used to expand innovation in areas that are currently not being adequately investigated and implemented, such as the heart attack-aspirin and ulcer-antibiotic examples mentioned above, and to allocate innovative medicines quickly to patients at marginal cost while rewarding innovators.

Determining the size of the preannounced drug innovation rewards would not be technically difficult, and would be based on cost-effectiveness and cost–benefit analysis. There is a large domestic and international base of pharmaceutical cost-effectiveness researchers (e.g., www.ispor.org). For each therapy the government could convene an independent panel of experts to establish patent reward values based on marginal cost drug pricing and a societal perspective on drug costs and benefits. The government or international agency could preannounce rewards in areas of particular need (e.g., HIV/AIDS, cancer, heart disease) or establish rewards at the time of regulatory approval for safety and efficacy. Presumably the reward would be in line with what the monopoly producer reasonably anticipates in terms of future monopoly profits. In some cases (e.g., new life-saving uses of older generic drugs), the rewards would substantially exceed what the innovator could expect in the market, to stimulate valuable but unpatentable innovations.

An advantage of using this reward approach for pharmaceuticals is that there is a clear decision point at which the reward can be earned and paid. This is the point where the FDA determines that the drug is safe and effective in meeting a specific clinical indication for marketing approval. Should the drug later turn out not to have the precise safety and efficacy characteristics established at the time of FDA approval, the reward payments could be pro-rated based on new clinical evidence. The simplest way to accomplish this is to make the rewards payable over a multiyear period with out-year payments contingent on future knowledge.

The application of cost-effectiveness and cost–benefit analysis in establishing a reward system for new drug innovation could dramatically expand the development and use of new therapies. When patients and payers are paying the marginal cost of medications, rather than the monopoly-protected price, the number and range of cost-effective applications for these new therapies will increase dramatically. Moreover, with the Medicare program projected to spend hundreds of billions of dollars for medications annually, it will actually be less expensive for the taxpayer to buy out patents or reward the drug innovators with lump sum payments, rather than pay exorbitant monopoly prices for these drugs year after year. Medicare drug payments alone will exceed total pharmaceutical industry profits within a few years, and can thus be more efficiently allocated to generate both greater levels of drug innovation through rewards and patent buy-outs and also much lower and fully competitive drug costs for patients and payers. Alan Garber has proposed a parallel application of cost-effectiveness analysis to ensure that health plan coverage decisions and benefit structures ensure efficient use of resources which would neatly complement a drug patent buy-out system, ensuring that cost-effective innovations spread quickly into medical treatment guidelines.[84]

CONCLUSIONS

Cost-effectiveness analysis and cost–benefit analysis have migrated from mere academic curiosities to wide-scale use in mainstream medical decision making by clinicians, governments, and third-party payers in dozens of countries including the United States and several EU countries. These techniques ensure that limited healthcare resources are being used efficiently to accomplish explicit clinical outcomes reflecting the preferences of patients, payers, and medical decision makers.

Because the cost-effectiveness and cost–benefit analytic models are (or should be) fully transparent, it is possible for critics and users to understand what assumptions, evidence, and preference measures are utilized. The structure of medical decision making can thus be challenged and re-evaluated in a scientific and rigorous fashion. Issues that are particularly controversial can be identified and targeted for additional research. Because healthcare allocation decision alternatives to using these economic analytic approaches are more inequitable, secretive, and inefficient, they are not feasible in open democratic societies.

It is clear that these economic evaluation techniques provide some hope for the future in the pharmaceutical marketplace as drug spending continues to grow rapidly, and as governments struggle to deal with the financial burdens of coping with aging populations and patients with expectations of ever-expanding and improving medical technologies. It is also likely that cost-effectiveness analysts and cost–benefit analysts may provide new ways of fundamentally restructuring the payment systems for pharmaceuticals and healthcare benefits generally, where rewards are directly tied to value. These new payment paradigms are badly needed, because the existing health financing systems will be increasingly politically unsustainable as cost and coverage pressures escalate.

PART III

PATENTS, PRICING, AND EQUAL ACCESS

Introduction to Part III

Michael A. Santoro

INTRODUCTION: INTELLECTUAL PROPERTY RIGHTS VERSUS HEALTHCARE RIGHTS

The most controversial ethical and public policy issues involving the pharmaceutical industry arguably derive from the dynamic tension between healthcare's dual status as an economic commodity and a moral right. Fundamentally, this tension is an ongoing dialogue about competing rights, i.e., property rights versus the right to affordable healthcare. This section considers the conflicts arising from the pharmaceutical industry's assertion of strong intellectual property rights and the attempts by some advocates to erode these rights in order to honor the right to affordable access to drugs.

A recurring theme of this book has been the disjunction that sometimes exists between public health needs and the profit-maximizing behavior of pharmaceutical companies. In the case of intellectual property this disjunction is not only a function of free-market dynamics; it is also a result of deliberate government intervention. The patent system is a not-so-finely tuned government regulatory mechanism that can, in effect, ratchet up the intensity of this gap. Patent laws grant state-protected monopolies to inventors in order to spur innovation. The exercise of those patent rights, however, also leads to higher prices and limited access.

Some industry leaders well understand that the fates of their companies are inextricably bound with the healthcare needs of the communities in which they operate. In his chapter, William Weldon, the CEO of

251

Johnson & Johnson, one of the world's largest diversified healthcare companies with significant interests in the pharmaceutical industry, argues that the fundamental source of tension between industry and society is a "basic conflict: between funding priorities for providing access to *current* healthcare, and the need to provide incentives for developing better treatments in the future." Weldon believes that this gulf can and must be bridged because the public and the pharmaceutical industry ultimately share a common goal of ensuring continued innovation and new products while broadening access to the fruits of drug research. Weldon notes that patent protection is but one of a wide array of government policy levers such as reimbursement policies, price controls, and safety and efficacy review standards that impact public health outcomes and costs. He goes on to describe in some detail a number of specific areas in which government and industry can cooperate and play complementary roles in meeting current and future healthcare challenges.

According to one study regularly cited by pharmaceutical executives, it costs $802 million to bring each new drug to market.[1] This figure includes, among other things, capital costs, the cost of basic research, clinical testing, and obtaining regulatory approval, as well as the costs associated with drug investigations and trials that fail to come to fruition. Because the marginal costs of manufacturing a drug are very small in proportion to the overall costs of research and development, without patent protection a so-called "generic" manufacturer could profitably bring a drug to market at a much lower price than the innovating firm. In such a case, there would be insufficient financial incentive for the drug company to make the investments necessary to invent a new drug and bring it to market. With patent protection, an innovative company essentially holds a state-protected exclusive monopoly, enabling it to restrict output, set prices to maximize profits, recoup the cost of developing the drug, and achieve an attractive rate of return for the enormous sums that need to be invested in the risky business of drug development.

Although for industry a strong patent system is unambiguously essential, from a social perspective, the economic effects of patents are more complex. Society as a whole shares with pharmaceutical companies the goal of creating financial incentives for innovation, and the existence of the patent system reflects that goal. High costs and limited access to novel drugs, however, remain of paramount concern.

To be sure, the social benefits of innovation in the pharmaceutical industry have been considerable. Even in the past quarter of a century, a period that some critics say has been marked by "me too" drugs and an excessive emphasis on the marketing of "lifestyle" drugs, the pharmaceutical industry has developed numerous medically significant new drugs.[2] AZT, Saquinivir, and Fuzeon, for example, have prolonged life for AIDS patients; Cyclosporine has allowed organ transplantation to become a reality; and cancer treatments such as Rituximab are helping more patients to achieve remission.

The development of drugs to treat HIV patients represents both the triumph and tragedy of pharmaceutical patent protection. The drugs sadly came too late for too many. Eventually, however, useful drugs were invented to treat HIV and AIDS patients. Many factors contributed to development of these drugs, including inventions developed in government and university laboratories. Without a doubt, however, one of the principal factors was the patent system and the profits that pharmaceutical companies could earn by bringing these drugs to market. At the same time that patent protection made such drugs possible, however, it also meant that the drugs would be priced beyond the reach of many patients.

As one of history's foremost advocates for the rights of HIV/AIDS patients, Martin Delaney is uniquely positioned to comment on the human toll of high drug prices. As Delaney details in his chapter, the pitched battles that AIDS activists fought with pharmaceutical companies over drug prices were literally a matter of life and death for countless patients. Delaney also recounts how AIDS activists contributed to the development of HIV treatment regimens, and how ultimately some activists decided to attempt to work cooperatively, albeit warily and reluctantly, with pharmaceutical companies on drug development. Noting that such cooperation is becoming increasingly common, and worried that it has the potential to co-opt and undermine effective patient advocacy, Delaney offers an important set of ethical principles that delineate the appropriate parameters of such cooperative relationships. These principles represent one of the most important contributions to a central theme of this book – the need for private, governmental, and nongovernmental actors in the healthcare system to work together to achieve positive outcomes in addressing medical needs and problems.

PRICE CONTROLS AND INNOVATION: CAN THEY CO-EXIST?

The basic tension between the need to encourage innovation through intellectual property protection and the resulting high prices and restricted access is at the core of many of the public policy debates that have dominated the news in recent years. These debates have all, either overtly or under the surface, been about price controls. One of the most labyrinthine manifestations of this basic conflict is the debate over Canadian drug reimportation. Unable and unwilling to pay high drug prices, many Americans have turned to Canada as a source for drugs. Stories about beleaguered senior citizens taking the bus to Canada to make bulk purchases have become a news industry staple. As many commentators have noted, however, the Canadian route is a very roundabout way of dealing with the basic problem of high drug prices. Hank McKinnell, Chairman and CEO of Pfizer, recognized this when he boldly proclaimed that "re-importation is a false promise. If we want to import price controls we should have that discussion."[3]

The tension between innovation and access has even spilled over into international trade. Europe, Canada, Australia, and other developed countries have enacted strong price controls to provide greater access for their citizens. The net effect of this has been that American citizens have shouldered the burden of paying for innovative drugs. As a result, then FDA Commissioner Mark McClellan, arguing that the "average price of important medical breakthroughs ought to bear some relation to a nation's income," has suggested developing some kind of international trade provision that would effectively tie price controls to a nation's ability to pay.

The basic tension between spurring innovation and ensuring access has also been manifest in the debate over the Medicare drug benefit passed by Congress at the end of 2003. A controversial provision of that bill prevented the Secretary of Health and Human Services from "interfering" in negotiations over drug prices. In practice, this means that the various drug benefit providers are required to negotiate individually for drug discounts. Preventing the federal government from leveraging the combined purchasing power of the entire Medicare population inevitably means that the American taxpayer will pay more for the Medicare drug program, especially for drugs without adequate substitutes. In contrast, the Department of Veterans Affairs has achieved over $200 million in savings in two years because of its willingness to use its bulk purchasing power and competitive bidding.[4]

How can saving the federal government money be a bad idea? After all, no one is forcing the drug companies to sell drugs to the Medicare system. Surely, they will not lose money by selling to the government. One way to interpret the proscription against using the government's bulk purchasing power is as a triumph of lobbying by industry and as a failure by the Congress to mind the public interest. If there is any public policy argument to be made for this proscription, however, it is possibly one that regards the government's use of bulk purchasing power as essentially tantamount to price controls.

This, in turn, raises a host of difficult economic questions. Can we have the benefits of innovation while imposing price controls on companies? Or do price controls frustrate the purpose of the patent law by undoing the very economic incentives the patent system is set up to create? In his chapter, Sidney Taurel, the Chairman and CEO of Eli Lily & Co., tackles these issues head-on and argues that efforts to control drug prices, such as one finds in Europe and Japan, will inevitably lead to reduced investment in research and ultimately diminished innovation in the future. Accordingly, Taurel argues, any form of direct or indirect or de facto price controls will have a devastating effect on the discovery of new drugs to meet future medical needs. He makes a vigorous argument that the ability of pharmaceutical companies to set prices freely is essential to continued innovation in the industry and ultimately, therefore, in the public interest.

Although the public shares with industry a strong interest in innovation, broad access to the fruits of that innovation also weighs heavily in the public interest. In the future, as the United States government takes on a larger role in paying for prescription drugs, it seems inevitable that fiscal and political pressures will make it more and more likely that "de facto" price controls will emerge from the government's powerful bargaining position. For this reason, the pharmaceutical industry may come in the fullness of time to regard the Medicare drug benefit as a double-edged sword. How can we achieve greater access through lower prices and at the same time provide sufficient economic incentives to encourage investment and innovation? Policymakers will be dealing with this delicate social balancing act well into the twenty-first century.

Lessons from the Flu Vaccine Scare of 2004:
The Impact of Price Controls

In the winter of 2004, the FDA suspended vaccine-maker Chiron's license to import vaccines into the United States because of production quality issues at its Liverpool, England manufacturing facility. This action triggered a flu vaccine shortage that commanded substantial media attention and caused significant worries among vulnerable groups such as the elderly, for whom the flu can be fatal.

The unpredictability of the vaccine market made it inevitable that a shortage would occur in one flu season. During the 1999–2000 flu season, supply and demand were nearly perfectly matched. In contrast, between 2000 and 2004, manufacturers disposed of 35 million unused doses, often at a significant financial loss, due to overestimation of market demand.[5]

The unpredictable nature of a market in which demand is based not only on the severity of the virus, but also on the varying amount of media attention given to it each year, is only one of the problems that has forced out several vaccine manufacturers, leaving the United States with only two suppliers. Vaccines, as biological products, are much more difficult to produce and are subject to much greater scrutiny than other pharmaceutical products. For example, the production process for the influenza vaccine can take eight to nine months, an expensive cycle that must be repeated every year due to changes in the dominant influenza strain. Vaccine manufacturers are not, however, operating in a free market, in which they can set higher prices to offset costs. The government purchases most childhood vaccines sold in the United States through the Childhood Immunization Initiative, which sets price ceilings.[6] Government is also a major purchaser of other vaccines through the military and other government healthcare services. In its role as the primary purchaser of these vaccines, the government has extraordinary power to influence prices for the rest of the market. As a result, manufacturers have pleaded that it is difficult for them to make a profit from vaccine production.[7]

Few are as qualified to address the public health implications of the 2004 influenza vaccine shortage as Dr. Gary Noble, a twenty-nine-year veteran of the Centers for Disease Control and Prevention, during which time, as a virologist, he was actively involved in trying to discover the cause of AIDS. Dr. Noble, who went on to work for a large pharmaceutical industry after retiring from the CDC, sounds a sobering note in his chapter. He warns that a flu pandemic rivaling the 1918–19 swine flu which took between 40 and 100 million lives worldwide, is a real possibility. In addition, Noble emphasizes the major public health stakes in developing detection mechanisms and vaccines for a wide array of infectious diseases from HIV to Ebola to SARS.

Noble argues that insufficient financial incentives are discouraging private investment in a vaccine for HIV and other infectious diseases. Sounding a recurring theme of this volume, Noble goes on to suggest that public–private partnerships, working in collaboration with international agencies, foundations, and nonprofit organizations, are the most effective means to develop vaccines to meet the public health needs of the future. He analyzes a number of successful examples of such cooperation and offers some pointed guidelines for how agencies of government such as the CDC, NIH, and Department of Defense can effectively collaborate with private industry to meet pubic health needs. The threat of pandemic infectious diseases and bioterrorism is too great and the consequences are too severe for the world to ignore Dr. Noble's advice. Such public–private collaboration and partnerships may in the future be the key to our very survival.

INTELLECTUAL PROPERTY RIGHTS AND THE THIRD WORLD

The challenges to intellectual property rights are especially pronounced in the third world. Many leaders of less economically developed countries do not regard strong patent protection for pharmaceuticals as being in the best interests of their citizens. They reason that their populations are too poor and their healthcare needs too pressing to suffer the high prices accompanying pharmaceutical patents. Moreover, their weak scientific and industrial infrastructures make it extremely unlikely that any innovative gains will result from a strong patent regime. Accordingly, from the perspective of many third world countries the optimal policy is to eschew patent protection for pharmaceuticals developed by innovative firms in advanced economies and to import cheap generic versions of drugs from countries such as India and Brazil, where there are firms that have sufficient technical resources to manufacture generic drugs.

In the 1980s, the weak patent protections in third world countries placed them on a collision course with big innovative pharmaceutical companies that were not happy about losing profits in what they regarded as small but fast-growing markets. Mounting a vigorous global public relations campaign, the pharmaceutical industry successfully pressured many third world nations to strengthen patent protection, most crucially by passing legislation that granted product patents for drug compounds themselves. (Patents that protect only the process by which a drug was manufactured are insufficient because most drug compounds can be manufactured through a variety of processes.) Although enormously successful in accomplishing its aims, the pharmaceutical industry engendered deep resentment in the third world, in large part because the intellectual property campaign was bolstered by heavy-handed use of bilateral trade sanctions by the United States government.[8]

With the formation of the World Trade Organization in 1995, the dispute between the pharmaceutical industry and third world nations achieved an uneasy compromise. The pharmaceutical industry succeeded in making strong patent protection laws a WTO requirement, but third world countries won a reprieve through provisions that allowed them until 2016 to phase in such protections fully. With the advent of the global AIDS crisis, however, the issue of generic manufacturing and patent protection re-emerged as a source of bitter controversy between the pharmaceutical industry and much of the third world.

In August 2003 a WTO ministerial meeting held in Doha, Qatar declared the right of third world countries to import generic drugs when there are public health concerns. Many hailed the so-called Doha Declaration as a broad victory for the third world because it did not restrict generic imports to emergency situations or a short list of drugs, but some NGOs such as Oxfam and Médecins Sans Frontiéres have criticized the agreement for imposing onerous bureaucratic obstacles.[9]

In his chapter, Professor James Gathii, a native of Kenya now teaching in an American law school, provides a penetrating third world perspective on the issue of intellectual property. Gathii examines in detail the role that patent law plays in the lack of access to antiretroviral drugs in third world countries. He argues that strong patent regimes remain the principal stumbling block to expanded access to drugs, and that the poverty of many third world countries, although an obvious factor, is not an insurmountable obstacle to treatment. Gathii goes on to offer his thoughts on the lessons we can learn from the tragically slow implementation of AIDS therapies in sub-Saharan Africa.

In their chapter, Professors Patricia Werhane and Michael Gorman examine the moral underpinnings of intellectual property. They argue that ideas are normally the result of "a long history of scientific or technological development and numbers of networks of creativity, not the act of a single person or a group of people at one moment in time." As such, it is a mistake to grant a proprietary and exclusive right to the person or group of persons who brought an idea to fruition in the final stage of its development in the same manner in which one would grant such a right to the use of physical property. Werhane and Gorman conclude that, under these circumstances, relaxing the enforcement of the intellectual property rights of pharmaceutical companies (for example, by allowing parallel importing or compulsory licensing) would not violate any strong moral claim on the part of the pharmaceutical companies. They then go on to analyze the moral responsibilities of multinational pharmaceutical corporations in responding to the AIDS pandemic in sub-Saharan Africa. Echoing a theme that appears in many chapters of this book, they propose a cooperative model for addressing a global medical problem, in this case for action that "engages companies, donor organizations, NGOs, local villages, and countries in a systemic networking approach" to the problem of AIDS.

15

Intellectual Property Rights, Access to Life-Enhancing Drugs, and Corporate Moral Responsibilities

Patricia H. Werhane and Michael E. Gorman

INTRODUCTION

Since the publication of John Locke's *Second Treatise on Government*,[1] individual rights to property, and in particular private property, have become one of the philosophical tenets of rights theory and one of the foundations for the justification for Western-style free enterprise. Out of a Lockean notion of property, Western thinking has developed the idea of *intellectual* property rights, proprietary rights to what one invents, writes, paints, composes, or creates.

Despite their origins in a strong rights tradition, intellectual property (IP) rights are now being challenged across the globe in a number of areas. These challenges include:

- copying music and other works of art without permission;
- "knock-off" copies of designer products;
- generic brands of well-known drugs and other products;
- copying products by reverse engineering;
- challenges to gene patenting and genetic engineering;
- conflicting ownership claims to products developed from tacit knowledge of indigenous populations;
- copying patented drugs without permission or license – for national security, in health emergencies, in life-threatening epidemics, to reduce costs to end-users, or simply to make money.

Focusing on the last challenge, in this essay we shall develop four points.[2] We will analyze two arguments defending intellectual property: a standard rights-based defense and utilitarian justifications. We will outline some of the challenges to these ideas that raise questions concerning ownership, competition, and sharing. In the first section, we shall present another way to think about intellectual property that both challenges and preserves that tradition. We shall then apply our arguments to one particular issue: the protection of intellectual property rights by pharmaceuticals, the extent of corporate responsibilities, and access to HIV drugs in less developed countries.

RIGHTS TALK AND THE STATUS OF INTELLECTUAL PROPERTY RIGHTS

Rights talk is grounded on a set of assumptions that human beings have intrinsic value; that is, they are of value because of their human status, regardless of particular historical, religious, or cultural situations or abilities. It follows that human beings have certain basic rights, ordinarily called *human rights* or *moral rights*. Traditionally, basic rights include rights to life, to survival, and to liberty, and the right not to be harmed. According to rights theorists, human rights are so fundamental and so inviolable that every person should be entitled to them, regardless of his or her particular social, political, historical, or even cultural situation, although in fact they are not recognized or honored everywhere (thus the term "moral" rights).[3]

Locke included the right to work and to own property in his list of natural rights. But early on, David Hume, Adam Smith, and Thomas Jefferson, among others, claimed that property rights were conventional, not natural rights, recognizing that the notion of property is a social convention differing widely in societies and in different historical periods.[4] Still, according to Hume and Smith, property rights, however socially defined by a particular society, create obligations on the part of others and the state to protect property interests.

During the early advent of the industrial revolution it became apparent that ideas as well as material property needed to be protected.[5] Jefferson, in particular, recognized that patent protection encourages invention and creativity by protecting ownership of new ideas, and allows the inventor or creator to reap benefits from that idea, just as the farmer benefits from good agricultural practices on her land.

However, Jefferson distinguished farm land from ideas:

> ... ideas should freely spread from one to another over the globe, for the moral and mutual instruction of man, and improvement of his condition, seems to have been peculiarly and benevolently designed by nature.... Inventions, then, cannot, in nature, be a subject of property.[6]

Unlike the farmer, the inventor is encouraged to make public her or his innovation while protecting the right to copy or reproduce the invention. Jefferson defended time-limited intellectual property protection on two rather different grounds. The first, from the rights perspective of Locke, is that inventors have rights to what they create. The second argument links rights and utility; that is, without IP protection inventors will be less likely to be creative since they will not necessarily reap honor or the benefits of their inventions.

Thus there developed a set of patent and copyright laws that "protect some (or most) products of the human mind *for varying periods of time*, against use by others of those products in various ways"[7] (our italics). Many nations, including the United States, have developed complex trademark, copyright, and patent laws to protect intellectual property. Genetically engineered products, designs, trade secrets, plant breeder rights, databases, and a variety of other forms of intellectual property are also protected by various laws, as least in most Western developed countries.[8]

Rights-Based Defenses of Intellectual Property

The view that intellectual property is a form of ownership in which one has exclusive rights to use, copying, or distribution is often the way intellectual property is conceived, particularly in countries and companies that sponsor the development of new processes or products. From this perspective, if a person or company creates a patentable (i.e., new, usable, and not obvious) process or product, it is argued that because of the creativity and work involved, the person or organization has exclusive rights to that creativity.

Despite the treatment of intellectual property (IP) rights as time-limited protected claims, IP rights, at least in some Western contexts, are sometimes taken to be perfect rights such that violations of copyrights, trademarks, or patents are always wrong without exception. Ayn Rand summarizes this view:

Patents and copyrights are the legal implementation of the base of all property rights: man's right to the product of his mind . . . patents are the heart and core of property rights, and once they are destroyed, the destruction of all other rights will follow automatically, as a brief postscript.[9]

Rand contends that IP rights are the most basic rights, such that without them all other rights are threatened. If so, then property, or at least intellectual property rights, might even preempt other important rights, say, to life and liberty. But do I give up my liberty when I relinquish control or some control over products of my mind? What basic liberty rights are we giving up when our intellectual property agreements are violated? Here we should distinguish liberty and creativity, allegedly acts of the mind, from the productivity or products of the mind. I can sell, give away, or sacrifice my property or my creation, but I cannot, without being enslaved, give up my entitlement to liberty and free choice. Admittedly without IP rights we might lose recognition of our creativity and the "fruits" or our labor, but whether we are giving up all our basic liberties is more questionable. Locke's idea is that because we have rights to our bodies and to liberty, we "own" our own labor and its productivity, and are able to exercise and entitled to property rights. But Locke also argues that life, labor, and liberty are the *bases* for property rights and not the converse. Without rights to liberty, I can be enslaved, and slavery erodes the justification for the natural or human right to private ownership and thus for ownership of "products of the mind."

If one makes the case that intellectual property rights are the basis for liberty, as Rand implies, then those without property are less free. And could intellectual property rights, in some cases, override rights to life? While it has been argued (whether or not all agree) that liberty rights could override rights to life, it is more difficult to argue that property rights, even the right to the "product of our minds," override rights to life *or* liberty. Thus it is more justifiable to argue that intellectual property rights develop out of, but are not the basis for, rights to life and liberty. The importance of this conclusion will be elaborated upon in a later section.

Utilitarian Defenses of Intellectual Property Rights

There are number of strong arguments for the protection of intellectual property from a more utilitarian point of view. It is commonly argued that protection of intellectual property is critical for the continued discovery, creation, and development of new ideas. Many inventors and companies argue that they have rights to patent protection to control access to that process and product because without such protections there will be few incentives for new product or idea development. Few people will write new material, create new art, or invent new products without such protections, because there is little in the way of honor, recognition, or profit in such activities.

There are other facets of a utilitarian defense of intellectual property. The importance of patent protection, for example, is contended to be particularly important to pharmaceuticals, whose survival and creativity depends on large amounts of money for research and development. Patent protection allows companies to develop ideas, to profit from that development, and thus to have funds for further research and development. Whether or not such development would take place without IP protection is an interesting question.

A third argument focuses on consumer benefits. In a paper titled "'Napsterizing' Pharmaceuticals...," Hughes, Moore, and Snyder argue that, in the short term, consumers would be much better off if we eliminated present patents on drugs, thus increasing competition with generic products. Costs of all drugs would be lower. However, as they demonstrate, in the long run we would all be worse off. This is because without revenues, pharmaceutical firms could not finance research and development that are critical for the development of new products. So gradually the development of new drugs would decline, and new life-saving and life-enhancing possibilities would be unavailable to future generations.[10]

There is a fourth set of utilitarian arguments defending IP protections. C. L. Clemente, a Senior Vice President at Pfizer Corporation, contends that without intellectual property protection companies such as Pfizer, which depend on patent protection for profits and product development, will not go into countries such as India, since the reverse engineering of the product development, not illegal under Indian patent law (and thus giving Indian companies the ability to copy their products), decreases market share and prevents recouping company R&D investments.[11] Indeed, according to Clemente, one early 1990s World Bank survey of international executives allegedly shows that tax rates and intellectual property protection were the main factors in determining global corporate investment decisions.[12]

The World Bank survey finding that companies such as Pfizer will not invest in countries where there are no enforced patent protections appears to lead to the conclusion that, if the World Bank data are correct, lack of IP protection hurts investment in less developed countries (LDCs).[13] Dr. Harvey Bale at Pfizer argues that

[w]ithout strong and effective global intellectual property rules, the gap between developed and developing countries will only grow in the future.[14]

This is also the argument of the World Intellectual Property Organization (WIPO). In a new book sponsored by the WIPO, Kamil Idris argues that the transformation of natural resources and products produced by indigenous populations into intellectual property and the protection of those ideas and others with a rule of law can contribute substantially to the wealth of any nation.[15] Still, as we shall see, there are challenges to this view, particularly as it is used to argue for the patenting of indigenous products; this makes it unclear, at best, whether the Western notion of IP and IP rights should be applied universally in all settings and for all ideas, processes, and products.

CHALLENGES TO INTELLECTUAL PROPERTY RIGHTS

The preoccupation with individual and corporate protection of IP is one way to frame our thinking, a mindset or mental model, a social construction of experiences that predominates in developed countries. But it is only one worldview.[16] There are other worldviews that account for property, products of the mind, and intellectual property differently. Let us give some examples.

The neem tree is indigenous to India and other hot, arid, climates where it flourishes. Its extensive roots stabilize soil erosion, and because it grows quickly it is also a renewable source of lumber. In India it has played a central role in the Hindu culture for thousands of years. Its leaves are supposed to preserve health and it is prescribed for a number of medicinal purposes. The twigs are often used as toothbrushes and the leaves are chewed for paste. The leaves, when spread on plants, also serve as a pesticide. Because of these qualities, in the 1980s W. R. Grace, with the permission of the Indian government, developed and patented a commercial pesticide, Neemix, made from neem leaves. This product is patented under Indian law and produced in India. However, Neemix and other products developed from the tree are often considered public indigenous property, communally owned and shared, and thus not subject to patents or patent rights. A number of villages in India have protested this patenting, claiming that the neem tree and its products are communally owned, and its pesticidal and medicinal qualities have been well known for centuries; thus Neemix cannot be owned by a specific company nor protected by patents, since no new innovation was required to create the product. According to opponents of W. R. Grace's patent, Indian villages have rights to all proceeds from Neemix sales, because the product is theirs.[17]

Neemix is one of hundreds of products developed from indigenous plants.[18] This thinking about property and intellectual property rights is iterated in a story closer to the United States. The yellow Mayacoba bean has been grown in Mexico since the Aztecs developed the plant. Until recently yellow beans were a common export to the United States. In 1990, Larry Proctor, a farmer from Colorado, imported and planted some Mayacoba beans and began a complicated process of selecting out the most yellow for replantation. Proctor also renamed his beans Enola beans, and in 1999 the U.S. Patent Office awarded Proctor a patent for his very yellow bean. As a result, because of Proctor's patent control, Mexican Mayacoba beans can no longer be imported, despite their popularity among the Hispanic populations in this country. The case was settled out of court in 2002. An undisclosed sum was paid to Pod-Ners, a company representing Mexican bean growers.[19]

These cases, and there are many others, raise the question: whose property is the neem tree? The yellow bean? Do patents infringe on communal property rights of indigenous people? Should communal property rights take precedence or, from a more utilitarian point of view, would patent protection contribute to economic development, often needed in remote areas of the world or in India? Underlying these debates is a difference in mindsets. Western industrial nations have adopted a Lockean individualistic mindset about property and property rights. From that sort of thinking, improving neem products or the color of beans should give property rights to those who improve these natural products in innovative and creative ways.

But the mindsets of those who defend communal property rights may be different. Their worldview is one in which certain properties, including ideas, and their characteristics are shared commodities, a commons, to be used by everyone. In 1968 Garrett Hardin made famous the expression, "tragedy of the commons." In an article in *Science*, Hardin argued that shared resources, the unowned commons such as air, land, forests, and water, suffer from overuse. This is because, since the commons belong to no one, none of us takes responsibility for its conservation. Hardin defended the idea that sharing common property usually leads to overgrazing and misuse, since no one owns and thus is responsible for it.[20]

Belying Hardin's predictions, the neem tree still flourishes in India despite population increases and its common "over" uses. And beans are a major crop in Mexico, despite soil erosion and little horticultural innovation. This is because in these cultures the commons are thought of as communally owned property, and thus everyone in the community is responsible for its use and preservation – a mindset different from that to which Hardin was referring.

A similar mindset may exist in parts of China. According to Philip Altbach,

Chinese culture, which has dramatically influenced the culture of most Asian nations, has traditionally emphasized that individual developers or creators are obliged to share their development with society.... [21]

Although this may simply be an excuse, the Chinese habit of copying CDs, clothing, and other consumer products without paying royalties or acknowledging that these are copies may have its roots in that idea of sharing.

One last example, from the United States: Until recently patent rights to pharmaceuticals were protected under U.S. patent laws and under similar legislation in other developed countries. These rights are thought to be inviolable, and are included as one of the reasons pharmaceutical companies have resisted giving drugs away, for example, to the impoverished HIV-infected.

However, after the anthrax scares in 2001 and 2002, the allegedly inviolable nature of IP rights was brought into question by the U.S.

government. The antidote for anthrax is a highly powerful antibiotic called Cipro, patented and manufactured exclusively by Bayer. Because there was little demand for this drug, Bayer did not stockpile Cipro. During the anthrax scare it appeared that Bayer would be unable to manufacture enough Cipro to satisfy U.S. government demands. So on the grounds of a national emergency, the U.S. government threatened to override Bayer's patent of Cipro and license its manufacture elsewhere. As a result of that threat, Bayer responded with increased manufacturing capacity and produced enough Cipro.[22] Still, a precedent was set – that patents can be overridden in cases of national emergency when lives may be at stake. Thus the inviolability of patent protections was questioned, and patent rights were treated as *prima facie* rights, which can be justifiably overridden in certain circumstances. When lives or liberty are at stake, these most basic rights override property rights, or should do so. Intellectual property has no special claim to this exemption.[23]

It is on similar grounds that Brazil and India are manufacturing generic versions of a number of HIV drugs to respond to the HIV epidemics in their countries, and the impossibility of these and other countries to pay full price for those drugs. This is done despite protests of pharmaceutical firms concerning their patent protections, although recently most companies producing antiretroviral HIV drugs have now licensed this Brazilian manufacture.

To conclude this section, there is much to be learned from a mindset that places the commons as a priority over individual property claims. Although this thinking appears to be alien to the protection of individual intellectual property rights, inroads to that sort of protection are being made, albeit on an ad hoc basis, globally through a movement to protect rights of indigenous populations to their traditional uses of natural products, with Chinese and other cultural sharing customs, and in the United States with the anthrax scare.

THE TRAGEDY OF THE ANTICOMMONS, AND A NETWORK APPROACH TO INTELLECTUAL PROPERTY

The pharmaceutical company Pfizer, in a recent publication, links its intellectual property rights (its ownership of patents) to control of the *processes* that produce these products as well as to any products produced from those processes.[24] But in another article, recalling Garrett Hardin's earlier worries about the tragedy of the commons, Michael A. Heller and Rebecca S. Eisenberg argue that some intellectual property protections, in particular, patent protections of biomedical and software innovations, have created what they call the "tragedy of the anticommons."

Patent laws protect ownership and control while making the patent itself public knowledge. It is the control of the use of knowledge that Heller and Eisenberg challenge. Heller and Eisenberg argue that in some cases (although not in every case) overprotection of IP rights creates a "resource ... prone to underuse ... a 'tragedy of the anticommons' when multiple owners each have a right to exclude others from a critical resource [or essential element of a process or technology] and no one has an effective privilege of use."[25] Focusing on biomedical research, Heller and Eisenberg contend that privatization and patenting of IP in biomedicine can create fragmented, overlapping patents for discoveries and restricted access to these fragments, access that is necessary for and linked to other research. For example, patent protection of DNA sequences and gene fragments can block their use in other applications or research, except via expensive licensing agreements or through bundling multiple patents and licenses. The lack of immediate availability of such research and/or the expenses of licensing agreements can produce barriers that often discourage research development.

Part of this "tragedy" of the anticommons is a result of how we ordinarily protect intellectual property. IP protection is allegedly granted to the source of the innovative idea. But what is that source? Is it the person who created or discovered the idea? The innovator of an idea or the person or company who developed it? Some companies, universities, and other institutions, through employee agreements, receive patents for products and processes their researchers develop on the grounds that they funded the project and will market it.

Ownership of IP, depicted as "mine" or as belonging to a company, is a picture of homesteading that presents a distorted mindset about IP and IP rights. Intellectual property is different from ordinary material property. The development of IP – a so-called new idea or creation – is a result of a network of interrelationships, discoveries, research and development, and exchanges of ideas, some passed down over time.

IP phenomena are not single or even corporate creations; they are results of a buildup of research and exchange of ideas. This is as true of genome research as it is of Neemix and yellow beans. Centuries of research made the discovery of DNA possible; the idea did not drop from the sky into the minds of Watson and Crick. Out of that came years of research and networking relationships underlying the human genome projects. This is the case for every "new" scientific discovery or technological innovation. Ownership of these IP rights is not the same as owning and developing land, for example, even if it can be shown that the inventors or discoverers have found or created new intellectual property. This is because land development can be done by an individual independently of others. IP claims, at least in science, are derived from a series of other intellectual property developments and a complex chain of human creativity. Even if only two people discovered DNA (and that in itself is a questionable conclusion), the discovery could not have been possible without the contributions of thousands of researchers, foundations, dollars, and companies and a long history of research.

Although credit for the final "aha" might be given to the person or group of persons who brought the idea to fruition, simple patent protection may not be the proper vehicle for protecting this discovery or creation, since the property in question has many ancestral "owners." IP is a result of numbers of inputs, not all of which can ever be acknowledged or traced. AZT, for example, was first synthesized as a cancer drug in 1964 by Dr. Jerome Horwitz at the Detroit Institute. Later the National Institutes of Health tested the efficacy of the product on HIV before it was developed and patented as a marketable drug by Burroughs Wellcome (now GlaxoSmithKline).

Recognizing the communal qualities of IP might help us in recrafting protections of that kind of property. Part of this recrafting is parsing out the distinction between ownership, control, and sharing. Kenneth Goodman challenges this idea more dramatically. He argues that the conclusion that patenting creates incentives for inventors, researchers, and companies, is subject to reexamination. According to Goodman "the history of research shows that [at least] university research for centuries yielded major results without the incentive of patents and still does."[26] Moreover, he contends, the sharing of information may yield more ideas than its control.

Notice that the restrictions on sharing, not patenting per se, are what is at issue. A better way to think about this that takes into account the costs and incentives for expensive research is to distinguish patent ownership from sharing. In scientific circles worldwide there is a tradition of sharing new information, new discoveries, and new inventions. This sharing of knowledge ordinarily has one proviso: ownership of the idea, recognition for the final "aha," is given proper credit.

What we suggest is the following. The approach to IP as an individual or corporate exclusive proprietary right to products of the mind leads to oversimplified thinking about IP. IP is almost always a result of a long history of scientific or technological development and numbers of networks of creativity, not the act of a single person or a group of people at one moment in time. So-called ownership of an idea is different from ownership of a piece of property, because the development of intellectual property is part of a historical, cultural, and scientific network, a system of the interchange of ideas. Thus thinking about and evaluating IP requires at least recognizing that IP rights are *prima facie* not natural rights, and that it may be necessary to evolve new forms of shared rights. Although credit can be given to the discoverer or discoverers, absolute control of processes and products is at issue.

This approach is crucial in thinking about IP, both in its development and in multicultural settings, because of the network of interlocking relationships out of which ideas develop and because from a multicultural point of view, each social perspective usually "reveals insights . . . that are not obtainable in principle from others."[27] Although there are family resemblances, that is, intellectual property has some of the characteristics of other forms of property, intellectual property is not identical to material property, and thus its ownership and control should be distinctive as well. A network approach to IP challenges a traditionally Western view of IP.

To conclude, there are many good reasons for protections for intellectual property. But we need to disengage ourselves from mindsets that contend that intellectual property is identical to material property, that property rights of any form "trump" other basic rights, or that rights to intellectual property are perfect rights that can never be overridden with justification. Discovery or creativity is a result of multiple sets of events, networking, interactions, and other discoveries. That historical and networking trail needs to be acknowledged even while giving credit to Watson and Crick for discovering the double-helix structure of DNA. Because of the interdependence of ideas, patent and copyright laws should themselves not be so restrictive as to create a tragedy of the anticommons.

IP RIGHTS, CORPORATE RESPONSIBILITIES, AND ACCESS TO HIV DRUGS IN LESS DEVELOPED COUNTRIES

The Dilemmas

We have argued that IP rights are time-limited conventional rights that can be overridden in times of life-threatening emergencies of worldwide epidemics. IP develops out of networks of relationships, thus distinguishing it from ordinary property rights. It would appear, then, that we should arrive at the following conclusions. In times of life-threatening epidemics such as the worldwide HIV epidemic,[28] IP rights can be overridden with justification. Either pharmaceutical companies with antiretroviral HIV drugs should give them away, or countries with high HIV infections should be able to produce or buy generic drugs with impunity.

As satisfying as these conclusions appear to be, the issues are more complex. Underlying this discussion is the looming question of protecting IP rights, rights that some pharmaceutical firms are attempting to protect as they worry about giving away these drugs to poor countries with high HIV infection rates. They are worried too, about recouping costs of research and development, a legitimate worry but one that is sometimes couched in terms of rights language rather than in the utility of patent protections. And no company, on its own, could tackle the HIV epidemic without depleting all of its own resources.

It turns out, however, that patents are not protected in at least two-thirds of those less developed countries with high HIV infections.[29] These countries then, *could*, in theory, make generic versions of antiretroviral drugs without violating their own laws.[30] So either the IP issue is a red herring in this debate, or much more is at stake.

What is at stake is the fact that most countries with high infection rates have no money to buy anything, and what is at stake for companies is the loss of patent protections if generic drugs become widely used. What is also at stake is the long-term, never-ending demand for new drugs and the costs of developing those new drugs. In the long term, patent protection is important to encourage the development of new drugs, and thus for the well-being of our and future generations.

Another complication arises out of the mission of pharmaceutical companies. These companies are in the business of reducing pain and/or curing disease. This is what they do and if they do it well, focusing on customers as their primary stakeholders, they are generally profitable.[31] These companies are always faced with a series of dilemmas. Which research should they fund? On which diseases should they concentrate? And if they have a drug or a set of drugs that are effective, how do they serve infected communities that have no money to pay for these drugs? The dilemma is acute in the case of HIV. Although HIV/AIDS is fatal, we have effective life-prolonging and life-enhancing drugs to address this disease. Isn't it the responsibility of companies that have these drugs to give them away to their poor customers? Isn't that part of their mission?

In most sub-Saharan African countries with HIV infections, countries that account for two-thirds of worldwide infections, the question of whether or not they have laws protecting intellectual property is moot. There is little in the way of financial resources, except in South Africa, to underwrite the manufacture of drugs, even generic drugs. There is also no money to finance the purchase of HIV drugs from anywhere. Worse, in most of these countries, with the possible exceptions of Botswana and South Africa, there is little in the way of medical infrastructure in place to distribute and monitor the use of these drugs.

Even if pharmaceutical firms forego profits and quit worrying about patent copying, companies dealing in LDCs cannot simply give away HIV drugs; there is no place to send them, no central authority, no distribution channels, few medics to administer and monitor the drug use, and no adequate delivery and follow-up systems in place in most of these countries. Even if the drugs reached the ill, without medical assistance they would be misused. Giving away the drugs even in countries with a semblance of a medical system is dangerous because often these drugs get into the black market. They are then diluted and/or sold back to developed countries at discount prices. For instance, according to one report, as much as two-thirds of the AZT now virtually given away in many African countries by GlaxoSmithKline finds its way back to Europe through black markets.³² Moreover, just giving away these drugs without controls opens the way for unbridled development of generic drugs, thus threatening patent protections and profits in industrialized countries that can afford to buy these drugs.

So what should companies with antiretroviral drugs do? These companies did not start or perpetuate the HIV epidemic, and surely the countries in which this disease flourishes have responsibilities to their citizens to address this problem. Faced with what appear to be overwhelming challenges, these companies could follow the easy path of doing nothing, which in fact is what was happening until recently. But given the mission of pharmaceutical firms, the overwhelming extent of this epidemic, the pressure of their researchers and public opinion to address the HIV epidemic, the hopelessly poor countries in which the epidemic is prevalent, and the efficacy of HIV drugs, this option is morally irresponsible.

There are other alternatives. Countries could be encouraged to focus on prevention: the use of condoms and/or abstinence. This sort of program has been somewhat successful in Uganda in reducing infection rates, but men in most of these areas of the world are loath to use condoms. The growing use of female condoms in many countries has helped stem the spread of HIV but this, too, is a small step. Companies could focus on drugs for pregnant women and newborns, a project that GlaxoSmithKline and other companies have done. However, even if those drugs get to infected mothers (and not to the black markets) and newborns are not infected, an infected mother's lifespan is short, and orphans proliferate. Companies could license the production of their products or develop joint ventures, but again, to and with whom? Companies could develop a vaccine, and there are a number of such initiatives in process. However, an effective vaccine is probably ten years away. In the meantime, under the present circumstances, if nothing is done by 2020, it is projected that approximately 100 million people will have died of HIV/AIDS.³³

HIV/AIDS is not simply a problem for countries with high infection rates. It is a disease that is spreading worldwide. It is a global issue that requires a more global or systems approach. Drug distribution is not merely the responsibility of companies who have these drugs; yet because HIV is controllable with drugs, it is a responsibility they cannot avoid either. This is not an epidemic; it is a pandemic.

An Alliance Model

The previous discussion of issues surrounding the HIV pandemic in sub-Saharan Africa is too simplistic. We have presented the problems as either-or dilemmas, but the issues are much more interrelated and intractable. This pandemic presents unique challenges. It presents challenges to pharmaceutical firms, not to their expertise or to the quality of their products, but to their way of thinking through these issues. The pandemic presents similar challenges to those governments, donor organizations, and NGOs that deal with these issues on a daily basis and to other individuals, governments, and international organizations that at least pay lip service to the problem.

To wrestle with this issue requires companies, governments, donor organizations, and NGOs to reconceive their traditional approaches to problems in LDCs and revise their "standard operating procedures" or traditional mindsets that have worked well in other situations. What is needed is a new way of thinking about intellectual property, IP protection, drug distribution, and disease control, an approach that could create a template for future corporate, government and donor activities. That is, all of these organizations need to employ a great deal of moral imagination and conceive of this and future projects using a systemic networking approach.

The first challenge for pharmaceuticals is to disengage themselves from past practices of drug distribution with a more morally imaginative approach. What do we mean by moral imagination? Elsewhere Werhane has defined moral imagination as

the ability in particular circumstances to discover and evaluate possibilities not merely determined by that circumstance, or limited by its operative mental models, or merely framed by a set of rules or rule-governed concerns.[34]

Moral imagination is by and large a facilitating reasoning process that helps us out of a particular framing box, leading us to refocus our attention, to critique, revise, and reconstruct other operative mental models, and to develop more creative normative perspectives. Moral imagination requires the ability to disengage – to step back from a particular situation and take on another perspective, or at least to begin a critical evaluation of the situation and its operative mindsets. Thus part of being morally imaginative is perceiving the ethical dimensions of a managerial or corporate situation. Of course, no one and no company can ever disengage completely. Our revisions, critiques, and evaluations are still context-driven by historical circumstances, culture, surrounding political and social pressures, and values perspectives.

Moral imagination, however, is not merely "second guessing." It also should entail work at developing fresh solutions based on revised or even different mindsets. Finally, being morally imaginative involves evaluating these new possibilities or solutions from a normative perspective, judging not only the possibilities but also the way in which they are framed and the kinds of outcomes they are likely to produce.[35]

The HIV/AIDS pandemic involves another dimension. This pandemic is embedded in a complex network of relationships themselves embedded in a complex set of systems and subsystems, including the diverse cultures and practices of indigenous people in every infected country, distribution issues, financing and funding, pressures from shareholders and NGOs, and the ever-present worry about protection of patents. For pharmaceutical firms with antiretroviral drugs to protect their patents and address this crisis requires more of companies that we ordinarily expect. It requires developing and implementing a truly systemic approach to this problem.

The model we propose engages companies, donor organizations, NGOs, local villages, and countries in a systemic networking approach to this problem. A multiple-perspective systems approach should include the following:

- a multiperspective analysis, spelling out the networks of relationships and viewing them from the perspective of each kind of relationship. This would include an attempt to understand these issues from the point of view of pharmaceutical companies with antiretroviral drugs, country and cultural perspectives, traditions, funding agencies, NGOs and delivery mechanisms, and the global perspective of the pandemic;
- an evaluative perspective, prioritizing the value priorities of each stakeholder and of the pandemic;
- a multistakeholder model for structural change that will attack and work to alleviate the pandemic by distributing (but not avoiding) the risks and responsibilities.

The model is an alliance model developed by Mary Ann Leeper, COO of the Female Health Company, a for-profit company that distributes female condoms to protect women against HIV infection in over 100 less developed countries. The model was developed in response to a huge demand by women first in Zimbabwe and now in many countries for protection against infection in cultures where men are averse to condom use themselves. The dilemma for this small company was obvious. They had a fine product, a large customer demand for the female condom, and adequate supplies. But the customer base was penniless, and as we have mentioned, governments in countries with high infection rates, at least in Africa and India, have few or no funds for this or any other product. So Dr. Leeper begin finding donor organizations to support supplying this product. She solicited monies from UNAID, USAID, Difid, social marketing organizations that deeply discount products such as condoms, and other international organizations. But even with money for the product the company was faced with a second challenge: getting governments in these countries to support the distribution of the product. And there was a third difficulty: training villagers and local health personnel on how to use the product and how to instruct others. By working with NGOs they are gradually overcoming this problem through training and education, village by village, in the 100 countries where the FHC distributes its product.[36] Figure 15.1 represents this alliance graphically.

A similar model has been adapted by Merck & Co. and the Gates Foundation in attacking HIV in Botswana. Merck has partnered with the Botswanan government and the Gates Foundation in its HIV project in Botswana. It could not merely give its HIV drug, Crixivan, away, even if it had the financial resources and will to do so. Although Botswana has better medical facilities and government than most of the rest of sub-Saharan Africa, its complex culture is such that education, medical infrastructures, and monitoring are not adequate, nor are tribal traditions aligned with modern medical treatment. Without a systems approach Merck's and the Gates Foundation's attempts to work on the HIV crisis in this country and other less developed countries will fail, whether or not IP is preserved.[37] In Tanzania, Abbott Laboratories Fund has partnered with the Tanzanian government and the Axios Foundation (a U.S. NGO) in a multiyear multimillion-dollar project to upgrade and improve the medical care infrastructure, to train health

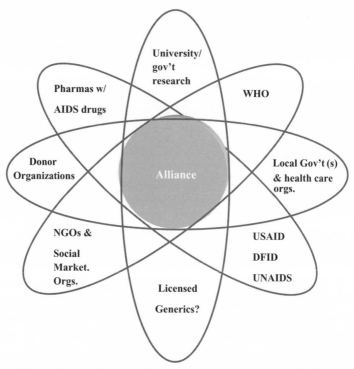

Figure 15.1. Alliance Model for Pharmas: Marketing a Program, Not a Product. *Source*: Model courtesy of Mary Ann Leeper, COO, Female Health Company.

care professionals, and to expand access to treatment for HIV-infected citizens.[38]

This model requires thinking of this enterprise as a program, not merely as delivering a product. Employing this model requires proactive corporate initiatives, because these initiatives have not been forthcoming from those countries with widespread epidemics. One has to find international donor organizations for funding, elicit government cooperation in the countries most afflicted with HIV, and work with NGOs to set up delivery, medical, and monitoring systems. This requires developing alliances with local and state governments, NGOs, and donor organizations, and it requires hands-on interaction in the infected communities. It requires training local villagers to deliver and monitor drug intake. This is currently being done in Haiti, where hundreds of local people are being trained in the rudiments of drug delivery and sent out to villages daily to deliver and monitor drug use for the

HIV-infected.[39] This model is also being tried by the World Health Organization in a number of other countries.[40] And of course, companies have to provide the drugs and monitor the process of delivery and use themselves.

A hands-on alliance approach to drug distribution in LDCs protects company patents and ensures that products are to be used properly and by those for whom the program is aimed, because companies are in control of distribution and use. But is it unfair to those of us who pay full price for drugs or who pay for this giveaway through buying other expensive drugs? We would argue that it would be unfair if we lived in a global egalitarian society where everything was distributed equally and if we adapted that model as the fairest for distributive justice. But we neither live nor will live in such a society, nor, as Ronald Dworkin argued some years ago, is equal distribution the fairest method for distribution. Dworkin argues, in brief, that the fairest means of societal distribution is not based on equality but rather on the principle of treating every individual as an equal. So for example, if I have a small supply of medicine and three children, I give the medicine to the sickest. Only if they were all equally sick would I distribute it equally. It would be unfair to distribute the medicine equally if only one child was sick. This is because that sick child is disadvantaged and needs to be brought up to the healthy status of the others.[41] Similarly, providing transportation to people who otherwise cannot get to the voting booths is not unfair to those of us who can, for the same reasons. So those indigent people dying of HIV/AIDS are owed more than the rest of us just to bring them up to the same level, that is, the level of the living. This would be unfair only if they could provide for themselves; but they cannot.

Still, we must ask, why would any company engage in this program? These programs take a great deal of time, effort, and ingenuity, and positive outcomes are slow to be realized. In Botswana, for example, so far Merck and the Gates Foundation are providing treatment for only about 40,000 HIV-infected. In Tanzania, Abbott has only begun to make a difference for the two million HIV-infected in that country. Other companies that are engaging in these processes are also finding that this enterprise is enormously difficult.

Still, there are a number of good reasons why engaging in this enterprise is worthwhile. First, and most obviously, from the point of view of rights and justice, it is the right thing to do. One does not have the right to die needlessly, and those who can help have obligations to come to the aid of the dying. Unless one imagines that IP rights override the right to life, it is difficult to justify ignoring this pandemic. Second, this is a worldwide pandemic that endangers all of us. So even from a self-interested perspective, companies and countries that can engage in this process need to do so for their own long-term interest. Third, as we have said repeatedly, only a systemic approach with an alliance model protects patents for the engaged companies. Without that involvement, drugs will be copied and distributed anyway by companies that disregard patent law, products will be misused, and black market drug sales will thrive. Fourth, HIV/AIDS is a heterosexual disease destroying the young middle-class population in sub-Saharan Africa. This is a tragic loss to these economies, a loss to companies marketing to these people, and a long-term loss to global economic development, so important for free enterprise. Finally, if pharmaceutical companies are in the business of *healthcare*, they ignore that mission with peril. It is what they do.

CONCLUSION

Jefferson's goal, in setting up the U.S. Patent Office, was to provide limited protection for the innovator in exchange for publication of the idea in a forum in which others could improve on it. Following his lead, we conclude that intellectual property is a form of community-developed property with naming opportunities and limited rights for the final discoverer/creator, but not absolute rights to further development and use. Proprietary control of knowledge ignores the distinctive features of intellectual property as forms of innovation with many historical, social, and cultural ancestors and thousands of parents, cousins, sisters, and aunts. Moreover, from a rights perspective, when millions of lives are at stake, not to share benefits is morally unthinkable.

Such a conclusion assumes that intellectual property protection is a *prima facie* right that is important, but not primary, particularly when lives are at stake. It is advisable for societies to grant certain IP rights, in order to stimulate creativity, but therefore these societies have the obligation to withdraw or amend those rights when the consequences to the overall system are negative. Furthermore, in an increasingly global economy, negotiation of IP rights will have to involve multiple societies. For example, an innovator who publishes core knowledge about the neem tree or the yellow Mayacoba bean deserves credit for organizing the knowledge and making it available beyond the original cultures. But this credit should not compromise the cultures that have developed and used this knowledge for hundreds or even thousands of years.

The HIV/AIDS pandemic represents an international emergency analogous to, but much larger than, the anthrax scare, where individual rights may have to be overruled – but where it is reasonable for the individual firm to expect to be involved in a partnership and to formulate some protection for its patents. A systems approach can achieve these ends. The challenge today is to operationalize such an approach globally before the projection of 100 million HIV deaths becomes a reality.

Note: A different version of this paper is published under the title "Intellectual Property Rights, Moral Imagination, and Access to Life-Enhancing Drugs," *Business Ethics Quarterly*, 15 (2005), pp. 595–613.

16

A Future Agenda for Government–Industry Relations

William C. Weldon*

INTRODUCTION

Running a research-driven health company in the twenty-first century is both exciting and challenging. We've discovered and developed clinically valuable modern medicines, devices, and diagnostics to improve the lives of millions of patients and their families; these advances also provide economic value by decreasing hospital stays, reducing the use of other expensive healthcare services, and increasing individuals' productivity.[1–4] Yet, the media and politicians routinely identify the industry as a major societal problem. This image is reinforced because insurers and others are shifting costs, so patients are paying more for medicines than for hospital stays or doctor visits. Consequently, the public's appreciation of our contributions is at an all-time low.

As individuals and governments face real economic challenges in paying for healthcare, the clinical and economic benefits of new medicines often fail to make a favorable impression on the public. Growing premiums, co-payments, and administrative burdens are what the public and many healthcare providers generally focus on, because these are the challenges confronting them daily. And the overall value of new treatments is often obscured by segmental budgeting and cost shifting within our healthcare system. For example, a clinically important new treatment may allow a patient to leave the hospital sooner. Clearly, this is a good thing for patients, as well as their employers, if

* The author gratefully acknowledges the contributions to this chapter of Patricia Molino and Michael Miller.

it allows them to return to work earlier. But financially, this break-through can have multiple effects. Insurance companies may save money because outpatient care is less expensive than hospital care. Conversely, the patients may end up spending more if they are required to pay more co-payments for doctor visits, prescription drugs, and other services and supplies. Finally, the breakthrough treatment may undermine the hospital's financial health by cutting its revenue stream. These types of innovations, with multiple big and small economic effects, are common in our modern healthcare system. These advances bring clinical benefits to patients, but can cause financial gains or losses to healthcare providers and payers because few of them are responsible for the total healthcare costs of an individual's illness or disability.

In discussing the future of government and industry relations, I will first briefly examine the general roles of the pharmaceutical industry and governments within our entire healthcare system, and then look at specific areas where the industry and governments at the state, national, and global levels can work together to improve the value of healthcare for patients and society.

ROLES OF INDUSTRY AND GOVERNMENTS IN HEALTHCARE

Healthcare companies discover and develop new medicines, devices, and diagnostics that are then used by the patients, healthcare professionals, and institutions, such as hospitals, that make up our healthcare *delivery* system. Paying for the majority of this healthcare are the governments, employers, and individuals that comprise our healthcare *financing* system. These healthcare delivery and financing "systems" interact to meet society's twin goals of providing healthcare to those who need it and creating incentives for improving the quality of that healthcare.

Besides paying for healthcare, governments regulate the sale and marketing of new treatments and diagnostics, fund basic research, conduct disease monitoring, epidemiology, and public health activities, and decide ownership of intellectual property. In the United States, these functions occur primarily through agencies of the Department of Health and Human Services (such as the Food and Drug Administration, the National Institutes of Health, and the Centers for Disease Control and Prevention), state and local public health agencies, and the Patent and Trademark Office. Other countries have similar government entities, but they also have more unified government-centric healthcare financing or delivery systems than the United States. Although most of my discussion will focus on the United States, I will address these international differences where appropriate.

Industry is often squeezed between society's two priorities of delivering care and creating incentives for improving the quality of care. This pressure is caused by several factors: first, the 40-plus million without health insurance are paying directly for most of their healthcare, whereas people with insurance are shielded from most costs. And whereas insurance companies negotiate discounts from healthcare providers and pharmaceutical companies on behalf of insured individuals, the uninsured are not represented and consequently pay the highest prices. Second, the prices paid for brand-name medicines reflect the resources needed to develop the next generation of new medicines much more than their direct production costs. Last, unlike doctors and hospitals, the industry is faceless in the healthcare delivery system because it has very little direct patient contact.

Even though pharmaceuticals comprise only about 11 percent of all healthcare costs, it is easy for the industry to be vilified or marginalized in discussions about how to improve our entire healthcare system because the pharmaceutical industry represents a large share of personal healthcare spending and is one step removed from patient care. But precisely because modern treatments are so effective and important to quality healthcare, I believe there need to be more open discussions and debates about how we can manage our limited resources and improve both our healthcare delivery and financing systems. Industry executives need to become more engaged in these debates, and to work actively with governments at all levels toward achieving a better societal consensus about how to balance resource allocation between the two competing priorities of increasing access and promoting future innovation and quality.

FUTURE ACTIONS

As I stated above, the industry (along with other providers and payers) must work in partnership with governments at all levels in candid discussions about improving our system so that it better serves the public's needs. And all participants in these discussions need to be prepared to contribute both intellectually and economically toward making these improvements. In addition, industry and governments can and should work together on issues related to basic research, translating this research into advanced medical treatments, and ensuring that the public benefits from these new developments. Below are some higher priority issues where common ground and joint or synergistic actions can and should take place. This list is certainly not exhaustive and could change as new discoveries or challenges confront our society in the future.

Managing Uncertainty

The clinical or economic value of a new treatment may not be recognizable during its development. Managing this uncertainty is one of the greatest ongoing challenges for industry and government decision makers, who must constantly balance risk–reward and risk–benefit information and uncertainties.

Early in clinical development, uncertainties exist because the trials may not have the size to demonstrate significant value, or because clinical trials test the efficacy of potential new treatments under controlled conditions rather than their real world effectiveness. Uncertainties also exist after FDA approval because new or expanded uses may be discovered years after a medicine is introduced, dramatically broadening its benefits. For example, Bactrim's™ use in prophylaxis for AIDS-related pneumonia was discovered after it had been used for years as a mainstream antibiotic for urinary tract and other common infections. Similarly, the HIV/AIDS pandemic brought new uses for antifungal medicines, while immunosuppressive chemotherapies have found valuable broader uses in cancer treatment and organ transplantation. The downside of uncertainty occurs when unforeseen side effects or toxicities appear. Such unexpected side effects cause the withdrawal of about 1 to 2 percent of all medicines approved by the FDA. Overall, for company executives and government leaders, the need to balance what is known about the value of a potential new treatment against what may still be unknown about its risks and benefits strongly directs how they manage resource allocation among R&D areas and projects, and at what point they determine it is appropriate for an experimental compound to be approved for widespread use.

Balancing uncertainty versus known benefits is a business challenge for companies, a regulatory challenge for governments, and a clinical challenge for physicians and patients. Several steps could be taken to better manage and reduce this uncertainty without delaying the approval of new treatments. First, the current MedWatch system for collecting reports about adverse events related to drugs and devices could be improved and expanded. For example, more staffing and other resources for the FDA's office responsible for the MedWatch program would help more quickly separate adverse events caused by a drug or a device from those that are unrelated to the treatment. Reforming our medical tort system would also support better analysis of adverse events. The current legal environment creates negative incentives for healthcare providers to report potential errors because it seeks to penalize every poor outcome as a preventable mistake rather than recognizing it as a real-world occurrence. I recognize that there are great controversies surrounding legal system reforms, but these are certainly important issues that governments and industry should be discussing to help improve our healthcare system to benefit patients and society.

Second, new science in the area of bioinformatics is likewise providing us with ways to anticipate areas of clinical risk even before products are used in humans. This is another area where government and industry should collaborate.

Third, more Phase IV post-approval trials should be conducted to look at longer-term side effects that may occur in real-world use, with Phase IV trials being required in some situations. We have already moved forward to promote more research on the use of medicines in children with incentives for Phase IV trials.[5] A similar dialogue and consensus could be reached about Phase IV trials in other areas because information from such trials would aid physicians and benefit patients. When to require and how to create incentives for conducting such Phase IV trials are issues industry and governments should seriously discuss.

Similarly, industry and governments should address the challenge of how and when to conduct more head-to-head clinical trials comparing existing medicines. Such trials should be structured so that they evaluate the real-world effectiveness of treatments rather than their clinical trial efficacy. This is an important distinction, because some innovations that reduce side effects or otherwise increase patient compliance result in medicines that produce better clinical outcomes, though their efficacy in clinical trials may be similar to that of older medicines. This was the case with the modern SSRI antidepressants compared with the older TCA class of antidepressants. Medicines in both classes generally result in improvement of depression in 60 to 70 percent of patients in clinical trials, but the TCAs have more frequent serious side effects that cause many patients to stop taking them.[6–8] Thus, the SSRIs are more effective than the TCAs for real-life patients, consistent with the clinical rule, "a medicine that a patient doesn't take is unlikely to do them any good."

Some people have advocated for longer-term and head-to-head trials before a new medicine is approved. In some cases, depending upon the disease and the existing treatment options, such trials are appropriate and the regulatory process already requires them. However, routinely calling for longer or more complex trials will delay wider access to new treatments and unnecessarily tie up finite clinical trial resources and researchers. In contrast, because Phase IV trials are simpler in design and intended to look at different questions than pre-approval Phase III trials, they can be conducted using fewer resources while collecting information from many more patients. Determining the appropriate scope and extent of these testing requirements are among the challenges industry and governments face in assessing how much risk and benefit information is enough, because delaying approval to conduct more testing effectively means delaying patients' access to new treatments.

Striving to Recognize Innovation

As discussed above, it can be difficult to recognize the magnitude of an innovation while a new treatment is being developed. However, despite uncertainties during development, once a new healthcare product comes to market, government reimbursement policies and other decisions that reflect the perceived overall value of a treatment significantly affect companies' revenues. In some countries where the government acts essentially as a sole purchaser, direct price or profit limits are imposed. In the United States, where the situation is much more varied, the government's reimbursement policies still have a significant impact. In some instances, the U.S. government has eliminated market forces from the process and taken direct control over pharmaceutical pricing. For example, in 1990, with Medicare expecting to pay for 95 percent of the U.S. consumption of erythropoietin (a biotechnology medicine for anemia developed by Amgen and co-marketed by the Ortho Biotech unit of Johnson & Johnson), Congress passed a law setting the price Medicare would pay for this drug.[9] Congress later reduced payment amounts even further, while Medicare itself instituted a variety of administrative actions to limit reimbursements for this medicine.[10] Another example of U.S. governmental action to control prices is the pharmaceutical system created by the Veterans' Health Care Act of 1992, which requires companies, if they want to participate in the Medicaid program, to sell medicines at a maximum of 76 percent of the average price paid by private sector purchasers in the United States to the Veterans Healthcare Administration and three other agencies of the federal government.[11]

To create incentives to spur on future innovation, governments (and other payers) should work with industry quickly to create adequate reimbursement amounts and simple procedures that facilitate the use of new treatment. If companies perceive that future reimbursements might fail to justify the development of innovative treatments, their internal investments may well become more conservative, concentrating on less innovative and less financially risky areas of research, such as nutritional supplements that are nonpharmaceutical treatments that can be purchased outside of the insurance system. Similarly, if small biotech and other biomedical research companies cannot project adequate reimbursement for their products, they may find it difficult or impossible to obtain the outside funding on which they rely. The result would be fewer new breakthrough treatments – particularly for diseases that currently lack good therapies.

Medicare has traditionally been slow to create new reimbursement codes and payment amounts for innovative treatments. And because many private U.S. payers follow Medicare's lead, such delays can impede both the development and use of new treatments for everyone. In recent years, however, Medicare has begun to act faster. For example, Medicare quickly responded to the FDA's approval of Johnson & Johnson's innovative coated stent system for opening narrowed coronary arteries. Medicare's speed in establishing the new code and payment amount also signaled the government's recognition that, despite their higher cost, these new stents provide superior clinical and economic value, keeping patients out of the hospital and the operating room. This action also provided incentives for physicians to use these new stents, and for other companies to push forward rapidly with their own versions of these device-drug combination treatments. Availability of these other systems spurs on both competition and further innovation – both of which benefit patients.

The opposite is also true. When governments fail to support an area of treatment, the effect can be seen in clinical care and the less-than-robust development of new treatments. For example, Medicare's 50 percent co-payment requirement for outpatient mental health services not only has served as an access barrier to obtaining mental health services, but also limits incentives for developing new diagnostics and treatments for mental illnesses.

Governments create other types of incentives for specific areas of research and development. For example, the 1983 U.S. Orphan Drug Act provides tax and market-exclusivity incentives to companies that develop medicines for conditions affecting fewer than 200,000 individuals in the United States. This law has proven to be a huge success, leading to a dramatic increase in the number of available treatments for rare diseases: more than 200 of these medicines have been approved in the past two decades, compared with less than 10 in the decade prior to 1983.[12]

Industry needs to match the commitment shown by Medicare and other payers to support innovation by acknowledging the difference between truly innovative treatment advances and those that provide more focused clinical benefits. This acknowledgment should be both in our rhetoric and in our expectations for reimbursement. For example, even though considerable effort and resources may have been expended in developing a new medicine, the fact that it is a novel chemical compound, with unique clinical characteristics, does not make it a major piece of innovation. In fact, the market reflects this reality because only about three of every ten medicines that are new chemical compounds ever return the average development cost.[13]

It would be great if I could create a definition of what major innovation is, and what it is not, but pharmaceutical science and clinical medicine are too complex and rapidly changing for a static definition. The nature of innovation is that this year's innovation may very well be tomorrow's run-of-the-mill treatment. However, there are certain characteristics of innovative treatments that can be described, including a new way to attack a disease, a significant difference in side effects (or drug–drug or drug–food interactions), a new way to administer or dose a medicine so that it can be used by a different patient population, or other features that improve patient compliance and hence the clinical value of the medicine. Another type of innovation is discovering that an older medicine can be used to treat a different disease than that for which it was originally developed. These innovations may be broad in scope and involve relabeling of the medicine to include the new use, or small and involve so-called "off-label" uses that are clinically important to individual patients. One dramatic example of this is the off-label use of Viagra® for a small number of women with fertility problems arising from a thin uterine lining.[14]

Last, in thinking about ways to make improvements in how industry and governments respond to and create incentives for future innovation, it is important to remember that government initiatives, market forces, and company actions are seldom perfect, and there are generally significant time delays before societal priorities can be translated into real actions. An all-too-apt example can be seen in recent efforts to develop treatments for possible bioterrorism agents – a clear national priority since the 2001 anthrax attacks. Some smaller companies have applied significant resources toward this goal. Nonetheless, long-term government funding and other components of the "Bioshield" program remain uncertain. Considering the length of the R&D process, which can take up to decades, it requires a leap of faith to assume that a government-guaranteed market will exist when the treatments are eventually approved, particularly since one of the Federal government's responses after the anthrax attacks was to propose taking away patent rights for the leading treatment for anthrax exposure.[15]

Focusing on Unmet Needs

To fulfill society's priorities, industry and governments focus on diseases that cause significant morbidity and mortality.[16] I believe our attention should also include diseases important to populations in developing countries. Wealthier nations have an ethical imperative to support healthcare for poor populations. In addition, governments and industry need to expand their global perspectives because the increasingly global nature of diseases will affect international public health and economic development. The risk of Asian bird flus, for example, is so real that the World Health Organization convened a global summit of governments and industry in November 2004 to discuss how to prepare for this potential pandemic. As was reported in *The New York Times*, the role of scientists in addressing this challenge will be expansive and include diplomatic as well as scientific skills: "[I]n a globalized world where peripatetic germs hitch rides in the lungs or luggage of unwitting airline passengers, where sick chickens in Asia can threaten to topple third-world governments, where the role of politics and money can obscure the free flow of medical information, [epidemiologists at the Centers for Disease Control and Prevention] cannot do their job – preventing the spread of deadly flu viruses – by being scientists only."[17]

In the past, governments and industry faced many challenges concerning healthcare's impact on economic development and vice versa. Both industry and government should expect similar opportunities in the future: in the 1300s, plague epidemics devastated local workforces in Europe, leading first to abundance for the survivors, and then to economic disruptions due to manpower shortages.[18] The robust economies of developed countries in the early 1900s following the industrial revolution allowed for vastly improved public health and sanitation systems. And a recent review of 30 years of data from more than 100 countries found that a 1 percent improvement in a population's life expectancy translates into a 4 percent rise in the country's economic output.[19]

Like the avian flu threat, twenty-first century globalization will undoubtedly have a huge impact on health. Global transmission of other infectious diseases, such as SARS and West Nile Virus, will only become more frequent. As globalization raises the economic standards of developing countries, their middle-class populations and life expectancies will increase, resulting in significantly more people with cancer, arthritis, cardiovascular illnesses, and other chronic diseases. Delivering healthcare to the world's population will increasingly test the economic resources, political leadership, and capabilities of healthcare industries in both developed and developing countries.

Still, if developing countries institute market-oriented healthcare systems with adequate reimbursement opportunities, globalization may well provide companies with the opportunity and incentives to tackle the diseases more common in these emerging economies.

In addressing challenges in this area, governments should also recognize that the support of global economic development and healthcare capabilities worldwide will affect industry's research activities. Industry needs to factor in globalization when setting its priorities, allocating research resources, and choosing locations for its clinical trials and business centers. Both groups also need to consider how healthcare delivery will be affected by local social and cultural practices, as well as genetic differences in disease susceptibility and drug metabolism.

Addressing Needs of Uninsured Individuals

I firmly believe that healthcare companies have a responsibility to help the poorest members of society with access to appropriate healthcare products and services. Companies and governments have to work together in this regard. In the short term, health products companies must continue to operate their Patient Assistance Programs (PAPs), which provide free medicines for low-income individuals without adequate insurance. Recently, the industry took steps to extend these access programs to many more Americans through the several state-based programs and the Partnership for Prescription Assistance, a collaborative effort with doctors, nurses, and community groups across the United States, to enroll eligible individuals in these programs. The industry must also continue to develop programs that offer discounts to uninsured individuals who may not qualify for PAPs. One such program, Together Rx Access™, was introduced this year in the United States. Similarly, governments must maintain the viability of safety net programs such as Medicaid and the State Children's Health Insurance Programs in the United States. Johnson & Johnson has long offered Patient Assistance Programs to provide medicines at no charge to low-income individuals. We were among the founders of the original Together Rx™ discount card, which allows Medicare enrollees to obtain discount medicines from multiple pharmaceutical companies; we worked with other companies to create the Together Rx

Access™ program for the uninsured, and we supported the creation of a Medicare prescription drug benefit that provides assistance to seniors and the disabled. Globally, healthcare companies, such as Johnson & Johnson, collaborate with governments and nongovernmental organizations in delivering free medicines and building healthcare delivery capacity to address endemic diseases such as AIDS and malaria, as well as responding to natural disasters such as floods, hurricanes, and earthquakes.

As we transition into the new Medicare prescription drug benefit, governments and industry will need to step up our efforts to work with individuals and advocacy groups to facilitate the use of the new benefit and to help patients obtain the maximum value from the benefit. In part, this will involve coordinating patients' new Medicare benefit with other prescription drug coverage options, including companies' Patient Assistance Programs.

For these efforts to be fully effective, governments and industry need to be consistent partners, supporting both short- and long-term solutions with sound operational practices and financing. In the long term, industry needs to work in tandem with governments to expand private-sector insurance options to give more individuals reliable, affordable, and comprehensive access to integrated healthcare services. As part of this long-term improvement, patient education must be integrated with our efforts to help individuals make informed choices.

Another area of concern for underinsured patients, governments, and the industry is the recent trend of purchasing lower-priced medicines over the Internet or from other countries where governments control retail prices. Aside from real concerns about fraud and counterfeit medicines, these purchases have hidden costs because importation removes local health professionals from the patient's healthcare team. A pharmacist in Canada or Australia, for example, is unlikely to contact a physician in Kansas to discuss a patient's multiple medicine regimen, nor is the patient likely to call the foreign pharmacy with concerns about how to use the medication. Safety concerns are of vital importance to the pharmaceutical industry, since we do not want our medications used in ways that make them less effective or potentially harmful.[20] At a time when safety issues in healthcare are of increasing concern, promoting importation is a step backward. Discussions of importation have also generally ignored the disturbing reality that importing medicines undercuts incentives for developing new medicines because it is also importing *de facto* price controls. The bottom line is that patients in the United States would be much better served by having good insurance coverage that would dramatically reduce their costs while supporting innovation, rather than facing the uncertainty of imported medicines that would offer few savings, stifle innovation, and promote the export of U.S. manufacturing jobs. These are all areas that need to be openly discussed as we consider all options for improving access to care for the uninsured and underinsured.

Improving Outpatient Care

The trend toward more outpatient care will help us use our healthcare resources more efficiently. Opportunities for increasing the delivery of higher-quality, more patient-focused care need to be supported by both governments and industry. Governments and industry can foster this trend with better data collection to measure more accurately and rapidly the quality of care. This information will then allow more resources to be directed toward healthcare interventions and public health strategies that produce the best clinical and economic outcomes. Increased use of information technologies such as electronic medical records and e-prescribing will aid in this data collection and resource management, while also helping to reduce medical errors that arise from communications problems.

Industry should support these efforts by participating in the development of appropriate technologies and disease-management programs with governments and other payers. Governments and other payers can help promote the development and use of disease-management programs by doing more system-wide management of healthcare spending. By taking more integrated approaches to healthcare budgeting, governments will be able to make more informed decisions about allocating resources toward more valuable outpatient care.

Industry should also continue to support the development of less toxic, less invasive treatment options, such as the recent introduction of essentially nontoxic cancer treatments and minimally invasive surgical instruments. Tools such as these can reduce patients' need for lengthy hospital stays and allow more resources to be applied toward therapeutic care.[21]

Prevention is another area where both industry and governments should increase their efforts, because it is a much more efficient use of our healthcare resources than disease treatment. Although the public tends to focus more on treatment-related R&D than on prevention, governments and industry should increase their support for educational activities aimed at prevention, including efforts to understand what forms of educational outreach are most effective in changing individual behaviors for vaccinations, diet, smoking, and exercise. As Rudyard Kipling said, "Words are the most powerful drug used by man." Industry needs to be a part of these efforts and to continue working with patient advocacy organizations and governments to educate the public about chronic diseases such as arthritis, diabetes, and high blood pressure. These public education campaigns need to include initiatives emphasizing that treatment is a means of delaying or preventing serious consequences such as heart attacks, strokes, kidney failure, and blindness.[22]

Increasing Use of Genomic Knowledge

Genomics research and other advances in biomedical science will continue to provide new information about serious diseases and present new opportunities for developing better and more cost-effective treatments.[23] Because this area of science has broad and potentially far-reaching consequences for society, industry and governments need to continue discussing how generic discoveries should be approached and managed. For example, pharmacogenomics and surrogate markers of disease progression may increase the specificity and speed of developing new treatments. Also, information about the genetic components of diseases is slowly enabling physicians better to guide patient care so that the most appropriate treatments are used. The industry and the U.S. Food and Drug Administration are currently collecting and analyzing data to understand the best ways to utilize these advances for improving healthcare delivery and drug development. Both sides need to continue these efforts.

One stumbling block to using genetic information for individual patient care is the scarcity of trained genetic counselors and other clinicians who can educate patients about the implications of specific genetic tests. Governments and others need to increase their educational activities for healthcare professions so that as new genomics-based diagnostics and treatments become available, clinicians will be able to use them to their patients' greatest advantage.

Increased genomic knowledge might also potentially be used to discriminate against individuals – particularly for health insurance or employment. Governments need to take the lead in ensuring that individual genetic information will be used to benefit patients, not to penalize them. If individuals are wary of obtaining genetic tests that could improve their healthcare, then the value of these scientific and clinical advancements will be undermined, and the incentives for further development will be reduced.

However, from a financing perspective, knowledge of underlying genetic causes of diseases may segment treatment recommendations for common conditions. This segmentation of patient populations may increase costs for treating individual patients and decrease a company's potential revenues from the new treatment. Improved diagnostics and treatments developed with greater genomic information may also result in shifting resources from one part of the healthcare system to another, for example, from inpatient care to outpatient treatment. In addition, if these new treatments lead to overall increases in longevity, they may increase the burden on public retirement systems such as Social Security. Again, these are reasons why I believe the leadership of research-based healthcare companies must be involved with the broader debate about how to improve our national and global healthcare delivery and financing systems.

Reducing Development and Approval Times

Industry–government interactions start early in the research process and extend past the approval of new treatments and diagnostics. Historically, getting a new treatment approved has been a bottleneck in bringing a new medicine to waiting patients. But a 1992 United States law hastened the process considerably by creating a mechanism whereby the FDA receives a "user fee" from companies with each new drug application in exchange for a commitment to conduct the review process within certain defined time targets.[24–26] The revenue from these fees has enabled the FDA to hire more personnel and meet its review targets. The original initiative has already been augmented several times, most recently in a 2002 measure for new medical device applications.[27] Other countries also have been looking toward the U.S. model in hopes of improving their own pharmaceutical approval processes.[28]

The success of the U.S. prescription drug user fee law teaches us a valuable lesson about government–industry cooperation: shortening the time for moving a treatment from the lab bench to the patient – without compromising on safety standards – helps improve patient care and reduce future costs for research and healthcare. Faster development and approval times also enable industry to investigate more treatments for a greater range of diseases over the same time. We need to apply these lessons both toward further collaborative improvements in the drug approval process, and toward helping other countries to improve their own systems.

One way to shorten the R&D timeline is through the use of validated markers of disease progression. Progress in the development and validation of surrogate markers relies on the sort of government–industry collaboration that produced the prescription drug user fee law, and that is currently happening with genetic information being collected and analyzed by the FDA. Markers are needed that accurately reflect the progression of many chronic illnesses, such as high blood pressure, and provide a reliable prognosis for the development of devastating outcomes, such as a stroke. Such markers would allow companies to better focus research efforts. They also would allow government agencies, such as the FDA, to evaluate clinical research data sooner. But because these research programs can take many years for any single disease, and to be truly useful these markers must be validated and agreed upon by all parties, developing them will require broad alliances.

The government also can act as an effective and enthusiastic research partner in areas ranging from basic biochemistry to epidemiology, whereby scientists from industry, government, and academia collaborate on projects that none of them could accomplish alone.[29–31] Although most of this research is performed without restrictions on publication or other use, a small percentage is done on an exclusive basis or license.[32] Despite the success of these collaborations, there is one potential downside for drug companies. When a joint project does lead to a successful new medicine, the public may protest the drug's price, thinking that a private company is profiting from government research. This perceptual problem persists in the face of the actual circumstances: research has shown that when a new medicine arises from these collaborations, the private company is the one that has overwhelmingly spent the majority of money and time in the development and approval processes.[33] To secure more public support for continuing these joint activities, there should be greater openness about the extent of these collaborations and their value, so that credit can be given where credit is due.

A final broad avenue for increasing the value patients and society receive from biomedical research and the industry is intraindustry collaboration. Although specific business partnerships for approved and late-stage medicines are common, and broad industry collaborations such as the Forum for Collaborative HIV Research[34] have been undertaken with government approval, real and perceived concerns about antitrust laws present barriers to other opportunities where the industry could collectively improve patient care. This has been the case with patient assistance and discount medicine programs where broader collaboration has been stymied by antitrust concerns. These same concerns may be presenting similar challenges in developing treatments for tropical diseases and the diagnostic-drug combinations needed for genetically linked diseases. I do not see a single answer to how to improve this situation, but since it was possible to create the Forum for Collaborative HIV Research, it should be possible for industry, governments, and others to discuss how to facilitate similarly productive activities when not faced with public health emergencies such as the HIV pandemic.

CONCLUSIONS

The future holds great promise for improving the quality and efficiency of healthcare – in both developed and developing countries. The challenge will be in effectively allocating public and private resources to support healthcare delivery and financing systems that will both provide access while also promoting industry to aggressively turn the scientific discoveries coming out of industry, academic, and government laboratories into real-life diagnostics, devices, and drugs.

Over the next several years, governments and health products companies can take steps, individually and in tandem, to improve the process of delivering new medicines to the public. We need to work together to improve how we develop new medicines, get them approved, and make them more readily available to patients, while also investing in the future.

For us to accomplish our common goal of providing better, more efficient healthcare, I believe all participants need to work together as collaborators, rather than antagonists. This is essential if we are to achieve a convergence of minds, hearts, and spirits that will lead to healthier, happier, and more productive societies and greater economic and social advancement for communities around the world.

17

AIDS Activism and the Pharmaceutical Industry

Martin Delaney

The AIDS epidemic is widely recognized as a turning point in the relations between the people directly affected by a disease and the many groups, agencies, and institutions that respond to the disease. People with AIDS and their advocates are credited with spearheading several fundamental changes in how society and its institutions behave when confronting a new, life-threatening illness. Some of these changes include:

- Reforms in the way new drugs are approved by the U.S. Food and Drug Administration;
- Greatly enhanced communication between patients and their physicians;
- A new emphasis on patient empowerment in all aspects of the healthcare system;
- New inclusion of patients and advocates in scientific decision-making and the conduct of clinical research;
- Greater involvement of the public at every level in the management of research at the National Institutes of Health;
- More political oversight of how research is funded by taxpayers and how research dollars are divided between disease interest groups;
- An unprecedented degree of interaction between patients, their advocates, and the pharmaceutical industry in the development, testing, pricing, and marketing of new therapies.

Given today's increasing concerns about the cost of healthcare, and the public's demand for ever better solutions to medical problems, this chapter will focus on the last item on the list, the dramatic changes that have occurred in how a patient community interacts with the pharmaceutical industry. Although the pharmaceutical industry has long maintained significant relations with the public and with various disease-interest, nonprofit foundations, there is little precedent for the ways in which companies now interact routinely with AIDS groups. This chapter will explain how and why this new relationship evolved, and examine the benefits and potential pitfalls it presents. Finally, it offers guidelines for developing policies and practices that will protect and maintain ethical standards. Upholding these standards will sustain a mutually supportive, respectful, and productive relationship between the advocacy/patient community and the pharmaceutical and biotech industry. In order to comprehend how and just how far this relationship has evolved, it is necessary first to take a quick course in AIDS history.

A SHORT HISTORY OF AIDS, ACTIVISM, AND INDUSTRY

When AIDS first appeared in the early 1980s, the part initially visible was the most dramatic and virulent form of the disease, or "full-blown AIDS." What scientists, patients, government, and the public saw was a relatively swift and horribly aggressive disease that seemed likely to kill everyone infected. One common presentation of the disease was sudden weight loss, followed by a life-threatening bout of pneumocystis carini pneumonia, or PCP; another was the rapid spread of red lesions, or Kaposi's Sarcoma, often called the "gay cancer." Both most often afflicted young gay men in their twenties through forties, and led to almost universal death in a relatively short time.

Given this picture, and the fact that thousands of gay men had succumbed to the disease by the middle 1980s, the fight to find treatment for AIDS was a desperate challenge. We soon saw how people were also infected through blood transfusions and how hemophiliacs had become unwitting victims through the use of inadequately tested Factor VIII. All too swiftly the rates among women, hemophiliacs, African Americans, Latinos, the homeless, IV drug users, and others began to add to the numbers. Sometimes spurred on by overly pessimistic predictions, the general public was lead to fear that the disease would soon break out everywhere. After all, what other infectious disease had ever remained confined to specific groups?

This naturally set the stage for demands to speed up the drug development and approval process. But even before the first drugs were approved, patient groups sought access to some – any – form of treatment. By 1986, four drugs were being tested as possible treatments for HIV disease. Two of these, products of American companies, were already marketed in many countries that had less strict drug approval requirements. One was approved for limited use in the United States against respiratory syncytial virus, a childhood disease. As these drugs were hurried into clinical trials against AIDS, it was inevitable that people with HIV would soon come calling on the pharmaceutical companies. Patients primarily from California and Texas began a weekend ritual of trips to Mexican border towns where both American medications could be purchased. Although there was no proof that either drug worked, even the hope of some benefit was more than doctors could offer at the time.

Ironically, the issue that first brought the AIDS/HIV community into direct contact with the pharmaceutical industry was the very one that still causes the greatest conflict today: drug pricing. Due to a logarithmic collapse in the value of the Mexican peso in 1986, the price of one of the drugs tripled almost overnight. AIDS advocates, many with backgrounds in the business community as well as the various protest movements of the Vietnam era, almost instinctively marched on the headquarters of ICN Pharmaceuticals in Irving, California, demanding that the price increase be rolled back. It was a moral issue and an emotional issue, and it established a model of what was to come. It was a warning to the pharmaceutical industry that "business as usual" would be challenged on every front. Rather than face the prospect of a public confrontation, the company worked with activists to create a bulk-purchasing process that effectively eliminated the price increase. Activism had its first small victory in its relations with the pharmaceutical industry.

Little more than a year later, another drug (zidovudine or AZT), a product of the British firm Burroughs Wellcome, became the first drug approved by the FDA as a treatment for AIDS. Instead of being overjoyed at the approval, as the company expected, AIDS advocates instead quickly organized to fight the drug's unexpectedly high price of $10,000 per year. This was considered particularly outrageous in light of the fact that the government had paid a great deal of the cost of studies that supported the drug's approval and use. Others almost immediately questioned the design and conclusions of the clinical trials that lead to approval. Because the drug was associated with chemotherapy-like side effects (it had initially been developed as a potential cancer treatment twenty years earlier), activists wanted assurance that the claimed benefits were real and worth the risk of the side effects. Within weeks, angry activists confronted company officials at conferences and scientific meetings, challenging both the price and the company's data. Later, a few activists met with the company at its headquarters, just as others had done at ICN the previous year. When their efforts were rebuffed by company officials, the "other side" of activism took over and activists eventually marched on the headquarters, temporarily shutting the company down. The drug's price was scaled back a step at a time, with some reductions occurring as a result of reduced dosage recommendations and later an actual reduction in the retail price of the drug. Activists had a second victory and had laid the groundwork for challenging companies on their science as well as their prices.

Early meetings between the HIV/AIDS patient community and the pharmaceutical industry were typically either "ad hoc" and angry (to protest a perceived grievance) or informal and concerned with the future. From the beginning, though, it was evident that anger and protest alone would not take us far enough. We also needed to talk to and influence the industry. A balance was struck that holds to this day, a balance that recognizes that industry and patient groups are at once both partners facing great challenges together, and opponents with often conflicting interests.

The relationship between activist groups and the industry matured substantially around the approval of the second drug for HIV, didanosine from Bristol Myers. While clinical studies of the drug were occurring, activists were making efforts to speed the drug development process and to make such experimental drugs available for people who couldn't take part in clinical trials.

In this era, the interests of the HIV community and the pharmaceutical industry greatly overlapped. Both wanted to see the drugs approved more quickly. Both saw a need to make drugs available outside clinical trials. Both sought a more efficient, responsive process at the FDA. Both believed that drugs should be approved on the basis of surrogate markers (lab tests) as predictors of eventual clinical benefit, without waiting for proof of that benefit.

A new type of triangulation evolved to address these needs:

- A small group of activists began to meet formally and informally with scientists and managers from the company to iron out differences and find common ground where possible;
- Company officials and activists met with FDA and NIH officials, in formal meetings at the agency and informally at conferences and public meetings;
- Larger groups of activists brought media attention to the issues through public protests and staged events.

The companies, scientists, and government officials faced, on every front, a well-informed, highly motivated activist and patient community prepared to collaborate, debate, or confront.

These forces came together over a period of a few years, leading up to a critical FDA Advisory Committee meeting called to decide whether surrogate markers, in this case T-cell numbers, could be used as a basis for approval. The debate had become critical because the limitations of the first drug, zidovudine (AZT), had quickly become evident, while the development of the second drug, didanosine, had dragged on far longer that expected. AIDS activists carried the day at the Advisory Committee meeting, successfully arguing that the urgency of the situation warranted taking reasonable chances and not waiting for the traditional proof of clinical benefit. A similar public committee meeting a few months later focused on the presentation of data aimed at getting didanosine approved by the FDA.

The situation had become urgent even for the sponsor, Bristol Myers. Details had been worked out between activists, the FDA and the company for emergency but wide-scale access to didanosine for the neediest patients under a system then called the "parallel track" (in addition to traditional drug approval studies, another "track" would provide the drug to people who could not participate in the clinical trials). Because there were no other drugs available except for AZT, the number of people in need was dramatic. Bristol Myers ended up supplying didanosine to some 16,000 people outside of clinical trials, at the company's expense. The company was as anxious as the activists to get the drug approved so they could finally start charging for it. For the moment, the interests of the company and the interests of the activist and patient community were almost entirely aligned.

The FDA drug approval process was also changed forever in this drama. It became routine to see the patient community represented on FDA and industry advisory panels and to see community spokespeople consulted on every step in the drug development and approval process. The procedures that were developed in and around the approval of didanosine became the framework for what was eventually codified as the Accelerated Approval process at the FDA. This process has been used for every subsequent drug developed for treatment of HIV and has quickly been applied to other life-threatening illnesses.

The relationship between industry and the activist/patient community was most productive during the development and subsequent approval of the new class of drugs called protease inhibitors. These drugs reached the pharmacies in mid-1996, after news of their dramatic benefits was announced at the International AIDS Conference in Vancouver Canada that year. The fact that the drugs, used in combination with two of the older generation AIDS therapies, were highly successful had leaked out of early research studies beginning in 1993 and 1994. Without the input of the activist/patient community, however, the drugs might never have made it to market. When they were first developed, the sponsors really believed they were approaching a cure for the disease and were thinking only in terms of a dramatic "home-run" success by the individual drugs. Combining them with the older drugs was not part of the plan, at least initially.

The early dramatic success of protease inhibitors in small studies, however, collapsed quickly when the virus began to develop resistance to the drugs, just as it had to the earlier generations of drugs. Although the protease inhibitors were indeed more potent, it made little difference in the long run. This sobering observation led at least a few of the companies to consider abandoning the drugs' development altogether. A number of prominent scientists echoed their disappointment.

The activist/patient community, however, focused on the fact that the drugs still offered greater potency for a while than anything previously seen. The answer was obvious to many activists and physicians: add the drugs in combination. The continued enthusiasm for the protease inhibitors by activists and patients was a decisive factor in continuing, rather than abandoning, their development. Once the drugs were studied in three-drug combinations, they produced one of the most dramatic advances ever seen against a fatal illness, cutting the death rate in half in their first year on the market. By the end of their second year of use, the reduction in mortality approached 80 percent. Throughout the middle 1990s, the value of the input provided by the activist/patient community in scientific, clinical, and regulatory matters was proven time and again.

MODELS OF INTERACTION

Over the twenty-year history of AIDS drug development, a variety of models of industry–community communications has evolved. In some cases, companies created "community advisory boards" made up of activists known to specialize in drug development. In others, interested community activists formed their own groups and initiated meetings with the companies whenever an issue warranted it. In the early to middle 1990s, the burgeoning activist–company relationship was seen as a business opportunity. Several small public relations companies were created, often by members of the HIV community. These companies worked to manage the interface between the pharmaceutical companies and the community, arranging meetings, managing communications, advising, and identifying people for inclusion. These were particularly useful for pharmaceutical companies new to the HIV/AIDS field or whose internal cultures were ill-prepared to deal with a public that was well-informed, often angry, and almost entirely unimpressed by corporate titles and positions. The PR firms, rooted as they were in the patient community, offered a unique conduit.

In the first fifteen years of treatment activism in the United States, the groups representing "community activists" were entirely self-identified and self-selected. In the first five years, the entire spectrum of "treatment activists" was made up of a few people on the East Coast who were a subset of ACT-UP New York and a parallel group on the West Coast mostly housed at Project Inform, a nonprofit education and advocacy organization. Although there were many "AIDS activists" working on a variety of issues in public policy matters, only this small squad focused on treatment issues, research, and the pharmaceutical industry.

By the late 1980s and into the early 1990s the size of this group swelled rapidly on both coasts, many joining under the banner of ACT-UP (which wasn't really an organization as such, but rather a point of affiliation), and many others simply creating their own new groups. There were no rules, no formal procedures for meeting with the pharmaceutical industry, the FDA, or researchers. People became part of the effort simply by showing up. This raw democracy was in some ways the movement's greatest strength and in others one of its greatest weaknesses. It permitted anyone to take part, but it tended to favor the best informed, the most charismatic, and the best connected. The meek found it hard to be heard.

In Europe, a more structured, perhaps more bureaucratic model evolved in which a formal coalition of activists was created (the European Treatment Activist Group, ETAG) to manage both the relationships with industry and the relationships between community organizations. The activist community came from several countries, each with its own problems, rules, languages, and cultures. No single country had a large enough or strong enough activist movement to effect change in ways parallel to the American movement. Out of necessity as much as design, the European effort grew as a coalition, with all the procedural overhead that implies, but also with the strength of greater organization. Although the style of the European process was perhaps more polite than that of its slightly disorganized, more forceful American counterpart, the outcomes were similar.

Beginning around the late 1990s, American activists had begun to experience the pains typical of an aging movement. Many key players had themselves died of AIDS and those who had not were getting older. Most significantly, fewer new people were joining the movement, partly due to the success of therapy. The sense of urgency felt strongly in earlier years was diminished; fewer people each year seemed interested in treatment activism. In response, a coalition of community members (the AIDS Treatment Activists Coalition, ATAC) was created that fairly well bridged the gap between the previously unstructured U.S. approach and the bureaucratic model of the Europeans. For the first time in the United States, the activist movement became organized, with planned meetings, committees, and a formal process of membership. The path for joining the national treatment activism effort was clearly laid out for those who wished to join.

Areas of Collaboration

Out of this mix of conflicting and common interests has grown a complex, multilayered relationship between industry and the HIV/AIDS patient community. Beginning with the development of the second drug for HIV, every drug's development process has included deep involvement by the patient community. Patient advocates expect to be included or at least consulted in all scientific and procedural decision-making, including the design of clinical protocols. As relationships with industry have developed, the community's involvement has come to include:

*   Influencing companies' development priorities;
*   Selection of drug candidates for development;
*   Oversight of study demographics and site selection for clinical trials;
*   Expanded access in all its forms (methods for making experimental drugs available to patients outside of clinical trials);
*   Initial pricing of new drugs and subsequent price changes and increases;
*   Oversight of advertising and promotion;
*   Collaborations with other pharmaceutical companies.

It is this set of expectations, which are routinely fulfilled, that make the relationship between the HIV/AIDS community and the pharmaceutical industry so nearly unique. In recent years, a few disease interest groups, particularly breast cancer and hepatitis organizations, have developed similar relationships with industry. Even these lack the comprehensiveness of the HIV–industry connection.

Why does the pharmaceutical industry permit or even seek such involvement? On one level, it is because it has no choice in the matter. From the earliest days, government agencies and regulators took a sympathetic approach to the HIV/AIDS community. Groups such as the FDA and the NIH made it clear that they welcomed an in-depth consumerism from the patient community, at least as long as it was directed primarily at industry (they were a little slower to accept it when they themselves were the target). Perhaps more importantly, companies chose to work with advocates because they got something out of it. The most common benefits to the companies included:

- Learning from the collective experience of advocates, who over the years had accumulated a great deal of practical experience in drug development.
- Early identification of potential problems: close contact with the patient advocate community served as an early warning, bringing problems to companies' attention more quickly and before regulators were forced to act.
- Opportunities to discuss and promote the company's point of view: while listening was an important expectation from advocates, the companies also used meetings and communications with advocates to promote their own views on their products, the policies, and pricing.
- Seen favorably by the FDA: the FDA views itself as a consumer protection agency and, as such, it welcomes the flow of information from consumers to the industry.
- A focal point for input: some aspects of this new relationship with patients raised complex issues, such as the design of expanded access to drugs prior to their approval by the FDA. By ten or more years into the AIDS epidemic, the core group of activists and patients knew more about the benefits and pitfalls of these programs than any consultant a company could hire.
- Exposing company culture to the community (for better or worse): the better the public understood a company, the more likely they would be to accept it.

Not everything works to the benefit of the companies once the door is opened to communication. A company may not like what it hears when it asks for input. But once input is given, it is a lot more difficult for the company to charge off in its own contrary direction. Companies need to really be open to change. Entering into this kind of give and take with "customers" may set false expectations if company management still plans to do things its own way. A related problem is that pharmaceutical companies can all too easily get conflicting input from the many kinds of advisors they solicit. Most companies also maintain close relations with a large number of physicians in every medical discipline related to their products. These relationships range from primary care doctors to the leading researchers in the field. There is no guarantee that the activist/patient community and the physician advisors will come up with the same kinds of advice.

When all works right, the relationship between industry and the activist/patient community can lead to many potential payoffs. Some examples from the AIDS experience include:

- Well-planned expanded access programs can meet the needs of patients without slowing recruitment in clinical trials and without creating painful "lotteries" to distribute limited supplies of a new drug.
- Community can become a vocal ally at approval hearings and meetings of advisory committees. The opposite can also happen if a company mismanages the relationship, and the FDA is generally reluctant to give a company what it wants when the relevant patient community opposes it.
- A unique example of cooperation was an unprecedented two-year "price freeze" negotiated on most AIDS drugs in 2002–2003. The freeze was so successful that the companies did their best to avoid public recognition of it, for fear that consumer groups would demand the same for other medical fields in their portfolio.
- A similar collaboration evolved between industry and activists over federal funding for the AIDS Drug Assistance Program (ADAP), which provides drugs to people not covered by Medicaid or private insurance. The ADAP Working Group was formed as a joint effort to lobby Congress and the states for the necessary funding. Industry could not conduct such efforts on its own without appearing self-serving. Activists on their own often lacked the skills and political clout needed to influence large financial decisions on the state and national level. Working together seemed a natural way to build on the strengths of each group.
- Educational efforts are another area where the patient community and the industry share similar, though not identical, goals. Both seek the development of educational tools to inform newly affected patients. Each company, of course, has its own view of the best strategy, which drugs to use first, which are the best choices. The patient community educators, in contrast, view their job as countering the

spin of individual drug companies and letting the science speak for itself. Many companies, however, have great skill and experience in the educational field, as well as enormous resources, so wherever possible, collaboration is invited.

Areas of Conflict and Potential Abuses

Despite the advantages offered by the unique levels of collaboration that have evolved between the activist/patient community and the pharmaceutical industry, the relationship has not always been peaceful. It was inevitable from the first fight over drug pricing that conflicting interests would surface. These have taken many forms over the last twenty years. The most common areas of conflict have included the following.

The Cost of Drugs. The pharmaceutical industry expects the public simply to be grateful for new drugs, without questioning the company's overall profitability or reinvestment in new drug development. The Pharmaceutical Manufacturers Association regularly claims that the average cost of developing a new drug is somewhere between $800 million and $1.2 billion. Several independent analyses contest these figures and argue the true cost is much lower. The actual cost is difficult, if not impossible, to calculate because there is no agreed-upon standard of accounting for determining the cost. (See Chapter 14, by Joel Hay, for a more detailed discussion of the economics of the cost–pricing issue.) At the very least, the manufacturers believe that the cost of every successful drug must also reflect a portion of the costs of all the drugs that failed during development. Just how much was spent on failed drugs is impossible to calculate without complete access to a company's books and a complex auditing process. No matter how independent auditors might add things up, industry can always claim they haven't accounted for all the costs. The real cost of drug development largely remains a "black box" of indeterminate proportions; some say "just as the industry wants it."

The battle between the industry and AIDS activists goes on continually. Today, it is largely channeled through a group called the Fair Pricing Coalition (FPC), a subset of the treatment activist community, joined by a cadre of people managing AIDS Drug Assistance

Programs on a state level. The FPC meets with every company prior to its pricing of new drugs and attempts to talk with them whenever price increases are made. The Fair Pricing Coalition is unique in its ability – and demands – to meet only with the senior company executives directly responsible for setting prices. Many of those who attend FPC meetings come from the heady ranks of corporate senior management, a group that is still typically reluctant to meet with the consumers of its products. The primary goal of the FPC has been to keep pricing decisions at least "cost-neutral," meaning that each new drug should be priced no higher than the existing drugs in its class. Prior to the efforts of the FPC, industry made sure that each new drug was priced somewhat higher than previous drugs of the same kind, leading to an ever-escalating cost of treatment for AIDS.

The Portfolio of Studies a Company Uses to Seek FDA Approval. For most companies, the goal has been to find the fastest path toward some kind of approval, even if it leads to a narrowly defined medical application. So-called "off-label" uses of a drug can easily become a larger portion of sales than the specific indication for which the drug was originally approved. In AIDS, this has meant conducting studies that show a drug's activity in "naïve" patients, or people who are using anti-HIV therapy for the first time. The advantages to the company are evident:

- The drug is used in people who are the "easiest" targets for therapy.
- The studies will seldom include people with advanced disease or a high risk of suffering the most severe side-effects or complications.
- The drug will only be compared to other drugs tested in the same relatively gentle environment.
- The drug will not be exposed to the forms of the disease with the greatest likelihood of producing drug resistance.

Unfortunately, this kind of approval leaves a great deal to be desired from the patient's point of view. The drug reaches the market with only minimal knowledge of how to use it across the spectrum of the disease. Little is known about how it will interact with the wide variety of drugs with which it may be used. Once a drug is approved on the "easy" path, the company has only minimal incentive to conduct further studies in other stages of the disease. On the contrary, it has strong incentives not to, since additional studies will almost certainly show less effectiveness, greater development of resistance, and more frequent and more severe side effects.

As a result, the activist/patient community has learned to insert its views into the drug development process from its earliest stages. Over time, most pharmaceutical companies working in AIDS have come to expect the involvement of the activist/patient community in all stages of drug development. A few have acted responsibly on their own, without inviting much public input, whereas a few others have actively resisted input, leading to contentious relations and a lack of support for their cause when the drug goes before the FDA. The activist/patient community has become remarkably sophisticated in its knowledge of drug approval and companies ignore its input at their peril. At most a company (and any of its regulatory or clinical research staff) will work on four to six drugs over the span of its work in AIDS, whereas some activists have been involved in the development of more than twenty.

Using the Activist/Patient Community to Battle with the FDA. This phenomenon was relatively common in the early years of AIDS drug development, when companies and activists alike were testing the ways in which they could collaborate. The relationship between industry and the FDA was anything but cooperative and industry welcomed a new friend who shared its feelings about faster drug approval. Until then, the most vocal consumer voices, such as Public Citizen, opposed any effort to make drug approval easier. Yet the industry's early use of its new friend was hardly its wisest move. When talking with the FDA, activists quickly began to notice there were at least two versions of a story: the FDA's and the companies'. To hear it from the FDA, the problems that were delaying the approval of a drug could always be attributed to some failure on the part of the sponsor/company. To hear it from the sponsor, the problem was always due to inactivity or mindless bureaucracy at the FDA. Activists quickly learned to force both sides to communicate with each other in public whenever possible so at least the "who said what" part could be verified.

This behavior has never completely ceased, though it is now more often due to poor communication than to deliberate malice. Still, activists work to get everything in writing whenever possible and demand that communication be as public as possible.

Promotion of "Selected" (Biased) Community Members to Speak at Hearings. In a related attempt to manipulate the FDA, companies have sometimes sought to use members of the activist/patient community to make their arguments for them at meetings and Advisory Committee Hearings. In some cases, where interests were truly held in common, no one minded as long everyone remained committed to the truth. But in several cases, famous in the oral history of AIDS activism, some companies inserted "ringers" into the process, people who were not regular members of the activist community, but were hand-selected from the broader patient community to make a specific claim or point. A company might have several hundred patients in clinical trials at any one time and most would be relatively neutral about the benefits of the drug under study. But a few would always become enthusiastic "true believers." When they are needed, companies will fly such people anywhere, put them up in the best hotels, and pay them for their time. When asked, they perform on cue, fully believing what they say. What they lacked, however, was any perspective but their own personal experience. Industry has long used the public in this fashion. The difference that evolved in AIDS is that once such a tactic was recognized, activists came publicly to demand disclosure of any company support from everyone who sought to speak at hearings and approval meetings. The offending companies were later singled out and their misdeeds widely communicated, often permanently shattering any trust that might have developed between activists and the company.

Using Community People to Say Things Forbidden to Company People. Some, if not most, AIDS treatment activists are also involved in treatment education. In recent years, the task has grown far larger than the supply of activists; many community educators today lack the hard-edged background of the activists. This has presented an opportunity for industry, which seeks to exert as much influence as possible on the

educational materials and viewpoints delivered to the patient community. While industry may not be able unduly to influence the treatment
activists, the person engaged solely in education is an easier target. The
goal of unscrupulous sales reps has simply been to put words in their
mouths, words that they themselves cannot utter by decree of the FDA.
The FDA carefully monitors and controls every word spoken by industry sales and marketing reps. If a sales person working a promotional
booth at a conference crosses the line, making claims not accepted by
the FDA, someone walking the floor will almost always report it to the
regulatory agency. That is, unless the sales rep gets someone else to
say it, perhaps at a community meeting. Educators not skilled in the
possible wiles of industry can easily become unwitting purveyors of
messages forbidden to company personnel. Activists can only root out
such misbehavior within their own organizations, as it rapidly becomes
inappropriate to challenge the actions of other agencies.

Feeding False or Misleading Data into Community Channels. There is
more than one way to look at or interpret the significance of most clinical studies. There is always a conservative way, championed by the best
scientists and usually by the FDA. And there is always the company's
way, a way usually guaranteed to put everything in the terms most
favorable to the company. Since the FDA and a company's competitors
are always watching at scientific conferences and events, there is little opportunity there. Instead most companies have created organized
tours in which a team of sales and clinical personnel is sent around to
meet with community agencies one at a time or in geographic groups.
Usually there is no one present who can challenge the spin on the
data. Whenever possible, activist-oriented agencies try to send "truth
squad" personnel to these meetings, serving notice to the company that
someone is indeed listening.

"Cherry-Picking" Nonprofit Agencies in Financial Need. One of the
worst forms of abuse occurs when a company uses its considerable
financial clout to "help" financially troubled community agencies, for
a price. The price is typically creating a package of educational materials on subject matter carefully selected by the company. The package goes out under the agency's name and may or may not mention

that it was funded by a specific company, to address a specific topic. This mechanism is callously used by companies trying to change public perceptions about their product or to promote some new theme of interest. There is nothing inherently wrong with industry providing funding for independently produced educational materials, but when the host agency is selected primarily on the basis of its financial needs, it is difficult not to become suspicious of a company's motives.

Shaping Agency Behavior by Rewarding Good Behavior, Punishing "Bad". This is one of the most contentious actions taken by companies, and only a few have resorted to such tactics. The game works like this: the more favorably a particular agency portrays a company or its products, the more generous the company becomes with grants for that agency. Conversely, when an agency takes highly critical positions or writes articles the company feels unfair, spoken or unspoken threats are made with regard to future funding potential. In the worst examples, funding has been abruptly canceled. When funding is used to manipulate the actions of an activist or educational group, the entire relationship of industry and the AIDS community is threatened.

These are but some examples of the areas in which conflict have arisen in the relationship between industry and AIDS activism. All such matters are "on the table" in the relationship. They range from matters of pricing and science to fundamental questions of ethics. And this brings us to the final and perhaps most important area of conflict.

The Biggest Conflict of All: Conflict of Interest

The most difficult challenge faced by the activist/patient community in its relations with industry affects everything discussed in this chapter. Ideally, AIDS activists would be entirely independent, with their own means of support for their organizations. Sadly, to the contrary, the great majority of AIDS treatment activists work for organizations that receive varying percentages of their income in the form of "unrestricted educational grants" from the very pharmaceutical companies they seek to influence. Even those activists who do not work for AIDS organizations typically have their travel expenses reimbursed for attendance at drug company meetings. Perhaps most startling, the new U.S. AIDS

Treatment Activist Coalition is almost entirely funded by the pharmaceutical industry.

Such a situation would be unheard of in some forms of public interest activism. It is the norm in AIDS, and for that matter, in most other disease interest areas. This implication is obvious: there is at least an appearance of some conflict of interest affecting the rank and file of AIDS treatment activism. Despite its use of protest, despite the fights waged over conflicting interests, one cannot escape the observation that few AIDS treatment activists could function without industry funding. The activist/influencer is subject to the most powerful form of influence.

In AIDS, the pharmaceutical industry has been extraordinarily generous in its outreach to community organizations. Without financial support from industry, the impressive nationwide network of AIDS service agencies would be hard pressed to meet the needs of the epidemic. Taken to an extreme, however, this network of financial relationships can stretch the limits of ethical behavior. In many medical interest fields, for example, nonprofit agencies posing as "watchdog" groups have sometimes been found to be little more than wholly owned or funded fronts for individual companies or industries. More commonly, industries frequently contribute to related nonprofit agencies in hopes of influencing their beliefs and behavior. Such relationships create at least the perception of a conflict of interest, especially when advocacy groups become solely or mostly dependent upon industry funding.

The AIDS epidemic has put a bright spotlight on both the problems and opportunities presented by the relationship between industry and nonprofit service and advocacy agencies. The pharmaceutical industry spends billions annually in efforts to influence physicians and health-care workers through an endless stream of marketing materials, promotional junkets, gifts, and research funding. Since the beginning of the epidemic, many have argued that the simplest way to prevent any perception or opportunity for conflict of interest is to steer clear of all industry funding. Although this may work, it may be unnecessary. It also would have a serious impact on the delivery of services to people with AIDS, because industry has indeed been a good giver to AIDS-related causes, probably the single largest source of funding other than government. Those who support the use of industry funds argue that because the pharmaceutical industry is one of the few groups profiting, and handsomely, from AIDS, it has a moral obligation to turn a large portion of those profits around to help support community-based services, advocacy, and education.

AIDS activists have debated long and hard and, for the most part, have come to the conclusion that it is possible to accept industry funding without compromising one's positions and activities. Those who choose to believe that any acceptance of industry funding automatically compromises an advocate's or agency's integrity have a right to their views, but must recognize that others of good will may see things differently and with good conscience. Those who choose to take advantage of the opportunities presented by industry funding should not be accused of compromising their integrity unless there is clear evidence that this has been the case.

This decision to "have it both ways" brought with it the obligation to ensure that the community of nonprofit agencies engaged in activism does its best to establish ethical standards that attempt to address the ethical questions that may be raised by industry funding. Good faith alone may not guarantee that industry funding will not affect the objectivity and balance of organizations and people. The following general principles and guidelines are suggested as a starting point for a discussion about how to achieve the highest possible ethical standards, while acknowledging the legitimacy of industry. These guidelines, first proposed in 1999 by Project Inform in San Francisco, have been implemented, in part or in full, by many AIDS organizations across the United States and Canada.

GUIDING PRINCIPLES

The following ethical guidelines derive from a set of three Guiding Principles. Each of these principles, in turn, provides a series of Related Guidelines for individuals and agencies.

The Three Guiding Principles that generate the Related Guidelines are:

1. Disclosure;
2. Structured Communication;
3. Independence and Ownership.

Guiding Principle 1: Disclosure

All significant financial relationships between the pharmaceutical and biotech industries and any for-profit or nonprofit community service agencies should be explicitly stated and acknowledged.

This is the simplest of the principles. It merely asks that community agencies be entirely up front about their sources of funding in general and with regard to specific materials. It also asks agencies to develop internal guidelines to govern this aspect of their funding, and to make those guidelines publicly available.

Related Guidelines

- *Major grants should be announced publicly at the time they are received.* The definition of "major" remains unspecified here because dollar amounts are relative to individual agencies. 10K might be major to a small group and all but insignificant to a larger one. Agencies know for themselves what constitutes a larger donation.
- *Any documents or educational materials explicitly paid for by pharmaceutical and biotech industry support should be clearly identified as such in those materials.* Materials or documents funded by "nonrestricted educational grants" should also be identified in the materials themselves, if such materials were specifically mentioned or called for in the related grant request.
- *A summary of all pharmaceutical and biotech industry support should be published annually and provided to supporters and the public.* This summary should define what is and is not included as "pharmaceutical support." For example, some agencies list only major grants, not counting industry purchase of tables at fund-raising dinners, etc. Others acknowledge (or do not acknowledge) reimbursement for travel to company and product-specific meetings, and related honoraria. Some do or do not list solicited reimbursements for travel to scientific and medical conferences not specific to the company's products.
- *On an annual basis, nonprofit agencies should describe how they used funding received from the pharmaceutical and biotech industry.* This can be achieved as part of the process for disclosure.

- *Agencies should develop and make publicly available a statement of their policies regarding pharmaceutical and biotech industry support or funding.* A few examples of policy positions:
  - Some agencies set a specific limit for the percentage of their funding from the pharmaceutical and biotech industry.
  - Some require that neither board members nor staff may own stock in pharmaceutical and biotech companies that are engaged in developing products for HIV disease (except perhaps in the form of 401K retirement plans where the individual does not choose specific stocks).
  - Some require that any honoraria offered by industry for speaking engagements or participation in meetings be paid to the agency rather than the individual.

Guiding Principle 2: Structured Communication

This is a multifaceted principle designed to establish effective communication pathways between agencies and the members of the pharmaceutical and biotech industry. This is necessary because companies' proprietary interests and views often conflict with those of other companies. Each company seeks to influence agency positions and perspectives on its products and interests. This principle speaks about all the ways in which industry seeks to communicate with and influence agency views and practices. In the earlier years of the epidemic, there was little direct contact between agencies and members of the pharmaceutical and biotech industry. Contact happened, if at all, at the request of advocates or educators chosen for this task by their organizations. This process has now been reversed, and most contact occurs at the request of industry members seeking to influence the positions taken by local and national agencies.

In many cases, members of the pharmaceutical and biotech industry target not only the agencies themselves, but also people within agencies, particularly those who directly influence patient treatment choices or advocacy positions that might affect the industry. These individuals are sometimes targeted for in-depth relationships with the company, including invitations to special meetings, travel reimbursement for industry meetings and scientific conferences, industry-developed materials, and marketing promotions. This often places individuals in untenable positions, especially if they are the ones specifically designated by their agencies to address such matters. Several companies have further facilitated this "relationship-oriented" process by hiring community people once associated with local agencies as adjuncts to their marketing staff. At best, this may provide a helpful form of input to industry; at worst, it can allow industry to put a friendlier face on its proprietary interests and to take advantage of individuals and their relationships within the community.

If pharmaceutical or biotech industry representatives are permitted without restriction to contact and work with any and all agency personnel, they gain the ability to influence treatment knowledge and advocacy positions taken throughout an agency. This may easily create conflicting viewpoints within an agency depending on how effectively the company "sells" its message to those individuals. This is a dangerous formula for running an agency or serving a clientele and it often creates a "divide and conquer" strategy for companies that seek to manipulate an agency's views. A company that does not like an agency's "official" position on an educational or advocacy issue may whittle away at the position, one person at a time, sowing dissent and confusion.

The personnel of nonprofit agencies providing treatment information and advocacy services need to work as a team, providing consistent messages to constituents and uniform positions on advocacy matters. Every agency needs to create its own structure for processing information and taking positions. Accountability must be a part of that process. The agency, and only the agency, should decide how to communicate with the pharmaceutical and biotech industry. Both agency and industry must then respect and adhere to the chosen channels of communication.

Often an agency's interests in an advocacy issue and in grant-seeking can collide. An agency providing treatment information may find serious fault with the data or promotion of a given company's product, at the same that the agency is seeking funding from the same pharmaceutical or biotech company. Those working in advocacy or treatment information must be free to take positions without concern for how this might affect potential funding from a company. Companies must not be permitted to use funding as a way to leverage an agency's views on treatment or other issues. Agencies need to find a way to keep funding and advocacy/education on separate tracks. Industry must be willing to support agencies solely for the good and necessary work they do, and never as a reward for the positions they take regarding the company or its products.

Related Guidelines

- Agencies should establish clear and explicit lines of communication to govern all contact between their personnel and members of the pharmaceutical and biotech industry.
- Agencies should determine, in advance, who will attend meetings sponsored by pharmaceutical and biotech companies.
- Members of the pharmaceutical and biotech industry should proactively ask agencies to define their "rules of engagement" and should respect them without question.
- Whenever feasible, agencies should separate the channels of contact regarding financial/development matters and regarding educational or advocacy matters by assigning different personnel to each.
- Members of the pharmaceutical and biotech industry should support and mimic this process by assigning separate teams of people responsible for financial/development matters and others responsible for educational and advocacy matters.

Guiding Principle 3: Independence and Ownership

The goal of seeking funding from the pharmaceutical and biotech industry should be the same as that for funding from any other source: to help the agency fulfill its mission of service to the HIV-affected communities. The agency and the agency alone, under the auspices of its board, should determine what the agency does.

Unfortunately, funding sometimes comes with strings attached, no matter what the source. Government funding brings with it certain requirements and responsibilities and is seldom if ever directed at general support for the recipient agencies. Instead, government offers funding to meet needs that have been determined by government agencies, sometimes with the input of nonprofit agencies. Major foundation funding, likewise, is often directed toward specific, predetermined goals. The most difficult form of funding, and perhaps the most important to many agencies, is the kind of funding that permits the agency and its leadership, staff, and board to determine how the money will be used. The pharmaceutical and biotech industry has, in some instances, offered this type of funding, though only with considerable reluctance. Only the largest or most established agencies routinely have the ability to attract funding with virtually no strings attached. Nonetheless, the goal of independence and ownership of the services and programs of an agency remains a guiding principle for financial and funding relationships.

Since the advent in 1996 of highly effective combination therapy, industry funding largely has been directed at supporting programs that provide information about treatment or advocating the use of treatment – an area in which it has a strong vested interest. Although nonprofit agencies are seldom in a position to tell industry what it must fund, they often have the power to influence how industry will fund this particular area. Ideally, industry support is given in the form of an unrestricted educational grant. At the opposite extreme, industry itself sometimes supplies finished program content packages to agencies along with funding to support the delivery of the programs to the agency's constituents. This brings the risk that the funder's proprietary interests will be woven into the program content, perhaps in ways that are not transparent to the casual viewer. At the very least, such programs are unlikely to describe the comparative benefits of products from competing companies, or to acknowledge that for some people at certain stages in the course of HIV disease, no treatment at all may be as effective or more effective than the treatment.

The compromise between these extremes combine financial support from industry with varying degrees of technical support and oversight in the creation of educational programs. This supposedly balanced approach may be the most invasive of all, because it depends upon regular, intensive contact between industry and the participating agencies. In this context, it is all but impossible to avoid the influence of a wealthy and highly skilled major corporation. Thus, the integrity of the process depends almost entirely upon the intentions of the company.

The greatest trust in the quality and accuracy of information comes when community groups are able to develop and produce their own materials without outside interference. This must be the goal when seeking funding, and independence and community ownership must be the guiding principles in the development of materials and programs. The greater the influence of industry in the development of the programs or content of educational efforts, the greater the risk of conflict of interest, whether intended or merely permitted on a relatively unconscious level.

Related Guidelines

- Whenever possible, community agencies should seek support in the form of unrestricted grants or (second best) unrestricted educational grants, with little or no input by industry into program content.
- Avoid unsolicited offers of funding from members of the pharmaceutical and biotech industry in return for developing industry-determined programs.
- Avoid offers of support to distribute industry-created educational packages.[1]
- Before participating in industry-sponsored educational programs or permitting use of the agency's name on such programs, insist upon the right of rejection over program content.

CONCLUDING COMMENTS

These Guiding Principles and Related Guidelines represent an effort to establish an ideal relationship between community agencies and the pharmaceutical and biotech industry. Ideals cannot always be achieved, and it is likely that not every relationship can meet the standards defined here. Nonetheless, they can serve as goals and as standards for comparison in any situation. The more agencies insist upon such an ethical framework, the more likely industry will operate with the same concerns and values as the agencies they support.

The first two decades of the AIDS epidemic have launched a new era of relationships between the pharmaceutical industry and the patients it serves. For the most part, these relationships have been extraordinarily productive, bridging gaps that were once thought insurmountable. Yet as these relationships have evolved, building greater influence for the public on the companies, they have also created increasing opportunities for the companies to exert undue influence over the public. In the first decades of the AIDS epidemic, the passion and determination of activism prevented wide-scale abuse of the relationships. But as we move into the third decade, new voices not grounded in the lessons of the past inevitably will take over. It is our duty to codify, to whatever extent possible, the principles that have permitted us to maintain integrity in the balance of common and conflicting interests. It is the duty of a new generation to learn what came before them and to understand the delicately balanced tools of collaboration they are inheriting. The benefits of extensive consumer involvement in the drug development process can only be maintained if the public side of the relationship is able to maintain its independence. It is my hope that this chapter will contribute to that goal.

18

The Campaign Against Innovation

Sidney Taurel*

The issues I'll address in this chapter – basically, the tension between society's desire for better medicine and its aversion to higher healthcare costs – may be familiar. But I hope to offer an angle of view on these issues that may not be so familiar. I want you to look over my shoulder and see how the various choices in the policy environment affect the choices available to a CEO in my industry.

Let me start with a question: Do you believe we already have all the medical innovation we need? That may sound like a purely rhetorical question, but it's not. For one thing, there are some influential commentators who are on record as saying, in essence, "yes." If actions can be taken as answers, I have to assume that many policymakers, here and in other nations, must agree with that view.

The two most important preconditions for innovation in my industry are market-based pricing and intellectual property protection. But when I look at healthcare systems around the world, I see that policies that support innovation are dwindling, whereas policies that discourage it are proliferating. A third-party observer trying to make sense of this, without access to other data on the motives involved, might reasonably conclude that this amounts to a worldwide campaign against pharmaceutical innovation.

These measures are almost always advocated and adopted in the name of cost control. I don't really believe that there is some global conspiracy or even that the proponents of any single measure

* This chapter is adapted from a speech by the author to the American Enterprise Institute in Washington, D.C., on March 18, 2003.

actually intend to stop medical progress. Nonetheless, that may turn out to be their end effect. If these trends continue, especially here in the United States, we could see the collapse of true innovation in biomedicine.

Leaders in my industry have made this point before, but apparently we have not been able to make the case for it successfully. I want to attempt to make the case by sharing with you the business logic that anchors it. First, let me give you a very quick tour of what a company like Lilly faces as an innovation-driven business in a global pharmaceutical market.

The market restrictions that pharmaceutical companies face in Germany and Japan are unique only in their particulars. In general, they reflect a global pattern. Throughout Europe, the pharmaceutical industry labors under various kinds of price controls, of which the simplest and most onerous is a price set by government fiat. This is the practice in all of southern Europe, including France. Canada also has price controls. The United Kingdom substitutes profit controls for direct price controls and also has a number of mechanisms to restrict access and limit demand.

In the developing world, intellectual property protection is the burning issue. After years of slow, steady progress in improving intellectual property protection, the recent trade negotiations have put the whole patent system into jeopardy. Participants in the ongoing TRIPS (Trade-Related Aspects of Intellectual Property Rights) negotiations are now contemplating proposed revisions, which would essentially allow developing countries to abrogate pharmaceutical patents almost at will.

Despite the way this issue has been featured in the press, the drug companies are not worried about a poor country overriding patents to meet an internal public health emergency. The concern is over the potential to legalize intellectual property theft in places such as India and Brazil, where low-cost manufacturers would exploit wider latitude to produce knock-off drugs for export.

When all is said and done, there is only one market in the world that supports pharmaceutical innovation – the United States. We still speak of it as the "last free market," and indeed, though hardly "free" of government intervention, it is the one market where global innovators find the incentive they need to keep pushing the boundaries.

But those incentives are now threatened on a number of fronts, as various kinds of cost-control legislation find new proponents – notwithstanding Dr. Frank Lichtenberg's work showing that the benefits of new drugs greatly exceed their costs.[1] Congress has actually passed legislation to allow U.S. pharmacies to import U.S.-made drugs from Canadian wholesalers, essentially importing Canada's price controls as well. The only thing holding it back from implementation is FDA concerns about potential safety problems.

We see many states adopting a variety of price measures and access controls to reduce their Medicaid drug costs. In some cases, they are trying to extend Medicaid drug rebates to a larger segment of their population.

The debate over Medicare reform and especially over the addition of an outpatient drug benefit is in many ways a debate over a market-based model versus the current central planning approach, with its attendant price controls.

Finally, we have seen a variety of measures that would weaken intellectual property laws in the United States. A bill was passed in the Senate last year that would tilt the playing field heavily in favor of generic companies and very much against the research-oriented innovators.

Given the discouraging climate for innovation already established around the world, I believe that any of these more drastic proposals would, if implemented in the United States, lead to a "death spiral" in our ability to find and develop new treatments. When I make this point to elected officials, I realize that many don't believe me. Perhaps they hear it as a threat and think it's really a bluff. Perhaps they think it's just a gross exaggeration. Perhaps what they won't quite say out loud is roughly this: "Are you saying you'll stop doing R&D? You won't. That's what you do. You don't have any other business to be in."

It's true that we would not turn out the lights in our labs – we would continue to do some form of R&D – but it would be very different from what we are doing today. My key point is that, under a regime of weaker IP protection or harsher market controls, our R&D would no longer be able to deliver true innovation. To understand why, one needs to take a look inside the machinery of pharmaceutical innovation and understand the genesis of medical breakthroughs.

Major pharmaceutical companies are built upon and driven by blockbuster drugs. At this point, those are defined as products with sales of above a billion dollars a year. All the "Big Pharma" companies have some of these very big drugs anchoring their portfolios, and most have grown by developing or acquiring a series of them over the years.

Blockbusters tend to be highly innovative drugs, often breakthroughs. They are big because they represent the first or best treatment for a major medical need. At the same time, they are very elusive and very rare. No company has ever found a way to produce big, innovative drugs efficiently, economically, or even predictably. For all its technological sophistication, the business model centered on innovation is pretty primitive.

Think of a funnel, with the wide end representing the discovery stage and the narrow end representing the launch point of a new product. Thousands of compounds enter the top of the funnel and begin to undergo testing. A large percentage fail very early. More fail at each stage of development. But ultimately a few do make it through. The attrition statistics are well-known in the industry – for every 5,000 entering the top, one comes out the bottom. This is part of the reason why it costs $800 million to $1 billion to produce a new drug.

Of those that make it to market, not all are big drugs by any means. In fact, only one in three makes back its cost of development. So the true blockbusters are a fraction of the fraction that survive the journey. Yet these few throw off enough value to make the innovation model work. Among other benefits, they pay for all the failures, but also for the lesser innovation that occurs along the way. These discoveries may have smaller markets and thus represent a lower return to the companies. But they are critically important to those who suffer from these diseases, and, as long as we can continue to find some big new drugs, we can afford to bring these lesser ones to market as well. Most importantly, blockbusters finance the search for more breakthroughs, which makes our innovation engine run something like a breeder reactor, the nuclear energy system that produces fuel even as it consumes fuel. This is not simply a matter of having the resources to reload the top of the funnel. Rather, the key resources are those required to keep moving a "critical mass" of compounds through the R&D funnel. It's the "D" (development) that's rate limiting, not the "R" (research). This is a key to understanding where innovation comes from, so let me take it one layer deeper.

Think of the funnel again. Superimposed over the funnel of scientific attrition, there is an inverse funnel of cash outlays, a stream that gets wider and wider as the molecules move forward. It's well known that the greatest expense occurs in the third and final phase of clinical trials and so this is the part of the innovation process that most people associate with the capabilities of the big companies. But there is an earlier, less visible stage of development that really defines the engine room in the innovation machine.

This is the period between candidate selection, where one molecule is selected for further development from a "family" of kindred compounds, and the stage where a surviving drug candidate is tested for efficacy in patients, which is the beginning of Phase II clinical trials. In between, the candidate is tested for toxicity and for all sorts of other properties that determine whether it can be moved into human beings and, ultimately, commercialized as a marketable product.

The key thing about this part of drug development is that it combines high costs with high technological risk. Moving a compound from candidate selection through first human dose involves a lot of people putting in a lot of hours in many disciplines. By the time you reach the end of Phase I, you may have something like $100 million invested in that compound when you include the cost of all failures and the cost of capital. Yet 70 percent of the molecules that make it this far will never make it to market, and none of this work tells you what you most want to know – will it work?

But you have to be willing and able to place your bets, despite the uncertainty. The chances of succeeding are improved by having a lot of candidates to move forward. But that means proportionally greater expenditures. Unless you have one or more big drugs on the market to give you these resources, you cannot afford the risks that go with a sustained pursuit of innovation.

Incidentally, this explains why the vast majority of new drugs come from pharmaceutical companies and not from university or government labs. That claim has been advanced in several recent attacks on the industry, but it is simply not true. These scientists can do the early part of the "R," and in fact they do contribute a lot of new ideas for the top of the funnel. But they are simply not staffed, funded, or organized to do the "D." The capabilities really don't exist outside the industry. Even smaller pharmaceutical companies and most biotechs typically partner with the major companies to bring their molecules through the development process.

Obviously, this business of finding significant new pharmaceutical treatments is a very high-risk proposition. The only thing that induces people to put their money and their time and talent into it is the prospect of a return commensurate with the risks. Nobody, under any circumstances, is ever guaranteed that such a return will be achieved. But what guarantees that such a return is possible are the two key principles noted at the beginning of this chapter: intellectual property protection and market-based pricing.

The patent system gives inventors a period of exclusivity in which to try to get their return. Market-based pricing allows successful innovators actually to achieve the level of return their investors require. The question our policymakers need to ponder is what happens to biomedical research and development if those two principles are compromised to any significant degree? What changes in the model I've described, if we get price controls in "the last free market"? I believe pharmaceutical companies would focus first on how to survive and later on how to succeed in the new environment. The first thing they would likely do is to focus much more attention and resources on maximizing sales of existing products. That means much greater marketing expenditures to try to gain market share, and the only place that money can come from is the research budget.

As the importance of marketing grows, the number of marketers would shrink in an intense wave of consolidation. Many would have no choice but to combine operations and cut costs. But even relatively successful companies would see consolidation as a key strategy for gaining leverage to counter the greater power of the government buyers.

The net result would be that the industry's total R&D effort would shrink tremendously. Instead of twenty or so medium-to-large companies spending $30 billion a year on research, there might be four or five huge conglomerates spending half or one-quarter of that amount.

Furthermore, whatever the total amount spent on R&D, it would be allocated much differently than it is today. In the aftermath of new controls, companies would shift resources away from early stage R&D and focus them on developing new indications or line extensions for existing products and on trying to accelerate development of late-stage molecules. Those are the potential new products that you know the most about and that can come to market soonest. They may be the last new products you'll ever see, so you'd better get everything out of them you possibly can.

Over time, a number of other strategies would emerge to try to offset the lower potential returns by pursuing lower risk ventures. The likely dominant strategy would center on deliberate imitation and incremental improvements to existing products. The pharmaceutical market would become a world of "me-toos." There are already quite a few companies that haven't been successful at innovation and so already depend heavily on this kind of incrementalism. Ironically, they might actually have an advantage in the new world. To the extent that new research still continues, it will be very much more concentrated, in terms of disease targets, than it now is.

In the current innovation model, where blockbusters are so rare but so valuable, most companies will follow a promising lead even into a therapeutic territory where they have no presence. Over the last twenty years, in fact, 50 percent of pharmaceutical innovations have come in areas where the inventors had no prior experience. That exploration of the "white space" will disappear. Companies will try to leverage their existing knowledge base. What are physicians in this specialty really looking for? What are the critical success factors for a clinical trial in this class? Companies thus would stick closely to the therapeutic areas they know best.

Another very likely adaptation would be an effort to diversify beyond pharmaceuticals. To escape oppressive regulation, companies may move toward the over-the-counter market or nutritional supplements or any other similar opportunity for which consumers pay out of pocket.

It's hard to see where the industry might go in a new wave of diversification. But if marketing indeed turned out to be the key competency in the price-controlled environment, companies would probably try to leverage that skill in new areas of comparatively low risk, perhaps in areas such as home healthcare or nursing homes or other areas of healthcare delivery. Finally, we have to assume that, for some companies, none of these adaptations will work. They will fail and disappear.

Those most vulnerable in a price-controlled future would logically be those that, today, are most committed to innovation. The biotech industry, in particular, would see terrible attrition. It's no coincidence that 70 percent of the world's biotech capability is located in the United States. That concentration is directly tied to the potential for profits in the United States pharmaceutical industry. Take away that incentive and the investors will pull out and biotech will wither away.

That will only accelerate the downward spiral in innovation, because, collectively, biotech companies are a very important source of new ideas, new technology, and new molecules for the broader pharmaceutical industry. The cumulative impact of all these effects is not hard to see: the innovation engine runs out of fuel; true medical breakthroughs will be few and far between, if they come at all.

This scenario of the choices pharmaceutical companies might make in the face of price controls or patent erosion is what the economic logic suggests to me. But it is not merely hypothetical. There is plenty of empirical evidence from the experience of other nations and from our own experience in the United States suggesting that the pursuit of innovation would no longer be a choice.

France may be the "poster child" for the campaign against innovation. In the second half of the 1960s, French pharmaceutical companies matched U.S. firms in producing new drug substances – 92 for France, 93 for the United States. This was double the innovation output for German firms in the same period, which in turn was double the output of the United Kingdom. Over the next three decades, U.S. innovation continued to outpace all others. Production of new drugs held steady in the United Kingdom, declined sharply in Germany, and all but collapsed in France. In the five-year period from 1990 through 1994, U.S. firms produced 85 new drugs. French firms produced 14.

What are the forces behind such an extraordinary decline? A great part of the answer has to be the impact of price controls. The French system aims to force the lowest possible unit price for pharmaceuticals, and, in pursuit of this, it takes very deliberate aim at innovation. When a genuinely new product is approved, its price is set based, in part, on its expected sales volume. If the sales exceed expectations, the maker is required to cut the price to offset the incremental costs to the government. In other words, innovation is punished if it is successful.

Ultimately, the industry that has emerged in France is just what our hypothesis would predict. Their industry has seen huge consolidation over the last twenty years, as French companies have become less and less able to generate the innovation desired in the developed world. Two of the surviving companies have acquired the critical mass necessary to try to discover and develop drugs for the U.S. market. But the majority have concentrated on their home market and on exports to developing nations. They have fitted themselves to these markets by pursing a strategy of low-cost, minimal innovation, and heavy promotional spending.

Finally, this kind of reaction to the threat of controls, this flight from innovation, has happened before in the United States – twice, in fact. In the 1960s, in the aftermath of the notorious Kefauver hearings, we saw pharmaceutical companies rapidly diversifying into all sorts of business lines – agricultural chemicals, animal health products, cosmetics, medical devices, and diagnostics. That's how Lilly came to be, for a number of years, the owner of Elizabeth Arden cosmetics.

The same thing happened in the early 1990s in reaction to the Clinton administration's proposed healthcare reforms, which many thought would end market pricing in U.S. healthcare. There was a very rapid response within the industry. Internal R&D spending began to decelerate very rapidly. Industry investments in research had been increasing at more than 10 percent per year. All at once that rate fell to under 3 percent per year.

Wall Street had a similar response. Venture capital for biotech companies all but dried up. And investors bailed out of pharmaceutical stocks, wiping out billions of dollars of market capitalization in a very short span of time. In that climate, pharmaceutical companies were following the logic laid out here, shifting budgets to the late-stage pipeline and redirecting investment into other business lines.

In that period, Lilly and the other majors began to invest in things such as disease management and pharmaceutical benefits management and even entered the generics business. Because the threat arose and disappeared so quickly, we promptly shed these new branches and resumed our core pursuit of innovation. But there is no doubt in my mind that the industry would be forced down that same path if the incentives to innovate were dismantled by new legislation.

In short, pharmaceutical innovation for the entire world hinges on the policy choices of the American people and their elected representatives. The question we must ask as a society is – do we already have all the innovation we need? As healthcare costs continue to rise, as our society tries to cope with the retirement of 76 million baby boomers, there will be some voices willing to argue in the affirmative. For the other side, we must imagine the voices of all who suffer from illnesses we cannot yet defeat: the millions who suffer from heart failure, from Alzheimer's, from a dozen deadly cancers, from the complications of diabetes, and on and on. How do they vote?

The terrible irony of the campaign against innovation is that it is coming at precisely the moment in history when medicine is poised for a great leap forward. For all our amazing advances in the last 50 years, we are still working with the tools of the first pharmaceutical revolution. That is, we are still mostly using advanced chemistry to treat disease symptoms. In the new age we are now entering, we will increasingly use advanced biology to actually cure or even prevent disease from occurring.

The fruits of genomics and other new disciplines in biomedicine will clearly take some time, longer than we first thought, to transform therapeutics. But that transformation will come if we do not interdict it with short-sighted controls. To do that would forsake millions of sufferers and yet never deliver effective cost control. It would leave us stranded partway along the curve of progress – advanced enough to do some good at great cost but not enough to really begin to shrink the massive cost of disease.

We need to understand, once and for all, that innovation is not the problem. It is the solution.

19

Third World Perspectives on Global Pharmaceutical Access

James Thuo Gathii

INTRODUCTION

This chapter has two primary objectives.[1] First, it critically appraises the efficacy of the claim embraced in U.S. policy and by brand name pharmaceutical companies that poverty is by far the most critical barrier to affordable antiretrovirals in the third world. The chapter contextualizes the affordability of antiretovirals within a broader crucible of factors that include extremely strong legal protection of patents, lack of or slow third world government attention to the crisis, and economic programs that have greatly lowered funding for public health infrastructure.

Second, the chapter looks to the future, particularly with a view to assessing what lessons can be learned from missteps and policies in addressing the question of access to antiretrovirals. For example, the lowering of prices of patented antiretrovirals and the wider availability of generic antiretrovirals in the last five years have increased the number of people who have access to the drugs. Lower prices and increased access, though modest, undermine the claim that patents are *not* integral to lack of access to affordable antiretrovirals. Wider and broader access to antiretrovirals requires re-examining these and other assumptions that have been challenged by experience and whose revision is required to arrest the pandemic's already disastrous effect on the third world.

EXTREMELY STRONG LEGAL PROTECTION OF PATENTS PLAYS A ROLE IN LIMITING ACCESS TO ESSENTIAL MEDICINES

Strong patent protection is founded on the view that patents are private property rights that confer unconditional rights over inventions and discoveries. The basis of this strong patent protection view is that such a level of unimpeachable protection is a precondition or guarantee that patent holders, such as pharmaceutical companies, reap returns on their investments in research and development so that they have the incentive to continue investing in research and development for new drugs.[2] According to this view, any form of governmental control, including initiatives to make essential drugs affordable and accessible to indigent persons, is regarded as inconsistent with the unconditional rights of patentees in a way that would discourage investment in the development of new drugs. Strong patent protection is achieved not simply by protecting the property interest in the patent from any form of regulatory control, but also by means of a monopoly period of twenty years within which a patent holder is protected from the sale of the patented product by any competitiors.[3]

This view of strong patent protection undervalues the fact that the patent monopoly is granted to an inventor in return for the inventor producing a benefit to the society. In other words, patents have both a private as well as a public essence. To refer to patents only as a form of private property right is therefore to downplay the balance between the interests of the inventor and the public consuming the patented product contemplated in many national jurisdictions.[4] For example, the patent and copyright clause of the U.S. Constitution[5] embodies such a balance as interpreted by the Supreme Court. In *Brenner v. Manson*, the Supreme Court held that the "basic quid pro quo contemplated by the Constitution and the Congress for granting a patent monopoly is the benefit derived by the public from an invention with substantial utility."[6]

In the context of international intellectual property law, patents are protected as private property rights with a twenty-year monopoly and with several procedural safeguards protecting the patentee, but that protection is understood to serve public policy objectives such as the promotion of technological innovation in developing countries.

Patents, in essence, are understood to serve to the mutual advantages of both producers and users of technological knowledge, to promote social and economic welfare, and to balance rights and obligations.[7]

The Doha Declaration on TRIPS (Trade-Related Aspects of Intellectual Property Rights) and Public Health recognizes this dialectical character of patents in the following terms: "[W]e recognize that intellectual property protection is important for the development of new medicines. We also recognize the concerns about its effect on prices."[8] Further, the Declaration notes that members recognize that although the TRIPS Agreement confers flexibilities such as the freedom to establish their own regimes of international exhaustion and to engage in compulsory licensing, members are still required to maintain their "commitments in the TRIPS Agreement."[9] Hence, although the Declaration recognizes the importance of interpreting and construing the TRIPS Agreement in a manner that would allow countries to enable access to essential HIV/AIDS drugs through processes such as compulsory licensing, it nevertheless affirms the importance of patent protection. Professors Werhane and Gorman also embrace this balanced view in Chapter 15. This balance between the rights of patentees and those of consumers of pharmaceutical products is a far cry from the strong conception of patent protection argued to be embodied in the TRIPS Agreement by the United States and by brand-name pharmaceutical companies. Pharmaceutical companies and Western governments such as the United States, opposed to a dialectical understanding that would allow even extremely narrow exceptions to patent protection for essential drugs, have sought to disentangle the relationship between patents and high prices for such essential drugs by overstating the barriers posed by poverty in limiting access to HIV/AIDS drugs.[10] In this context, the world can rest reassured that the thousands who die of HIV/AIDS every day in sub-Saharan Africa are dying because they are poor, and not because they did not have access to expensive drugs.[11]

The United States, rather than directly defending the exclusivity of patents from regulatory controls to facilitate access to essential drugs, now emphasizes that poverty – not the high price of patented HIV/AIDS drugs – is the explanation for lack of access to these drugs in sub-Saharan Africa.[12] This position shifts the focus from pharmaceutical companies and Western governments and instead shines light on endemic poverty in developing countries. Implicit in this shift is the view that poverty, rather than access to essential drugs, accounts for the fact that less than 2 percent, or 30,000, of the more than 28.5 million Africans living with HIV/AIDS virus in 2001 have access to life-prolonging patented drugs.[13] This tactic also ensures that the United States is not defending the unpopular policy supporting the impregnability of patents as millions of people who need the drugs die every year.

PHARMACEUTICAL COMPANY PROFITS VERSUS
AIDS PATIENTS IN U.S. POLICY

The conclusion that the United States and major pharmaceutical companies would disfavor overriding patents to facilitate access to essential drugs is best demonstrated by the American response to South Africa regarding the protection of patent rights. In 1997, South Africa passed an amendment to its Medicines and Related Substances Act, authorizing the use of compulsory licensing and parallel importing to provide low-cost medications to South Africans in need.[14] Over 30 percent of the South African population is infected with HIV.[15] With the high mortality and morbidity rate, the enactment of this law signaled some willingness on the part of the government to begin laying a framework for facilitating access to antiretrovirals.[16] This amendment was never implemented as intended, in large part because the U.S. government and the multinational pharmaceutical industry opposed overriding patents to begin the process of enabling access to essential drugs in the world capital of the HIV/AIDS crisis.[17] Instead, the United States added South Africa to the infamous Section 301 watch list, under which countries that the U.S. Trade Representative (USTR) reports to have violated patents granted in the United States are subject to trade sanctions prior to a determination of violation under the TRIPS Agreement.[18] Section 301 authorizes the use of unilateral trade sanctions as a retaliatory measure by the United States. To illustrate further the U.S. support for a policy of strong patent protection even in cases of dire humanitarian need, an additional factor informing the USTR's citation of South Africa under Section 301 was South Africa's support of a proposal at the World Health Organization to add HIV/AIDS drugs to the WHO's essential medicines list.[19] The USTR report on South Africa also bore a striking resemblance to the February 16, 1999,

Pharmaceutical Research and Manufacturers Association (PhRMA) submission to the USTR urging the USTR to take action against South Africa for taking action inconsistent with the protection of U.S. intellectual property rights.[20]

Following these actions, the U.S.-South Africa binational panel, which then Vice President Al Gore and Deputy President Mbeki co-chaired, became the forum that produced a framework for resolving South Africa's listing by the USTR under Section 301.[21] As a result, and in light of his connections to the pharmaceutical industry, especially in terms of the funding of his 2000 presidential bid, Gore became a target for AIDS activists seeking to reform U.S. policy toward developing nations facing the HIV/AIDS pandemic.[22] As a result of the resulting media attention, U.S. Trade Representative Charlene Barshefsky announced on September 17, 1999, that an agreement was reached with South Africa that would lead to their removal from the Section 301 watch list.[23]

On December 1 of that same year, President Clinton announced that the United States would change its trade policies to support greater access to medications for developing nations facing an AIDS crisis.[24] In an Executive Order signed on May 10, 2000, President Clinton stated that the United States would not seek the revocation or revision of any intellectual property law in sub-Saharan African nations, so long as they promoted access to HIV/AIDS medication or treatments. This Executive Order, however, requires sub-Saharan African countries to provide adequate and effective intellectual property protection as a precondition for increasing access to HIV/AIDS drugs.[25] This condition reflects how the U.S. foreign policy of increasing access to antiretroviral drugs gives shelter to the priority of strong patent protection. On the one hand, there is a willingness to succumb to pressure and to acknowledge that patents do not trump public health. Conversely, there is continuity in insisting that any access to essential medicines should not compromise providing adequate and effective intellectual property protection.[26]

Lobbying the United States for Greater Empathy before President Bush's 2003 State of the Union Address

The tactics and efforts of activists to bring attention to the U.S. policy of strong patent protection and to the HIV/AIDS crisis have been similar under both the Clinton and Bush administrations. Thus, at the XIV International Aids Conference in Barcelona in 2002, the U.S. Health and Human Services Secretary Tommy Thompson was shouted down by pro-treatment/anti-U.S. activists who stormed the stage when he rose to address the conference.[27] The United States was also accused of misrepresenting and being "miserly" with its contributions to the Global Fund for AIDS, Tuberculosis and Malaria.[28] The amount the fund has raised so far is around $2.8 billion, well short of the stated $10 billion a year needed to bring AIDS under control.[29] The criticisms aimed at the United States are a result of the fact that it contributes less per capita than other leading industrialized countries, and it counts some bilateral assistance as contributions to the fund, thereby overstating U.S. support towards addressing the global HIV/AIDS pandemic.[30] In addition, the Global Fund is still far short of funds to make new grants until 2007.

2003: U.S. $15 Billion for Fighting HIV/AIDS

In his 2003 State of the Union address to Congress, President Bush announced an unprecedented initiative on the part of the United States to support the global effort to combat the HIV/AIDS pandemic. This $15 billion initiative was stated to provide AIDS drugs for 2 million people infected with the virus, care for 10 million AIDS patients and orphans, and provide education to prevent the epidemic from spreading further.[31] This widely applauded plan[32] eventually was approved by the Senate on May 16, 2003 when it voted to appropriate just over $3 billion in the first installment of this five-year initiative.[33] However, President Bush's 2004 budget only proposed to spend less than half of that amount in twelve African countries and two in the Caribbean.[34] The Bill as passed also required that a third of the money go to programs to promote abstinence until marriage,[35] although there is no empirical evidence that abstinence is more effective than condom use in preventing the spread of the pandemic or even of sexually transmitted diseases.

The Bush plan has also been criticized for compromising rather than working with the Global Fund to Fight AIDS, Tuberculosis and Malaria, which would have much more expeditiously disbursed it, and for introducing religious priorities that limit addressing transmission of HIV/AIDS through condom use.[36] Most important, the critics have observed that to the extent that the new initiative will buy drugs from brand name companies rather than encouraging cheaper generics, the expense will limit the number of people that it can benefit.[37] In 2004, the U.S. Congress tripled President Bush's request for the Global AIDS Fund after threatening to cut U.S. commitments to the Fund for the year 2005.[38] In the 2006 budget, President Bush proposes to cut spending on his global AIDS initiative from the Congressionally approved figure of $38 billion to $3.2 billion.[39] It is estimated that President Bush's pledge of $2.9 billion in 2007 will only meet 14 percent of the estimated cost of AIDS services needed.[40]

POVERTY – THE LATEST FAD IN THE UNITED STATES'S
POLICY OF STRATEGIC AMBIGUITY

The Discovery of Poverty: From the IIPE 2000 Study to the Gillespie-White/Attaran 2001 Paper

In line with its policy of strong patent protection, the latest explanation given by the United States for lack of access to HIV/AIDS drugs in sub-Saharan Africa is poverty.[41] In its initial submission to the TRIPS Council regarding a solution to paragraph 6 of the Doha Declaration on TRIPS and Public Health, the USTR relied on the 2001 World Health Organization's *Macroeconomics and Public Health* report to argue that poverty, rather than patents, was the major factor inhibiting access to "needed medicines at any price."[42] The premise of this position is that there is no necessary relationship between patents and access to patented antiretroviral drugs because millions of Africans with HIV/AIDS could not afford these drugs even if their prices were dramatically lowered.

The first soundings of the move to delink negligible access to essential drugs from strong patent protection came from the International Intellectual Property Institute (IIPI), a pro-intellectual-property think tank based in Washington, D.C., that was established in 1999.[43] In a report issued in 2000, IIPI examined the prevalence of the HIV/AIDS pandemic in Africa in the context of three other major considerations. First, it analyzed the response of the international community and, in particular, the levels of foreign assistance provided by Western countries such as the United States.[44] Second, it examined patent regimes across the African continent. Third, it examined the number of patented HIV/AIDS drugs in these countries.[45] The conclusions of this study seemed rather benign when compared to subsequent work that built upon this initial work. Unlike the initial work, the subsequent work concluded that poverty was a primary barrier.[46] Thus, in its 2000 report, the IIPS had concluded that access to essential drugs involves "numerous and complex issues, including healthcare infrastructure, international pricing mechanisms, financing, debt, tariffs and patents."[47]

In addition, the report specifically concluded that the TRIPS Agreement was "not an impediment to the distribution of HIV/AIDS pharmaceuticals" for at least three reasons. First, the TRIPS Agreement was not in force in "a majority of sub-Saharan Africa countries." Second, the TRIPS Agreement "permits sufficient flexibility for countries to avoid negative effects." Third, "most drug companies have not obtained patents widely in Africa."[48] Hence, rather than elevate poverty as the primary barrier to access of HIV/AIDS drugs, the report emphasized that the real issue "is that of adequate financing of the overall health system and the development of healthcare infrastructures." The report therefore remained open to further research to establish whether or not patents and the TRIPS Agreement played any role with regard to access to affordable drugs.[49]

Lee Gillespie-White, one of the contributors to the IIPI report, and Amir Attaran, affiliated with the Center for International Development and the Kennedy School of Government at Harvard, conducted a further survey relying on responses from drug companies.[50] Unlike the 2000 IIPI study, which examined a number of patented HIV/AIDS drugs alongside donor funding and availability of patent protections in sub-Saharan Africa, the Gillespie-White/Attaran study was much narrower, primarily focusing on the relationship between patents and access to drugs. Some of its conclusions coincided with those of the 2000 IIPE study. For example, the Gillespie-White/Attaran study confirmed that patent protection was not extensive in Africa.[51]

The Gillespie-White/Attaran study made several assumptions, particularly regarding the reliability of patent status data from patent holders and licensees, concluding that "pharmaceutical research and development will always require the incentive of patentability in poor countries ... [since] the entire African pharmaceutical market, at 1.1 percent is commercially negligible, as is the market share of antiretroviral drugs sold to the poorest of the third world."[52] The study argued that nonpatent barriers to access to antiretrovirals – including insufficient financing, lack of political will among countries, poor medical care and infrastructure, regulatory barriers, and high sales taxes and tariffs, among other inhibitions – were more important than patents in preventing access to antiretrovirals.

Perhaps this paper's most significant assumption was that the annual cost of a full regiment of antiretroviral treatment per patient, per year, is U.S. $1,200,[53] although they acknowledged that prices for some antiretroviral combinations range between $350 and $1,000 outside the United States.[54] This, the authors conclude, puts treatment out of reach for many of Africa's economies, the annual health budgets of which spend $8 or less per person. Hence, the authors' statement that "even if health budgets were radically expanded and all waste and corruption banished, Africa's impoverished economies could never afford more than a few percent of the cost of treatment and this is true even if antiretroviral drug prices continued to decline significantly, which is unlikely." Gillespie-White and Attaran therefore concluded that the "extreme dearth of international aid finance, rather than patents, is most to blame for the lack of antiretroviral treatment in Africa."[55]

Since the publication of the Gillespie-White/Attaran study, pharmaceutical companies,[56] press reports, and the USTR's office in particular[57] have much more loudly used the legitimacy given to poverty as a barrier to access to antiretrovirals to deflect the blame from patents.[58] A press report in a South African paper even went so far as to conclude that "[i]f developing country governments are serious about resolving the issue [of access to antiretrovirals], they should be encouraging greater protection of private property, the rule of law and other market-based reforms."[59] The Gillespie-White/Attaran paper's statements to that effect had the caveat that although patents might create market conditions "in which it could become lucrative to patent antiretroviral drugs more widely in future," even where patents do exist in sub-Saharan Africa, there is still a need for an infusion of foreign assistance based on the recognition that "countries ought to respect patent laws, but that patent holders reciprocally supply medicines to the global poor without profit, but also without loss."[60]

Limits of the Gillespie-White/Attaran Poverty Thesis

There are several limitations inherent in the Gillespie-White/Attaran thesis. First, the authors make a circular argument. For example, they find that patents are not a major issue inhibiting access to antiretrovirals because poverty is a more important factor. But, then, they take for granted that the cost of these drugs is an immovable baseline. Their argument implies that nothing can be done about the drug prices other than in terms of increasing donor assistance.[61] In essence, the goose that lays the golden eggs must be protected from governments seeking to override patent rights. Second, Gillespie-White and Attaran assume that the only "reciprocal" obligation pharmaceutical companies have towards poor countries is that of voluntarily reducing prices of expensive antiretrovirals, and no more.

I have several reservations regarding the aforementioned arguments and claims advanced by Attaran and Gillespie-White. First, recent research undertaken by the World Bank demonstrates that the WTO's new commitments, such as TRIPS, impose expensive implementation costs that undermine poverty reduction and growth, especially in the least developed countries.[62] To that extent, the links of barriers access to HIV/AIDS drugs to poverty, and to lack of donor support, must necessarily account for the fact that the very implementation of new regimes of intellectual property protection do not contribute positively toward the eradication of poverty, but rather serve to undermine antipoverty programs in these countries.

In addition, the Gillespie-White and Attaran assumption that the adoption of patent regimes to protect intellectual property would necessarily create market conditions under which access to antiretrovirals would be enhanced underestimates the fact that the economic programs that accompany such policy shifts also call for contractionary macroeconomic policies. These would reduce public spending on areas such as health and encourage the imposition of user fees.[63] For example, in its 1993 World Development Report entitled *Investing in Health*, the World Bank recommended that patients pay user fees for health, with the exception of a limited range of essential services.[64] The report does not acknowledge, however, that there was a "disastrous" resurgence of tuberculosis in China in direct and almost immediate response to the reintroduction of user fees for tuberculosis tests.[65] Evidence shows dramatic declines in hospital visits in countries undertaking these reforms, particularly for pre- and antenatal care, preventive tests, and infant deliveries.[66] In large-scale commercial farming areas, the introduction of user fees coincided with a 64 percent drop in patient registration at health clinics.[67] If such programs have the effect of discouraging the poor from taking preventive steps to avoid tuberculosis, clearly they would have a similar effect with HIV/AIDS, especially because it is associated with cultural and social stigma, more so than tuberculosis.[68]

Second, there is much that is unknown in countries that have only recently upgraded their intellectual property systems in conformity with the WTO's intellectual property rules. Specifically, it is difficult to establish with certainty whether there have been changes in activity patterns that affect prices of HIV/AIDS drugs, either upward or otherwise.[69] Such a determination would be critical because strong patent protection presumes the creation of market conditions that would encourage more research and development to make drugs more readily available. The difficulty of establishing such activity patterns is evidenced by the fact that the TRIPS Agreement is not yet formally binding in most of sub-Saharan Africa until 2005. It is premature to presume that the adoption of patent regimes would necessarily create market conditions under which antiretrovirals would be more readily available even before the TRIPS Agreement was actually implemented. Indeed, Attaran and Gillespie-White acknowledge that after 2005, patents will likely impede access to antiretroviral AIDS medications.[70]

In addition, recent research on retail-pricing patterns of patented antiretrovirals in East Africa shows that their actual availability, as opposed to access, varies greatly from country to country.[71] This, in and of itself, would make it hard for anyone to conclude, without additional verifiable evidence, that cost or poverty is a significant issue barring access to antiretrovirals, given that they are often not even available although patented. More importantly, though, where the drugs were available, there was a wide price divergence within the region for the same drug.[72] For example, for the same antiretroviral, there was a price divergence of 35 to 100 percent between the lowest and the highest price.[73] This seems rather odd because such differences cannot be attributed to variations in per capita income. Furthermore, the same study found that antiretrovials such as aciclovir and neverapine were twice as expensive in Kenya as in Norway,[74] and zidovudine was 35 percent more expensive in Tanzania than in Norway.[75] The conclusions of studies such as these should serve as a warning to those making definitive links between poverty and lack of access to drugs, for if pharmaceutical pricing is "about the law of the jungle," price levels, and not merely poverty, are key to access to these drugs. These disparities mean that a Tanzanian worker would have to earn 500 hours of wages to get a course of first-line tuberculosis treatment, compared with the one hour of wages necessary for a Swiss worker.[76] Needless to say, although poverty is not a static phenomenon, it seems foolhardy to argue that it is the major deterrent to access, drug pricing does not seem to reflect just the cost of research and development, but also ancillary and inflated costs that cannot be justified even under market conditions.[77]

Third, the premise that the cost of drugs or poverty is as big a factor inhibiting access to AIDS medications, as Gillespie-White and Attaran and their supporters claim, is frighteningly consistent with the non-responsiveness of Western countries towards humanitarian disasters in Africa. Indeed, the HIV/AIDS pandemic is not the first time that millions of Africans have died.[78] Over 30,000 people lost their lives daily during the genocide in Rwanda in the early 1990s as the world watched.[79] Today, 5,000 people die every day in the Democratic Republic of Congo and countless others throughout sub-Saharan Africa with little or no response from the West.[80] The world has learned to watch tragedy in Africa and do little or nothing about it. The contemporary case is Sudan, where thousands of Africans continue to be brutally displaced, killed, and raped by Arab militia, as a mute world, including the African Union, stands by. President Clinton's attempts at apologizing for doing little about the well-publicized genocide in Rwanda when he visited Kigali for only about an hour says a lot about what needs to change concerning U.S. foreign policy towards Africa generally, and the HIV/AIDS epidemic particularly. More than window-dressing and appearances is needed.[81]

Fourth, attempts by the Bush administration to address the HIV/AIDS epidemic in Africa primarily as an issue involving strategic security, state destabilization, and national economic distress removes the urgency of dealing with the egregious lack of access to healthcare and to AIDS drugs in sub-Saharan Africa. This is a human, and not simply a strategic foreign policy, issue. Even with the $15 billion five-year initiative launched by President Bush, only 2 million people in twelve African and two Caribbean countries (out of the more than 29 million in sub-Saharan Africa and the Caribbean in need of access to HIV/AIDS care and support, including drugs) will be serviced.[82] While this initiative was planned to benefit 2 million people, less than one-tenth of 1 percent of this number are benefiting from treatment.[83] Thus, contrary to President Bush's pledge, there has been no significant increase from the fewer than 30,000 people in sub-Saharan Africa who were estimated to be benefiting from antiretroviral drugs by the end of 2001.[84]

Happily, too, advances in access to care and drugs in resource-limited settings make it possible now more than ever to ensure that a larger number of Africans, who compose over 70 percent of those infected globally,[85] are reached.[86] The WHO's guidelines, seeking to have a three-in-one pill,[87] together with its treatment guidelines once such drugs are available, are based on an analogous experience in the United States, where the introduction of the triple therapy in 1996 led to a 70 percent decline in AIDS deaths.[88] New research and the hope of new drugs also continue to abate fears of drug resistance.[89]

In addition – and quite significantly contrary to the Gillespie-White and Attaran paper, which together with the Macroeconomics and Health report discussed below, are cited as the leading studies supporting the proposition that poverty is the largest barrier to access to AIDS drugs[90] – most of the drugs under patent in Africa are not "practical as first-line treatments" in most of sub-Saharan Africa because of the need for constant monitoring as well as cumbersome dietary requirements.[91] Furthermore, the AZT/3TC combination, which is the one of the "most practical and sought after" treatments, is patented in thirty-seven out of fifty-three countries, whereas nevirapine, a leading non-nucleoside used for preventing mother-to-child infection, is patented in twenty-five out of fifty-three countries.[92] In those countries, the Attaran and Gillespie-White study, when read against evidence of falling prices of generic triple therapies, only confirms the high correlation between patents for brand-name drugs and high prices. A more recent study also tends to confirm this.[93] If the cost of these drugs were to drop, African employers, particularly corporations, might be better able to buy them for their employees with HIV/AIDS.[94] In addition, more Africans, as well as governments on the continent, might extend coverage to more and more people because lower prices would stretch foreign assistance and corporate health programs further, since lower drug prices might mean that increased volumes of the drugs would be affordable.[95] Furthermore, the Attaran and Gillespie-White study did not anticipate the emergence of Triomune® a first-line triple combination therapy produced by the Indian company Cipla, which Doctors Without Borders has now demonstrated to be safe, effective, and simple to administer. Triomune® costs U.S. $20 a month in Cameroon, whereas a similar combination using brand name drugs costs U.S. $35.[96] In effect, a first line of treatment in Cameroon can cost $240 a year, indicating rather obviously the cost barriers that patents place on facilitating wider access to antiretrovirals.

The WHO's Commission on Macroeconomics and Health, which was chaired by economist Jeffrey Sachs, has also argued that the United States can do better by increasing foreign aid significantly to increase access to HIV/AIDS drugs among other public health goals in developing countries. The report observes that if the United States were to increase its foreign aid budget from its current levels of less than one-tenth of 1.1 percent of the U.S. GNP to two-tenths of 1 percent, an extra $10 billion would be available for disease control, primary school education, clean water, and other important needs in developing countries such as those of sub-Saharan Africa.[97] The report in essence notes that a tiny share of rich-country income would translate into 8 million lives saved each year in poor countries.[98] Should the United States have the political will to raise its foreign aid budget by such an amount, this would in turn become a significant bargaining advantage with the European Union and Japan to direct even more money toward this end. As U.N. Secretary General Kofi Annan has suggested, the Global AIDS Fund would need $7 billion a year from the United States to be effective.[99] It seems that such a goal is clearly within the reach of the international community with proper leadership from the United States.[100] The U.S. initiative pledging $15 billion over five years is a big first step in that direction. Although this is a significant pledge as Jeffrey Sachs noted in response to the initiative, it is by no means enough to win the battle against HIV/AIDS.[101]

CONCLUSIONS

By beating the drum of poverty, pharmaceutical companies and Western governments, such as the United States – that are opposed to making exceptions to patent protection to facilitate access to HIV/AIDS drugs to indigent populations, while arguing that this is consistent with the provisions of the TRIPS Agreement – have sought to marginalize the access issue by suggesting that solutions lie largely outside the patent regime. In this context, the world can rest reassured that the thousands who die of HIV/AIDS every day in sub-Saharan Africa are dying because they are poor, not because they did not have access to drugs. Yet it is clear that the policy of strong patent protection prevents widespread access to antiretroviral drugs to treat HIV/AIDS.

Although all the members of the WTO unanimously acceded to the passage of the Doha Declaration on TRIPS and Public Health,[102] which recognized that the TRIPS Agreement envisions a balance between the rights and interests of consumers and producers of intellectual property rights, there has yet to be even one instance of a country in Africa using this flexibility to facilitate access to affordable antiretrovirals, such as through compulsory licensing. This seems to suggest strongly that the United States's view of strong patent protection, supported by many TRIPS-plus sanctions such as Section 301, has transformed pharmaceutical patents into impregnable private property rights. That strong patent protection, therefore, seems to enjoy unassailable persistence, even in the face of one of the most serious public health crises in historical memory, in my view, reflects a lopsidedness favoring pharmaceutical profits over the lives of millions of Africans unnecessarily dying without dignity. In addition, the United States was a critical objector to expanding compulsory licensing at the World Trade Organization toward the end of 2004. A compromise, known as the "Motta text,"[103] was developed, but it contained restrictions on the importation and exportation of generic drugs that were as burdensome as Article 31 of the TRIPS Agreement, which it was intended to moderate. These burdensome requirements resulted in what authors Jawara and Kwa called a "cosmetic" and "painful two-year exercise" to make the United States "appear sympathetic towards development and deflect international criticism, while in reality protecting its own commercial interests."[104]

The variety of ways in which patents have been removed from the equation of access to essential medicines reflects not only the asymmetrical nature of power in international relations, but also the structural power of strong patent protection over the most vulnerable populations of the global economy. The discourse of charity and humanitarianism accompanying the uncompromising support for patents at any cost simply disguises the American priorities in ensuring that multinational pharmaceutical companies acquire markets for their drugs without any threat to their profitability, even in the face of heart-wrenching human need.

It is precisely because of the needs of the millions without access to drugs that the following lessons from the missteps and policies of the past addressed above must become part of future policy deliberations. First, the lowering of prices of patented antiretrovirals in the last five years has increased the number of people with access to the drugs and this has happened without any threat to patent protection or returns to research and development. These lower prices and increased access, though modest, undermine the claim that patents are *not* integral to lack of access to affordable antiretrovirals. Indeed, this wider and broader access to antiretrovirals calls for a re-examination of other assumptions that have been challenged by experience. These assumptions must be revised in order to arrest the pandemic's already disastrous effect on the third world. Second, the potential behind reinterpretating the provisions of the TRIPS Agreement on patent protection and the $15 billion pledge by the Bush administration in 2003 to combat the global HIV/AIDS pandemic suggest that political will can overcome virtually any barrier to access to essential drugs. Yet we must always be vigilant to ensure that the implementation of donor pledges has the most impact on the ground possible, not only because such support is contingent on annual appropriations, but also because the balance between prevention and access to antiretrovirals remains a thorny issue. Finally, it must be acknowledged that although many developing country governments are now much more vigorously involved and committed to addressing the pandemic, the economic programs that Western multilateral and bilateral donors require them to implement often result in reductions in public spending on health. As such, any HIV/AIDS policy, to be truly effective, must be comprehensive in examining the multitude of factors affecting and influencing access to essential drugs.

20

The Promise of Vaccines and the Influenza Vaccine Shortage of 2004

Public and Private Partnerships

Gary R. Noble

INFLUENZA VACCINES

The shortage of influenza virus vaccine in the United States in late 2004 illustrates the major challenges that the United States faces in consistently providing reliable supplies of vaccines. The lack of a reliable market and a return on investment left only two manufacturers of inactivated influenza vaccine in the United States. The loss of vaccine supply from one of these manufacturers created a severe shortage of vaccine, with the result that many individuals considered to be at increased risk of complications from influenza infection could not obtain vaccination. (Although the recent introduction of an attenuated live influenza virus vaccine administered intranasally has added a third supplier in the United States, this vaccine has been approved for use only in otherwise healthy individuals between the ages of five and fifty years.[1] However, these age groups are not those at highest risk of complications from influenza virus infections.[2])

Millions of unused influenza vaccine doses are discarded over the years due to the vagaries of influenza epidemic severity and vaccine usage, as well as the complexities of vaccine production and the fact that the new vaccines produced each year must contain the most contemporary variants of the three strains of influenza expected to cause illness in the next influenza season.[3,4] Although vaccine liability concerns add additional uncertainty for manufacturers of vaccines, the National Vaccine Injury Compensation Program (VICP) has greatly reduced the liability risks for these manufacturers.[5]

The tenuous supply of influenza vaccines in the United States also reflects, to some extent, the complexity of the influenza virus vaccine strain selection and development process and the need to reformulate the vaccine each year. The process requires ongoing worldwide virus surveillance and strain characterization coordinated by a network of worldwide WHO Collaborating Centers for Influenza. This information is used in early winter each year to predict the direction that influenza viral antigenic variation is expected to take in the following ten to fourteen months. The vaccine manufacturers must then begin the time-consuming adaptation of the three strains of influenza virus to high-yield growth in fertilized (embryonated) hens' eggs, virus production, purification, testing, preparation, and approval by the FDA before initial distribution of the vaccine product.[6]

The shortage of influenza vaccine in the United States has raised again the question of how the supply of vaccine can be made more reliable while also ensuring some profitability for the suppliers of influenza vaccine. Incentives under consideration include increased annual purchase of vaccine by the government and increased tax incentives for the vaccine producers.[7] However, the political will to find such solutions may be difficult. Congressional approval for consistent purchase of vaccines is likely to be a slow and uncertain process.[8] Nonetheless, the federal government has stepped in this year to add to its usual purchase of influenza vaccine by obtaining small volumes of influenza vaccine from other countries, pending satisfactory review of the vaccine's safety by the FDA, as well as other initiatives.[9]

Future demand for influenza vaccine could be intense, if a major new variant of influenza virus were to infect the human population.[10] Scientists and public health officials have argued for many years that a reoccurrence of an influenza pandemic, similar to the 1918–19 "swine flu" pandemic that killed somewhere between 40 and perhaps 100 million people in the world, is a very real possibility.[11–13] The population would be largely susceptible, because most individuals would not be likely to have any substantial immunity to such strains of influenza virus as a result of prior vaccination or natural infection.

Improved methods for influenza vaccine delivery are also being considered,[14] as well as possibly more rapid vaccine production methods using tissue culture rather than embryonated hens' eggs.[15,16]

Antiviral drugs for treatment of patients with influenza infection are also available, and can be useful when infection occurs in the absence of immunity induced by vaccination. Here again, the pharmaceutical industry has an important role in producing treatments when primary prevention is either not available, has not been widely utilized, or is not completely effective.[17]

Clearly, there is much to occupy academic, federal, and industry scientists and administrators in collaborative efforts for years to come, if the United States and the global community are to be prepared to develop, produce, and make available the vaccines and treatments that will be needed for infectious agents known and yet unknown.[18]

Dr. Anthony Fauci, Director of the National Institute of Allergy and Infectious Diseases, NIH, has reviewed some of the emerging infectious diseases facing the world and has commented, "Fortunately, clinicians now have an ever-growing toolbox of sophisticated technologies and strategies at their disposal. These will help detect, prevent, treat, and respond to new and old infectious agents as they emerge, whether by an act of nature or by deliberate design."[19] Dr. Fauci continues by noting that the challenge is to "... rapidly develop new technologies and strategies to help in the detection, prevention, treatment, and containment of new infections."

Recognizing that vaccines are the most effective method for the prevention of disease, Dr. Fauci also comments, "Scores of vaccine candidates are now in the pipeline to prevent infection by emerging microbes such as HIV, Ebola, West Nile virus, dengue virus, H5N1 avian influenza virus, and the virus that causes severe acute respiratory syndrome (SARS). The first new tuberculosis vaccines in sixty years recently entered clinical trials, and vaccines against the most menacing bioterrorist threats are being developed."

Even hepatitis B virus infections, which have been a major source of chronic liver disease and liver cancer, can be prevented with hepatitis B virus vaccine. Cancer of the liver caused by hepatitis B virus infections has been a significant problem among some populations, such as the Inuit (Eskimos) and Chinese. Thus, hepatitis B virus vaccine has proven to be a first effective vaccine against cancer. A second vaccine to prevent cancer may be possible, with reports of successful early trials of a Merck vaccine against some strains of human papilloma viruses (HPV) that cause much of the cervical cancer of women.[20]

IMPACT OF VACCINES FOR CHILDREN AND ADULTS

Vaccines against infectious diseases of children and adults are among the many powerful tools for primary prevention of illness and death.[21] The remarkable success of smallpox eradication demonstrates just how effective vaccination can be, when the contributions of scientists, the private pharmaceutical sector, international bodies and governments at national and local levels are brought together with large numbers of volunteers.[22,23]

Vaccines have also brought much benefit to the children of the world, although the gap in vaccination coverage globally remains far too large. Vaccination against polio has rendered this scourge of earlier generations a forgotten problem for many children and parents of the world. However, the threat of polio has not entirely disappeared, because it remains endemic in six countries, primarily as a result of interruptions in vaccination programs caused by lack of adequate government resources and commitment, public education, armed conflicts, and cultural barriers. Thus, while polio virus remains in circulation anywhere in the world, there is a potential for spread back into countries where polio vaccinations are incomplete.[24] There is great hope that polio can become the first disease to be eradicated from the face of the earth in the twenty-first century, but great effort is required by individuals and organizations from many sectors of the global community to achieve that goal.

Vaccines have made remarkable changes in the occurrence of serious childhood viral infections in the United States. Pertussis (whooping cough), measles, rubella, chicken pox, to name a few childhood diseases, occur rarely among the youth of the United States today. (See Table 20.1.)

However, an adequate, reliable supply of vaccines in the United States has been of concern for many years.[25] A report in 2003 from the Institute of Medicine (IOM) stated that "...recent shortages of vaccines have highlighted the fragility of vaccine supply. Currently, public funds pay for more than half of all childhood vaccine purchases in the United States. Government purchasing policies have sought to limit expenditures and decrease the cost of vaccines. Companies face declining financial incentives to develop and produce vaccines, and the number of producers of recommended vaccines for the United States

Table 20.1. *Comparison of Twentieth-Century Annual Morbidity and Current Morbidity for Vaccine-Preventable Diseases in the United States*

Disease	Twentieth Century Annual Morbidity[1]	2003[2]	Percent Decrease
Smallpox	48,164	0	100
Diphtheria	175,885	1	99.99
Measles	503,282	56	99.99
Mumps	152,209	231	99.85*
Pertussis	147,271	11,647	92.09
Polio (paralytic)	16,316	0	100*
Rubella	47,745	7	99.99*
Congenital rubella Syndrome	823	1	99.88
Tetanus	1,314	20	98.47*
H. influenzae, type b and unknown (<5 yrs)	20,000	259	98.71

Source: Walter A. Orenstein, M.D., Director, Emory Vaccine Policy and Development and Associate Director, Emory Vaccine Center; former Director, National Immunization Program, Centers for Disease Control and Prevention

[1] *Source:* CDC. *MMWR* 1999. 48 (12): 242–264

[2] *Source: MMWR* January 9, 2004. 52, No 53 (provisional data); final data provided by B. Sirotkin, CDC, via email 9/3/04

* Record lows

market has declined from more than twenty-five, thirty years ago, to only five today."

"In order to sustain the achievements of the national immunization system to date and enhance the development of vaccines against new diseases for the future, the national immunization system must balance the need for better access to recommended vaccines with enhanced incentives for investment in vaccine development and production."[26]

This IOM report clearly lays out the major achievements of vaccinations in reducing disease and death caused by the eleven common childhood diseases, as well as providing "important protection across the lifespan, from infancy to death." It also details the challenges of maintaining the important private–public sector partnership that will enable the continued production of vaccines.[27]

HIV VACCINE

Of all the vaccines that could contribute to the future health of the world, a vaccine to prevent HIV infection is near the top of any list.

The worldwide HIV pandemic starkly challenges multiple segments of the world's health community, from the pharmaceutical industry to national and international governments, nongovernmental agencies, and the scientific community. Because the burden of HIV disease now is concentrated so heavily in the least developed countries, the approach to prevention and treatment requires a broad coalition of responders. An impressive group of leading scientists has called for a global HIV vaccine enterprise, commenting that "Commercial, academic, and research institutes must work together to solve the scientific challenge."[28] These authors also argue that one of the features critical to success includes "collaborative arrangements with the private sector and/or the vaccine development centers (VDCs)." They observe that sufficient resources are not currently available, and some of the needed disciplines are "largely found in the private sector."

The incentives and barriers to commercial development and production of HIV vaccines are critically evaluated by Kremer and Snyder[29] and the International AIDS Vaccine Initiative (IAVI).[30] The IAVI Policy Brief points out that "Private investment in R&D for an AIDS vaccine remains seriously inadequate – IAVI estimates that less than 20 percent of the $646 million spent on vaccine R&D in 2002 came from private sources...." They go on to question, "What can be done to stimulate the private sector to discover, develop, and manufacture an AIDS vaccine, so that scientific and financial risks are reduced and the expected financial returns can be brought more into line with the very large health and social benefits of a vaccine that prevents HIV infection, illness, and death?"

A critical evaluation of "push" and "pull" financial mechanisms is outlined in the IAVI Policy Brief, recognizing that, although private sector expertise and capacity are critical to progress in this arena, the large costs and relatively small and uncertain profits of vaccine development and production are a large impediment to the private sector's major investment, unless mechanisms to lessen these risks are addressed.

An effective HIV vaccine could provide a most powerful tool for primary prevention of HIV infection, when compared with other primary prevention tools that require behavior modification, that is, sexual abstinence or mutually faithful monogamy and elimination of risky injections of illicit drugs. The scientific and financial challenges for successful development of an HIV vaccine, however, remain formidable. A collaborative effort is essential if success is to be achieved.

PARTNERSHIPS AND THE ROAD AHEAD

People work hard for rewards, be they monetary, recognition by peers and society, or the rewards of doing something good for others. Without the opportunity for fair rewards for hard work, incentives disappear and productivity declines, as attempts at total government management of the workplace have demonstrated throughout history.[31]

Thus, the challenge is to find the best balance between what are fair rewards for the hard work of individuals and companies, and the needs of society. Professor Santoro and other authors have stated this very lucidly elsewhere. Clearly, willingness to listen to – and understand – the arguments of different points of view must prevail if progress is to be made.

Availability and access to the tools and resources that increase health and quality of life in the less developed world remain great challenges. However, poverty, armed conflicts, and corruption are among the most basic and difficult barriers to better health in many countries.[32,33] Despite the barriers, many examples of collaborative success do exist. These examples include the program to treat river blindness, involving dozens of organizations and the donation of Mectizan® by Merck, which is a model for collaborative approaches to tackling other diseases in the less developed world.[34] Dr. Bill Foege also describes this and other successful partnerships in his contribution to this book.

Many other examples exist, such as the program to provide treatment for HIV/AIDS in Botswana, led by the Merck Foundation, the Bill and Melinda Gates Foundation, and the national government of Botswana;[35] the treatment and training center for care of people with HIV/AIDS in Kampala, created with substantial funding by Pfizer in collaboration with the government of Uganda and dedicated in October 2004;[36,37] the trachoma elimination initiative coordinated by the Edna McConnell Clark Foundation with support largely funded by Pfizer;[38] and many other collaborative programs supported by pharmaceutical companies.[39]

As other authors have argued so well, collaboration, a partnership, a dialogue must be developed and maintained that allows these competing interests and needs to be satisfied in a way that can be sustained for the long term. This system should stimulate and reward innovation and also ensure maximum product safety, efficiency of oversight regulation, and the effective delivery and access to services and goods for the greatest number of those in need.[40]

But such an initiative, to be effective, requires a more fundamental understanding and appreciation of what motivates these systems to be most efficient and productive. A system that is overly bureaucratic and regulated, a system that stifles incentives for risky investments and limits competitive rewards for those willing to make the risky investments, will be less efficient and less productive in the long run.

The causes of tension between the pharmaceutical industry and society described in the introduction to this book are also operative in the relationships between the pharmaceutical industry and those working in the public health community. We must foster an active partnership that will enhance and promote successful outcomes for all participants, including those who are in need and those who are in a position to effect positive change. This will require patience and a much greater understanding than now exists on the part of many participants in the heated debates about how to create greater access, availability, and affordability of products for the diagnosis, prevention, and treatment of diseases.

There has been criticism that the pharmaceutical industry takes advantage of the intellectual capital funded by the taxpayers of the country. The costliest part of bringing products to market, however, lies in the ever-expanding size and complexity of the clinical studies required to demonstrate whether or not products are safe and effective, followed by costly production through a highly regulated environment. Rare side effects may be exceedingly difficult to recognize, although postmarketing monitoring and reporting of adverse events and careful scrutiny of these are essential.[41,42]

Thus, partnerships remain vital to the research, development, and production linkages that lead to marketed tools for the prevention and treatment of diseases. The government sector rarely has a mandate, nor has it developed the capacity or expertise, for any large-scale development and production of products for diagnosis, treatment, or prevention of disease. Thus, collaboration with the private sector is almost always necessary to see that discoveries in the public sector eventually become FDA-approved, marketable products. However, agencies such as the CDC, NIH, and the U.S. Department of Defense, also working in collaboration with the private sector, do play a key role in developing diagnostic and even treatment tools for some of the most exotic and dangerous diseases, such as anthrax, severe acute respiratory syndrome (SARS), and Ebola-Marburg African hemorrhagic fevers.[43]

In conclusion, the world is becoming a better healthier place to live for many, and it can be much better with collaboration between public and private sectors of the world, working with international agencies, foundations, nonprofit organizations, and private citizens to make the most of the creative, innovative, openly competitive entrepreneurial energies that combine to improve the health of all. Each sector of society and each individual with a potential to effect change for better health has an important role and responsibility.

PART IV

CONCLUDING THOUGHTS

Charting a Sustainable Path for the Twenty-First Century

Introduction to Part IV

Michael A. Santoro

The goals of this book have been to understand the factors behind the growing tension in the relationship between the pharmaceutical industry and society and to chart a sustainable path for that relationship in the twenty-first century. The extraordinary authors assembled in this volume have gone a long way toward achieving these goals. The insights and recommendations offered by these authors have been diverse, multifaceted, and far-reaching, and it would do them an injustice to attempt to summarize them pithily. Nevertheless, it is possible to discern a few basic themes. The chapters in this final section underscore these themes and point out paths to a sustainable future for the industry.

PUBLIC HEALTH AND PRIVATE ENTERPRISE: AN IMPERFECT MATCH

One theme that has emerged is that the tensions between the industry and society derive from real conflicts that are endemic to the free market economic system and the current regulatory environment. Many of the authors have in one manner or other made the case that the interests of the pharmaceutical industry and society are imperfectly aligned. What is good for the bottom line of the drug companies is not always good for society. In this volume we have seen numerous examples of this divergence, such as research agendas that are guided by market size rather than medical need; marketing practices and objectives that emphasize increasing sales without regard for the medical priority of conditions treated; and monopolistic pricing policies that maximize revenue at the explicit cost of broad access.

363

One aspect of this divergence of private and public interests concerns the very idea of intellectual property rights. On one side, some authors such as Gathii and Werhane and Gorman have argued for according weak protection to intellectual property rights in order to fulfill the rights of patients in third world countries to AIDS medications. On the other side, Weldon and Taurel have argued with equal conviction that strong intellectual property protection is needed to provide sufficient incentives for innovation. In his chapter, Nien-hê Hsieh, a business ethicist and economist who teaches at Wharton Business School, considers these arguments and asks whether the demands being placed on the pharmaceutical industry are compatible with the idea of private property. In Hsieh's account, bridging the gap between public and private interest need not mean the erosion of private property rights. Indeed he sees danger in weakening property rights, particularly with respect to meeting future health crises beyond AIDS. Hsieh argues, conversely, that even under strong property rights assumptions pharmaceutical companies have a "duty of rescue" to provide AIDS medications to citizens of third world countries.

Not every success for industry is a thorn to society. In many respects a prosperous industry creates corresponding public health benefits. A number of authors in this volume have reminded us, for example, that the pharmaceutical industry has discovered and developed important drugs that can reduce expensive hospital admissions and expenditures; that advertising can create public awareness about underappreciated medical conditions; and that the patent system has made possible a flow of life-saving and life-enhancing drugs, not the least of which are those which have been developed to combat the scourge of AIDS. The fact remains, however, that in a system that relies so heavily on private enterprises to serve public health needs, there will always be significant misalignment of interests. From a public policy perspective, therefore, the task is somehow to enable the creative forces unleashed by the private sector to flourish while devising strategies for closing the inevitable gap between public and private interest. Many of the authors in this book have offered suggestions to accomplish precisely this goal.

A focus on the problems caused by the systemic misalignment of public and private goals offers a surer path to progress than the manner in which many critics have characterized the tension between industry and society. Consider the titles and subtitles of some recent books about the pharmaceutical industry – *On the Take*; *How They Deceive Us*; and *The Big Fix*. All of these titles imply that the source of the problem lies in the venality and moral turpitude of pharmaceutical executives. There indeed are many examples of failed morals and lapsed integrity among drug companies and their executives. The authors in this volume, however, have pushed us to look deeper into the systemic reasons that separate public from private interest. We have learned that even honest executives pursuing legal ends will find themselves at odds with the public interest. This is a simple, but profoundly important insight. It leads us to understand that the most progressive way to bridge the gap between public and private interest is not to point fingers at presumably corrupt individuals whose morals need to be reformed. Instead, progress will come from changing the business environment and the regulation system so that the public good is better served.

PROFESSIONALIZING THE PHARMACEUTICAL INDUSTRY

One potential way to change the existing business environment is through industry self-regulation. Industry advocates and lobbyists would do well to heed the emphasis that the authors place on the divergence of public and private interest. Too often industry defenders and apologists have adopted a myopic view of public criticism. They presume too much about the public benefits of private profits. They have tended to view the problem as one of perception and bad press instead of a fundamental one that requires mutual understanding and compromise. The industry as a whole has adopted a defensive and often arrogant posture. Far too many industry advocates arrogantly assert that the problem of public perception is due to the ignorance of the public: "If only they understood all the good things we do. If only the press would not emphasize the negative. If only we could make everyone understand how important patents and innovation are. The problem is that we are just misunderstood." The authors in this volume, including the CEOs of two major pharmaceutical companies, have issued a bold challenge to such solipsistic and self-satisfied thinking. The pharmaceutical industry has much to contribute to the public health and it has a social responsibility to do so. Only by embracing this goal and acknowledging that it has a long way to go toward achieving it can industry work itself out of the low public esteem that it currently suffers.

So what is the socially sustainable path for the pharmaceutical industry in the twenty-first century? First, it must be said that on a number of issues the industry needs to get its own house in order or else the government is going to get it in order for them. Two obvious areas where there is much work to be done are in DTCA and the truthful and timely disclosure of unfavorable clinical trial results. As we have seen in this volume, in both of these areas current practices fall significantly short of what the public interest demands.

Many have questioned the friendly relationship between industry and the FDA and have called for stricter and broader regulatory oversight.[1] Unless industry boldly undertakes significant self-regulatory steps, the pressure for stronger and more comprehensive governmental regulation will be over time impossible to resist. One effective way to achieve this objective is through an overhaul and strategic reform of the industry's principal membership organization. The Pharmaceutical Manufacturers Association of America (PhRMA) has over time developed into a powerful lobbying organization. It has helped to deliver many tactical successes for its members, but its heavy-handed and aggressive style has served to reinforce the public's perception that the pharmaceutical industry exercises excessive power over the political system at the expense of the public good.

PhRMA can make a valuable contribution to recapturing respect for the pharmaceutical industry by transforming itself from a purely lobbying organization into a professional organization that maintains standards of conduct among its members. What would this entail? A small but important step was taken with PhRMA's adoption in 2002 of a voluntary code of conduct governing contacts with physicians and other healthcare professionals. This was followed in 2005 by a proposed code to govern DTCA. In addition to promulgating such standards, the industry needs to put some teeth in its self-regulatory efforts. Unfortunately, thus far voluntary efforts such as the promises of pharmaceutical companies to provide public information about clinical trials have fallen far short of expectations.[2] Adherence to these voluntary codes, therefore, should be monitored and over time should become mandatory for members.[3] This is, to be sure, a significant departure from the current pure advocacy mission of PhRMA. The transformation is necessary, however, because the public is judging the industry according to the least common denominator of behavior and PhRMA or some organization needs to take steps to rein in those companies that tarnish the reputation of the entire industry.

If PhRMA can somehow transform itself from a typical Washington lobbying association into a credible *professional* association that looks out for the public interest in addition to the interests of its members, it can help the industry as a whole to regain some of its credibility. If PhRMA is not able to evolve in this manner or if it adopts transparently cosmetic and superficial efforts at self-regulation, then the industry's credibility as a whole will continue to suffer and stronger and broader government regulation will become necessary to bridge the current gulf between public and private interests.

TACKLING MEDICAL NEEDS THROUGH MULTI-STAKEHOLDER COOPERATION AND PARTNERSHIPS

Another theme that emerges in this volume is the need for the pharmaceutical industry to increase dialogue and cooperation with various stakeholder groups. A number of authors, including those from within the industry, emphasize that to repair their relationship with society, drug companies must learn to see advocacy groups, the medical and scientific community, governments, NGOs, and international institutions as essential partners in developing useful drugs to solve medical problems that often have social and transnational implications.

The virtue of such partnerships is that they draw upon the insights, talents, and resources of diverse groups. In his chapter, William Foege, a physician who has been the head of the Centers for Disease Control and Prevention and who is currently the Medical Director of the Bill and Melinda Gates Foundation, reflects upon a distinguished career at the epicenter of global public health problems. He points to a future where the most pressing public health problems can be solved through cooperative ventures among private and public actors. In a wonderful formulation that serves as a fitting capstone for this volume he notes that "leadership is no longer the result of someone having a title, but rather leadership goes to the person who develops an effective coalition."

In his chapter, Tom Gorrie, a co-editor of this volume, also takes up the theme of cooperation. As the Corporate Vice President in charge of global public affairs for Johnson & Johnson, Gorrie describes how in his career he has worked with diverse constituencies to fashion solutions to healthcare problems. Gorrie offers some pointed recommendations for how such partnerships can work most effectively to serve public needs. Gorrie, Foege, and other authors all point to a future where industry works in partnership with governments, NGOs, patient groups, the medical community, and other stakeholders to meet the world's healthcare needs.

Ultimately, the pharmaceutical industry needs to understand that its own survival and well-being depend on the survival and well-being of the patients it serves. This is a truth that the industry's founders such as George W. Merck understood perfectly well, but that seems sometimes to be lost in the megamerged faceless corporate giants of today. The men and women who occupy positions of power in the industry need to lead their companies back to the simple and profound vision of their founders. Improve healthcare and profits will follow.

BALANCING PEOPLE, PROFITS, AND PRINCIPLES

The final chapter, by noted physician and former government public health officer Greg Koski, offers a synthesis of many of the themes in the book. It is fitting that the last word in this book comes from a medical professional. For it is the doctors, nurses, pharmacists, and other healthcare professionals who are most dedicated and attuned to the needs and interests of patients. Koski argues that the early twenty-first century represents the "greatest period of opportunity" in the pharmaceutical industry's history. Following a number of other authors in this volume, he challenges the pharmaceutical industry to realign itself more closely with the public interest. If it can do so, Koski argues, it can secure a meaningful and profitable role for itself well into the century. If the industry proves incapable of making this transition, however, further regulation is inevitable to make it serve the public interest. This is likely to result within a very few decades in an industry configuration and business environment that are radically different from what we find today.

21

Evolving Approaches to Healthcare Challenges

Thomas M. Gorrie*

Disease and illness have always challenged human existence, and healthcare has mirrored humanity's social evolution and acquisition of scientific knowledge. As cities grew, populations multiplied, and long-distance travel increased, larger outbreaks of infectious diseases became possible. As our activity level, diet, and longevity have changed, we have increasingly had to treat diseases of the joints, cardiovascular diseases, and cancers. Similarly, our understanding of what causes these and other diseases has evolved from attributing their origin to demonic forces and the imbalance of elements such as the four bodily humors to today's scientific understandings of microbiology, cell biology, and genetics. With our increased knowledge came vastly improved treatments. The days of bleeding patients to treat fevers are gone. We have vaccines to prevent infections. But as society and science have advanced, we continue to be challenged by new diseases and providing access to healthcare for all people. These are two of today's greatest healthcare challenges, and this chapter, like the others in this book, focuses on various aspects of how we can be more successful in addressing them.

To overcome the unmet health needs throughout the world, we need new approaches based upon sound principles. We are in an era of tremendous innovation with great potential for increasing access to quality healthcare around the globe. With nearly 60 percent of the growth in worldwide GDP through 2020 expected to occur in emerging

* The author gratefully acknowledges the contributions to this chapter of Brian Moran and Michael Miller.

markets such as China, Brazil, India, Mexico, and Russia, new collaborative approaches and new ways of working in global partnerships across geographies and companies will be required if we are to successfully address our healthcare challenges.

From their unique perspectives, the authors in this book look at specific issues about how we should address these challenges. Interestingly, they all come to the same basic precept: what is right for the individual patient is central to ethical leadership and our common interests in galvanizing society to improve healthcare. The fact that these authors, despite their diverse backgrounds, all arrive at similar conclusions shows that there is the possibility of cohesive leadership in the medical and scientific communities, the pharmaceutical industry, government, and academia that can generate consensus options for improving healthcare and access to treatment. Through deliberation, collaborative thinking and planning, and finding common ground on how to address our major issues, we can begin to work on a strategy for improving access to affordable and effective health for all. This chapter will focus on how we can create and support such collaborations, empower leadership to address these challenges, and successfully execute ethical strategies to meet our current and future healthcare challenges.

FACING OUR CHALLENGES

Enormous economic and operational burdens are being placed on our society by shifting demographics, aging populations, and technological advances, with globalization potentially turning a local infectious outbreak into a pandemic. Sound strategies encompassing the viewpoints of all major stakeholders will be needed to manage these burdens. Successfully implementing these strategies will require strong leadership that can work both locally and globally among diverse populations and address issues to find common ground for the key groups of healthcare payers, providers, and patients.

Moving forward will require us not only to work together, but also to recognize and agree upon what constitute the major healthcare challenges we are facing. For example, the U.S. healthcare system is traditionally touted as being one of the finest in the world. Yet it leaves approximately 40 million people without health coverage. The indigent, elderly, mentally ill and chronic care patients are typically seen as challenging populations for whom to provide services in the United States because their care is often delivered and financed through multiple governmental and private sources. Improving the quality and efficiency of care for these groups will allow more equitable and efficient distribution of resources. The result will be to provide healthcare for a greater number of people, and it should be part of our systemic approach to improving and streamlining the U.S. healthcare system.

On a global scale, the HIV/AIDS pandemic continues to grow and threaten the lives of tens of millions of people. We must ensure that the infrastructure is available for the effective delivery of HIV/AIDS medications to combat this insidious threat to humankind. This is a daunting endeavor on every level. Broad coalitions are needed to address education and prevention, as well as effective treatment.

These are no small tasks, and much work remains to be done in order to tackle these complex problems. By addressing these and other major healthcare issues through substantial financial, intellectual, and infrastructure investments in nongovernmental organizations (NGOs) and national public health systems, we will also be structurally improving our healthcare system's ability to respond to healthcare and, in turn, to economic challenges, such as avian flu epidemics, bioterrorism, and natural disasters.

CHANGING THE FUTURE WITH SOUND SCIENCE

From theory to therapy, and discovery to delivery, healthcare begins with science directed toward meeting the needs of patients. Science is the basis for discovering new and innovative medicines. Similarly, our strategies and goals for improving healthcare access and affordability should be focused on improving patients' lives, and should be developed and directed by sound evidence and proven methods for changing the behavior of individuals, organizations, and governments.

Turning scientific advances into practical healthcare applications requires in-depth analyses and a sophisticated understanding of the complexities of how our healthcare system operates and is financed. Despite this inherent system-wide complexity, progress can be made by applying practical solutions to discrete problems. Collaborations using this approach have historically been successful in addressing healthcare challenges, and should serve as templates for us in the future. Examples of this would include the development of the polio vaccine, the Mectizan® distribution program for the treatment of river blindness, and more recently the royalty-free agreement for the development and distribution of TMC120, a microbicide for the prevention of HIV/AIDS in women. These cases illustrate how collaborative efforts of pharmaceutical companies, governments, providers, and nongovernmental organizations (NGOs) have led to vastly improving the quality of life for millions of people.

The polio vaccine was first developed by Jonas Salk in the mid-1950s, and just ten years later, with an improved oral vaccine, the incidence of polio within the United States dropped from 38,000 cases per year to less then 600. By 2004, only 1,170 cases were reported worldwide. The rapid distribution of the polio vaccine and the near-worldwide eradication of polio that followed could not have happened without the cooperation of a number of different constituents.

Merck's Mectizan® Donation Program for the treatment and eradication of "river blindness" (also discussed by Professor Santoro in his Introduction to Part I and by Dr. William Foege in Chapter 23) is a remarkable achievement.[1] Through the partnering of several NGOs, the World Health Organization, numerous ministries of health, UNICEF, and thousands of small communities in less developed countries, Merck has been able to make tremendous inroads in helping to eradicate river blindness, a disease that affects millions of people every year. Since its inception in 1987, the Mectizan® Donation Program has distributed more than 850 million doses to more than 30 million people.

Another exciting and life-saving scenario success story in the making is the accelerated discovery, development, and distribution of the compound TMC120, a microbicide gel for the prevention of HIV infection in women and girls, who account for about half of all HIV infections worldwide. The Johnson & Johnson (J&J) subsidiary Tibotec recently partnered with the International Partnership for Microbicides, an NGO, on a royalty-free agreement where J&J is carrying the costs of developing TMC120 through Phase II testing in order to promote its rapid development and distribution to resource-poor countries.

These are just a few of the many stories surrounding the ability of pharmaceutical innovation to serve as a starting point for dramatically improving people's lives. As we move further into the twenty-first century, we can look to these success stories as proof that by working together we can solve the most difficult public health problems throughout the world. The key to success will come from the fundamental idea that due to our ever increasingly connected healthcare systems and global economies, solving the world's health problems will benefit all people and therefore all countries. In order to succeed in this initiative, we must first work on finding common ground on the most difficult issues. By creating partnerships, based on a foundation of trust and well-intentioned visions, we can continue to promote health and prosperity while maintaining standards of civic responsibility. This may seem idealistic, but from looking at the contributions to this book, it is evident that this concept already has support from many vantage points.

CHANGING APPROACHES

In order to successfully resolve the larger issues facing the healthcare system, several steps must be taken. First, we will need collaborative efforts from the major constituents that make up the fragmented systems of healthcare delivery in this country and around the world. Second, a thoughtful and well-orchestrated campaign will be needed to raise public support for tackling these issues. Finally, the healthcare system's key stakeholders must agree upon a comprehensive strategy with clear timelines to addresses manageably sized issues and objectives within the wide realm of our healthcare system's problems. Attempting to build a structure to overhaul and address all of our healthcare system's problems comprehensively at the same time will inevitably fall under its own weight. Only by working in partnership for clear and defined goals can we expect to succeed in improving the many issues that affect the global health of all people.

Another challenge we face is entrenched thinking and historical blame-gaming. For many decades, as healthcare costs have grown faster than GDP and the percentage of the U.S. population without insurance has increased, our healthcare system has been characterized as one in "crisis," and arguments raged about who must take the responsibility, or the blame, for the many basic problems. The pharmaceutical industry often is the focus of the majority of complaints on many different issues.

Over and over, both through personal experience and in historical reading, I have found that bickering and retreating to ideological positions results in an impasse, especially as it pertains to increasing healthcare coverage. The result of such impasses is a stalemate: no progress is made, big problems get bigger, and those in need continue to suffer.

Although diverse groups have often failed to reach consensus, movement forward will require collaboration among groups representing the various healthcare constituencies, including payers, patients, and providers. Historically, pharmaceutical companies have been part of these discussions because we have an obligation to ensure that patients are receiving safe and effective medicines. But companies also have an obligation to employees and shareholders to generate profits. Governments have responsibilities to their entire constituencies, but they must also weigh the costs of social programs versus economic development, and factor in the effects of putting burdens on the rich to assist the poor and the elderly. Physicians strive to provide the best care for patients, but in today's complex healthcare scheme, they often are given the task of being economic "gatekeepers" by managed care organizations. They are rewarded for controlling costs and limiting the use of potentially expensive tests, procedures, and treatments. At the same time, they must worry and prepare for the possibility of medical liability. Patients, of course, are involved in this debate too. They often are taken to task for their lifestyles, eating habits, and other issues that can lead to increased health problems and long-term costs. It is apparent that finger pointing does little to address the underlying problems of our healthcare system. Rather, all of the partners of the world's healthcare system must accept some level of responsibility and accountability in the development of solutions to these problems. Only when this multilateral kind of cooperation exists can we institute an overarching strategy to resolve these issues.

As the person entrusted with government affairs and policy at Johnson & Johnson, I have learned over many years that the only way progress is made is through collaboration. The way to gain buy-in from the many different stakeholders is to find common ground on reasonably containable issues or problems where successful improvements will lead to benefits for everyone involved. Using the ideas in this book as one starting point, we can create a dialogue among the researchers, physicians, managed care organizations, healthcare providers, pharmaceutical industry, nongovernmental organizations, governments, employers, and patients as a way to find common ground as we work better and more effectively as partners to improve the healthcare system for everyone.

For the past six years, I have been a part of an effort that captures the essence of the collaborative attitude. That effort is known as the Health Sector Assembly (HSA). The initiatives undertaken by this collaborative and diverse organization are focused on generating positive reform in today's healthcare system. The HSA is a group of approximately 60 concerned leaders from public and private sector corporations, organizations, and institutions that meet voluntarily to discuss issues of broad national significance. Leaders from the U.S. Chamber of Commerce, the American Association of Retired Persons, The Robert Wood Johnson Foundation, the American Medical Association, the National Alliance for Hispanic Health, the Catholic Health Association, Families USA, the National Consumer League, the National Rural Health Association, the Healthcare Leadership Council, a few businesses, and many other associations, academic institutions, governments and healthcare organizations have attended these meetings. Over the past several years, this broad group of healthcare experts have made recommendations to improve the overall quality and availability of healthcare for all people. By spending time with each other, developing trust, and finding common ground, we have eliminated the bottleneck of win/lose. We have developed broad consensus statements to deal with issues such as care for the growing elderly population, improving the healthcare safety net, caring for patients with chronic conditions, providing access for the uninsured, Medicare reform, and national and global reforms to address access and affordability. Pulitzer Prize-winning columnist David Broder of *The Washington Post* commented on the Health Sector Assembly, stating that *"A more substantive approach to finding agreement (in healthcare) has been taking place in recent years under the auspice of the Health Sector Assembly...."*[2] The HSA's success demonstrates that the status quo is no longer a sustainable option after one's self-interest. The diversity of its contributing members is critical to creating viable consensus opinions and recommendations that can gain majority support outside the group and foster change in the current system.

Care of the Elderly

Improved care for the elderly has been one of the focal points of the Health Sector Assembly. By starting with clear goals in mind, the HSA outlined the major principles surrounding the three core issues of coverage, delivery, and financing of healthcare for the elderly. The HSA's proposal identifies the key challenges and unresolved issues that need to be addressed in order to ensure the successful movement forward. The challenges that remain are creating a sense of urgency based on future expected access and affordability challenges for the elderly, establishing trust among key stakeholders to get them to work toward solutions, and reconciling the proposal with the current Medicare program to implement successful changes. These are no small hurdles. The leadership that has assembled at the HSA has taken on the task of mapping out a potential path to solutions, but it is still going to take the collaboration of many different public and private institutions to see this process to fruition.

Chronic Care

Chronic care patients garner the largest percentage of healthcare resources. As the size of this population increases, it is crucial that we act to create an integrated system to manage the many different areas involved in chronic care. From initial acute clinical intervention and diagnosis to long-term home care, the need for an integrated care paradigm is evident.

The future of chronic care treatment is patient-focused. This entails implementing education systems for the patient as well as for the individuals directly involved in assisting them in managing their care. This education will empower patients to monitor their symptoms and successfully manage their own complex treatment regimens, including their multiple medications, hospital visits, and diagnostic tests. This idea of an increased "health literacy" was mentioned by Dr. Valentine Burroughs earlier in the book, and it applies not only to compliance in clinical trials, but also to disease prevention and the care and treatment of the chronically ill.

Healthcare Safety Net

The healthcare safety net that currently exists in the United States has been a topic of much discussion by the Health Sector Assembly. It is agreed that the best way to solve the problems of the deteriorating safety net in the United States is to reduce the need for it by providing healthcare coverage to all people. Having set a practical ten-year goal of 97 percent coverage, the HSA understands that given world events and economic challenges, the safety net is a necessary part of the healthcare delivery system and will remain so for a long time to come.

The safety net currently is made up of a fragmented group of public and private institutions and organizations that provide healthcare services to those in need. This patchwork system operates mainly at the local level and varies dramatically in accessibility and quality, depending on location.

Improving the infrastructure and ensuring adequate financing are two of the most pressing challenges facing the system. Determining the components needed to enhance the infrastructure should be done on a local basis to best tailor the needs to the individual region. The goal should be to locate treatment services within the patient's community, offer a choice of providers, and place a strong emphasis on health promotion and disease prevention. The financing of the safety net should continue to draw from the philanthropy of providers and institutions that traditionally donate services, medication, and other resources, but the greatest burden will fall on the local, state, and federal governments.

The HSA has taken on these initiatives in hopes that it will bring a broad national awareness to the problems and spur local and national actions. By doing so, we are creating a platform for further dialogue and laying the groundwork for collaboration by the key stakeholders in order to improve the overall state of the healthcare system. In many ways, this book reflects the philosophy of the HSA. It raises for discussion a broad range of issues that affect the healthcare system, in general terms, and the pharmaceutical industry in particular.

CONCLUSIONS

Many of the issues raised throughout this book have the potential to be highly divisive in nature. When groups with mutual concerns are not willing to work to find common ground on issues, it often leads to an impasse or stasis, prolonged systemic inefficiencies, and ultimately a decline in the quality and accessibility of healthcare. In order to avoid these pitfalls, we must have strong leadership that is able to overcome the emotional and philosophical differences and work across a broad spectrum of constituencies to find issues of manageable size that can be foci for practical collaborative thinking and action. The strategic initiatives derived from these collaborations should follow the fundamental ethical principle that actions need to be based upon the best interests of the patient.

Obviously, much more remains to be done. This book is just one piece of the beginnings of a mosaic outlining what we need to do to successfully provide adequate healthcare for all people. Partnerships such as the Health Sector Assembly, and the programs developed to deliver medications to third world countries, such as those for polio, river blindness, and HIV/AIDS, can serve as examples and templates to build upon. The leadership of the key stakeholder groups, scientists, physicians, patients, pharmaceutical companies, governments, insurers, and providers, must continue on this path to address the challenges facing our healthcare system. The risk for many of these groups is that, if impasses remain, and problems compound, stakeholders may lose the ability to provide input about decisions made to improve healthcare. The result could be that payers and governments make unilateral decisions that will ultimately hurt patients, undermine innovation, and erode the quality and stability of our healthcare system. It is in everyone's best interest to work together to improve our healthcare system. As Ben Franklin said at the signing of the Declaration of Independence, "We must all hang together, or most assuredly we will all hang separately."

22

Property Rights in Crisis

Managers and Rescue

Nien-hê Hsieh

The chapters in this book present a challenge under the current property rights regime. On one hand, the case has been made that the dire plight of persons suffering from HIV/AIDS in developing countries requires relaxing the protection of patent rights held by pharmaceutical companies for essential HIV/AIDS medicines. On the other hand, relaxing protection of those patent rights appears to call into question the philosophical foundations of the current intellectual property rights regime and the for-profit nature of the pharmaceutical industry.

This chapter takes up this challenge. Specifically, the chapter aims to ground the pharmaceutical industry's response to the HIV/AIDS crisis in a way that takes the current property rights regime as a given. Central to this account is an examination of the nature of property rights in the context of a crisis.

PROPERTY RIGHTS AND THE HIV/AIDS CRISIS

In Chapter 19, James Thuo Gathii criticizes the argument that the problem of access to HIV/AIDS medicines in developing countries is best addressed by alleviating the widespread poverty in those countries. As part of his account, Gathii chronicles steps taken by Western governments to enforce the protection of patent rights on medicines to treat those afflicted by HIV/AIDS. He describes, for example, the U.S. response to the passage in 1997 of an amendment to South Africa's Medicines and Related Substances Act to improve access to essential HIV/AIDS medicines for South African citizens by authorizing compulsory licensing and parallel importing. Gathii concludes that in the end, increasing access to essential HIV/AIDS medicines in developing countries requires allowing exceptions such as these to the protection of patent rights. To enforce patent protection under the existing regime of intellectual property rights and to focus attention on the issue of poverty is to miss the point.

In their chapter (15), Patricia Werhane and Michael Gorman analyze the arguments given in defense of the current regime of intellectual property rights. The current regime of intellectual property rights is consistent with treating intellectual property as though it were similar to real or physical property. Rights to real or physical property are often taken to grant the possessor exclusive and proprietary use of that property. Ideas, however, as Werhane and Gorman argue, are normally the result of "a long history of scientific or technological development and numbers of networks of creativity, not the act of a single person or a group of people at one moment in time." As such, it is mistaken to grant an exclusive and proprietary right to the person or group of persons who brought an idea to fruition in the final stage of its development in the same manner as one would grant such a right to the use of real or physical property. Instead, according to Werhane and Gorman, intellectual property should be understood from the perspective of a "network approach." A network approach to intellectual property would reflect the shared nature of discovery in the development of intellectual property and thereby weaken the claim of patent holders to the protection of intellectual property rights.

Taken together, these chapters outline one way in which to ground a response to the HIV/AIDS pandemic on the part of the pharmaceutical industry. In particular, these chapters suggest that adopting a network approach to intellectual property would justify the use of mechanisms such as compulsory licensing and parallel importing to increase access to essential HIV/AIDS medicines in developing countries. Although there is much to recommend it, grounding a response in this way may encounter certain objections.

To begin, William Weldon argues in Chapter 16 that the profits earned by pharmaceutical companies under the current intellectual property rights regime provide both the incentive and the means to fund the development of new medicines. Extending Weldon's argument, to change the current regime of patent protection in order to address the HIV/AIDS crisis is to run the risk of undermining the very system that gives rise to the developments that allow the alleviation of the suffering from HIV/AIDS in the first place. Furthermore, calling for relaxed patent protection, and thereby reduced profits for the pharmaceutical industry, would appear to suggest calling upon the pharmaceutical industry to reconsider its nature as a for-profit business enterprise. As Greg Koski notes in Chapter 24, however, the Institute for OneWorld Health is the only nonprofit pharmaceutical company to date. Until there are other such nonprofit pharmaceutical companies, the development and provision of medicines will involve for-profit companies that are responsible not only to persons in need of their medicines, but also to their shareholders.

These potential objections are compelling reasons to ground a response on the part of the pharmaceutical industry to the HIV/AIDS crisis in a manner that will not challenge the fundamental features of the current property rights regime. These potential objections reflect two features of the current property rights regime, broadly understood. The first is the granting of enforceable patent rights to pharmaceutical companies for HIV/AIDS medicines. The second feature is the for-profit nature of pharmaceutical companies, the managers of which have responsibilities to shareholders. Grounding a response to the HIV/AIDS crisis that takes these two features as given is not to suggest that these or other features of the current property rights regime should not be reconsidered. Instead, the point is to make the case that a response by the pharmaceutical industry to the HIV/AIDS crisis need not be a radical departure from the current property rights regime.

THE RESCUE PRINCIPLE

The starting point of the analysis is framing the issue of the pharmaceutical industry's response to the HIV/AIDS crisis in terms of the decisions made by managers of pharmaceutical companies. Focusing on what managers of pharmaceutical companies are permitted and required to do within the current property rights regime then allows consideration of a response to the HIV/AIDS crisis that incorporates the two features of the current property rights regime outlined above.

The dire plight of those afflicted by the HIV/AIDS pandemic is motivating the challenges to the current property rights regime and its enforcement. As Werhane and Gorman write, with a projected 100 million HIV deaths, the HIV/AIDS pandemic represents an "international emergency." The critical nature of this plight grounds an approach that calls upon managers of pharmaceutical companies to help alleviate that suffering within the current property rights regime. This approach avoids fundamentally undermining the two features of the current property rights regime outlined above. Central to this argument is the claim that there is a duty to engage in rescue in cases of emergency. Call the principle specifying this duty the *Rescue Principle*.

The Rescue Principle has been articulated by a number of philosophers. According to one formulation, as put forward by T. M. Scanlon, "if you are presented with a situation in which you can prevent something very bad from happening, or alleviate someone's dire plight, by making only a slight (or even moderate) sacrifice, then it would be wrong not to do so."[1] There are three criteria for the duty of rescue to apply to a person. First, the nature of the plight is dire. Second, the person in question is able to help alleviate the plight. The ability to alleviate the plight is taken to refer both to the fact that the person is in a position to alleviate the plight and has the means by which to do so at his or her disposal. Third, the alleviation of the plight is limited by the sacrifice that it requires of the person in question. That is to say, if alleviating the plight would require the person to incur a sacrifice above some threshold, then he or she would not be considered bound by a duty of rescue to alleviate that plight.

In the context of the HIV/AIDS crisis in developing countries, there is reason to think that these three conditions apply to managers of pharmaceutical companies. First, if the plight of those suffering from HIV/AIDS does not count as dire, then it is unclear what does. Second, pharmaceutical companies are well positioned to help alleviate the plight in ways that other parties are not. As discussed in the previous chapters, in addition to relaxing the enforcement of patent protection, pharmaceutical companies are in a position to provide donations of essential HIV/AIDS medicines to persons in developing countries. Third, although engaging in these activities requires a degree of sacrifice on the part of pharmaceutical companies, there is reason to think that the sacrifice is moderate relative to the plight that they are in a position to help alleviate. The reasoning is as follows.

At first, it may seem that the sacrifice required of pharmaceutical companies in relaxing patent protection and donating essential HIV/AIDS medicines is far above the threshold beyond which the duty of rescue no longer applies. Many of the persons suffering from the HIV/AIDS pandemic lack the resources to purchase essential HIV/AIDS medicines at current market prices and live in conditions that make the administration of treatment difficult. It would at first appear that the amount of assistance that can be justified by the Rescue Principle on the part of pharmaceutical companies is not that great relative to the degree of suffering resulting from the HIV/AIDS pandemic.

In response, however, it may be pointed out that the development of essential HIV/AIDS medicines has already occurred and that pharmaceutical companies were not anticipating the sale of these medicines to persons in developing countries at market prices. One could argue, therefore, that pharmaceutical companies incur relatively little sacrifice by providing these medicines for free, or at manufacturing cost, to developing countries and by relaxing the enforcement of patent protection. To be clear, this assumes that the HIV/AIDS medicines remain within those countries and are not sold in developed country markets, which, as Werhane and Gorman point out, is a distinct possibility. With that said, the general point remains that the cost to pharmaceutical companies is the profit forgone on the sale of essential HIV/AIDS medicines to the poor in developing countries. But because these sales were never anticipated, the sacrifice required of pharmaceutical companies is much lower than might initially be thought to be the case. This would suggest that the amount of assistance that can be justified by the Rescue Principle is not as insignificant as one might initially think.

On the basis of the argument thus far, the response by managers of pharmaceutical companies to the HIV/AIDS crisis can be justified by a duty of rescue to help alleviate the suffering in the HIV/AIDS crisis. Grounding their response in this way avoids undermining the two, assumed features of the property rights regime – namely, the granting of enforceable patent rights and the for-profit nature of pharmaceutical companies.

With regard to the granting of enforceable patent rights, relaxing the enforcement of patent protection for reasons of rescue need not represent a challenge. As discussed by Werhane and Gorman in Chapter 15, human beings have basic rights that are fundamental and inviolable. These include rights to life, liberty, and survival. The Rescue Principle applies to individuals and the resources at their disposal that enable them to engage in rescue. When a person comes under a duty to rescue, the exercise of his or her right to liberty is curtailed in one sense. There is a moral duty that takes priority over the liberty right in the instance of rescue. It seems mistaken, however, to conclude that the right to liberty is any less basic a right. Similarly, it seems mistaken to conclude that because a person is under a duty to use the resources at his or her disposal to engage in rescue, his or her property rights over those resources are weakened in any fundamental sense. Accordingly, whereas the Rescue Principle requires the relaxation of the enforcement of patent protection, this does not imply that the patent rights granted to pharmaceutical companies are weakened in any fundamental sense.

Grounding the pharmaceutical industry's response with reference to the Rescue Principle also preserves the second, assumed feature of the property rights regime, which is the for-profit nature of pharmaceutical companies. The Rescue Principle does not require a person to relinquish personal pursuits to become a full-time provider of assistance to others. The point of the Rescue Principle is that when confronted with an instance to engage in rescue in the course of normal activities, a person comes under a duty to engage in rescue. Similarly, the claim is not that pharmaceutical companies need to become nonprofit enterprises, but rather that given the crisis situation in which they find themselves, the responsibility to engage in rescue arises. Engaging in an act of rescue need not require pharmaceutical companies to alter in any fundamental way their purpose as for-profit business enterprises.

At this point, one might argue that by engaging in rescue, managers of pharmaceutical companies are violating their responsibilities to shareholders by imposing a cost on them. In response, it may be pointed out that there are situations in which persons are required to engage in rescue even if this involves a cost to others. To be certain, there are limits to how much cost it is permissible to impose upon third parties to engage in rescue, and the responsibilities of managers to shareholders may place further limits on how much assistance can be required of managers to address the HIV/AIDS crisis. That there are limits to the amount of assistance that can be required of managers, however, does not imply that there is no responsibility to engage in rescue.

By focusing on the role of managers of pharmaceutical companies and the Rescue Principle, this discussion argues that it is possible to adopt an approach that will allow a pharmaceutical industry response to the HIV/AIDS crisis that does not also challenge the current property rights regime. Relaxing the protection of patent rights and donating essential HIV/AIDS medicines, if done on grounds of rescue, need not undermine fundamental features of the property rights regime. In short, in moments of crisis, the dire plight of persons may take priority over property rights in a way that need not call into crisis the idea of property rights themselves.

FUTURE CHALLENGES

The Rescue Principle is limited in what it requires of persons. The HIV/AIDS pandemic, however, is not the only crisis situation that the pharmaceutical industry is able to help alleviate. Looking forward into the twenty-first century, it is also hard to imagine that there will not be additional healthcare crises. Moreover, responding to crises is only one of the many issues to consider with regard to property rights and the pharmaceutical industry. One issue to consider is the development of medicines specifically targeting problems unique to developing countries. In the light of these points, a more comprehensive framework will be required to evaluate the nature of the property rights regime and the role of the pharmaceutical industry, governments, and other private-sector actors in addressing healthcare needs.

Other chapters in this book have considered elements of this broader framework. The aim of this chapter has been to ground a near-time response to the HIV/AIDS crisis in a way that avoids having first to address this broader debate about property rights. However, it would be a mistake to wait until another crisis to settle this broader debate, because by then, it may be too late.

23

Blurring the Lines

Public and Private Partnerships Addressing Global Health

William H. Foege

INTRODUCTION

It is common to think of public/private partnerships as the latest chapter in global health improvement, and it is true that such partnerships are much in the news. But it is also true that few things are truly new.

Several thousand years ago, the Greek and Roman historian Polybius (Greek by origin, but as a captive of Rome he also chronicled Roman history) pointed out that the world is a dynamic whole where everything is interconnected. This has been true for public health and global health, where every advance has combined private initiatives and public efforts. Although some would interpret blurring the lines as the result of being out of focus, the real interpretation is that there is no distinct line because we are all in this together.

The immunization program in the United States has been only one example. Almost fifty years ago the announcement that the Salk polio vaccine could actually prevent the disease was one of the great days in public health. Much of the funding came from donations of individuals to the "March of Dimes." Work was done in both public and private laboratories, private companies produced the vaccine, and the announcement was made at a public university, the University of Michigan. There Tommy Francis coordinated the largest field trial ever attempted, which involved both public and private institutions and workers.

But the next few days were even greater because the announcement of an effective vaccine led the U.S. government to seek public funds for the purchase of vaccine. At first the intent was to purchase vaccine for poor children, but by the time the debate ended, there was an understanding that vaccines provided both personal protection and a social good. Again the line between public and private had been blurred by the realization that we are in this together. During the early 1980s when immunization programs were reaching maturity in this country, approximately half of the immunizations given to children were given in public clinics, the other half in private offices. Often the vaccine given by a private physician was purchased with public funds. Although the public and private lines were crossed repeatedly in the research, development, and then production of polio vaccine, the line between public and private became blurred entirely in the purchase and delivery of the vaccine, to the point of benefit for the children of this country.

In global health there have been attempts recently to catalog the programs where success can be shown and proven by tracking inputs and outcomes and showing that an intervention led to an improvement of health. Many programs have demonstrated success and, as expected, there are many ways to organize such successful programs. What is the one characteristic in common? Every success was the result of a successful coalition, almost always including public and private partners.

EXAMPLES OF GLOBAL HEALTH SUCCESS

Although examples are plentiful, the brevity of this chapter allows only short examples. Smallpox eradication was possible because of cooperation that crossed political boundaries and the boundaries of specialties, as well as the involvement of governments, public health workers, medical facilities, faith groups, volunteers, foundations, and private companies. Many private groups were heavily involved, manufacturing vaccine, bottles, needles, and jet injectors, as well as all of the materials needed to conduct a campaign involving millions of people. The actions of Wyeth are but one example of the private contribution to this public goal, but they symbolize the crucial role of the private sector. On developing the bifurcated needle, which made it possible to train vaccinators easily, improve the effectiveness of vaccination techniques, and consistently deliver safe vaccine, Wyeth obtained a patent on July 13, 1965, Patent 3,194,237, and then gave the patent to the World Health Organization, forgoing its own profit. It was a crucial contribution for which they sought no recognition and there is no way to properly thank them. Even in the countries with smallpox, private industry came to the assistance of the program in helping with transport, materials, and publicity, or even in larger ways, as when Tata Industries in India took responsibility for eradication in a large geographic area, at their own expense. These are two of countless stories.

Another example is the use of Mectizan® in the treatment and reduction of transmission of onchocerciasis (river blindness), which is also discussed above by Professsor Santoro (in his introduction to Part I) and Dr. Gorrie (in Chapter 21). Twenty-five years ago, Merck & Co. developed a drug for heartworm in dogs. They could have stopped at that point but they proceeded to test the drug against onchocerca in humans. Although the drug turned out to be very effective in removing micofilaria when given once a year, thereby preventing blindness and the systemic effects of the microfilaria, it was realized immediately that there was no viable market for an inexpensive drug, used once a year, by some of the poorest people in the world. Merck could have stopped at that point, but they made a decision to donate the drug for use by any group that could deliver it effectively. Some 300 million treatments have now been given in the last 17 years, leading to a reduction in misery and blindness that is beyond comprehension. This has required the coordination of many public groups such as WHO, UNICEF, the World Bank, and ministries of health with dozens of private groups, including foundations, medical mission organizations, and nongovernmental agencies. But the program has only been possible because a private company, Merck, donated the medication free.

When Glaxo-Wellcome developed a new antimalarial drug, Malarone, they recognized the extraordinary potential for the drug because it was a combination of two drugs. This immediately reduced the chance of resistance developing quickly. However, the drug is costly to manufacture and would therefore be less useful in the areas of the world where the need is greatest. Glaxo offered to provide a million treatments if there were a way to identify a way to treat those in most need rather than those most able to pay. Studies in Africa have demonstrated it is possible to identify patients who have been shown to be resistant to other antimalarial drugs and to provide Malarone under direct observational therapy. These studies are convincing that it is possible, under field conditions, to get Malarone to the people who need it, successfully treat malaria resistant to other medications, and reduce the possibility of resistance to Malarone by appropriate and full therapy.

The Mectizan Expert Committee was meeting in France to review the progress of Mectizan® delivery and to approve new applications when a presentation by Dr. Eric Ottesen, of the World Health Organization, caused great excitement. Dr. Ottesen reported on a study using both Mectizan® and albendazole in the treatment of lymphatic filariasis. The use of the drugs separately had not been impressive, but when combined the drugs showed promise. The discussion immediately focused on the possibility of securing albendazole for large programs against this disease. Further encouragement was found in the latest reports on the clinical care of patients with lymphatic filariasis to reduce infections and to reduce the edema accompanying such infections. It was decided that the group should find a way to make an overture to SmithKline for free or subsidized albendazole.

No one at that meeting could have anticipated the serendipitous moment for that report. The next morning with the meeting again under way, President Jimmy Carter called to say that although it was 5 A.M. in Atlanta, he was so excited that he needed to talk about a new possibility in global health. The night before, while having dinner with the CEO of SmithKline, President Carter had been asked if there was anything SmithKline could do in the global health area. After being briefed on the presentation heard the day before, President Carter called the CEO of SmithKline and that began the process that has led to two pharmaceutical companies combining their efforts with those of the World Health Organization, universities, ministries of health, and nongovernmental organizations in a global effort to reduce the enormous toll extracted by lymphatic filariasis.

Returning to the story of polio, the early public/private efforts leading to a vaccine and use in the United States finally led to the logical conclusion with a global effort under way. Again, the power of the story is found in the public and private cooperation that developed. In 1985, Rotary International, a service organization, pledged to raise $120 million for global polio efforts by their centennial in 2005. Rotary members are found around the world combining public and private in each local organization with members who are small business people, teachers, and others representing public life. Rotary members found polio such a compelling project that the time frame for raising the money was gradually reduced from twenty to ten and then to five years. Then when they realized that they had pledges for the total amount, Rotary began to increase the monetary goal, and they had soon raised $300 million, then $400 million, and now they have raised over $500 million. Much of the funding, privately raised, goes to public organizations, such as UNICEF for the purchase of vaccine, or the Centers for Disease Control for the provision of epidemiological services. Local business leaders often provide transportation, printing, and massive support for National Immunization Days. Again, the lines between public and private have been totally blurred and this blurring has been for the benefit of the children of the world.

The success of these programs, plus dozens of others at both global and local levels, has encouraged dozens of public/private ventures for vaccine production, new drug development, health delivery programs in developing countries, and micronutrient fortification programs.

THOUGHTS FOR THE FUTURE

It is apparent that the best improvements in health can be expected only with public/private partnerships. Leadership is no longer the result of someone having a title, but rather leadership goes to the person who develops an effective coalition. It is also clear what the benefits are for health and for those in the public sector, which is always lacking in resources but holds a responsibility to improve health. But then the question is asked, "What is the benefit to the private sector?" As demonstrated at Merck and now other corporations, the real benefit is engagement in the problems of the world and a work force that takes a new pride in working for a company willing to do such work. This is a tangible benefit to the corporation as it provides new meaning for its work force.

AIDS now requires the best we have to offer in partnerships, not only to make drugs more effective and more affordable, but also to promote what would not seem to be in the interest of the private sector, namely prevention. Prevention will lead to improvements in development, the work force, product demands, and stability. Not one of us is as powerful as all of us in improving the health of the world. To improve global health by effectively controlling AIDS requires us to develop seamless cooperation between public and private efforts. The opportunities for such cooperation are clear in treatment and prevention, but they also exist in providing a more hopeful future for the many children left orphans by the epidemic. The NOAH's Ark project (Nurturing Orphans of AIDS for Humanity) in South Africa, a non-governmental organization, is an example of what corporate support can do in strengthening communities to respond in a positive way to the care and nurture of the orphans in their own communities.

Public/private cooperation needs to extend to agreements on the selection of global research priorities and the willingness of decision makers in public policy both to fund such global research priorities through the National Institutes of Health and universities, but also to contract for certain types of research best done in the private sector.

It means not only urging countries to contribute to the Global Fund but also to encourage corporate giving to the Global Fund. In addition, the future should include more attempts to merge the expertise of both public and private groups as has been done with the AIDS project in Botswana where Merck, the Bill and Melinda Gates Foundation, Harvard University, the Centers for Disease Control, and others have formed a venture with the government of Botswana to seek answers as to how best to deliver the science now available, under the conditions in Africa.

Repeatedly it has been found that the biggest barrier now encountered in providing some equity in global health is the scarcity of management skills. The difference between scientific knowledge improving the health of a group of people or not improving their health finally comes down to management. It is difficult for ministries of health to compete with the private sector for the best managers and it is difficult for them to train an excess of workers with the knowledge that many will go to the private sector.

But if corporations, both pharmaceutical and others, continue to be willing to assume a role in solving this problem, it might be possible for them to provide not only their best scientists but also their best managers for limited periods of time as part of career development. If promising managers were expected to spend a year or two working on the improvement of health delivery systems in developing areas, supervising field workers, and developing health training programs, the training component for global health could be strengthened and corporations would have executives with a new understanding of the world.

The marketplace is not the answer to all questions facing society. Likewise, the public sector cannot solve all social problems. But the combination of public and private efforts, when harnessed together in an effort to achieve a clear and shared health objective, provides a powerful force that exceeds the sum of its separate efforts. We owe the future nothing less than our best efforts to combine these efforts for health.

24

Renegotiating the Grand Bargain

Balancing Prices, Profits, People, and Principles

Edward Grèg Koski

At the close of the nineteenth century, the pharmaceutical industry bore little resemblance to the industry we know today, except for the widespread public concern for the safety of compounds sold for treatment and prevention of disease. Much of this concern stemmed from unacceptable marketing practices of "snake-oil salesmen" hawking their goods to a hopeful but uninformed populace, with false claims of efficacy for untested products, many of which were devoid of benefit and actually harmful to human health. Tragedy and public outcry led to legislative action, ultimately taking form as the Food, Drug and Cosmetic Act, the law that forever changed the industry by establishing a regulated approach to testing and marketing of pharmaceutical products in the United States under the Food and Drug Administration (FDA).

The thalidomide tragedy of the late 1960s resulted in major reform of the FDA, requiring that all products be thoroughly tested for both safety and efficacy before they could be approved for marketing. Over the years, FDA regulations have become ever more detailed, complex, and invasive, to the point that today, many in the industry, as well as scientists, government, and even patient advocacy groups, complain that this onerous regulatory burden has stymied the introduction of new products to the detriment of the industry, medical progress and human health. William Weldon reflects this view in Chapter 16, "A Future Agenda for Government–Industry Relations."

At the same time, however, the pharmaceutical industry is being intensely criticized both in the United States and abroad for a host of perceived failures, including unethical research practices (as described by Dr. Valentine Burroughs in Chapter 5 and Glenna Crooks in Chapter 6), unlawful marketing practices (discussed by Tom Abrams, an FDA director, in Chapter 9), unfair pricing practices (questioned by Joel Hay in Chapter 14), suppression of critical safety and efficacy data, and manipulative business practices (such as abuses of direct-to-consumer advertising, the subject of Chapter 10, by Professors Meredith Rosenthal and Julie Donahue) to name but a few. These topics have been thoughtfully considered by the several authors of this volume. When one reads this collection of chapters covering a diverse range of issues – from ethics and economics (which Jürgen Drews explores in Chapter 1) to global health disparities (the subject of James Gathii's Chapter 19) – one cannot help but be moved by a sense that the time has come to renegotiate what Professor Santoro has referred to (in the Introduction to this volume) as "the grand bargain."

THE PHARMACEUTICAL INDUSTRY'S DECLINING PUBLIC IMAGE

As the pharmaceutical and related biosciences industries emerged as engines of economic growth and innovation in medicine during the twentieth century, the people of the world watched with great hope, awaiting the next breakthrough, believing that virtually any disease could be cured or prevented by drugs. Both the promise and the productivity of research and development in the laboratories of our academic institutions, our government research facilities and our pharmaceutical companies warranted the optimism and support of the public. That support was provided in the form of investment capital and willing participation in the studies necessary to demonstrate the safety and efficacy of new products, whether drugs or devices, and the pharmaceutical industry enjoyed a position of esteemed respect. For nearly two decades, the industry enjoyed a measure of public confidence and respect that overshadowed all other industries, and with that respect, enjoyed a margin of unprecedented profitability. Today, neither of these privileged positions remains. Rising costs, declining profits, spreading price controls, dwindling pipelines, expiring patents, and corporate scandals have eroded investor confidence, and the public's regard for the industry and its practices continues to plummet faster than even that for the tobacco industry.[1] What is perhaps most tragic and ironic is that these declines were both predictable and preventable.

Along the way, there have been some notable detours from the path toward decline of the industry – for example, the laudable handling of the Tylenol-tampering case by the McNeil subsidiary of Johnson & Johnson, still cited by many as the ultimate example of corporate responsibility and an equally dramatic demonstration that even in business, good deeds can be rewarded. The company sustained a temporary blow, but emerged with not only its integrity, but its profitability intact, and its reputation for ethical conduct enhanced. A visitor to its corporate offices still finds its now famous code of ethics prominently displayed at the main entrance as a daily reminder to everyone who enters there that J&J is committed to responsible conduct of its affairs.[2] Many companies have undertaken initiatives to address the need to make their products available to some who cannot pay for, or otherwise access them, and too frequently, these good deeds have not been given the credit and recognition they deserve.

Despite these noble deeds, we know even the very best and most altruistic industry efforts to be good citizens are frequently greeted with suspicion and cynicism by a skeptical public that sees them as just another clever marketing ploy. Legitimate efforts for the industry to support worthy organizations and causes are today avoided or rejected out of hand, solely because of the perception that they are tainted by the industry's "dirty money." An industry-sponsored educational conference, even if it is an honest effort to educate physicians, is somehow denigrated by the words "sponsored by." Although perception is not reality, reality often shapes public perception – when one's motives are subject to suspicion, there is usually a reason. This phenomenon is the hallmark of mistrust. As has been said before, trust is earned, not purchased, and once lost, is terribly difficult to restore. Today, the pharmaceutical industry is not trusted, and many see it as the victim of greed.

The erosion of public respect for and trust in the pharmaceutical industry can be attributed to its failure to conduct its business activities in an ethical manner. Although some would consider the concept of "business ethics" an oxymoron, John Maxwell contends that business conduct ought to be governed by the same ethical principles that apply to other endeavors. In his popular book *There's No Such Thing as Business Ethics*, he asserts that the Golden Rule, or the notion of treating others as one would oneself want to be treated, is a fundamental principle of all human interaction, and that "business ethics" is no exception.[3] Simply restated, this is the principle of respect for persons, the first principle of ethical conduct of human research set forth in the so-called Belmont Report of the National Commission for the Protection of Human Subjects in Biomedical and Behavioral Research. To the principle of respect for persons, the Commission added the principles of beneficence (to do good) and justice (to be fair).[4] Although the principles identified in the Belmont Report were intended to provide a framework for the ethical conduct of human research, including clinical research, they can usefully be applied to the broader conduct of the pharmaceutical, device, and biologics industries.

It is obviously easier to talk about ethical principles than it is to act faithfully and consistently in accord with them. Nevertheless, had the life sciences industries adopted and abided by this ethical framework in the overall day to day conduct of the activities over the past thirty years, they probably would not find themselves in the unfortunate positions they occupy today. Consider, for example, the recent controversy surrounding the approval and marketing of antidepressants for use in children. Although the industry was aware of an association between an increased risk of suicidal thoughts and behavior in adolescents and children taking selective serotonin re-uptake inhibitors (SSRIs), it continued to pursue approval for marketing of the drugs for treatment of childhood depression, and even chose not to disclose to regulatory officials the results of completed trials that failed to demonstrate efficacy of the drugs in this patient population. This and other issues of child safety are addressed in Chapters 3 and 4, in the chapters by Dianne Murphy and Sara Goldkind and Robert Nelson. This behavior directly violates all of the ethical principles set forth above. It is obviously disrespectful and unjust to withhold information that any parent would reasonably want to have if a child were seeking safe and effective treatment for depression. And what good could possibly be done by bringing to market a drug that not only was ineffective, but might also have carried with it an increased risk of suicide? Even some ethicists would argue on utilitarian grounds that depriving the many who might benefit from a drug an opportunity to receive it because of potential adverse side effects observed in only a few, would be equally unjust. In fact, this was the argument used by the U.S. FDA, an agency charged first and foremost with protecting public safety, to justify its suppression of an internal analysis that cast doubt on the safety and efficacy of these drugs in children. The principles of respect and beneficence would dictate that such information be appropriately disclosed so that parents, young patients, and their doctors are given the autonomy to make treatment decisions for themselves, allowing those who were demonstrably receiving benefit from the drugs to continue taking them.

On the corporate side, one might well ask why disclosure of information would have been undesirable for a company that had pledged to conduct its activities in an ethical manner. To many, the answer is clear – that in this case, it was not principles of ethical conduct that drove the actions of the companies, or for that matter the FDA, but a desire to protect first the market for the product and the company's profitability. There can be no doubt that application of the simple principles of ethical conduct in this case would have avoided a major Congressional investigation and another unflattering scenario for an industry whose actions have once again been characterized as driven by self-serving corporate greed, rather than a commitment to doing good.

TOWARD A SUSTAINABLE AND ETHICAL PHARMACEUTICAL
INDUSTRY IN THE TWENTY-FIRST CENTURY

If one reviews the chapters in this volume with these simple ethical principles in mind, one can begin to appreciate that it may be possible to modify the practices of the global pharmaceutical industry, governments, scientists, and the public toward a more sustainable and ethical pharmaceutical industry as the twenty-first century progresses, with positive consequences for all. Of course, change never comes easily, particularly when the diverse and often competing interests of so many are at stake. But that does not mean that we should not try – indeed, some already are, but the present efforts are inadequate in both scope and number. Power to initiate change usually rests with the leaders of industry and government. Unfortunately, if history is our guide, we cannot expect these leaders to initiate change until events and public pressure forces them to do so. In this case, people have enormous power, and even ultimate control to affect reform. We see a historically recent example in Martin Delaney's account of the AIDS crisis in Chapter 17. Similarly, were an informed public suddenly to boycott participation in clinical trials, the industry would be forced to change its practices overnight. This scenario is not all that unlikely if public trust in the industry continues to decline.

Tragedy, scandal, and abuse are frequently the catalysts of reform. In the United States, "reform" generally means that laws and regulations are introduced to prohibit what are deemed to be the offending practices. One cannot look at the current landscape of the pharmaceutical industry, with the recent surge of high-profile lawsuits and settlements, without noticing the dark clouds of reform on the horizon. One may predict with some measure of confidence that several aspects of industry practice are likely to become subjects of reform efforts. The specter of price controls in the United States, the only unregulated market for pharmaceutical products in the industrialized world, is lurking at every turn, despite what many view as the pro-industry orientation of the present administration in Washington. In a very short period after disclosure of the SSRI data-suppression incident described above, powerful members of Congress (Reps. Henry Waxman, D-Calif., and Edward Markey, D-Mass.) introduced very strong legislation that would require the establishment of a public registry of all clinical trials and their results, and that trials be registered before an institutional review board (IRB), or ethics committee, could approve their initiation.[5] Despite resistance from some parts of the industry, public pressure is likely to enable passage of this bill, which would bring about what many would consider to be radical change in industry practice. With state and municipal governments and private citizens across the country already flouting regulations to import lower cost prescription drugs from Canada and other countries where prices are already controlled, and with the U.S. Congress already considering legislation that would freely permit such importation, we may be entering an era of *de facto* price controls, even in the absence of specific regulatory action. This fact is surely not lost on the leaders of the industry or their minions among the ranks of Washington's abundant lobbyists.

Although the industry steadfastly maintains that its primary mission is to develop new drugs for the benefit of humanity, drugs to improve the duration and quality of our lives, these claims evoke cynical laughter among critics who see profits as the industry's primary goal and motivation. On the other hand, one must take note of the endorsement of proposals for registration of clinical trials by pharmaceutical leaders such as Johnson & Johnson. Perhaps the notion that the industry could actually jump from the swamp onto the path of righteousness is not sheer folly, or even as unlikely as most would imagine. Even today, there are giants among the leadership of the industry who could accept the mantel of leadership, such as Roy Vagelos, the former CEO of Merck during much of the golden era of Merck's tenure as the most highly respected company in the industry.

Some professional organizations already have paved the way by adopting very strong codes of ethical conduct to which their members attest their support. Two of these, the Association of Clinical Research Professionals and the American Academy of Pharmaceutical Physicians (on whose boards I serve as a trustee), are striving to raise awareness and standards of conduct while enhancing professionalism in the clinical trials process through training and independent certification of their members. As this modest innoculum begins to proliferate, these efforts could be joined by other professional organizations that share their principles and motivation, thereby altering the environment of the clinical research community to facilitate movement toward more responsible ethical conduct. Recently, the editors of many of the most prestigious medical journals issued a position statement endorsing the call for open registration of clinical trials before inception as a condition for subsequent publication. This is a highly laudable move that will leverage the possible passage of the enabling legislation – one can only wonder with some well-deserved cynicism what took them so long to get to this position. Regardless, their action supports the contention that we may indeed be entering a period of "facilitated evolution" toward a culture of conscience. The really big question is whether industry itself will join the march.

Major repositioning within the industry will require some realignment of incentives and liabilities. Business is still business, and money still talks. If the industry can envision ways in which good practices and deeds can work in its favor in the long term, the likelihood of significant change occurring is heightened.

A full-scale global assault on drug prices and industry profits is not the answer. As William Weldon so eloquently writes in Chapter 16, the possibility of reasonable return on investment fuels innovation and discovery. Accordingly, we should strive to preserve a robust market-driven approach to the discovery process, with full expectation of appropriate rewards. Those returns, however, should be based on true costs of discovery and development, with full recognition that only a few test articles will ever make it to market, and even fewer will be blockbusters. But the cost basis should not be inflated by the costs of widespread, expensive advertising and detailing activities that undermine rational, data-driven prescribing practices and subvert efforts to reduce overall health costs. In the twenty-first century, given the vast disparities that persist in healthcare resources and access to them around the world, we cannot continue business as usual. With so much being spent on the needs and desires of so few, while so many disadvantaged and suffering people go without, the global community must develop and implement ways to address these inequities. The entire burden, however, should not fall upon the pharmaceutical industry's profitability, nor should it stifle innovation.

A MODEL FOR ADDRESSING GLOBAL PUBLIC HEALTH NEEDS

The expansion of information technology affords an opportunity for more detailed and meaningful analysis of medical effectiveness, including diagnosis, prevention, and therapy. In a just and rational world, particularly one with limited health resources, all medicines would be used according to the best available outcomes analyses to achieve the greatest and most equitable improvements in health at the most reasonable cost. This standard will probably never be achieved, given contemporary economic and political realities, but steps can be taken in that direction. The notion that healthcare is a right rather than a privilege will probably remain little more than an idealistic expression of that intangible goal; but in a more limited sense, we may be able to achieve at least a first approximation of that ideal. The advent of the world's first not-for-profit pharmaceutical company, the Institute for OneWorld Health, is evidence that there are some in the industry who would prefer to "make drugs for people, not for profit." This concept may be applicable for providing at least a basal level of drug therapy to regions and people of the world who currently have little or no access to prescription drugs. Even today, major pharmaceutical companies that derive their profits primarily from their brand-name blockbusters have developed their own capacity for manufacturing and marketing generic drugs. These drugs, which are no longer patent-protected profit-makers, generate some income on their own. Suppose the industry, signaling a new commitment to the beneficence of its core mission, were jointly to develop and fund mechanisms and facilities for production and distribution of safe and effective nonpatent drugs needed for treatment of diseases afflicting those parts of the world community that are currently neglected.

This is in effect is what the San Francisco-based Institute for OneWorld Health[6] is attempting to do, combining industry support and philanthropic donations to enhance the availability of much needed drugs in the developing countries of the world. Further growth of a not-for-profit sector in the pharmaceutical industry could still provide meaningful and extensive employment opportunities, as well as much-needed quality pharmaceuticals at dramatically reduced prices. Much of this investment and capacity development could even take place in developing countries, thereby fueling local economic development. Growth of this sector could be fostered by appropriate incentives to industry that would encourage free licensing of off-patent drugs to such not-for-profit entities, rather than the current practice of extending for as long as possible, through any means possible, the patent-life of a drug. Any new incentives should, to the fullest extent possible, be directed not toward enhancing industry profits, but toward achieving global public health goals. The long-standing tendency of governments to rely upon patent-preservation incentives to influence pharmaceutical company practices perpetuates a profit-only mentality that is antithetical to achieving a new balance of principles and practices that the global community needs to address more effectively the world's health problems – an effort in which industry, government, philanthropists, and the public must all contribute.

CONCLUSION: REALIGNING PROFITS WITH PUBLIC HEALTH

In these brief, concluding remarks, one can only begin to imagine how we might realign the priorities and practices of the pharmaceutical industry with the needs of the people of the world. Many of us have reaped the benefits of innovation, discovery, and technological advances, particularly when they have been translated into new products. It is only fair to point out that the many who receive health benefits from the products themselves, while not insignificant to be sure,

generally receive far less and more indirect benefit than those corporate executives and shareholders who receive the financial rewards
associated with their sale and marketing. While this is not likely to
change – and while many would argue that it should not change, as it is
the nature of market economics – much of the world views this imbalance as unjust. Some see it as offensive. The "grand bargain" between
the twentieth century pharmaceutical industry and society has served
many of us well, and some of us very well indeed – but it has left
the vast majority of the world's people behind. In some respects, this
imbalance represents a microcosm of today's global reality. Too many
have been left behind in so many ways as technology and prosperity
have distributed themselves around the globe. In the early years of
the twenty-first century we find the world much smaller than it once
was, its people more directly intermingled and interdependent than
ever before, and its resources more limited and its environment more
threatened. We must ask ourselves what kind of world we want to
leave to our next generation – a world in which widespread suffering
and disease generate resentment, and even hatred among its peoples,
or a more compassionate world in which those who have been more
fortunate try to help those who have been less blessed through no fault
of their own.

   If the pharmaceutical industry, during this process of renegotiating its contract with society for the next century, can commit itself to
conduct guided by the same ethical principles that guide the human
experiments upon which the future of the industry depends, it can
preserve both its continued success and the goodness of its corporate
soul. The pharmaceutical industry uses people as a means to achieve
its desired goals, but it must not exploit them. This is what respect,
beneficence, and justice are all about, and these principles provide the
only acceptable foundation upon which the industry's grand bargain
with society can be morally justified and sustained.

   Contemporary business philosophers, including some of those in this
volume, argue that times of challenge are times of opportunity. This
being the case, one might well argue that the pharmaceutical industry
is facing the greatest period of opportunity in its history. I submit that
this is indeed the case, and that with leadership, courage, and a real
willingness to implement meaningful changes in those practices that
lie at the heart of current concerns, the industry can emerge revitalized

with its public image restored to respectability. In doing so, the industry can position itself to better meet the challenges of the new millennium and possibly avoid another round of reactive regulatory zeal.

This book offers many promising ideas about how to address the challenges facing the pharmaceutical industry and the global health crisis. Ideas become reality when they attract champions, people willing to invest the energy and take the risks to make things happen, to stimulate dialogue and to foster change. The time for change, for renegotiating the "grand bargain," is now. To do so, we must bring together the many stakeholders for an open and forthright discussion of the realities and proposed solutions, and work together to develop a comprehensive long-term vision for the industry, governments, and the people who look to them with hope for better lives. If we are willing, we will be able to find the right balance of prices and profits, people, and principles to re-create a just and sustainable pharmaceutical industry for the next century, and the payoffs will be well worth the effort.

Notes

Notes to General Introduction

1. Harris G, "Drug Companies Seek to Mend Their Image," *The New York Times*, July 8, 2004.
2. Ibid.
3. Available at www.harrisinteractive.com/news/allnewsbydate.asp?NewsID =814 Accessed May 18, 2005.
4. Schaffler R, "Gallup Poll Get Public's Image of Variety of Occupations," *CNNfn*, Transcript # 090911cb.l05, September 9, 2003: 1.
5. Rowland C, "An Ailing Image Drug Industry's Tenacious Price Protection Stirs Anger," *The Boston Globe*, July 11, 2003.
6. Harris G, "Drug Companies Seek to Mend Their Image."

Notes to Part I Introduction

1. Ethical considerations in the administration of placebos to patients in control groups are discussed in chapters by Idänpään-Heikkilä and Fluss, Murphy and Goldkind, and Nelson.
2. Bond E, "Malaria's Overlooked Resurgence," *The Washington Post*, July 12, 2004: A17.
3. For a seminal article calling for market solutions to reducing global poverty, see Prahalad CK, and Hammond A "Serving the World's Poor, Profitably," *Harvard Business Review*, September 2002.
4. See www.oneworldhealth.org Accessed May 18, 2005.
5. The information about the development of Invermectin comes from *Merck & Co., Inc.*, by the Business Enterprise Trust, reprinted in Donaldson T, Werhane P, and Cording M, *Ethical Issues in Business: A Philosophical Approach*, seventh ed. (Upper Saddle River, NJ: Prentice Hall, 2002). The quotation from George W. Merck can be found at www.merck.com/ newsroom/executive_speeches/120150.html Accessed May 21, 2005.

6. For a fascinating study of the development of the modern FDA, see Hilts P, *Protecting America's Health: The FDA, Business, and One Hundred Years of Regulation* (New York: Alfred A. Knopf, 2003).

7. See Joseph Needham, *Science in Traditional China* (Cambridge, MA: Harvard University Press, 1981), pp. 96–8.

8. Silverman E, "Judge Upholds $1 B Diet-Drug Verdict Against Wyeth," *Newark Star-Ledger*, May 18, 2004: 034.

9. Harris G, "Lawmaker Says F.D.A. Held Back Drug Data," *The New York Times*, September 10, 2004; Vedantam S, "Journals Insist Drug Manufacturers Register All Trials," *Washington Post*, September 9, 2004: A2. A trenchant source of further information about antidepressant safety issues is the Web site of the International Coalition for Drug Awareness. Available at www.drugawareness.org Accessed May 21, 2005.

10. Mathews AW, and Martinez B, "E-Mails Suggest Merck Knew Vioxx's Dangers at Early Stage," *The Wall Street Journal*, November 1, 2004: A1.

11. Martinez B, "Merck & Co. Offers Rationale, Context for Vioxx Memos," *The Wall Street Journal*, November 15, 2004: A5.

12. See, e.g., the comments on the FDA in the *Cato Institute's Handbook for Congress*. Available at www.cato.org/pubs/pas/pa-475es.html Accessed May 21, 2005.

13. See Benjamin Wilson, "The Rise and Fall of Laetrile." Available at www.quackwatch.org/01QuackeryRelatedTopics/Cancer/laetrile.html Accessed May 21, 2005.

14. See Martin Delaney's chapter (17) in Part III.

15. Pollock A, "Many See Hope in Parkinson's Drug Pulled from Testing," *The New York Times*, November 26, 2004.

16. For an account of the Gingrich-led assault on the FDA, see Hilts P, *Protecting America's Health: The FDA, Business, and One Hundred Years of Regulation*, pp. 295–308.

17. Bowe C, "Merck under Spotlight for 'Deal' with US Drug Regulators," *Financial Times*, October 16, 2004.

18. "FDA Releases Memo on Vioxx," *Bloomberg News*, November 3, 2004.

19. See Harris G, "FDA's Drug Safety System Will Get Outside Review," *The New York Times*, November 6, 2004.

20. Grady D, "Medical Journal Calls for a New Drug Watchdog," *The New York Times*, November 23, 2004.

21. See Harris G, "FDA's Drug Safety System Will Get Outside Review," *The New York Times*, November 6, 2004.

22. Iwasaki J, "Studies Struggle to Overcome Mistrust among Some Blacks," *The Seattle Post-Intelligencer*, August 31, 2003: A21.

23. Marchione M, "Medical Research Re-examined; 25 Years Later, Protecting the Vulnerable Still Vital," *Milwaukee Journal Sentinel*, May 24, 2004: Health and Science section, p. 1G.

24. Great controversy has arisen in the case of the use of placebos in studies of drugs to stop mother-to-child HIV transmission in third world countries. Many scientists argued that such methods were scientifically indispensable. Others have expressed concerns about the ability of vulnerable patients to consent freely to participate in such studies, particularly when a mother is desperate to seek therapy for her unborn child.
25. Pub. L. No. 105-115.
26. Pub. L. No. 107-109.
27. See, e.g., Pollack A, "Dying Man's Suit Tests a Drug's Availability," *The New York Times*, April 27, 2003: Section 3, p. 10; Noonan E, "Creating Hope out of Heartbreak after Its Loss, Santino Family Continues to Fight for Better Access to Experimental Drugs," *The Boston Globe*, March 21, 2002: 1; Tansey B, "Experiments on Humans; A Split Verdict on Clinical Trials; Studies Offer Hope – And Raise a Series of Ethical Questions." *The San Francisco Chronicle*, August 6, 2002: A1
28. See "Multiple Myeloma: Opportunities to Get More Patients Into Clinical Trials Is Being Missed." *Clinical Trials Week*, January 5, 2002: Editor's Choice section, p. 2.
29. "A New Medication Has Dramatically Reduced Mortality among African-American Patients Suffering from Heart Disease." Available at www.news-medical.net/?id=6213 Accessed November 26, 2004.

Notes to Chapter 1

1. Griffin JP, Ed., *Medicines: Regulations, Research and Risk*, 2nd edition (Belfast: Queens University of Belfast, 1992); The European Agency for the Evaluation of Medicinal Products, ICH – Technical Coordination, "EMEA: Common Technical Document for the Registration of Pharmaceuticals for Human Use: Organisation of Common Technical Document," CPMP/ICH/2887/99 (London, 1999).
2. Mooney G, and McGuire A, Eds., *Medical Ethics and Economics in Healthcare* (Oxford: Oxford University Press, 1988), pp. 5–22; Knessel J, *Medizinische Ethik aus Heutiger Sicht* (Basel, Boston, Berlin: Birkhäuser, 1989).
3. Medawar P, and Medawar J, *From Aristotle to Zoo* (Cambridge, MA: Harvard University Press, 1983).
4. A Service of Decision Resources, Inc., "Sepsis/Septic Shock, Infectious Disease Study," November 10, 1993.
5. Beers MH, and Berkow R, Eds., "Infectious Diseases," in *Septic Shock. Merck Manual of Diagnosis and Therapy*, 17th edition (Whitehouse Station, NJ: Merck & Co., 1999), Section 13, Chapter 156.

6. Rothmann DG, "Ethical and Social Issues in the Development of New Drugs and Vaccines," *Bulletin of the New York Academy of Medicine*, 1987, *63*: 557–68.

7. Kaitin KI, Mattison N, Northington FK, and Lasgna L, "The Drug Lag: An Update of New Drug Introductions in the United States and in the United Kingdom, 1977 through 1987," *Clinical Pharmacology and Therapy*, 1989, *46*: 121–38.

8. Drews J, *Grundlagen der Chemotherapie* (Vienna, New York: Springer, 1979), pp. 10–14.

9. Shanks RG, "The Discovery of Beta-Adrenoceptor Blocking Drugs," in Parnham MG, and Breuinvels J, Eds., *Discoveries in Pharmacology*, Vol. 2 (Amsterdam, New York, Oxford: Elsevier, 1984), pp. 46–70.

10. Drews J, *In Quest of Tomorrow's Medicines* (New York: Springer, 1999 and 2003).

11. Drews J, "The Economics of R & D," *Chimica Oggi*, 1993, *May*: 9–12.

12. "Tufts Center for the Study of Drug Development Pegs Cost of a New Prescription Medicine at $802 Million." Copyright 2004. Available at www.csdd.edu/NewEvents/RecentNews.asp?newsid=6 Nov. 30, 2001. Accessed Oct. 4, 2004.

13. Pilcher H, et al., "Snapshot of a Pandemic," *Nature*, 2004, *430*: 135–40.

14. Drews J, "Strategic Trends in the Pharmaceutical Industry," *Drug Discovery Today*, 2003, *8*: 411–20.

15. Drews J, "Orphan Drugs aus Europäischer Sicht," *Pharm. Ind.*, 1988, *50*: 803–5.

16. Orphan Europe SARL, France, "The Orphan Drug Legislations." Copyright 1997–2002. Available at www.orphan-europe.com/1038580716.html Accessed Oct. 4, 2004.

17. Available at www.theglobalfund.org/en/ Accessed May 25, 2005.

18. Bill & Melinda Gates Foundation. Available at www.gatesfoundation.org.

19. Waldholz M, "Fifteen Drug Firms in U.S. and Europe Plan to Collaborate on Tests of AIDS Medicines," *The Wall Street Journal*, April 21, 1993; and Tanouye E, "Pharmaceutical Consortium to Begin Clinical Trials of Combined AIDS Drugs," *The Wall Street Journal*, April 14, 1994.

Notes to Chapter 2

1. World Medical Association (WMA), *Declaration of Helsinki*, 2000. Available at www.wma.net Accessed May 25, 2005.

2. WHO, *Guidelines for Good Clinical Practice (GCP) for Trials on Pharmaceutical Products*, WHO Technical Report Series 850 (Geneva: WHO, 1999), pp. 97–137.

3. CIOMS, *International Ethical Guidelines for Biomedical Research Involving Human Subjects*, (Geneva: CIOMS, 2002). Available at www.cioms.ch Accessed May 25, 2005.
4. ICH, *ICH Good Clinical Practice Guideline*, 1996. Available at www.ich.org Accessed May 26, 2005.
5. The European Parliament and the Council, *Directive 2001/20/EC*, 2001. Available at www.europa.eu.int/eur-lex Accessed May 25, 2005.
6. The European Parliament and the Council, *Directive 2001/20/EC*; and Idänpään-Heikkilä JE, "Ethical Principles for the Guidance of Physicians in Medical Research – The Declaration of Helsinki," *WHO Bulletin*, 2001, 79: 279.
7. WHO, "Marketing Authorization of Pharmaceutical Products with Special Reference to Multisource (Generic) Products, a Manual for a Drug Regulatory Authority," Document WHO/DMP/RGS/98.5, 1999; and WHO, *Proceedings of the Ninth International Conference of Drug Regulatory Authorities (ICDRA), Berlin, April 1999* (Geneva: WHO and BfArM, 2000).
8. WHO, *Marketing Authorization of Pharmaceutical Products with Special Reference to Multisource (Generic) Products*; and WHO, *Proceedings of the Ninth International Conference of Drug Regulatory Authorities (ICDRA)*.
9. Nuremberg Municipal Museum, *The Nazi Party Rally Grounds in Nuremberg. Fascination and Terror*, 1996, pp. 43–4; and Fluss S, "Ethical Aspects of the Control of Human Subjects Research: A Brief Overview of the Current International Configuration," in Levine RJ, Gorovitz S, and Gallagher J, Eds., *Biomedical Research Ethics: Updating International Guidelines. A Consultation* (Geneva: CIOMS, 2000), pp. 248–68.
10. WMA, *Declaration of Helsinki*. The "Notes of Clarification" to paragraphs 29 and 39 clarify the circumstances under which placebo-controlled trials should not be used, as well as cases in which placebo-controlled trials could be considered ethically acceptable, and recommend the design of post-trial access to patients of treatments found to be beneficial in clinical trials. The WMA Web site provides the text of the Declaration in the version supplemented in Tokyo in September 2004. Available at www.wma.net/e/policy/b3.htm Accessed December 6, 2004. See also Carlson RV, Boyd KM, and Webb DJ, "The Revision of the Declaration of Helsinki: Past, Present, and Future," in the *British Journal of Clinical Pharmacology*, June 2004, 57: 6, 695–713.
11. Fluss S, "Ethical Aspects of the Control of Human Subjects Research."
12. CIOMS, *International Ethical Guidelines for Biomedical Research Involving Human Subjects*; Idänpään-Heikkilä JE, "Ethical Principles for the Guidance of Physicians in Medical Research"; and Levine RJ, "Revision

of the CIOMS International Ethical Guidelines: A Progress Report," in Levine RJ, Gorovitz S, and Gallagher J, Eds., *Biomedical Research Ethics: Updating International Guidelines. A Consultation* (Geneva: CIOMS, 2000), pp. 4–15.

13. Idänpään-Heikkilä JE, and Fluss S, "Revised CIOMS International Ethical Guidelines for Biomedical Research," *Journal of Commercial Biotechnology*, 2003, *10*: 140–46.

14. CIOMS, *International Ethical Guidelines for Biomedical Research Involving Human Subjects.*

15. WHO, *Guidelines for Good Clinical Practice (GCP) for Trials on Pharmaceutical Products.*

16. ICH, *ICH Good Clinical Practice Guideline.*

17. UNAIDS, *Ethical Considerations in HIV Preventive Vaccine Research,* (Geneva: UNAIDS, 2000).

18. The European Parliament and the Council, *Directive 2001/20/EC.*

19. The Council of Europe, *Protocol concerning Biomedical Research, Additional Protocol to the Council's 1997 Convention on Human Rights and Biomedicine,* 2004. Available at www.coe.int Accessed May 25, 2005.

20. UNESCO, Report by the Director-General on the Drawing Up of a Declaration on Universal Norms on Bioethics, Document 171 EX/13, March 9, 2005.

21. WMA, *Declaration of Helsinki*; WHO, *Guidelines for Good Clinical Practice (GCP) for Trials on Pharmaceutical Products*; CIOMS, *International Ethical Guidelines for Biomedical Research Involving Human Subjects*; ICH, *ICH Good Clinical Practice Guideline*; the European Parliament and the Council, *Directive 2001/20/EC*; UNAIDS, *Ethical Considerations in HIV Preventive Vaccine Research*; and the Council of Europe, *Protocol concerning Biomedical Research, Additional Protocol to the Council's 1997 Convention on Human Rights and Biomedicine.*

22. CIOMS, *International Ethical Guidelines for Biomedical Research Involving Human Subjects.*

23. WMA, *Declaration of Helsinki.*

24. WHO, *Marketing Authorization of Pharmaceutical Products with Special Reference to Multisource (Generic) Products*; WHO, *Proceedings of the Ninth International Conference of Drug Regulatory Authorities (ICDRA)*; and Nuffield Council on Bioethics, *The Ethics of Research Related to Healthcare in Developing Countries* (London: Nuffield Council on Bioethics, 2002).

25. WMA, *Declaration of Helsinki*; WHO, *Guidelines for Good Clinical Practice (GCP) for Trials on Pharmaceutical Products*; CIOMS, *International Ethical Guidelines for Biomedical Research Involving Human Subjects*;

ICH, *ICH Good Clinical Practice Guideline*; and the European Parliament and the Council, *Directive 2001/20/EC.*

26. WHO, *Guidelines for Good Clinical Practice (GCP) for Trials on Pharmaceutical Products.*

27. ICH, *ICH Good Clinical Practice Guideline.*

28. Ibid.

29. CIOMS, *International Ethical Guidelines for Biomedical Research Involving Human Subjects*; and the European Parliament and the Council, *Directive 2001/20/EC.*

30. WMA, *Declaration of Helsinki*; WHO, *Guidelines for Good Clinical Practice (GCP) for Trials on Pharmaceutical Products*; CIOMS, *International Ethical Guidelines for Biomedical Research Involving Human Subjects*; ICH, *ICH Good Clinical Practice Guideline*; the European Parliament and the Council, *Directive 2001/20/EC*; UNAIDS, *Ethical Considerations in HIV Preventive Vaccine Research*; the Council of Europe, *Protocol concerning Biomedical Research*; and Nuffield Council on Bioethics, *The Ethics of Research Related to Healthcare in Developing Countries.*

31. Idänpään-Heikkilä JE, "Ethical Principles for the Guidance of Physicians in Medical Research"; WHO, *Marketing Authorization of Pharmaceutical Products with Special Reference to Multisource (Generic) Products*; WHO, *Proceedings of the Ninth International Conference of Drug Regulatory Authorities (ICDRA)*; Nuremberg Municipal Museum, *The Nazi Party Rally Grounds in Nuremberg*; Qiu R-Z, "Asian Perspectives: Tension between Modern Values and Chinese Culture," in Bankowski Z, and Levine RJ, Eds., *Ethics and Research on Human Subjects* (Geneva: CIOMS, 1993), pp. 188–96; and Nuffield Council on Bioethics, *The Ethics of Research Related to Healthcare in Developing Countries*, 2002.

32. CIOMS, *International Ethical Guidelines for Biomedical Research Involving Human Subjects*; UNAIDS, *Ethical Considerations in HIV Preventive Vaccine Research*; Osuntokun BO, "An African Perspective," in Bankowski Z, and Levine RJ, Eds., *Ethics and Research on Human Subjects* (Geneva: CIOMS, 1993), pp. 173–6; and Marshall PA, "Informed Consent in International Health Research," in Levine RJ, Gorovitz S, and Gallagher J, Eds., *Biomedical Research Ethics: Updating International Guidelines. A Consultation* (Geneva: CIOMS, 2000), pp. 100–34.

33. Osuntokun BO, "An African Perspective"; Qiu R-Z, "Asian Perspectives"; Marshall PA, "Informed Consent in International Health Research"; and Hasan KZ, "An Eastern Mediterranean Perspective: Islamic and Cultural Influences," in Bankowski Z, and Levine RJ, Eds., *Ethics and Research on Human Subjects* (Geneva: CIOMS, 1993), pp. 198–200.

34. Qiu R-Z, "Asian Perspectives."

35. CIOMS, *International Ethical Guidelines for Biomedical Research Involving Human Subjects*; UNAIDS, *Ethical Considerations in HIV Preventive Vaccine Research*; Macklin R, "Reproductive Biology and Technology: Ethical Issues," in Levine RJ, Gorovitz S, and Gallagher J, Eds., *Biomedical Research Ethics: Updating International Guidelines. A Consultation* (Geneva: CIOMS, 2000), pp. 208–24; and Nuffield Council on Bioethics, *The Ethics of Research Related to Healthcare in Developing Countries.*

36. Qiu R-Z, "Asian Perspectives"; and Macklin R, "Reproductive Biology and Technology."

37. CIOMS, *International Ethical Guidelines for Biomedical Research Involving Human Subjects.*

38. Ibid.; and Macklin R, "Reproductive Biology and Technology."

39. CIOMS, *International Ethical Guidelines for Biomedical Research Involving Human Subjects*; Osuntokun BO, "An African Perspective"; Qiu R-Z, "Asian Perspectives"; Marshall PA, "Informed Consent in International Health Research"; and Nuffield Council on Bioethics, *The Ethics of Research Related to Healthcare in Developing Countries.*

40. WMA, *Declaration of Helsinki*; WHO, *Guidelines for Good Clinical Practice (GCP) for Trials on Pharmaceutical Products*; CIOMS, *International Ethical Guidelines for Biomedical Research Involving Human Subjects*; ICH, *ICH Good Clinical Practice Guideline*; and the European Parliament and the Council, *Directive 2001/20/EC.*

41. CIOMS, *International Ethical Guidelines for Biomedical Research Involving Human Subjects.*

42. WMA, *Declaration of Helsinki*; WHO, *Guidelines for Good Clinical Practice (GCP) for Trials on Pharmaceutical Products*; CIOMS, *International Ethical Guidelines for Biomedical Research Involving Human Subjects*; ICH, *ICH Good Clinical Practice Guideline*; and the European Parliament and the Council, *Directive 2001/20/EC.*

43. CIOMS, *International Ethical Guidelines for Biomedical Research Involving Human Subjects.*

44. WMA, *Declaration of Helsinki*; WHO, *Guidelines for Good Clinical Practice (GCP) for Trials on Pharmaceutical Products*; CIOMS, *International Ethical Guidelines for Biomedical Research Involving Human Subjects*; ICH, *ICH Good Clinical Practice Guideline*; the European Parliament and the Council, *Directive 2001/20/EC*; UNAIDS, *Ethical Considerations in HIV Preventive Vaccine Research*; the Council of Europe, *Protocol concerning Biomedical Research*; and Nuffield Council on Bioethics, *The Ethics of Research Related to Healthcare in Developing Countries.*

45. WHO, *Guidelines for Good Clinical Practice (GCP) for Trials on Pharmaceutical Products*; ICH, *ICH Good Clinical Practice Guideline*; and the European Parliament and the Council, *Directive 2001/20/EC.*

46. WHO, *Guidelines for Good Clinical Practice (GCP) for Trials on Pharmaceutical Products.*
47. Fluss S, "Ethical Aspects of the Control of Human Subjects Research"; and Levine RJ, "Revision of the CIOMS International Ethical Guidelines."
48. ICH, *ICH Good Clinical Practice Guideline*; WHO, *Marketing Authorization of Pharmaceutical Products with Special Reference to Multisource (Generic) Products*; and WHO, *Proceedings of the Ninth International Conference of Drug Regulatory Authorities (ICDRA).*
49. WHO, *Guidelines for Good Clinical Practice (GCP) for Trials on Pharmaceutical Products*; and ICH, *ICH Good Clinical Practice Guideline.*
50. WHO, *Guidelines for Good Clinical Practice (GCP) for Trials on Pharmaceutical Products.*
51. Ibid.; ICH, *ICH Good Clinical Practice Guideline*; and the European Parliament and the Council, *Directive 2001/20/EC.*
52. WHO, *Guidelines for Good Clinical Practice (GCP) for Trials on Pharmaceutical Products*; ICH, *ICH Good Clinical Practice Guideline*; and the European Parliament and the Council, *Directive 2001/20/EC.*
53. WMA, *Declaration of Helsinki.*
54. Ibid.
55. Ibid.

Notes to Chapter 3

1. Shirkey HC, "Therapeutic Orphans," *Pediatrics*, 1968, *72*: 119–20.
2. Biologics Control Act of 1902, Pub. L. No. 570244, 32 Stat. 328, 1902.
3. Federal Food, Drug and Cosmetic Act, Pub. L. No. 75-717, 52 Stat. 1040, 1938.
4. Drug Amendments of 1962, Pub. L. No. 87-781, 76 Stat. 780, 1962.
5. Beecher HK, "Ethics and Clinical Research," *NEJM*, 1996, *274*: 1354–60. One cited study involved deliberately infecting institutionalized children with hepatitis to ascertain more about its infectivity. The research had been justified because hepatitis was endemic in the Willowbrook facility, but ethical concern abounded, particularly because of the potentially coercive incentives for study, in that enrollment expedited placement in the institution.
6. "Labeling and Prescription Drug Advertising: Content and Format for Labeling for Human Prescription Drugs," *Federal Register*, 1979, *44*:37434.
7. Wilson JT, "Update on the Therapeutic Orphan," *Pediatrics*, 1999, *104*: 585–590.
8. "Specific Requirements on Content and Format of Labeling for Human Prescription Drugs; Proposed Revision of 'Pediatric Use' Subsection in the Labeling," *Federal Register*, 1992, *57*: 47423.

9. "Specific Requirements on Content and Format of Labeling for Human Prescription Drugs; Revision of 'Pediatric Use' Subsection in the Labeling," *Federal Register*, 1994, *59*: 64242.

10. Food and Drug Administration Modernization Act of 1997, Pub. L. No. 105–115. Available at www.fda.gov/opacom/7modact.html Accessed May 26, 2005.

11. Best Pharmaceuticals for Children Act of 2002, Pub. L No. 107-109.

12. "Regulations Requiring Manufacturers to Assess the Safety and Effectiveness of New Drugs and Biological Products in Pediatric Patients," *Federal Register*, 1998, *63*: 66631.

13. BPCA Section 9.

14. Available at www.fda.gov/medwatch/index.html Accessed May 26, 2005.

15. Food and Drug Administration Modernization Act of 1997, Section 111; National Institutes of Health policy and guidelines on the inclusion of children in research. Available at www.grants.nih.gov/grants/guide/notice-files/not98-024.html Accessed May 26, 2005. Pediatric Research Equity Act of 2003.

16. American Academy of Pediatrics, Committee on Drugs, "Guidelines for the Ethical Conduct of Studies to Evaluate Drugs in Pediatric Populations," *Pediatrics*, 1977, *60*: 91–101.

17. Beauchamp TL, and Childress JF, *Principles of Biomedical Ethics*, 5th ed. (Oxford: Oxford University Press, 2001), pp. 165–76.

18. Beauchamp and Childress, *Principles of Biomedical Ethics*, p. 115.

19. Emanuel EJ, Wendler D, and Grady C, "What Makes Clinical Research Ethical?" *JAMA*, May 24/31, 2000, *283(20)*: 2701–11.

20. Shah S, Whittle A, Wilfond B, Gensler G, and Wendler D, "How Do Institutional Review Boards Apply the Federal Risk and Benefit Standards for Pediatric Research?" *JAMA*, January 28, 2004, *291(4)*: 476–82.

21. The International Conference on Harmonised Tripartate Guidelines – Guidance for Industry, "E11: *Clinical Investigation of Medicinal Products in the Pediatric Population*," p. 3. Available at www.fda.gov/cder/guidance/index.htm Accessed May 26, 2005. The ICH Harmonised Tripartate Guidelines – Guideline for Good Clinical Practice guidances were adopted by the regulatory bodies of the European Union, Japan, and the United States. Good Clinical Practice is an international ethical and scientific quality standard for designing, conducting, recording, and reporting trials that involve human subjects.

22. Coffey MJ, Wilfond B, Ross LF, "Ethical Assessment of Clinical Asthma Trials Including Children Subjects," *Pediatrics*, January 2004, *113(1)*: 87–94.

23. The International Conference on Harmonised Tripartate Guidelines – Guidance for Industry, "E6: *Good Clinical Practice: Consolidated Guidance*," p. 9. Available at www.fda.gov/cder/guidance/index.htm Accessed May 26, 2005.

24. The National Commission for the Protection of Human Subjects of Biomedical and Behavioral Research, *Report and Recommendations: Research Involving Children.*

25. 21 CFR 50.3(k) and 45 CFR 46.102(i).

26. The National Commission for the Protection of Human Subjects of Biomedical and Behavioral Research, *Report and Recommendations: Research Involving Children*, p. 153; Report from NHRPAC, "Clarifying Specific Portion of 45 CFR 46 Subpart, D. that Governs Children's Research," p. 1. Available at www.hhs.gov/ohrp/nhrpac/doc-report.htm Accessed May 26, 2005. See also Field MJ and Behrman RE, Eds., *The Ethical Conduct of Clinical Research Involving Children: Institute of Medicine Report* (Washington, DC: The National Academies Press, 2004), pp. 4–9 and 4–11, Recommendation 4.1.

27. "November 15, 1999, "Consensus Statement." Available at www.fda.gov/oc/opt/default.htm Accessed May 26, 2005.

28. International Harmonised Tripartate Guidelines – Guidance for Industry, E6: *Good Clinical Practice: Consolidated Guidance*," April 1996, 4.8.14 lists for conditions for "nontherapeutic trials": (a) the objectives of the trial cannot be met by means of a trial in subjects who can give informed consent personally; (b) the foreseeable risks to the subjects are low; (c) the negative impact on the subject's well-being is minimized and low; (d) the trial is not prohibited by law; and (e) the approval/favorable opinion of the IRB/IEC is expressly sought on the inclusion of such subjects, and the written approval/favorable opinion covers this aspect. Such trials, unless an exception is justified, should be conducted in patients having a disease or condition for which the investigational product is intended.

29. FDA Docket No. 2004N-0337. Available at www.fda.gov/ohrms/dockets/dockets/04n0337/04n-0337-m000001.pdf Accessed July 20, 2005.

30. CIOMS, *The International Ethical Guidelines for Biomedical Research Involving Human Subjects*, The Council for International Organizations of Medical Sciences (CIOMS) in collaboration with The World Health Organization (WHO), Geneva, 2002. Available at www.fhi.org/fr/topicsf/ethicsf/curriculum/pdf_files/cioms.pdf Accessed May 26, 2005.

31. International Harmonised Tripartate Guidelines-Topic E8, *General Considerations for Clinical Trials*; The European Agency for the Evaluation of Medicinal Products, *Human Medicines Evaluation Unit*, July, 1997. Available at www.emea.eu.int/htms/human/ich/efficacy/ichfin.htm Accessed May 26, 2005.

32. The National Commission for the Protection of Human Subjects of Biomedical and Behavioral Research, *Report and Recommendations: Research Involving Children*, DHEW Publication No. (OS) 77-0004 (Washington, D.C.: U.S. Government Printing Office, 1977), p. 1.
33. Freedman B, "Equipoise and the Ethics of Clinical Research," *NEJM*, July 16, 1987, *317*: 141–5; Beauchamp and Childress, *Principles of Biomedical Ethics*, p. 323 and 327.
34. Kodish E, Eder M, Noll RB, Ruccione K, Lange B, Angiolillo A, Pentz R, Zyzanski S, Siminoff LA, and Drotar D, "Communication of Randomization in Childhood Leukemia Trials," *JAMA*, January 28, 2004, *291(4)*: 470–5.
35. Coffey, Wilfond, and Ross, "Ethical Assessment of Clinical Asthma Trials Including Children Subjects."
36. Available at www.wma.net/e/policy/b3.htm Accessed May 26, 2005.
37. A placebo-controlled trial may be ethically acceptable, even if proven therapy is available, under the following circumstances: (1) where for compelling and scientifically sound methodological reasons its use is necessary to determine the efficacy or safety of a prophylactic, diagnostic, or therapeutic method, or; (2) where a prophylactic, diagnostic, or therapeutic method is being investigated for a minor condition and the patients who receive placebo will not be subject to any additional risk of serious or irreversible harm. Available at www.wma.net/e/policy/b3.htm Accessed May 26, 2005.
38. www.fhi.org/fr/topicsf/ethicsf/curriculum/pdf_files/cioms.pdf Accessed May 26, 2005. The International Conference on Harmonised Tripartate Guidelines – Guidance for Industry, E10: *Choice of Control Group Related Issues in Clinical Trials* available at www.fda.gov/cder/guidance/index.htm; Emanuel EJ, and Miller FG, "The Ethics of Placebo-Controlled Trials – A Middle Ground," *NEJM*, September 20, 2001, *345(12)*: 915–19; Miller FG, Wendler D, and Wilfond B, "When Do the Federal Regulations Allow Placebo-Controlled Trials in Children?" *The Journal of Pediatrics*, February 2003: 102–7; Temple R, and Ellenberg SS, "Placebo-Controlled Trials and Active-Control Trials in the Evaluation of New Treatments, Part 1: Ethical and Scientific Issues," *Annals of Internal Medicine*, September 2000, *133(6)*: 455–63; and Temple R and Ellenberg SS, "Placebo-Controlled Trials and Active-Control Trials in the Evaluation of New Treatments, Part 2: Practical Issues and Specific Cases," *Annals of Internal Medicine*, September 2000, *133(6)*: 464–70.
39. Concern over newly identified or unquantified risks of current standard therapy may also warrant placebo-controlled studies. Without quantifying a therapeutic gain it is impossible to define a risk–benefit profile.

40. Temple R, and Ellenberg SS, "Placebo-Controlled Trials and Active-Control Trials in the Evaluation of New Treatments, Part 1: Ethical and Scientific Issues."

Notes to Chapter 4

1. "Additional DHHS Protections for Children Involved as Subjects in Research (45 CFR Part 46)," 48 FR 9818, March 8, 1983; 56 FR 28032, June 18, 1991; "Additional Safeguards for Children in Clinical Investigations of FDA-Regulated Products (21 CFR Parts 50 and 56)," 66 FR 20859, April 24, 2001. Hereafter "Subpart D."

2. "Directive 2001/20/EC of the European Parliament and of the Council of 4 April 2001 on the Approximation of the Laws, Regulations and Administrative Provisions of the Member States Relating to the Implementation of Good Clinical Practice in the Conduct of Clinical Trials on Medicinal Products for Human Use," *Official Journal of the European Communities*, January 5, 2001, *L121*: 34–44. Hereafter "EU Clinical Trial Directive."

3. Choonara I, and Conroy S, "Unlicensed and Off-Label Drug Use in Children: Implications for Safety," *Drug Safety*, 2002, *25(1)*: 1–5; Horen B, Montastruc JL, and Lapeyre-Mestre M, "Adverse Drug Reactions and Off-Label Drug Use in Paediatric Outpatients," *British Journal of Clinical Pharmacology*, 2002, *54(6)*: 665–70.

4. "Best Pharmaceuticals For Children Act (P. L. 107-109)," Statutes at Large 115, 1408–24, 2002.

5. "Pediatric Research Equity Act of 2003 (P. L. 108-155)," Statutes at Large 117, 1936–43, 2003.

6. Roberts R, Rodriguez W, Murphy D, and Crescenzi T, "Pediatric Drug Labeling: Improving the Safety and Efficacy of Pediatric Therapies," *JAMA*, 2003, *290(7)*: 905–11.

7. European Commission, "Proposal for a Regulation of the European Parliament and of the Council on Medicinal Products for Paediatric Use and Amending Regulation (EEC) No 1768/92, Directive 2001/83/EC and Regulation (EC) No 726/2004," Brussels, Belgium, 2004. Hereafter "EC Proposal."

8. Field MJ, and Behrman RE, Eds., *Ethical Conduct of Clinical Research Involving Children* (Washington, DC: The National Academies Press, 2004).

9. The National Commission for the Protection of Human Subjects of Biomedical and Behavioral Research, *Research Involving Children: Report and Recommendations* (Washington, DC: U.S. Government Printing Office, 1977).

10. Field and Behrman, *Ethical Conduct of Clinical Research Involving Children*, p. 4.

11. The National Commission, *Research Involving Children: Report and Recommendations*, p. 131.

12. World Medical Association (WMA), *Declaration of Helsinki* (Washington, DC, 2002). Available at www.wma.net/e/policy/b3.htm Accessed May 23, 2005.

13. FDA, "ICH: Good Clinical Practice: Consolidated Guideline." *Federal Register*, May 9, 1997, *62(90)*: 25692–25709. §4.8.14. Hereafter "ICH GCP."

14. FDA, "ICH: E11: Clinical Investigation of Medicinal Products in the Pediatric Population." *Federal Register*, April 12, 2000, *65(71)*: 19777–19781. Hereafter "ICH E-11."

15. "Pediatric Research Equity Act of 2003," Section 2, amending 21 USC 355a.

16. "Questions and Answers about the NIH Policy on the Inclusion of Children as Participants in Research Involving Human Subjects. March 1999." Available at www.grants.nih.gov/grants/funding/children/pol_children_qa.htm Accessed November 22, 2004.

17. 45 CFR 46.102(i); 21 CFR 56.102(i).

18. Shah S, Whittle A, Wilfond B, Gensler G, and Wendler D, "How do Institutional Review Boards Apply the Federal Risk and Benefit Standards for Pediatric Research?" *JAMA*, 2004, *291(4)*: 476–82.

19. Field and Behrman, *Ethical Conduct of Clinical Research Involving Children*, Recommendation 4.1.

20. The National Commission, *Research Involving Children: Report and Recommendations*, p. xx and pp. 153–54.

21. Chair, NIMH IRB, "Request to Forward NIMH Protocol to DHHS for Review," memorandum dated 3/5/04. Available at www.hhs.gov/ohrp/panels/jreview01/irbreq.pdf Accessed November 22, 2004.

22. Kopelman LM, "Children as Research Subjects: A Dilemma," *Journal of Medicine & Philosophy*, 2000, *25(6)*: 745–64.

23. CIOMS, *International Ethical Guidelines for Biomedical Research Involving Human Subjects* (Geneva: World Health Organization, 2002). Commentary on Guideline 4: Individual informed consent.

24. Field and Behrman, *Ethical Conduct of Clinical Research Involving Children*, p. 125.

25. 45 CFR 46.406; 21 CFR 50.53.

26. Freedman B, Fuks A, and Weijer C, "In Loco Parentis: Minimal Risk as an Ethical Threshold for Research upon Children." *Hastings Center Report*, 1993, *23*:13–19.

27. Ross LF, "Do Healthy Children Deserve Greater Protection in Medical Research?" *Journal of Pediatrics*, 2003, *142(2)*: 108–12.

28. Field and Behrman, *Ethical Conduct of Clinical Research Involving Children*, p. 130.

29. In the Court of Appeals of Maryland, September Term, 2000, No. 128, *Ericka Grimes v. Kennedy Krieger Institute, Inc.*

30. Canfield RL, Henderson CR Jr, Cory-Slechta DA, Cox C, Jusko TA, and Lanphear BP, "Intellectual Impairment in Children with Blood Lead Concentrations below 10 Micrograms per Deciliter." *New England Journal of Medicine*, 2003, *348(16)*: 1517–26.

31. See Nelson RM, "Justice, Lead and Environmental Research Involving Children," in Kodish E, Ed., *Pediatric Research Ethics: Learning from Cases* (New York: Oxford University Press, 2005).

32. CIOMS, *International Ethical Guidelines for Biomedical Research Involving Human Subjects*, Commentary on Guideline 4: Individual informed consent.

33. ICH GCP, §4.8.14.

34. 45 CFR §46.405, 21 CFR §50.52.

35. The National Commission, *Research Involving Children: Report and Recommendations*, p. 5–7.

36. EU Clinical Trial Directive, Article 4(e).

37. Personal communication, Peter Liese MP, January 25, 2002.

38. Council of Europe, "Convention for the Protection of Human Rights and Dignity of the Human Being with Regard to the Application of Biology and Medicine: Convention on Human Rights and Biomedicine." European Treaty Series, No. 164. Oviedo, 4.IV.1997. Article 17.

39. Field and Behrman, *Ethical Conduct of Clinical Research Involving Children*, p. 138.

40. WMA, *Declaration of Helsinki*, Paragraph 29.

41. FDA, "International Conference on Harmonisation; Choice of Control Group in Clinical Trials," *Federal Register*, September 24, 1999, *64(185)*: 51767–80. Hereafter "ICH E–10."

42. WMA, *Declaration of Helsinki*.

43. 45 CFR §46.405; 21 CFR §50.52.

44. Medical Research Council of Canada, "Tri-Council Policy Statement: Ethical Conduct for Research Involving Humans," August 1998: 7.1.

45. Shapiro G, Bronsky EA, LaForce CF, Mendelson L, Pearlman D, Schwartz RH, and Szefler SJ, "Dose-Related Efficacy of Budesonide Administered via a Dry Powder Inhaler in the Treatment of Children with Moderate to Severe Persistent Asthma," *Journal of Pediatrics*, 1998, *132(6)*: 976–82.

46. Ferdman RM, and Church JA, "Ethical Issues of Placebo-Controlled Trials," *Journal of Pediatrics*, 1999, *134(2)*: 251–2; Coffey MJ, Wilfond B, and Ross LF, "Ethical Assessment of Clinical Asthma Trials Including Children Subjects," *Pediatrics*, 2004, *113*: 87–94.

47. ICH E–10.

48. WMA, *Declaration of Helsinki*.
49. Miller FG, Wendler D, and Wilfond B, "When Do the Federal Regulations Allow Placebo-Controlled Trials in Children?" *Journal of Pediatrics*, 2003, *142(2)*: 102–7.
50. FDA, "BPCA Clinical Summary of NDA 20–548, SE8-018," June 4, 2003. Available at www.fda.gov/cder/foi/esum/2003/20548se8018BPCArev2.pdf Accessed November 22, 2004.
51. National Heart, Lung, and Blood Institute, "Guidelines for the Diagnosis and Management of Asthma," NIH Pub. No. 97-4051, July 1997. Available at www.nhlbi.nih.gov/guidelines/asthma/asthgdln.pdf Accessed November 22, 2004.
52. FDA, "BPCA Clinical Summary."
53. Personal communication, Diane Murphy, MD, September 15, 2004.
54. FDA, "ICH. E-4. Dose-Response Information to Support Drug Registration," *Federal Register*, November 9, 1994, *59(216)*: 55,972–6.
55. Murphy D, "Occurrence of Suicidality in Clinical Trials for Antidepressant Drugs in Pediatric Patients," September 13, 2004. Available at www.fda.gov/ohrms/dockets/ac/04/slides/2004-4065S1_01_FDA-Murphy.ppt Accessed November 22, 2004.
56. FDA Clinical Review, NDA: 20-031; S-037. Oct. 7, 2002. Available at www.fda.gov/cder/foi/esum/2004/20031s037_paxil_Clincal_BPCA_FIN.pdf Accessed November 22, 2004.
57. Laughren T, "Regulatory Background on Antidepressants and Suicidality in Pediatric Patients," September 13, 2004. Available at www.fda.gov/ohrms/dockets/ac/04/slides/2004-4065S1_02_FDA-Laughren.ppt Accessed November 22, 2004.
58. Duff G, "SSRI – Use in Children and Adolescents with MDD," December 10, 2003. Available at www.medicines.mhra.gov.uk/ourwork/monitorsafequalmed/safetymessages/cemssri_101203.pdf Accessed November 22, 2004.
59. Lenzer J, "FDA Panel Urges 'Black Box' Warning for Antidepressants." *British Medical Journal*, 2004, *329(7468)*: 702.
60. Hammad T, "Results of the Analysis of Suicidality in Pediatric Trials of Newer Antidepressants," September 13, 2004. Available at www.fda.gov/ohrms/dockets/ac/04/slides/2004-4065S1_08_FDA-Hammad.ppt Accessed November 22, 2004.
61. FDA Clinical Review for NDA 20-151 Supplement SE5-024, June 6, 2003. Available at www.fda.gov/cder/foi/esum/2003/20151se5024BPCA.pdf Accessed November 22, 2004.
62. Hammad, "Results of the Analysis of Suicidality in Pediatric Trials of Newer Antidepressants."
63. Rennie D, "Trial Registration: A Great Idea Switches from Ignored to Irresistible." *JAMA*, 2004, *292(11)*: 1359–62.

64. Steinbrook R, "Registration of Clinical Trials – Voluntary or Mandatory?" *New England Journal of Medicine*, 2004, *351(18)*: 1820–22.
65. De Angelis C, Drazen JM, Frizelle FA, et al., "Clinical Trial Registration: A Statement from the International Committee of Medical Journal Editors," *Lancet*, 2004, *364(9438)*: 911–12.
66. Steinbrook, "Registration of Clinical Trials."
67. Congressional Record – Senate, October 7, 2004, S10728–731; Congressional Record – Extensions of Remarks, October 11, 2004, E1882–83.

Notes to Chapter 5

1. A report of the Institute of Medicine found that these disparities exist even after adjustment for differences in socioeconomic status, insurance coverage, income, age, comorbid conditions, expression of symptoms, and healthcare access-related factors. IOM Report, *Unequal Treatment: Confronting Racial and Ethnic Disparities in Healthcare* (Washington, DC: National Academy Press, 2002).
2. Bach PB, Cramer LD, Warren JL, and Begg CB, "Racial Differences in the Treatment of Early Stage Lung Cancer," *New England Journal of Medicine*, 1999, *341*: 1198–1205.
3. Bernabei R, Gambassi G, Lapane K, et al., "Management of Pain in Elderly Patients with Cancer," *JAMA*, 1998, *279*: 1877–82.
4. Schneidger EC, Leape LL, Weissman JS, et al., "Racial Differences in Cardiac Revascularization Rate: Does 'Overuse' Explain Higher Rates among White Patients?" *Annals of Internal Medicine*, 2001, *135*: 328–37.
5. Freeman HP, and Payne R, "Racial Injustice in Healthcare," *New England Journal of Medicine*, 2000, *342*: 1045–7.
6. Morrison RS, Wallenstein S, Natale DK, et al., "'We Don't Carry That' – Failure of Pharmacies in Predominately Nonwhite Neighborhoods to Stock Opioid Analgesics," *New England Journal of Medicine*, 2000, *342*: 1023–6.
7. Lee S, Mountain J, and Koenig BA, "The Meanings of 'Race' in the New Genomics; Implications for Health Disparities Research," *Yale Journal of Health Policy, Law, and Ethics*, 2001, *1*: 33–75.
8. Veterans Administration Cooperative Study Group on Antihypertensive Agents, "Comparison of Propranolol and Hydrochlorothiazide for the Initial Treatment of Hypertension I: Results of Short-Term Titration with Emphasis on Racial Differences in Response," *JAMA*, 1982, *248*: 1996–2003; and Ahluwalia JS, and McNagny SE, "Smoking Prevalence and Desire to Quit in Inner City African American Walk-In Clinic Patients," *Clinical Research*, 1993, *41*: 752A.
9. Schwartz RS, "Racial Profiling in Medical Research," *New England Journal of Medicine*, 2001, *344(18)*: 1392–3; and Flack JM, Mensah GA,

and Ferrario CM, "Using Angiotensin Converting Enzyme Inhibitors in African-American Hypertensives: A New Approach to Treating Hypertension and Preventing Target-Organ Damage," *Current Medical Research and Opinion*, 2000, *16*: 66–79.

10. Lin KM, and Poland RE, "Ethnicity, Culture, and Psychopharmacology," in Bloom FF and Kupfer DJ, Eds., *Psychopharmacology, The Fourth Generation of Progress* (Nashville, TN: American College of Neuropsychopharmacology, 2000).

11. Strickland TL, Ranganath V, Lin KM, Poland RE, Mendoza R, and Smith MW, "Psychopharmacological Considerations in the Treatment of Black American Populations," *Psychopharmacology Bulletin*, 1991, *27(4)*: 441–8.

12. Meyer UA and Zanger UM, "Molecular Mechanisms of Genetic Polymorphisms of Drug Metabolism," *Annual Review of Pharmacology and Toxicology*, 1997, *37*: 269–96.

13. Xie HG, Kim RB, Wood AJ, and Stein CM, "Molecular Basis of Ethnic Differences in Drug Disposition and Response," *Annual Review of Pharmacology and Toxicology*, 2001, *41*: 815–50.

14. Lieberman JA, Yunis J, Egea E, Canoso RT, Kane JM, and Yunis EJ, "HLA-B38, DR4, Dqw3 and Clozapine-Induced Agranulocytosis in Jewish Patients with Schizophrenia," *Archives of General Psychiatry* 1990, *47(10)*: 945–8.

15. Schwartz RS, "Racial Profiling in Medical Research," *New England Journal of Medicine*, 2001, *344(18)*: 1392–3; and Wood AJ, "Racial Differences in the Response to Drugs – Pointers to Genetic Differences," *New England Journal of Medicine*, May 3, 2001, *344(18)*: 1394–6.

16. Poolsup N, Li Wan Po A, Knight TL, "Pharmacogenetics and Psychopharmacotherapy," *Journal of Clinical Pharmacology and Therapeutics*, 2000, *25(3)*: 197–220.

17. Vesell ES, "The Influence of Host Factors On Drug Response, I: Ethnic Background," *Rational Drug Therapy*, 1979, *13(8)*: 1–7.

18. Lin KM, and Poland RE, "Ethnicity, Culture, and Psychopharmacology."

19. Benowitz NL, "Substance Abuse: Dependence and Treatment," in Melmon KL, Morelli HF, Hoffman BB, and Nierenberg DW, Eds., *Clinical Pharmacology, Basic Principles in Therapeutics* (New York: McGraw Hill, 1992).

20. Resnicow K, Futterman R, Weston RE, Royce J, Parms C, Freeman HP, and Orlandi MA, "Smoking Prevalence in Harlem, New York," *American Journal of Health Promotion*, 1996, *10*: 343–46.

21. Caraballo RS, Giovino GA, Pechacek TF, et al., "Racial and Ethnic Differences in Serum Nicotine Levels of Adult Cigarette Smokers," Third National Health and Nutrition Examination Survey, 1988–91, *JAMA*, 1998, *280*: 135–9; and Perez-Stable EJ, Herrera B, Jacob P, and Benowitz

NL, "Nicotine Metabolism and Intake in Black and White Smokers," *JAMA*, 1998, *280*: 152–6.

22. Royce JM, Hymowitz N, Corbett K, Hartwell TD, and Orlandi MA, for the COMMIT Research Group, "Smoking Cessation Factors among African Americans and Whites," *American Journal of Public Health*, 1993, *83*: 220–6; Giovino GA, Schooley MW, Zhu BP, et al., "Surveillance for Selected Tobacco-Use Behaviors – United States, 1900–1994," in Centers for Disease Control Surveillance Summaries, November 18, 1994, *Morbidity and Mortality Weekly Report*, 1994, *43*: 1–43; Fiore MC, Novotny TE, Pierce JP, Hatziandreu EJ, Patel KM, and Davis RM, "Trends in Cigarette Smoking in the U.S., the Changing Influence of Gender and Race," *JAMA*, 1989, *261*: 49–55.

23. Royce JM, Hymowitz N, Corbett K, Hartwell TD, Orlandi MA, for the COMMIT Research Group, "Smoking Cessation Factors among African Americans and Whites."

24. Ahluwalia JS, Harris KJ, Catley D, Okuyemi KS, and Mayo MS, "Sustained-Release Bupropion for Smoking Cessation in African Americans. A Randomized Controlled Trial," *JAMA*, 2002, *288*: 468–74.

25. Noah B, "The Participation of Underrepresented Minorities in Clinical Research," *American Journal of Law and Medicine*, 2003, Summer–Fall. Available at www.findarticles.com/cf_dls/m6029/2-3_29/105518895/print.jhtml Accessed October 4, 2004.

26. Institute of Medicine Report, *Unequal Treatment: Confronting Racial and Ethnic Disparities in Healthcare.*

27. Kirsch IS, Jungebut A, Jenkins L, and Kolstad A, "Adult Literacy in America: A First Look at the Results of the National Adult Literacy Survey" (Washington, D.C.: Department of Education, 1993).

28. Ibid.; and Finkelstein JA, Brown RW, Schneider LC, et al., "Quality of Care for Preschool Children with Asthma: The Role of Social Factors and Practice Setting," *Pediatrics*, 1995, *95*: 389–94.

29. Williams MV, Parker RM, Baker DW, Parikh K, Coates WC, and Nurss JR, "Inadequate Functional Health Literacy among Patients at Two Public Hospitals," *JAMA*, 1995, *2714(21)*: 1677–82.

30. Nurss JR, el-Kebbi IM, Galliana DL, Zeimer DC, Musey VC, Lewis S, Liao Q, and Philips LS, "Diabetes in Urban African Americans: Functional Health Literacy of Municipal Hospital Outpatients with Diabetes," *Diabetes Education*, 1995, *23(5)*: 563–8.

31. Schillinger D, Grumbach K, Piette J, et al., "Association of Health Literacy with Diabetes Outcomes," *JAMA*, 2002, *288*: 475–82.

32. Williams MV, Baker DW, Parker RM, and Nurss JR, "Relationship of Functional Health Literacy to Patients' Knowledge of Their Chronic Disease: A Study of Patients with Hypertension And Diabetes," *Archives of Internal Medicine*, 1998, *158(2)*: 166–72.

33. Ibid.
34. Payer L, *Medicine and Culture: Varieties of Treatment in the United States* (New York: Penguin, 1988).
35. Kroll J, Linde P, Habenicht M, et al., "Medication Compliance, Antidepressant Blood Levels, and Side Effects in Southeast Asian Patients," *Journal of Clinical Psychopharmacology*, 1990, *10*: 279–83.
36. Mull JD, "Cross-Cultural Communication in the Physician's Office," *Western Journal of Medicine*, 1993, *159*: 609–13.
37. Landy D, Ed., *Culture, Disease, and Healing: Studies in Medical Anthropology* (New York: MacMillan, 1977).
38. Lin KM, and Shen WW, "Pharmacotherapy for Southeast Asian Psychiatric Patients," *Journal of Nervous and Mental Diseases*, 1991, *179*: 346–50; Westermeyer J, *Psychiatric Care of Migrants: A Clinical Guide* (Washington, DC: American Psychiatric Press, 1989).
39. Purnell LD, and Paulanka BJ, Eds., *Transcultural Health Care. A Culturally Competent Approach* (Philadelphia: F. A. Davis, 1998).
40. Cappuccio FP, Duneclift SM, Atkinson RW, and Cook DG, "Use of Alternative Medicines in a Multi-ethnic Population," *Ethnic Diseases*, 2001, *11(1)*: 11–18.
41. Bonkowsky JL, Frazer JK, Buchi KF, and Byington CL, "Metamizole Use by Latino Immigrants: A Common and Potentially Harmful Home Remedy," *Pediatrics*, 2002, *109(6)*: e98.
42. Mishra R, "Some Chinese Herb Remedies Called Toxic." Available at www.mdadvice.com/news/2001/02/01/medic/2531-0231-pat_ny-times. html Accessed July 30, 2002.
43. Noah B, "The Participation of Underrepresented Minorities in Clinical Research," *American Journal of Law and Medicine*, 2003, Summer–Fall.
44. Shavers VL, et al., "Factors That Influence African-Americans' Willingness to Participate in Medical Research Studies," *Cancer* 2001, *91*: 233; and "Vital African American Recruitment Low in Prostate and Breast Cancer Drug Clinical Trials," *NBC Nightly News*, September 15, 2002. Available at 2002 WL 3339803. Both cited in Noah, "The Participation of Underrepresented Minorities in Clinical Research" (note 25).
45. Heiat A, Gross CP, Krumholtz HM, et al., "Representation of the Elderly, Women, and Minorities in Heart Failure Clinical Trials," *Archives of Internal Medicine*, 2002, *162*: 1682, 1684, cited in Noah, "The Participation of Underrepresented Minorities in Clinical Research." Noah points to the finding in this study that "only 15 percent of patients enrolled in these studies were racial or ethnic minorities."
46. Svensson CK, "Representation of American Blacks in Clinical Trials of New Drugs," *JAMA*, 1989, *261*: 263–4, Table 1, cited in Noah, "The

Participation of Underrepresented Minorities in Clinical Research."
Noah points out that "The study did not suggest that African-Americans
had a lower incidence of the diseases in question than other population
groups overrepresented in the clinical trials."

47. Ahluwalia JS, and McNagny SE, "Smoking Prevalence and Desire to
Quit in Inner City African American Walk-In Clinic Patients," *Clinical
Research*, 1993, *41*: 752A.

48. King TE, "Racial Disparities in Clinical Trials," *New England Journal
of Medicine*, 2002, *346*: 1400, 1402; and Stone VE, "Race, Gender, Drug
Use, and Participation in AIDS Clinical Trials," *Journal of General Internal Medicine*, 1997, 12: 150. Both cited in Noah, "The Participation of
Underrepresented Minorities in Clinical Research."

49. Noah B, "The Participation of Underrepresented Minorities in Clinical
Research."

50. Taylor AL, Ziesche S, and Yancy C, "Combination of Isosorbide Dinitrate
and Hydralazine in Blacks with Heart Failure," *New England Journal of
Medicine*, 2004; *351*: 2049–57.

51. Kahn J, "How a Drug Becomes 'Ethnic': Law, Commerce and the Production of Racial Categories in Medicine," *Yale Journal of Health Policy,
Law, and Ethics 2004; 4*: 1–46.

Notes to Chapter 6

1. Bull JP, "The Historical Development of Clinical Therapeutic Trials," *The
Journal of Chronic Diseases*, 1959, *10*: 218–48.

2. Friedman LM, Furberg CD, and DeMets DL, *Fundamentals of Clinical
Trials*, 3rd ed. (New York: Springer Publishing, 1998).

3. Iber FL, Riley WA, and Murray PJ, *Conducting Clinical Trials* (New York:
Plenum, 1987).

4. NIH, *NIH Inventory of Clinical Trials: Fiscal Year 1979*, Vol. I. National
Institutes of Health, Division of Research Grants, Research Analysis and
Evaluation Branch, Bethesda, MD.

5. Although the increased growth in new compounds can be attributed
to a variety of causes, high-throughput screening stands out as a major
factor. Although it greatly increases the number of drugs that make it
to Phase I clinical trials, 30 percent fail to clear these trials. Primary
source: *Functional Genomics and Proteomics May Accelerate the Discovery of New Drugs and Therapeutic Molecules, News-Medical.Net*, April 29,
2004. Available at www.newsmedical.net/?id=1063 Accessed November
24, 2004.

6. Drennan K, "Have the Ultimate Benefits of Clinical Trials Been Maligned
beyond Repair?" *Drug Discovery Today, 6(12)*: 597–9.

7. The archive of NIH clinical trials can be searched at www.clinicaltrials. gov Accessed November 21, 2001.
8. Office of the Inspector General, Department of Health and Human Services, *The Globalization of Clinical Trials: A Growing Challenge in Protecting Human Subjects*, December 2001, OEI-01-00-00190. Available at www.oig.hhs.gove/oei Accessed December 5, 2004.
9. Standler RB, "Nonconsensual Medical Experiments on Human Beings," May 1999. Available at www.rbs2.com Accessed May 25, 2005.
10. Katz J, *Experimentation with Human Beings* (New York: Russell Sage Foundation, 1972), pp. 9–65.
11. The Willowbrook Hepatitis study was carried out from 1963 to 1966 at the Willowbrook State School, an institution for "mentally defective persons." Some children were deliberately injected with the hepatitis virus, others were fed extracts of stools from infected individuals, and still others received injections of purified virus. Information is available at www.hstraining.orda.ucsb.edu/training/willowbrook.htm Accessed December 5, 2004.
12. Jones JH, *Bad Blood: The Tuskegee Syphilis Experiment* (New York: Free Press, 1993).
13. Annas GJ, Glantz LH, and Katz BF, *Informed Consent to Human Experimentation* (Cambridge, MA: Ballinger, 1977).
14. Cited in Pernick MS, *A Calculus of Suffering: Pain, Professionalism and Anesthesia in Nineteenth-Century America* (New York: Columbia University Press, 1985), p. 156.
15. *Trials of War Criminals before the Nuremberg Military Tribunals under Control Council Law No. 10: Nuremberg, October 1946–1949*, 2 vols. (Washington, DC: U.S. Government Printing Office, 1949–53).
16. McNeill PM, *The Ethics and Politics of Human Experimentation* (Oakley: Cambridge University Press, 1993).
17. Shavers VL, Lynch CF, and Burmeister LF, "Knowledge of the Tuskegee Study and Its Impact on the Willingness to Participate in Medical Research Studies," *Journal of the National Medical Association*, December 2000, *92(12)*: 563–72.
18. Ibid.
19. Ibid.
20. Multiple sources, but primary discussions on subjects contained in Council for International Organizations of Medical Sciences (CIOMS), *International Ethical Guidelines for Biomedical Research Involving Human Subjects* (Geneva: WHO, 1993).
21. Speers MA, *Basic Protections for Human Subjects in International Research*, Centers for Disease Control and Prevention (CDC).
22. CIOMS, *International Ethical Guidelines for Biomedical Research Involving Human Subjects.*

23. Dickert N and Grady C, "What's the Price of a Research Subject? Approaches to Payment for Research Participation," *New England Journal of Medicine*, 1999, *341(3)*: 198–203.

24. Cumston CG, *An Introduction to the History of Medicine* (London: Dawson's of Pall Mall, 1968), p. 86.

25. Edgar I, *The Origins of the Healing Art: A Psycho-evolutionary Approach to the History of Medicine* (New York: Philosophical Library, 1978), p. 137.

Notes to Chapter 7

1. For a more complete discussion see, for example, National Institutes of Health, "Stem Cells: Scientific Progress and Future Research Directions," June 2001.

2. For a concise description and history of "cloning" see the Illinois Institute of Technology's Institute on Biotechnology & the Human Future web site: www.thehumanfuture.org Accessed May 26, 2005.

3. At least one company (Osiris Therapeutics) has protocols under review at the FDA for clinical trials with human mesenchymal stem cells (MSC). These are a form of human adult stem cells derived from bone marrow, which can be reproducibly isolated and expanded in vitro and can differentiate in vitro into cells with properties of cartilage, bone, adipose (fat), and muscle cells. Pittenger, M. F. et al., "Multi-lineage Potential of Adult Human Mesenchymal Stem Cells," *Science* 1999, *284*: 143–7.

4. Stem cell lines can be frozen for long periods of time. They can be thawed as required and cultured again.

5. However, the Act provides support for stem cell research using umbilical cord blood by making $10,000,000 available to establish a National Cord Blood Stem Cell Bank.

6. Prior to President Bush's ban on stem cell research, the NIH Human Pluripotent Stem Cell Review Group was formed to ensure compliance with guidelines for research. The group never met.

7. This decision has subsequent worldwide implications.

8. Although a number of bills have been introduced, such as H.R. 4682, "To amend the Public Health Service Act to provide for human embryonic stem cell research." The bill had 148 sponsors as of August 31, 2004.

9. See "In Memoriam: The Office of Technology Assessment, 1972–95," *Hon. Amo Houghton in the House of Representatives Congressional Record, Extension of Remarks – September 28, 1995*, Page E1868–1870.

10. *The New York Times*, December 6, 1994: Al; Gingrich N, *Contract with America* (New York: Times Books, 1994).

11. IVF is one of three other ART procedures. The other two are gamete intrafallopian transfer (GIFT) and zygote intrafallopian transfer (ZIFT).

12. See the Report of The President's Council on Bioethics, "Reproduction and Responsibility," March 2004, p. 47.
13. See "Does In Vitro Fertilization Work?" Available at the American Society for Reproductive Medicine Web site, www.asrm.org/Patients/faqs.html#Q4 Accessed May 26, 2005.
14. Society for Assisted Reproductive Technology (SART), "A Patient's Guide to Assisted Reproductive Technologies," www.sart.org/Text-Patients.htm Accessed May 26, 2005.
15. Hoffman D et al., "Cryopreserved Embryos in the United States and Their Availability for Research," *Fertility and Sterility*, 2003, *79*: 1063–69.
16. Other recent techniques for fertilization are gamete intrafallopian transfer (GIFT), zygote intrafallopian transfer (ZIFT), tubal embryo transfer (TET), and frozen embryo transfer (FET). As in IVF, the oocytes and sperm are combined in a culture dish in the laboratory with fertilization and very early embryo development occurring outside the body, rather than in the fallopian tube. See note 8.
17. American Society for Reproductive Medicine Web site: www.asrm.org/Patients/faqs.html#Q4, "Do Insurance Plans Cover Infertility Treatment?" Accessed May 26, 2005.
18. National Conference of State Legislatures, 50 State Summary of Legislation Related to Insurance Coverage of Infertility Therapy, www.ncsl.org/programs/health/50infert.htm Accessed May 26, 2005.
19. Sandel MJ, "Embryo Ethics – The Moral Logic of Stem Cell Research," *New England Journal of Medicine*, July 15, 2004, *351(3): 208.*
20. See, specifically, Section 553.
21. The APA defines "rule" as the whole or part of an agency statement of general or particular applicability and future effect designed to implement, interpret, or prescribe law or policy or describing the organization, procedure, or practice requirements of an agency and includes the approval or prescription for the future of rates, wages, corporate or financial structures or reorganizations thereof, prices, facilities, appliances, services or allowances therefore or of valuations, costs, or accounting, or practices bearing on any of the foregoing.
22. These procedural requirements do not apply to "interpretive rules, general statements of policy, or rules of agency organization, procedure, or practice." Although distinguishing certain classes of regulatory pronouncements from one another can be difficult, it has been stated that "regulations, substantive rules or legislative rules are those which create law, usually implementary to an existing law; whereas interpretive rules are statements as to what the administrative officer thinks the statute or regulation means."

23. Report on the Administrative Procedure Act, S. Rep. No. 79-752, at 15 (1945).

24. See Lubbers JS, *A Guide to Federal Agency Rulemaking, American Bar Association*, third ed., 1998, at 193, 205.

25. The administration can write or revise regulations largely on its own, whereas Congress must pass laws. For that reason, most modern-day presidents have pursued much of their agendas through regulation. Recently, the courts have struck down the administration's attempts to modify Congressional acts, such as the Clean Air Act, by changing or modifying regulations.

26. DeFrancesco L, "California Endorses Stem Cell Research," *The Scientist*, September 25, 2002. Available at www.biomedcentral.com/news/20020925/05/ Accessed May 26, 2005.

27. Among them are Louisiana, which is considering pro–stem cell legislation, and North Dakota, South Dakota, and Illinois. All four prohibit research on fertilized embryos.

28. Arizona, Indiana, North Dakota, Ohio, Oklahoma, and South Dakota.

29. For valuable tabular listing of current state laws on this, see *State Embryonic and Fetal Research Laws* and S*tate Human Cloning Laws*, published by the National Conference of State Legislatures (NCSL). Available at www.ncsl.org/programs/health/genetics/embfet.htm and www.ncsl.org/programs/health/genetics/rt-shcl.htm, respectively. Both accessed May 26, 2005.

30. The National Institutes of Health Stem Cell Information Web site on International Stem Cell Research has a condensation of international efforts in stem cell research and regulations. Available at www.stemcells.nih.gov/research/intlresearch.asp Accessed May 26, 2005.

31. "Global Therapeutic Cloning Ban Averted," NewScientist.com, December 10, 2003. Available at www.newscientists.com/article.ns?id=dn4471 Accessed May 26, 2005.

32. For a tabular listing of stem cell research among member states of the European Union, see the International Society of Stem Cell Research. Available at www.isscr.org/scientists/legislative.htm Accessed May 26, 2005.

33. Scott A, "EU Clarifies Stem Cell Rules," *The Scientist*, November 5, 2003. Available at www.the-scientist.com/news/20031105/06 Accessed May 26, 2005.

34. European Commission, "Stem Cells Cause a Stir," RTD Info Special Edition, November 2002: 5.

35. "France OK's Law Allowing Embryo Research," *The Las Vegas Sun*, July 9, 2003.

36. Stafford N, "Law Hinders German Research," *The Scientist*, May 10, 2004.

37. *Science*, May 28, 2004, *3094*:1239.
38. Liebowitz S, "Britain Moves to Supply Stem Cells for Research," *Boston Globe*, May 20, 2004
39. Payne D, "Canada Passes Cloning Law – Rules Are Part of Reproductive Technology Act That Some Say Leaves Confusion," *The Scientist*, March 16, 2004.
40. Canadian Institutes of Health Research, "Human Pluripotent Stem Cell Research: Guidelines for CIHR-Funded Research," March 4, 2002.
41. Hwang WS, Ryu YJ, Park JH, Park ES et al., *Science*, March 12, 2004; *303*: 1669–74; published online 12 February 2004 [DOI: 10.1126/science.1094515].
42. "Cloning Vote Pits Science vs. Naysayers," *The Asahi Shimbun*, June 25, 2004.
43. "Human Embryonic Stem Cell Research in China," September 2002 Report from the U.S. Embassy, Beijing.
44. "Dozens of Human Embryos Cloned in China," NewScientist.com, March 6, 2002. Available at www.newscientist.com/article.ns?id=dn2012 Accessed May 26, 2005.
45. Harvard University (under private funding from the Howard Hughes Foundation, the Juvenile Diabetes Foundation and the Naomi Berry Diabetes Center of Columbia University) has 17 lines of embryonic stem cells. *The New York Times*, August 24, 2004: D6.
46. For details of these stem cell lines, see Table 2, "NIH List of Human Embryonic Stem Cell Lines Eligible for Use in Federal Research," of the Congressional Research Service Report to Congress, "Stem Cell Research," RL 31015, July 22, 2004, p. 9.
47. Zerhoni E, Testimony before the Senate Committee on Appropriations, Subcommittee on Labor, Health and Human Services and Education, May 22, 2003, *Federal Funding for Stem Cell Research*, 108 Cong.
48. September 4, 2003 Hearings of the President's Council on Bioethics, available at www.bioethics.gov/transcripts/sep03/session4.html Accessed May 26, 2005.
49. *Federal Register*, Friday August 25, 2000, *65 (1666)*: 5179. These guidelines were first proposed at the end of the Clinton Administration but are no longer in effect.
50. "Materials for Congressional Meetings," Position paper, Juvenile Diabetes Research Foundation International, June 10, 2004.
51. McHugh PR, "Zygote and 'Clonote' – The Ethical Use of Embryonic Stem Cells," *New England Journal of Medicine* 2004, *351(3)*: 209–11.
52. Sandel MJ, "Embryo Ethics – The Moral Logic of Stem Cell Research," p. 10.

53. See Canadian Institutes of Health Research, "Human Pluripotent Stem Cell Research: Guidelines for CIHR-Funded Research," March 4, 2002.

Notes to Part II Introduction

1. See, e.g., Barlett DL, and Steele JB, *Critical Condition: How Health Care in America Became Big Business & Bad Medicine* (New York: Doubleday, 2004), pp. 195–233.
2. See Goozner M, *The $800 Million Pill: The Truth behind the Cost of New Drugs* (Berkeley, CA: University of California Press, 2004).
3. See data from IMS Health cited in Thomas Abrams, Chapter 9 of this book.
4. The FDA rules are available at 21 C.F.R. 202.1 (2000).
5. Available at www.pbs.org/wgbh/nova/doctors/oath_modern.html Accessed May 18, 2005.
6. For a thoughtful analysis of the threat posed by drug promotion by a practicing physician, see Abramson J, *Overdosed America: The Broken Promise of American Medicine* (New York: HarperCollins, 2004); See also Angell M, *The Truth about the Drug Companies: How They Deceive Us and What to Do about It* (New York: Random House, 2004), pp. 135–55.
7. Kassirer JP, *On the Take: How Medicine's Complicity with Big Business Can Endanger Your Health* (Oxford: Oxford University Press, 2005); Angell M, *The Truth about the Drug Companies: How They Deceive Us and What to Do about It*, pp. 115–34.
8. Fonda D, and Kiviat B, "Curbing the Drug Marketers," *Time*, July 5, 2004: 40.
9. Unfortunately, the Neurontin case is not an isolated one. In 1996, the drug dexfenfluramine, or Redux, swept the nation with its implied promises of significant weight loss. Though the drug carried the risk of pulmonary hypertension, and had questionable effectiveness, Redux was marketed for treatment of severe obesity. The companies that sold the drug claimed that the risk of pulmonary hypertension was offset by the fact that the severely obese suffer higher death rates and an increased frequency of other conditions. See Avorn J, M.D., *Powerful Medicines: The Benefits, Risks, and Costs of Prescription Drugs* (New York: Knopf, 2004), pp. 71–84.
10. Harris, G, "Guilty Plea Seen for Drug Maker," *The New York Times*, July 16, 2004.
11. AMA Ethical Guideline E-8.061, "Gifts to Physicians from Industry." Available at www.ama-assn.org/ama/pub/category/4001.html Accessed May 25, 2005.

12. "PhRMA Adopts New Marketing Code." (April 19, 2002) Available at www.pharma.org/mediaroom/press/releases/19.04.2002.390.cfm Accessed May 25, 2005.

13. Studdert DM, et al., "Financial Conflicts of Interest in Physicians' Relationships with the Pharmaceutical Industry – Self Regulation in the Shadow of Federal Prosecution," *New England Journal of Medicine,* October 28, 2004, *351(18):* 1891–900.

14. Levit K, Smith C, Cowan C, Sensenig A, Catlin A, and the Health Accounts Team, "Health Spending Rebound Continues in 2002," *Health Affairs,* 2004, *23(1):* 147–59.

Notes to Chapter 8

1. National Cholesterol Education Program, "Second Report of the Expert Panel on Detection, Evaluation, and Treatment of High Blood Cholesterol in Adults (Adult Treatment Panel II)," *Circulation* 1994, *89:* 1333–1445.

2. National Cholesterol Education Program, "Third Report of the Expert Panel on Detection, Evaluation, and Treatment of High Blood Cholesterol in Adults (Adult Treatment Panel III)." Available at www. nhlbi.nih.gov/guidelines/cholesterol/index.htm Accessed November 11, 2004.

3. Joint National Committee on Prevention, Detection, Evaluation, and Treatment of High Blood Pressure, "Seventh Report of the Joint National Committee on Prevention, Detection, Evaluation, and Treatment of High Blood Pressure (JNC 7)," NIH Publication No. 04-5230 (Washington, DC: National Institutes of Health, 2004). Also available at www.nhlbi.nih.gov/guidelines/hypertension/index.htm Accessed November 11, 2004.

4. Verma S, and Strauss M, "Angiotension Receptor Blockers and Myocardial Infarction," *British Medical Journal,* 2004, *329:* 1248–9.

5. United States Food and Drug Administration, Center for Drug Evaluation and Research, Office of Generic Drugs. Available at www.fda. gov/cder/ogd Accessed November 11, 2004.

6. Wal-Mart Pharmacy, Hudson, New York, October 2004.

7. Snow V, Barry P, Fihn SD, Gibbons RJ, Owens DK, Williams SV, Mottur-Pilson C, and Weiss KB for the American College of Physicians/America College of Cardiology Chronic Stable Angina Panel, "Primary Care Management of Chronic Stable Angina and Asymptomatic Suspected or Known Coronary Artery Disease: A Clinical Practice Guideline from the American College of Physicians," *Annals of Internal Medicine* 2004 *(141):* 562–7.

Notes to Chapter 9

1. IMS Health, IMS National Sales Perspectives, 2003, data extracted August 2004.
2. IMS Health, Integrated Promotional Services: Total Promotion Report.
3. 3 Fed. Reg. 3126, December 28, 1938.
4. Aikin KJ, Swasy JL, and Braman AC, "Patient and Physician Attitudes and Behaviors Associated With Direct-to-Consumer Promotion of Prescription Drugs: Summary of FDA Survey Research Results. Final Report," Center for Drug Evaluation and Research, Food and Drug Administration, Technical research report, 2004.
5. IMS Health, Integrated Promotional Services: Total Promotion Report. These percentages are based upon calculations by the Division of Drug Marketing, Advertising, and Communications at the Food and Drug Administration.
6. IMS Health, Integrated Promotional Services: Integrated Share of Voice Report. These percentages are based upon calculations by the Division of Drug Marketing, Advertising, and Communications at the Food and Drug Administration.
7. IMS Health, Integrated Promotional Services: Total Sampling Report.
8. 21 CFR §314.81(b)(3)(i).
9. Section 502(n)(3)(A); 21 U.S.C. §352(n)(3)(A).
10. Further information about these and other letters is available at www.fda.gov/cder/warn/index.htm Accessed May 25, 2005.
11. 21 CFR Parts 314.500 & 314.600.
12. 21 CFR §601.40 et seq.
13. 21 CFR §§314.550; 314.640; 601.45.
14. 21 CFR §202.1(j)(4).
15. Available at www.fda.gov/cder/guidance/5669dft.pdf Accessed May 25, 2005.
16. Available at www.fda.gov/cder/guidance/6019dft.pdf Accessed May 25, 2005.

Notes to Chapter 10

1. Angell M, and Relman A, "America's Other Drug Problem," *New Republic*, December 16, 2002.
2. Holmer AF, "Direct-to-Consumer Prescription Drug Advertising Builds Bridges Between Patients and Physicians," *JAMA*, 1999, *281(4)*: 380–82; Holmer AF, "Direct-to-Consumer Advertising – Strengthening Our Health Care System," *New England Journal of Medicine*, 2002, *46(7)*: 526–8; Bonaccorso SN and Sturchio JL, "Direct to Consumer Advertising

is Medicalising Normal Human Experience: Against" *British Medical Journal*, April 13, 2002, *324*: 910–11.

3. Hollon MF, "Direct-to-Consumer Marketing of Prescription Drugs," *JAMA*, 1999, *281(4)*: 382–4; and Wolfe SM, "Direct-to-Consumer Advertising – Education or Emotion Promotion?" *New England Journal of Medicine*, 2002, *346(7)*: 524–6.

4. Pitts PJ, "Turning Point or Tipping Point: New FDA Draft Guidances and the Future of DTCA," *Health Affairs*, 2004, W4–259.

5. Feather KR, Oral History Interview, U.S. Food and Drug Administration, Rockville, MD, May 7, 1997; and Terzian TV, "Direct-to-Consumer Prescription Drug Advertising," *American Journal of Law and Medicine*, 1999, *25*: 149–67.

6. Ruby LA, and Montagne M, "Direct-to-Consumer Advertising: A Case Study of the Rogaine Campaign," *Journal of Pharmaceutical Marketing and Management*, 1991, *6(2)*: 21–32.

7. Rothman DJ, "The Origins and Consequences of Patient Autonomy: A 25-Year Retrospective," *Health Care Analysis*, 2001, *9*: 255–64; Laine C, and Davidoff F, "Patient-Centered Medicine: A Professional Evolution," *JAMA*, 1996, *275(2)*: 152–6.

8. Emanuel EJ, and Emanuel LL, "Four Models of the Doctor–Patient Relationship," *JAMA*, 1992, *267*: 2221–6; and Roter DL, Hall JA, *Doctors Talking with Patients/Patients Talking with Doctors: Improving Communication in Medical Visits* (Westport, CT: Auburn House, 1992).

9. Rosenthal MB, Berndt ER, Donohue JM, Epstein AM and Frank RG, "Demand Effects of Recent Changes in Prescription Drug Promotion," in Cutler DM, and Garber AM, Eds., *Frontiers in Health Policy Research, Vol. 6* (Cambridge, MA: MIT Press, June 2003). Available at www.kff.org/rxdrugs/6084-index.cfm Accessed March 28, 2004.

10. Ling DC, Berndt ER and Kyle MK, "Deregulating Direct-to-Consumer Marketing of Prescription Drugs: Effects on Prescription and Over-the-Counter Product Sales," *Journal of Law and Economics*, 2002, *45*: 691–723; Narayanan S, Desiraju R, Chintagunta PK, "ROI Implications for Pharmaceutical Promotional Expenditures: The Case of Second-Generation Antihistamines," University of Chicago, Graduate School of Business, working paper, 2003. Available at www.gsb.uchicago.edu/fac/pradeep.chintagunta/research/Working%20Papers/ROI_pharmaceutical_promotional_expenditures.pdf Accessed September 2003.

11. Frank RG, "Prescription Drug Prices: Why Do Some Pay More Than Others?" *Health Affairs*, 2001, *20(2)*: 115–28.

12. *Prevention Magazine*, "Consumer Reaction to DTCA of Prescription Medicines" (Emmaus, PA: Rodale Inc., 2002/2003).

13. Ibid.

14. *Prevention Magazine*, "Consumer Reaction to DTCA of Prescription Medicines"; Food and Drug Administration, Office of Medical Policy, Division of Drug Marketing, Advertising and Communications, Center for Drug Evaluation and Research, "Attitudes and Behaviors Associated with Direct-to-Consumer Promotion of Prescription Drugs," 2001; and Weissman JS, Blumenthal D, Silk AJ, Zapert K, Newman M, and Leitman R, "Consumers' Reports on the Health Effects of Direct-To-Consumer Drug Advertising," *Health Affairs*, February 2003. Available at www.healthaffairs.org Accessed June 28, 2003.
15. Rosenthal MB, Berndt ER, Donohue JM, Epstein AM, and Frank RG, "Promotion of Prescription Drugs to Consumers," *New England Journal of Medicine*, 2002, *346(7)*.
16. *Prevention Magazine*, "Consumer Reaction to DTCA of Prescription Medicines."
17. Zachry W, Shepherd MD, Hinich MJ, Wilson JP, et al., "Relationship Between Direct-to-Consumer Advertising and Physician Diagnosing and Prescribing," *American Journal of Health-System Pharmacy*, 2002, *59(1)*: 42–9.
18. Iizuka T, and Jin GZ, *The Effects of Direct-to-Consumer Advertising in the Prescription Drug Markets*, mimeo, Vanderbilt University, 2003.
19. Weissman JS, Blumenthal D, Silk AJ, Newman M, et al., "Physicians Report on Patient Encounters Involving Direct-to-Consumer Advertising," *Health Affairs*, 2004, W4–219.
20. Teleki S, "Direct-to-Consumer Promotion of Prescription Drugs: The Case of Cox-2 Inhibitors," University of California Los Angeles, Ph.D. Dissertation, 2002.
21. Dubois RW, "Pharmaceutical Promotion: Don"t Throw the Baby Out with the Bathwater," 2003, *Health Affairs* W3–96.
22. Donohue JM, Berndt ER, Epstein AM, Rosenthal MB, Frank RG, "Effects of Pharmaceutical Promotion on Adherence to Treatment Guidelines for Depression." *Medical Care 42(12)*, 2004.
23. Swasy J, and Aiken K, "DTCA Physician Survey: General Practitioners vs. Specialists," Presentation at DTC National Conference, Boston, MA, March 26, 2003.
24. *Prevention Magazine*, "Consumer Reaction to DTCA of Prescription Medicines"; and Food and Drug Administration, "Attitudes and Behaviors Associated with Direct-to-Consumer Promotion of Prescription Drugs."
25. Wosinska M, "Direct-to-Consumer Advertising and Therapy Compliance," 2004. Forthcoming in *Journal of Marketing Research*.
26. Donohue JM, and Berndt ER, "Direct-to-Consumer Advertising and Choice of Antidepressant," March 2004. Forthcoming in *Journal of Public Policy and Marketing*.

27. Iizuka T, and Jin GZ, *The Effects of Direct-to-Consumer Advertising in the Prescription Drug Markets.*

28. *The Newshour with Jim Lehrer*/Kaiser Family Foundation/Harvard School of Public Health Survey, "National Survey on Prescription Drugs," September 2000. Available at www.kff.org/rxdrugs/3065-index.cfm Accessed June 28, 2003; *Prevention Magazine*, "Consumer Reaction to DTCA of Prescription Medicines"; and Weissman JS, Blumenthal D, Silk AJ, Zapert K, Newman M, and Leitman R, "Consumers' Reports on the Health Effects of Direct-to-Consumer Drug Advertising."

29. Weissman JS, Blumenthal D, Silk AJ, and Newman M, et al., "Physicians Report on Patient Encounters Involving "Direct-to-Consumer Advertising"; Murray E, Lo B, Pollack L, Donelan K, Lee K. "Direct-to-consumer advertising: Physicians' views of its effects on quality of care and the doctor-patient relationship." *Journal of the American Board of Family Practice*, 2003, *16*: 513–24.

30. Weissman JS, Blumenthal D, Silk AJ, Newman M, et al., "Physicians Report on Patient Encounters Involving Direct-to-Consumer Advertising."

31. Donohue JM, Berndt ER, Epstein AM, Rosenthal MB, and Frank RG, "Effects of Pharmaceutical Promotion on Adherence to Treatment Guidelines for Depression," *Medical Care*, December 2004, *42(12)*: 1176–85.

32. Wilkes MS, Bell RA, Kravitz RL, "Direct-to-Consumer Prescription Drug Advertising: Trends, Impact and Implications," *Health Affairs*, 2000, *19(2)*: 110–28.

33. Weissman JS, Blumenthal D, Silk AJ, Newman M, et al., "Physicians Report on Patient Encounters Involving Direct-to-Consumer Advertising."

34. Swasy J, and Aiken K, "DTCA Physician Survey: General Practitioners vs. Specialists."

35. Kaiser Family Foundation, "Understanding the Effects of Direct-to-Consumer Prescription Drug Advertising," November 2001. Available at www.kff.org/rxdrugs/20011129a-index.cfm Accessed May 2004.

36. Woloshin S, Schwartz LM, and Welch HG, "The Value of Benefit Data in Direct-to-Consumer Drug Ads," *Health Affairs*, 2004, W4-234.

37. Kaiser Family Foundation, "Understanding the Effects of Direct-to-Consumer Prescription Drug Advertising."

38. FDA, "Attitudes and Behaviors Associated with Direct-to-Consumer Promotion of Prescription Drugs."

39. Avorn J, Chen M, and Hartley R, "Scientific versus Commercial Sources of Influence on the Prescribing Behavior of Physicians," *American Journal of Medicine*, 1982, *73*: 4–8; Schwartz RK, Soumerai SB, and Avorn J,

"Physician Motivations for Nonscientific Drug Prescribing," *Social Science Medicine*, 1989, *28*: 577–82; and Ziegler MG, Lew P, and Singer BC, "The Accuracy of Drug Information from Pharmaceutical Sales Representatives," *JAMA*, 1995, *273*: 1296–8.

40. Swasy J, and Aiken K, "DTCA Physician Survey: General Practitioners vs. Specialists."

41. Huskamp HA, Deverka PA, Epstein AM, Epstein RS, McGuigan KA, and Frank RG, "The Impact of Incentive Formularies on Prescription Drug Utilization and Spending," *New England Journal of Medicine*, 2003, *394(23)*: 2224–32; and Wosinska M, 2002.

42. Rosenthal et al., 2002.

43. Avorn J, Chen M, and Hartley R, "Scientific versus Commercial Sources of Influence on the Prescribing Behavior of Physicians."

44. Avorn J and Soumerai S, "Improving Drug-Therapy Decisions through Educational Outreach: A Randomized Controlled Trial of Academically Based Detailing," *New England Journal of Medicine*, 1983, *308*: 1457–63; and Soumerai SB, and Avorn J, "Predictors of Physician Prescribing Change in an Educational Experiment to Improve Medication Use," *Medical Care*, 1987, *25(3)*: 210–21, and "Principles of Educational Outreach ("Academic Detailing") to Improve Clinical Decision Making," *JAMA*, 1990, *263(4)*: 549–56.

45. Food and Drug Administration, Office of Medical Policy, Division of Drug Marketing, Advertising and Communications, Center for Drug Evaluation and Research, "Guidance for Industry, Brief Summary: Disclosing Risk Information in Consumer-Directed Print Advertisements," January 2004. Available at www.fda.gov/cder/guidance/5669dft.pdf Accessed May 2004.

46. Chaloupka FJ, and Warner KE, "The Economics of Smoking," in Newhouse J, Culyer A, Eds., *A Handbook of Health Economics* (Amsterdam: Elsevier, 2000), pp. 1594–5.

47. Wosinska M, 2002.

Notes to Chapter 11

1. 21 U.S.C. §355(a).
2. 21 C.F.R. §310.3(h).
3. 21 U.S.C. §321(k) & (m).
4. 21 U.S.C. §352(f); 21 C.F.R. §§201.5, 201.100(d)(1).
5. 335 U.S. 345 (1948).
6. Ibid. at 350. In *United States* v. *Urbuteit*, 335 U.S. 355 (1948), decided the same day, the Supreme Court similarly held that leaflets describing a

therapeutic device were "labeling" even though the leaflets and devices were shipped separately from each other.

7. See 21 C.F.R. §202.1(1)(2). The FDCA specifically excepts advertising in newspapers, magazines, radio, television, and other electronic media from the definition of labeling.

8. 21 C.F.R. §201.128 ("The words *intended uses* or words of similar import . . . refer to the objective intent of the persons legally responsible for the labeling of drugs. The intent is determined by such persons' expressions or may be shown by the circumstances surrounding the distribution of the article. This objective intent may, for example, be shown by labeling claims, advertising matter, or oral or written statements by such persons or their representatives.").

9. Ibid. When an intended use for a product can be inferred from company promotional materials is a complex and often controversial issue, the complexities of which are not addressed here.

10. There are, however, a handful of narrowly defined exceptions to the general prohibition against communications about off-label topics that are recognized by the FDA. These exceptions describe categories of speech or conduct that the FDA has not traditionally regarded as promotional labeling. For example, the FDA has long recognized that companies may engage in "scientific exchange," such as the publication in the scientific literature of study results regarding new uses for approved drugs. The study results may diverge from the FDA-approved labeling for the drug product. In addition, companies are permitted to respond to unsolicited questions about drug products, including questions about off-label topics. Responses to unsolicited questions will not be regarded as labeling. And finally, materials disseminated to company consultants and clinical trial investigators are not regarded as labeling.

11. See, e.g., 59 Fed. Reg. 59820, 59821 (1994) (noting that the agency has restated this policy on numerous occasions).

12. See, e.g., *First National Bank of Boston* v. *Bellotti*, 435 U.S. 765, 784 (1978) (observing that the First Amendment does not support "the proposition that speech that otherwise would be within the protection of the First Amendment loses that protection simply because its source is a corporation").

13. "Commercial speech" is a category of speech that traditionally has received less constitutional protection than "core" political speech. *Virginia State Board of Pharmacy* v. *Virginia Citizens Consumer Council, Inc.*, 425 U.S. 748 (1976).

14. 447 U.S. 557 (1980).

15. Ibid. at 564.

16. *Washington Legal Found.* v. *Friedman*, 13 F. Supp.2d 51, 72–3 (D.D.C. 1998).

17. See Final Guidance on Industry-Supported Scientific and Educational Activities, 62 Fed. Reg. 64074 (December 3, 1997); Guidance to Industry on Dissemination of Reprints of Certain Published, Original Data, 61 Fed. Reg. 52800 (October 8, 1996); Guidance for Industry Funded Dissemination of Reference Texts, 61 Fed. Reg. 52800 (October 8, 1996).

18. While the case was before the district court, Congress passed the Food and Drug Modernization Act ("FDAMA"), which contained provisions allowing manufacturers to disseminate peer-reviewed off-label reprints under a narrow set of circumstances. *Washington Legal Found.* v. *Friedman*, 36 F. Supp.2d 16, 18 (D.D.C. 1999). The district court concluded that like the Guidance Documents, the FDAMA provisions violated the First Amendment. *Washington Legal Found.* v. *Henney*, 56 F. Supp.2d 81, 84 (D.D.C. 1999). When the case was appealed, FDA changed its position and stated that the Guidance Documents and FDAMA provisions were merely "safe harbors" and neither "independently authorizes the FDA to prohibit or to sanction speech." As a result, because there was no longer a constitutional question, the appellate court vacated the core holdings of the district court, but stated that it was not criticizing "the reasoning or conclusions" of the district court's First Amendment analysis. *Washington Legal Found.* v. *Henney*, 202 F.3d 331, 335 (D.C. Cir. 2000).

19. *FDA Response to Citizen Petition of Washington Legal Foundation*, Docket No. 01P-0250 (Jan. 28, 2002). Of course, if peer-reviewed reprints contain false or misleading information, FDA still has the authority to bring an enforcement action to prevent their dissemination.

20. 164 F.3d 650 (D.C. Cir. 1999) (*"Pearson I"*).

21. Ibid. at 658 (1999); see also 130 F. Supp.2d 105, 111–12 (D.D.C. 2001) (holding that FDA failed to comply with *Pearson I* and directing FDA to draft disclaimers); *Pearson v. Thompson*, 141 F. Supp.2d 105, 112 (D.D.C. 2001) (holding that FDA "again seem[s] to ignore the thrust of *Pearson I*").

22. 535 U.S. 357 (2002).

23. 535 U.S. at 371, quoting *Central Hudson*, 447 U.S. at 566.

24. Ibid.

25. 31 U.S.C. §3729.

26. Ibid. at §3730(b)(1).

27. Ibid. at §3730(d).

28. Ibid. at §3730(b)(1).

29. *"Qui tam"* is an abbreviation from the Latin *"qui tam pro domino rege quam pro sic ipso in hoc parte sequitur"* meaning "who as well for the king as for himself sues in this matter."

30. *United States ex rel. Franklin v. Parke-Davis*, 147 F. Supp.2d 39, 45 (D. Mass. 2001).

31. Reimbursement under the federal Medicaid program is, in most circumstances, available only for "covered outpatient drugs." 42 U.S.C. §1396r-8(k)(3). Covered outpatient drugs include drugs that are used for a "medically accepted indication." A medically accepted indication, in turn, includes a use "which is approved under the Federal Food Drug and Cosmetic Act" or which is included in specified drug compendia. ibid. §1396r-8(k)(6). Thus, unless a particular off-label use for a drug is included in one of the identified drug compendia, a prescription for the off-label use is generally not eligible for reimbursement under Medicaid.

32. The company disputed the relator's factual allegations, but because the court considered Franklin's allegations in the context of a motion to dismiss and motion for summary judgment, the court had to accept the relator's allegations as true. The U.S. Department of Justice filed a "statement of interest" in support of the relator, but did not intervene in the case.

33. *Franklin* v. *Parke-Davis*, 147 F. Supp.2d at 53.

34. *United States ex rel. Franklin v. Parke-Davis*, 2003 WL 22048255, *4-5. (D. Mass. August 22, 2003).

35. 2003 WL 22048255 at *1-2. Although ambiguous, this language suggests that both off-label promotion and financial incentives would be required for FCA liability.

36. Rx Compliance Report, Oct. 31, 2003.

Notes to Chapter 12

1. Detmer DE, Singleton PD, MacLeod S, et al., "The Informed Patient: Study Report," Cambridge University Health, Judge Institute of Management, March 2003.

2. Ibid.

3. Coulter A, Entwistle V, and Gilbert D. "Sharing Decisions with Patients," *British Medical Journal*, 1999, *318*: 318–22.

4. Nettleton S, Burrows R, O'Malley L, et al., (2004) "Children, Parents and the Management of Chronic Illness in the Information Age," ESRC End of Award Report, Award number L218252061.

5. Williams MV, Parker RM, Baker DW, et al., "Inadequate Functional Health Literacy among Patients at Two Public Hospitals," *JAMA*, 1995; *274(21)*: 1677–82.

6. Muss HB, White DR, Michielutte R, et al., "Written Informed Consent in Patients with Breast Cancer," *Cancer*, April 1979, *43(4)*: 1549–56.

7. Domenighetti G, et al., "Effect of Information Campaign by the Mass Media on Hysterectomy Rates," *The Lancet*, 1988, *ii*: 1470–73.

8. Heaney D, Wyke S, Wilson P, et al., "Assessment of Impact of Information Booklets on Use of Healthcare Services: Randomised Controlled Trial," *BMJ* 2001, *322*: 1218.
9. *Partners Health Initiative: Partners for a Healthy Community* (Boise, ID: Healthwise Inc., 2001).
10. National Audit Office, "NHS Direct in England" (London: The Stationery Office, 2002).
11. The full reports from "The Informed Patient" are available at www.jims.cam.ac.uk/research/health/tip/tip_f.html Accessed December 7, 2004.

Notes to Chapter 13

1. Ham C and Pickard S, *Tragic Choices in Health Care: The Case of Child B* (London: King's Fund, 1998).
2. Daniels N and Sabin JE, "The Ethics of Eccountability and the Reform of Managed Care Organizations," *Health Affairs*, 1998, *Sep/Oct*: 50–69; Daniels N, "Accountability for Reasonableness," *British Medical Journal*, 2000, *321(7272)*: 1300–01; Daniels N and Sabin JE, *Setting Limits Fairly: Can We Learn to Share Medical Resources?* (New York: Oxford University Press, 2002).
3. Burton SL, Randel L, Titlow K, and Emanuel EJ, "The Ethics of Pharmaceutical Benefit Management," *Health Affairs*, 2001, *Sept./Oct.*: 150–63; for an empirical study of drug rationales and conformance with accountability for reasonableness in a Canadian setting, see Martin DK, Pater JL, and Singer PA, "Priority Setting Decisions for New Cancer Drugs: A Qualitative Study," *The Lancet*, 2001, *358(9294)*: 1676–81.
4. Kleinke JD, "Just What the HMO Ordered: The Paradox of Increasing Drug Costs," *Health Affairs*, 2000, *Mar/Apr*: 76–91.
5. Reinhardt UE, "Perspectives on the Pharmaceutical Industry," *Health Affairs*, 2001, *Sept./Oct.*: 146. Even scientifically sound cost-effectiveness or cost–benefit analyses have distributive implications that require further ethical deliberation. See Russell LB, Gold MR, Siegel JE, Daniels N, and Weinstein MC, "The Role of Cost-Effectiveness Analysis in Health and Medicine," *JAMA*, 1996, *276(14)*: 1172–7; also Daniels N, "Distributive Justice and the Use of Summary Measures of Population Health Status," in Institute of Medicine, *Summarizing Population Health: Directions for the Development and Application of Population Metrics* (Washington, DC: National Academy Press, 1998), pp. 58–71.
6. Daniels N, *Just Health Care* (New York: Cambridge University Press, 1985); Daniels N, "Growth Hormone Therapy for Short Stature: Can We Support the Treatment/Enhancement Distinction," *Growth & Growth Hormone*, 1992, *8(Suppl 1)*: 46–8; Sabin J, and Daniels N, "Determining

Medical Necessity in Mental Health Practice," *Hastings Center Report*, 1994, *24(6)*: 5–13; Buchanan A, Brock DW, Daniels N, and Wikler D, *From Chance to Choice: Genetics & Justice* (New York: Cambridge University Press, 2000).

7. Daniels N and Sabin J, "Last Chance Therapies and Managed Care," *Hastings Center Report*, 1998, *28(2)*: 27–41.

8. Daniels N, "Rationing Fairly: Programmatic Considerations," *Bioethics*, 1993, *7(2/3)*: 224–33.

9. Daniels N and Sabin J, "Limits to Health Care: Fair Procedures, Democratic Deliberation, and the Legitimacy Problem for Insurers," *Philosophy & Public Affairs*, 1997, *26*: 303–50.

10. Daniels N, "The Profit Motive and the Moral Assessment of Health Care Institutions," *Business and Professional Ethics Journal*, 1991, *10(2)*: 3–30.

11. Teagarden JR, Daniels N, and Sabin JE, "The Need for Ethical Frameworks in Prescription Drug Benefit Allocation Policy," *Journal of the American Pharmaceutical Association*, 2002, *43*:1.

12. Steward WF, Shecter A, and Lipton RB, "Migraine Heterogeneity: Disability, Pain, Intensity, and Attack Frequency and Duration," *Neurology*, 1994, *44(Suppl. 4)*: S24–S39.

13. Where rationing is carried out under budget limits that require comparisons of drugs across different groups of patients, rather than for different drugs for the same diagnoses, other principles will be involved, such as "give priority to those who are sickest." See Daniels and Sabin, *Setting Limits Fairly*, Ch. 3.

14. In this case, the priority principle converges with concerns to avoid moral hazard. Pathological conditions are actuarial; we can assign probabilities to them based on experience. Conditions we simply would prefer to change are not.

15. In the United Kingdom, by contrast, there is currently controversy about whether to cover (at Level 1) several drugs on grounds of cost-worthiness. These are all new and expensive drug treatments of limited effectiveness for neurological conditions. (Personal communication, Tony Hope, professor of medical ethics at the University of Oxford and director of Ethox, 9 April 2002.)

16. *Boston Globe*, June 12, 1998: C3.

17. *Boston Globe*, June 28, 1998: A19.

18. Levine S, Campen D, Millares M, and Barrueta A, "Kaiser Permanente's Prescription Drug Benefit," *Health Affairs*, 2000, *Mar/Apr*: 185–90.

19. Simon GE, VonKorff M, Heiligenstein JH, et al., "Initial Antidepressant Choice in Primary Care: Effectiveness and Cost of Fluoxetene vs Tricyclic Antidepressants," *JAMA*, 1996, *275(24)*: 1897–1902.

20. Schneeweiss S, Walker AM, Glynn RJ, Maclure M, Dormuth C, and Sourmerae SB, "Outcomes of Reference Pricing for Angiotensin-Converting-Enzyme Inhibitors," *New England Journal of Medicine*, 2002, *346(11)*: 822–9.

21. Cohen JS, "Tablet Splitting: Imperfect Perhaps, but Better than Excessive Dosing," *Journal of American Pharmaceutical Association*, 2002, *42(2)*: 160–62.

22. Even in such settings, however, decisions to save money made within a pharmaceutical budgetary "silo" may increase costs in other "silos" that are budgeted separately.

23. Kleinke JD, "Just What the HMO Ordered."

24. Kleinke JD, "Just What the HMO Ordered," p. 84, citing B. Luce, "Pharmacoeconomics and Managed Care: Methodologic and Policy Issues," *Medical Decision Making*, 1998, *18(2)*: S6.

25. Nord E, *Cost-Value Analysis in Health Care: Making Sense out of QALYs* (Cambridge: Cambridge University Press, 1999).

26. Holm S, "Developments in the Nordic Countries – Goodbye to Simple Solutions." In Coulter A and Ham C, Eds., *The Global Challenge of Health Care Rationing* (Philadelphia: Open University Press, 2000), pp. 29–37.

27. Ham C and Robert G, *The Next Phase of Priority Setting in Health Care: Securing Fairness and Legitimacy* (in press).

Notes to Chapter 14

1. Levit K, Smith C, Cowan C, Sensenig A, Catlin A, and the Health Accounts Team, "Health Spending Rebound Continues in 2002," *Health Affairs*, 2004, *23(1)*: 147–59.

2. Ibid.

3. Kaiser Family Foundation, "Prescription Drug Trends: A Chartbook Update, June 2001." Available at www.kff.org/rxdrugs Accessed July 2004.

4. Reinhardt U, Hussey P, and Anderson G, "Cross-National Comparisons of Health Systems Using OECD Data, 1999," *Health Affairs*, 2002, *21(3)*: 169–81.

5. A superior good as defined by economists is a good for which an increase in income causes an increase in demand, and the income elasticity of demand is positive and greater than one. A superior good is also termed a luxury good.

6. Murphy KM, and Topel RH, Eds. *Measuring the Gains from Medical Research: An Economic Approach* (Chicago: University of Chicago Press, 2003).

7. Reinhardt U, Hussey P, and Anderson G, "U.S. Health Care Spending in an International Context: Why Is U.S. Spending So High, and Can We Afford It?" *Health Affairs*, 2004, *23(3)*: 10–25.

8. Chernew ME, Hirth RA, and Cutler DM, "Increased Spending on Health Care: How Much Can the United States Afford?" *Health Affairs*, 2003, *22(4)*: 15–25.

9. Available at www.schoolscience.co.uk/content/4/biology/glaxo/pmb1 trade1.html Accessed July 2004.

10. "The Trouble with Cheap Drugs," *The Economist*, January 29, 2004. Available at www.economist.com/displayStory.cfm?Story_ID=2388708 Accessed July 2004.

11. Krupnick AJ, "Valuing Health Outcomes: Policy Choices and Technical Issues," Resources for the Future Report. Washington, D.C., 2004.

12. Hay J, "Evaluation and Review of Pharmacoeconomic Models," *Expert Opinion on Pharmacotherapy*, 2004, *5(9)*: 1867–80.

13. Gold M, Siegel J, Russell L, and Weinstein M, *Cost-Effectiveness in Health and Medicine* (New York: Oxford University Press, 1996).

14. Weinstein M, "From Cost-Effectiveness Ratios to Resource Allocation," in Sloan F, Ed., *Valuing Health Care* (New York: Cambridge University Press, 1995).

15. Bureau of Labor Statistics, "Employer Costs for Employee Compensation – March 2004." Available at www.bls.gov/ncs/ect/home.htm Accessed July 2004.

16. Viscusi WK, and Aldy JE, "The Value of a Statistical Life: A Critical Review of Market Estimates Around the World," *Journal of Risk and Uncertainty*, 2003, *28(1)*: 5–76.

17. Wagstaff A, "QALYs and the Equity-Efficiency Trade-Off," *Journal of Health Economics*, 1991, *10*: 21–41.

18. Gold M, Siegel J, Russell L, and Weinstein M, *Cost-Effectiveness in Health and Medicine*.

19. Drummond M, Torrance G, and Mason J, "Cost-Effectiveness League Tables: More Harm Than Good," *Social Science and Medicine*, 1993, *37*: 33–40.

20. The Harvard Center for Risk Analysis maintains an updated list of cost-effectiveness results for many pharmaceuticals and other healthcare interventions. Available at www.hsph.harvard.edu/cearegistry/ Accessed July 2004.

21. Bingham M, Johnson FR, and Miller D, "Modeling Choice Behavior for New Pharmaceutical Products," *Value in Health*, 2001, *4(1)*: 1–13.

22. Hay J, "Conjoint Analysis in Pharmaceutical Research," *Journal of Managed Care Pharmacy*, 2002, *8(3)*: 206–9.

23. Johannesson M, "The Relationship between Cost-Effectiveness Analysis and Cost–Benefit Analysis," *Social Science and Medicine*, 1995, 41: 483–9.

24. Bleichrodt H, and Quiggin J, "Life Cycle Preferences over Consumption and Health: When Is Cost-Effectiveness Analysis Equivalent to Cost–Benefit Analysis?" *Journal of Health Economics*, 1999, *18*: 681–708.

25. Garber AM, and Phelps CE, "Economic Foundations of Cost Effectiveness Analysis," *Journal of Health Economics*, 1997, *16*: 1–31.

26. Klose T, "A Utility-Theoretic Model for QALYs and Willingness to Pay," *Health Economics*, 2003, *12*: 17–31.

27. Letourneau-Wagner J, Hay J, "The Cost Impacts of Vaccination in the United States: An Overview," *Managed Care Consultant* 2005, 4[2]: 11–25.

28. Topol E, "Good Riddance to a Bad Drug," Editorial Opinion, *New York Times*, October 2, 2004.

29. Spiegel BMR, Targownik L, Dulai GS, and Gralnek IM, "The Cost-Effectiveness of Cyclooxygenase-2 Selective Inhibitors in the Management of Chronic Arthritis," *Annals of Internal Medicine*, 2003; *138*: 795–806.

30. See www.hsph.harvard.edu/cearegistry Accessed July 2004.

31. Wennberg JE, "Dealing with Medical Practice Variations: A Proposal for Action," *Health Affairs*, 1984, *Summer*: 6–32.

32. Wennberg JE and Gittelsohn A, "Small Area Variations in Health Care Delivery," *Science*, 1973, *182*: 1102–8.

33. Available at www.rand.org Accessed July 2004.

34. Schuster MA, McGlynn EA, and Brook RH, "How Good Is the Quality of Health Care in the United States?" *Milbank Quarterly*, 1998, *76(4)*: 517–63, 509.

35. Leape LL, Park RE, Bashore TM, Harrison JK, Davidson CJ, and Brook RH, "Effect of Variability in the Interpretation of Coronary Angiograms on the Appropriateness of Use of Coronary Revascularization Procedures," *American Heart Journal*, January 2000, *139(1, Part 1)*: 106–13.

36. Schuster MA, McGlynn EA, and Brook RH, "How Good Is the Quality of Health Care in the United States?"

37. Reinhardt U, Hussey P, and Anderson G, "Cross-National Comparisons of Health Systems Using OECD Data."

38. Murphy KM, and Topel RH, Eds., *Measuring the Gains from Medical Research*.

39. Mushkin S, *Biomedical Research: Costs and Benefits* (Cambridge, MA: Ballinger Publishing Co., 1979).

40. Cutler DM, and McClellan M, "Is Technological Change in Medicine Worth It?" *Health Affairs*, 2001, *20(5)*: 11–29.

41. Murphy KM, and Topel RH, Eds., *Measuring the Gains from Medical Research*.

42. Available at www.washingtonpost.com/wp-dyn/articles/A27932-2004Jul4.html Accessed July 2004.

43. Available at www.phrma.org/issues/researchdev/ Accessed July 2004.
44. Cutler DM, and McClellan M, "Is Technological Change in Medicine Worth It?" *Health Affairs*, 2001, *20(5):* 11–29.
45. "The Trouble with Cheap Drugs," *The Economist*, January 29, 2004.
46. Similar concerns can be seen within the United States looking at the market for childhood vaccines. Unlike other pharmaceutical products, the federal Centers for Disease Control have purchased nearly half of all childhood vaccines used in the United States at heavily discounted prices for over a decade. As a result, vaccine R&D has grown more slowly than other pharmaceutical R&D, the number of U.S. vaccine manufacturers has dropped from dozens to five, severe vaccine shortages occur regularly, and many childhood vaccines have only a single supplier.
47. Lichtenberg FR, "Are the Benefits of Newer Drugs Worth Their Cost? Evidence from the MEPS," *Health Affairs*, 2001, *20(5)*: 241–51.
48. Lichtenberg FR, "The Impact of New Drug Launches on Longevity: Evidence from Longitudinal, Disease-Level Data from 52 Countries, 1982–2001," NBER Working Paper No. 9754, June 2003.
49. Garrison L, and Towse A, "The Drug Budget Silo Mentality in Europe: An Overview," *Value in Health*, 2003, *6(Supplement 1)*: S1–S6.
50. Horn SD, Sharkey PD, and Phillips-Harris C, "Formulary Limitations and the Elderly: Results from the Managed Care Outcomes Project," *American Journal of Managed Care*, 1998, *4(8)*: 1105–13.
51. Soumerai SB, Avom J, Ross-Degnan D, et al., "Payment Restrictions for Prescription Drugs under Medicaid: Effects on Therapy, Cost, and Equity," *New England Journal of Medicine*, 1987, *317(9)*: 550–56.
52. Soumerai SB, Ross-Degnan D, Avom J, et al., "Effects of Medicaid Drug-Payment Limits on Admission to Hospitals and Nursing Homes," *New England Journal of Medicine*, 1991, *325(15)*: 1072–7.
53. Soumerai SB, McLaughlin TJ, Ross-Degnan D, et al., "Effects of Limiting Medicaid Drug-Reimbursement Benefits on the Use of Psychotropic Agents and Acute Mental Health Services by Patients with Schizophrenia," *New England Journal of Medicine*, 1994, *331(10)*: 650–55.
54. Tamblyn R, Laprise R, Hanley J, et al., "Adverse Events Associated with Prescription Drug Cost-Sharing among Poor and Elderly Persons," *Journal of the American Medical Association*, 2001, *285(4)*: 421–9.
55. The input-focused paradigm is exemplified by the old saw, "the operation was successful, although the patient died."
56. Department of Health Housing and Community Services, Australia, *Guidelines for the Pharmaceutical Industry on the Preparation of Submissions to the Pharmaceutical Benefits Advisory Committee* (Canberra: AGPS, 1992).
57. Hill SR, Mitchell AS, and Henry DA, "Problems with the Interpretation of Pharmacoeconomic Analyses: A Review of Submissions to

the Australian Pharmaceutical Benefits Scheme," *JAMA*, 2000, *283(16)*: 2116–21.

58. Langley PC, "Focusing Pharmacoeconomic Activities: Reimbursement or the Drug Life Cycle?" *Current Medical Research Opinion*, 2004, *20(2)*: 181–8.

59. Hay J, "Pharmacoeconomic Guidelines: Where Do We Go from Here?" *Value in Health*, 2001, *4(3)*: 211.

60. Hjelmgren J, Berggren F, and Andersson F, "Health Economic Guidelines: Similarities, Differences and Some Implications," *Value in Health*, 2001, *4*: 225–50.

61. Siegel JE, Torrance GW, Russell LB, et al., "Guidelines for Pharmacoeconomic Studies. Recommendations for the Panel on Cost-Effectiveness in Health and Medicine," *PharmacoEconomics*, 1997, *11*: 159–68.

62. Drummond MF, and Jefferson TO, "Guidelines for Authors and Peer Reviewers of Economic Submissions to the BMJ," *BMJ*, 1996, *313*: 275–83.

63. Available at www.ispor.org/PEguidelines/COMP1.asp Accessed July 2004.

64. Fry RN, Avey SG, and Sullivan SD, "The Academy of Managed Care Pharmacy Format for Formulary Submissions: An Evolving Standard," *Value in Health*, 2003, *6(5)*: 505–21.

65. Dr. Mark McClellan, the CMS Administrator, has recently announced that Medicare will be demanding more rigorous outcomes evidence before approving new therapies for payment. See Kolata G, "Medicare Covers New Treatments with a Catch," *New York Times*, November 5, 2004.

66. Havighurst C, Public Law Research Paper No. 20, Duke Law School, *Indiana Law Review*, 2001, *34*: 395.

67. Available at www.nice.uk.org Accessed July 2004; see also Garrison L and Towse A, "The Drug Budget Silo Mentality in Europe."

68. This pre-NICE period is now referred to as the No Assessment or Utilization of Good Health Technology Years (NAUGHTY) era.

69. Available at www.ispor.org/peguidelines/COMP1.asp Accessed July 2004.

70. Chiou C-F, Hay J, Wallace J, Bloom B, Neumann P, Sullivan S, Yu H-T, Keeler E, Henning J, and Ofman J, "Development and Validation of a Grading System for the Quality of Cost-Effectiveness Studies," *Medical Care*, 2003, *41*: 32–44.

71. Ofman J, Sullivan S, Neumann P, Chiou C-F, Henning J, and Hay J, "Examining the Value and Quality of Health Economic Analyses: Implications of Utilizing the QHES," *Journal of Managed Care Pharmacy*, 2003, *9(1)*: 53–62.

72. Mather D, "Do Decision Makers Really Need Health Economic Data?" *Value in Health*, 2003, *6(4)*: 404–6.

73. Campen D, "The Bleeding Edge of Decision Making in Managed Health Care – Kaiser-Permanente's Model for Formulary Development," *Value in Health*, 2002, *5(5)*: 383–9.

74. Connolly C, "Drugmakers Protect Their Turf," *The Washington Post*, November 21, 2003.

75. Calfee J, "The Grim Economics of Pharmaceutical Importation," American Enterprise Institute, November 2003. Available at www. aei.org Accessed February 2004.

76. "2004 Annual Report of the Boards of Trustees of the Federal Hospital Insurance and Federal Supplementary Medical Insurance Trust Funds," March 23, 2004. Available at www.cms.hhs.gov/publications/trusteesreport/2004/tr.pdf Accessed July 2004.

77. Fumento M, *Bioevolution: How Biotechnology Is Changing Our World* (San Francisco: Encounter Books, 2003).

78. Liu L, Rettenmaier AJ, Saving TR, "How Large Is the Federal Government's Debt?" National Center for Policy Analysis, Policy Report No. 263, October 30, 2003. Available at www.ncpa.org/pub/st/st263/ Accessed July 2004.

79. Hay J, and Yu W, "Drug Patents and Prices, Can We Achieve Better Outcomes?" in Triplett J, Ed., *Measuring the Prices of Medical Treatments* (Washington, D.C.: Brookings Press, 1999), pp. 152–95.

80. Hay J, and Yu W, "Pharmacoeconomics and Outcomes Research: Expanding the Health Care "Outcomes" Market," *Value in Health*, 2000, *3(3)*: 181–5.

81. Kremer M, "Patent Buyouts: A Mechanism for Encouraging Innovation." *Quarterly Journal of Economics*, 1998, *November*: 1137–7.

82. Kremer M, 2000, "Creating Markets for New Vaccines. Part I: Rationale," NBER Working Paper, May 12, 2000. Available at www.nber.org Accessed May 26, 2005

83. Kremer M, 2000, "Creating Markets for New Vaccines. Part II: Design Issues," NBER Working Paper, May 12, 2000. Available at www.nber.org Accessed May 26, 2005.

84. Garber AM, "Cost-Effectiveness and Evidence Evaluation As Criteria for Coverage Policy," *Health Affairs* Web Exclusive, 2004, *W4*: 284–96. Available at www.healthaffairs.org/WebExclusives.php Accessed May 25, 2005.

Notes to Part III Introduction

1. See www.csdd.tufts.edu/NewsEvents/RecentNews.asp?newsid=6 Accessed November 21, 2004.

2. The fact that the current patent system yields considerable social benefits does not necessarily mean that it is doing so in a socially optimal

manner. From a social perspective, one must be concerned about providing too much as well as too little patent protection. It would be highly inefficient to provide more patent protection than is necessary because the resulting higher prices and reduced access would not be offset by any gain in innovation. (Indeed, in the worst-case scenario, a patent improvidently granted to one inventor can actually discourage innovation by blocking the superior inventions of others.) The patent system has a number of policy levers to fine tune incentives for innovation, e.g., variations in the breadth of claims allowed under a patent, the degree of innovation required to grant a patent and, most importantly, in the length of a patent. See generally, Jaffe A, and Lerner J, *Innovation and its Discontents: How Our Broken Patent System is Endangering Innovation and Progress, and What to Do About It* (Princeton, NJ: Princeton University Press, 2004).

3. Porter E, "Importing Less Expensive Drugs Not Seen as Cure for U.S. Woes," *The New York Times*, October 16, 2004. For a defense of free market pricing of drugs, see Ian Maitland, "Priceless Goods: How Should Life-Saving Drugs Be Priced?" *Business Ethics Quarterly*, 2002, *12(1)*: 451–80.

4. See Pear R, and Bogdanich W, "Some Successful Models Ignored as Congress Works on Drug Bill," *The New York Times*, September 4, 2003: A1.

5. Brown D, "How U.S. Got Down to Two Makers of Flu Vaccine," *Washington Post*, October 17, 2004: A1. Available at www.washingtonpost.com/wp-dyn/articles/A38776-2004Oct16.html Accessed November 10, 2004.

6. Noah L, "Triage in the Nation's Medicine Cabinet," *South Carolina Law Review* 2003, *54*: 741.

7. Foulkes A, "A Weakened Immunity," *The Independent Review*, 2004, *IX*:1, 31–54. Production and pricing issues have supplanted liability risks as the major explanation for vaccine shortages, at least in the case of childhood vaccines. Large punitive damage awards, which drove out many manufacturers in the 1980s, have been limited for childhood vaccines through the National Childhood Vaccine Injury Act, which set up a fund from excise taxes on vaccines to compensate those who experience vaccine-related injuries. For more information on the CVIA, see Scott EC, "The National Childhood Vaccine Injury Act Turns Fifteen," *Food and Drug Law Journal* 2001, *56*: 351.

8. For a description and analysis of the pharmaceutical industry's patent protection campaign (and the views of the third world nations on patents), see Santoro MA, *Pfizer: Protecting Intellectual Property in a Global Marketplace* (Harvard Business School Case Program, 1992).

9. For a summary of the Doha Declaration and reaction to it, see www.cid.harvard.edu/cidtrade/issues/ipr.html Accessed May 18, 2005.

Notes to Chapter 15

1. Locke J, *The Second Treatise of Government*, 1764, Laslett P, Ed. (Cambridge: Cambridge University Press, 1983).
2. Some of this thinking was stimulated by Bryan Maxwell from his unpublished thesis at the University of Virginia: "Access to Life: The Conflict between Public Health and Intellectual Property Protections on HIV/AIDS Drugs in Developing Countries," 2002.
3. Tuck R, *Natural Rights Theories* (Cambridge: Cambridge University Press, 1979); Werhane PH, Radin TJ, and Bowie N, *Employment and Employee Rights* (Malden, MA: Blackwell's, 2003).
4. Tully J, *A Discourse on Property: John Locke and His Adversaries* (Cambridge: Cambridge University Press, 1980).
5. Resnik DB, "A Pluralistic Account of Intellectual Property," *Journal of Business Ethics*, 2003, *46*: 319–35.
6. Jefferson T, "Letter to Isaac McPherson," 1813, reprinted in Kock A, and Peden W, *The Life and Selected Writings of Thomas Jefferson* (New York: Modern Library, 1972).
7. Vaver D, "Intellectual Property: State of the Art," *Law Quarterly Review*, 2000, *116*: 621.
8. Vaver D, "Intellectual Property: State of the Art," p. 622.
9. Rand A, *Capitalism: The Unknown Ideal* (New York: New American Library, 1966), pp. 125, 128.
10. Hughes JW, Moore MJ, and Snyder EA, "'Napsterizing' Pharmaceuticals Access, Innovation, and Consumer Welfare," National Bureau of Economic Research, Working Paper 9229, 2002.
11. Clemente CL, "Intellectual Property: The Patent on Prosperity," *Pfizer Forum*, 2001. Available at www.pfizerforum.com Accessed May 25, 2005.
12. World Bank, 1999. Available at www.worldbank.org Accessed May 25, 2005.
13. Interestingly, we are seeing huge Western investments in China, despite China's despicable record in protecting intellectual property of any sort. (China has developed some laws, but they are virtually unenforced and unenforceable.)
14. Bale HE Jr., "Patents and Public Health: A Good or Bad Mix?" *Pfizer Forum*, 2002. Available at www.pfizerforum.com Accessed May 25, 2005.
15. Idris K, *Intellectual Property – A Tool for Economic Growth* (Geneva, Switzerland: World Intellectual Property Organization, 2003).
16. This conclusion is based on the argument that all our experiences are socially constructed through a series of mental models or mindsets that

frame all our experiences. We do not simply take in experiences as if our minds were receptacles or "blank tablets." Rather, we focus, organize, select, and censor even our simplest perceptions so that all our experiences are framed by complex socially learned mindsets or cognitive schema. The argument is as follows. It is commonly (although not universally) concluded that human beings deal with the world through mindsets or mental models. Although the term is not always clearly defined, "mental model" encompasses the notion that human beings have mental representations, or cognitive frames, that model the stimuli or data with which they interact, and these frameworks set up parameters though which experience, or a certain set of experiences, is organized or filtered. See Senge P, *The Fifth Discipline* (New York: Doubleday, 1990), chapter 10; Gentner D, and Whitley EW, "Mental Models of Population Growth," in Bazerman M, Messick D, Tenbrunsel A, and Wade-Benzoni KA, Eds., *Environment, Ethics, and Behavior* (San Francisco: New Lexington Press, 1997), pp. 210–11; Gorman M, *Simulating Science* (Bloomington, IN: Indiana University Press, 1992); Werhane PH, *Moral Imagination and Management Decision-Making* (New York: Oxford University Press, 1999). Mental models take the form of schemas that frame the experience through which individuals process information, conduct experiments, and formulate theories.

17. Severance K, Spiro L, and Werhane PH, "WR, Grace & Co. and the Neemix Plant," in Gorman ME, Mehalik MM, and Werhane PH, Eds., *Ethical and Environmental Challenges to Engineering* (Upper Saddle River, NJ: Prentice-Hall, 2000), pp. 197–207; Vijayalakshmi K, Radha KS, Shiva V, *Neem: A User's Manual* (Madras, India: Centre for Indian Knowledge Systems, 1995).

18. It is estimated that there are about 70 such products produced from indigenous use in India alone. See Vijayalakshmi K, Radha KS, and Shiva V, *Neem: A User's Manual.* There are many other examples from other less developed countries.

19. Tolan S, "A Bean of a Different Color," *NPR Weekend Edition*: June 9, 2001. Transcript obtained from Livingston, NJ: Burrelle's Information Services; and Kegg A, "Has Bean: Patent Suit Settled Out of Court," *Northern Colorado Business Report*, November 29, 2002, p. 6.

20. Hardin G, "The Tragedy of the Commons," *Science*, 1968, *162*: 1243–5.

21. Altbach P, "Economic Progress Brings Copyright to Asia," *Far Eastern Economic Review*, 1988, *139*: 62–3; quoted in Diefenbach DL, "The Constitutional and Moral Justifications for Copyright," *Public Affairs Quarterly*, 1994, *8*: 229.

22. Wechsler J, "Bioterrorism Shines Spotlight on Pharma," *Pharmaceutical Executive*, 2001, December 1: 34.

23. Thurow LC, "Needed: A New System of Intellectual Property Rights," *Harvard Business Review*, 1997, September–October: 95–103.

24. Clemente CL, "Intellectual Property: The Patent on Prosperity."

25. Heller MA, Eisenberg RS, "Can Patents Deter Innovation? The Anti-commons in Biomedical Research," *Science*, 1998, *280*: 698.

26. Goodman K, "Intellectual Property and Control," *Academic Medicine*, 1993, *68(9)*: 588–92.

27. Mitroff I, Linstone H, *The Unbounded Mind* (New York: Oxford University Press, 1993), p. 98.

28. According to the World Health Organization, approximately 42 million people are infected with HIV, and last year alone there were 3.1 million deaths from this disease. Of the 42 million people approximately two-thirds live in sub-Saharan Africa. Unless this epidemic is addressed, it is estimated that by the year 2020 over 100 million people will have died of this disease. See World Health Organization and UNAIDS AIDS Epidemic Update 2003. Available at www.unaids.org/html/pub/publications/irc-pubob/jc943epiupdate2003_en_pdf.html Accessed May 31, 2005.

29. Attaran A, Gillespie-White L, "Do Patents for Antiretroviral Drugs Constrain Access to AIDS Treatment in Africa?" *Journal of the American Medical Association*, 2001, *286*: 1886–1892.

30. Although the World Trade Organization TRIPS agreement, which came into effect in 2000 and applies to all developing countries, protects patent and copyright laws, exceptions can be made in life-threatening public health situations such as the HIV/pandemic. So patent protection for antiretroviral drugs is not globally protected. See Curti AM, "The WTO Dispute Settlement Understanding: An Unlikely Weapon in the Fight Against AIDS," *American Journal of Law and Medicine*, 2001, December 22: 469–80.

31. Merck recognizes this in their mission as stated by George Merck, son of the company's founder. "We try never to forget that medicine is for the people. It is not for the profits. The profits follow, and if we have remembered that, they have never failed to appear. The better we have remembered it, the larger they have been." See Bollier D, Weiss S, Hanson K, "Merck &. Co, Inc," Harvard Business School Case No. 9-991-021 (Boston: Harvard Business School Publishing, 1991), p. 3. Similarly, Abbott Laboratories' stated mission is "to develop breakthrough health care products that advance patient care for diseases with the greatest unmet medical need." See Abbott Laboratories, "Touching Lives: 2003 Global Citizenship Report," 2004.

32. Friedman MA, den Besten H, Attaran A, "Out-Licensing: A Practical Approach for Improvement of Access to Medicines in Poor Countries," *The Lancet*, 2003, *361*: 341–4.

33. Dugger CW, "Rural Haitians Are Vanguard in AIDS Battle," *New York Times*, November 30, 2003: A1.

34. Werhane PH, *Moral Imagination and Management Decision-Making* (New York: Oxford University Press, 1999), p. 93.

35. Werhane PH, *Moral Imagination and Management Decision-Making*.

36. Yemen G, Powell E, "The Female Health Company (A) and (B)," UVA-BC-0182-3 (University of Virginia: Darden Business Publishing, 2003).

37. Weber J, Austin J, Barrett D, "Merck Global Health Initiatives (B): Botswana," HBS Case No. 9-301-089 (Boston, MA: Harvard Business School Publishing, 2001).

38. Abbott Laboratories, "Tanzania Care," 2003. Available at www.tanzaniacare.org Accessed May 25, 2005.

39. Dugger CW, "Rural Haitians are Vanguard in AIDS Battle," *New York Times*, November 30, 2003: A1.

40. Altman LK, "W. H. O. Aims to Treat 3 Million for AIDS" *New York Times*, December 1, 2003: A6.

41. Dworkin R, *Taking Rights Seriously* (Cambridge, MA: Harvard University Press, 1977), p. 273.

Notes to Chapter 16

1. Cutler D, McClellan, M, "Is Technological Change in Medicine Worth It?" in "The Value of Innovation," *Health Affairs*, Sept./Oct. 2001, *20(5)*: 11–29.

2. Lichtenberg FR, "Sources of U.S. Longevity Increase, 1960–1997," NBER Working Paper No. W8755 (February 2002).

3. DiMasi J, Hansen R, Grabowski, H, "The Price of Innovation: New Estimates of Drug Development Costs," *Journal of Health Economics*, 2003, *22*: 151–85.

4. PhRMA 2004 Industry Profile. Available at www.phrma.org/publications/2004-03-31.937.pdf Accessed May 25, 2005.

5. "Better Pharmaceuticals for Children Act" included in the FDA Modernization Act (PL 105–115) and the "Best Pharmaceuticals for Children Act" (PL 107–109).

6. Ables AZ, and Baughman OL, "Antidepressants: Update on New Agents and Indications," *American Family Physician*, February 1, 2003.

7. Hensley PL, and Nurnberg HG, "Formulary Restriction of Selective Serotonin Reuptake Inhibitors for Depression: Potential Pitfalls," *Pharmacoeconomics*, 2001, *19(10)*: 973–2.

8. Dunn R, Donoghue JM, Ozminkowski RJ, et al., "Longitudinal Patterns of Antidepressant Prescribing in Primary Care in the UK: Comparison with Treatment Guidelines," *Journal of Psychopharmacology*, 1999, *13(2)*: 136–43.

9. Omnibus Budget Reconciliation Act of 1990 established a payment rate of $11 per 1,000 units of erythropoietin effective January 1, 1991.

10. Greer JW, Milam RG, Eggers PW, "Trends in Use, Cost, and Outcomes of Human Recombinant Erythropoietin, 1989–98," *Health Care Financing Review*, Spring 1999, *20(3)*: 55–62.

11. Veterans' Health Care Act of 1992 (PL 102–585).

12. Lichtenberg FR, Waldfogel J, "Does Misery Love Company? Evidence from Pharmaceutical Markets Before and After the Orphan Drug Act," NBER Working Paper No. W9750 (June 2003).

13. Grabowski H, Vernon J, DiMasi J, "Returns on R&D for New Drug Introductions in the 1990s," *PharmacoEconomics*, 2002, *20(Supplement 3)*: 11–29.

14. Sher G, Fisch JD, "Vaginal Sildenafil (Viagra®): A Preliminary Report of a Novel Method to Improve Uterine Artery Blood Flow and Endometrial Development in Patients Undergoing IVF," *Human Reproduction*, April 2000, *15*: 806–9.

15. Calfee JE, "Bioterrorism and Pharmaceuticals: The Influence of Secretary Thompson's Cipro Negotiations" AEI, November 1, 2001.

16. Gupta RK, Taliento, L, "How Businesses Can Combat Global Disease," *The McKinsey Quarterly*, 2003, Number 4.

17. Reynolds G, "The Flu Hunters," *The New York Times*, November 7, 2004.

18. Ziegler P, *The Black Death*, Chapter 15, "The Social and Economic Consequences" (New York: Harper & Row, 1969).

19. Bloom DE, Canning D, Sevilla J, "The Effect of Health on Economic Growth: Theory and Evidence," NEBER Working Paper w8587, November 2001.

20. "Internet Pharmacies: Some Pose Safety Risks for Consumers and Are Unreliable in Their Business Practices," Government Accounting Office Testimony, GAO-04-888T, June 17, 2004.

21. Kleinke JD, "The Price of Progress: Prescription Drugs in the Health Care Market," *Health Affairs*, September/October 2001: 43–60.

22. Miller RD, and Frech HE, "Health Care Matters: Pharmaceuticals, Obesity and the Quality of Life," AEI Press, March 2004.

23. Banerjee PK, "The Mapping of the Human Genome: Where Next?" April 2002. Available at www.accenture.com/xdoc/en/industries/hls/pharma/reutersoverview8april02.pdf Accessed May 25, 2005.

24. U.S. Food and Drug Administration, "FY 2003 Performance Report to the President and the Congress for the Prescription Drug User Fee Act of 1992," 2003. Available at www.fda.gov/oc/pdufa/report2003/ Accessed May 25, 2005.

25. U.S. Government Accounting Office, "Effect of User Fees on Drug Approval Times, Withdrawal, and Other Agency Activities," Washington, DC, GAO Report 02-958, September 2002. Available at www.gao.gov/new.items/d02958.pdf Accessed May 25, 2005.

26. "User Fees Credited with 51% Drop in Average Approval Times since 1993," Tufts Center for the Study of Drug Development, Impact Report, October 2000, Vol. 2.

27. Lewis C, "User Fees and Medical Device Reviews," *FDA Consumer Magazine*, March–April 2003. Available at www.fda.gov/fdac/features/2003/203_mdufma.html Accessed May 25, 2005.

28. "FDI Specific Policy Recommendations #3 – Pharmaceuticals," American Chamber of Commerce in Japan, February 2004.

29. Toole A, "Does Public Scientific Research Complement Industry R&D Investment? The Case of NIH Supported Basic and Clinical Research and Pharmaceutical Industry R&D," Illinois State University Working Paper 0102, May 6, 2003.

30. Cockburn I, Henderson R, "Public-Private Interaction and the Productivity of Pharmaceutical Research," NBER Working Paper No. W6018, June 1999.

31. "How Government and the Rx Industry Cooperate for Benefit of Patients," PhRMA Quick Facts, October 17, 2000. Available at www.phrma.org/publications/quickfacts/admin/17.10.2000.178.cfm Accessed May 25, 2005.

32. "Technology Transfer: Number and Characteristics of Inventions Licensed by Six Federal Agencies," Government Accounting Office Report GAO/RCED-99-173, June 1999.

33. National Institutes of Health Response to the Conference Report Request for a Plan to Ensure Taxpayers' Interests are Protected. July 2001. Available at www.nih.gov/news/070101wyden.htm Accessed May 25, 2005.

34. See The Forum for Collaborative HIV Research, at www.hivforum.org Accessed May 25, 2005.

Note to Chapter 17

1. Some agencies lack the internal resources to create their own materials and the industry offer of professional, packaged programs is tempting indeed. A better solution may be to work with and share materials from other nonprofit agencies that practice fairness and objectivity.

Note to Chapter 18

1. Lichtenberg FR, "Are the Benefits of Newer Drugs Worth Their Costs? Evidence from the 1996 MEPS," *Health Affairs*, 2001, *20(5)*: 24–51; and Lichtenberg FR, "Benefits and Costs of Newer Drugs: An Update," National Bureau of Economic Research (NBER), Working Paper No. 8996, June 2002.

Notes to Chapter 19

1. This chapter discusses many of the themes presented in an earlier version of this paper, which was published as "The Structural Power of Strong Pharmaceutical Patent Protection in U.S. Foreign Policy," *Iowa Journal of Gender, Race and Justice*, 2003, 7: 267.

2. Doha Declaration on the Trade-Related Intellectual Property Rights Agreement & Public Health, Mar. 14, 2002, Communication from the United States, IP/C/W/340 1 ¶ 6; Sykes AO, *TRIPS, Pharmaceuticals, Developing Countries, and the Doha "Solution," Chicago Journal of International Law*, 2002, *3*: 47; and "The Legal Status of the Doha Declaration on TRIPS and Public Health Under the Vienna Convention of the Law of Treaties," *Harvard Journal of Law and Technology*, 2002, *15*: 291.

3. Article 33 of the TRIPS Agreement provides that "[t]he term of protection available [for patents] shall not end before the expiration of a period of twenty years counted from the filing date." Agreement on Trade-Related Intellectual Property Rights, Apr. 15, 1994, 31 Marrakesh Agreement Establishing the World Trade Organization, Annex 1C, Legal Instruments – Results of the Uruguay Round, 33 I. L. M. 81, 1994 [hereinafter TRIPS Agreement]. Available at www.wto.org/english/docs_e/legal_e/27-trips.pdf Accessed June 1, 2005.

4. Gathii J, "Construing Intellectual Property Rights and Competition Policy Consistently with Facilitating Access to Affordable Aids Drugs to Low-End Consumers," *Florida Law Review*, 2001, *53*: 727, 747–71.

5. Article 1, Section 8 provides that Congress shall make laws "To promote the Progress of Science and useful Arts, by securing for limited Times to Authors and Inventors exclusive Right to their respective Writings and Discoveries," U.S. Constitutions art. I, §8.

6. *Brenner v. Manson*, 383 U.S. 519, 534, 1966.

7. TRIPS Agreement, p. 86.

8. Declaration on the TRIPS Agreement and Public Health, WT/MIN(01)/Dec/2 ¶ 4, November 14, 2001 [hereinafter Doha Declaration]. Available at www.wto.org/english/thewto_e/minist_e/min01_e/mindecl_trips_e.pdf Accessed May 25, 2005.

9. Doha Declaration on the TRIPS Agreement & Public Health, ¶ 5.

10. For example, John L. McGoldrick, Executive Vice President of Bristol Myers-Squib which holds the patent on Zerit, an AIDS drug, commented that the AIDS pandemic "is not about profits; it's about poverty and a devastating disease . . ." See DeYoung K, and Brubaker B, "Another Firm Cuts HIV Drug Prices," *The Washington Post*, March 15, 2001: A1.

11. HIV/AIDS kills eight million people a year, mostly in sub-Saharan Africa. See Orbinski J, and Pecoul B, "G8: Drugs for Neglected Diseases." Available at www.msf.org/content/page.cfm?articleid=05c7c503-7f90-4bdf81fe0ad399cfcf44 Accessed June 24, 2003.

12. Doha Declaration on the TRIPS Agreement & Public Health at ¶ 6.
13. UNAIDS, *Report on the Global HIV/AIDS Epidemic* 2002, 1, 2002.
14. "Medicines & Related Substances Control Act 101 of 1965," amended by "Medicines and Related Substances Control Amendment Act 90 of 1997," South Africa Achmat Z, "We Can Use Compulsory Licensing and Parallel Imports: A South African Case Study." Available at www.sewer.law.wits.ac.2a/cals/OLPalp/tac/license.shtml Accessed June 10, 2003; Stoppard A, "Health – South Africa: Drug Companies Drop Lawsuit against Government," *Inter Press Service*. Available at www.aegis.com/news/ips/2001/IP010413.html Accessed Apr. 19, 2001.
15. Fredriksson J and Berry S, "South Africa HIV/AIDS Statistics." Available at www.avert.org/safricastats.htm Last updated October 21, 2003.
16. Berger JM, "Tripping Over Patents: AIDS, Access to Treatment and the Manufacturing of Scarcity," *Connecticut Journal of International Law*, 2002, *17*: 157.
17. Park RS, "The International Drug Industry: What the Future Holds for South Africa's HIV/AIDS Patients," *Minnesota Journal of Global Trade*, 2002, *11*: 125, 136–9.
18. "Trade Act of 1974," 19 U.S.C. §2242, 2000, amended by "Omnibus Trade and Competitiveness Act of 1988," Pub. L. No. 100–416, 102 Stat. 1105. Under this, the United States Trade Representative (USTR) is required within thirty days after the submission of the annual National Trade Estimates (foreign trade barriers) to report to Congress those foreign countries that (1) "deny adequate and effective protection of U.S. intellectual property rights" and (2) those countries under (1) "that are determined by the USTR to be priority foreign countries." The USTR identifies as priorities only those countries "that have the most onerous or egregious acts, policies, or practices that . . . have the greatest adverse impact on the relevant United States products and that are not entering into good faith negotiations or making significant progress in bilateral or multilateral negotiations to provide adequate and effective intellectual property rights" protection. In a challenge at the WTO, this notorious legal provision of U.S. law was sustained. See "World Trade Organization Report of the Panel," United States–Sections 301–310 of the Trade Act of 1974, WT/DS152/R ¶ 7.22, Dec. 22, 1999.
19. USTR report listing South Africa under §301 dated April 30, 1999. Available at www.ustr.gov/releases/1999/04/99-41.html Accessed June 10, 2003.
20. Available at www.phrma.org/issues/nte/safrica.html See also Love J, "Annotated USTR 301 Report Against South Africa." Available at www.lists.essential.org/pharm-policy/msg00078.html Accessed June 10, 2003.
21. Davis B, "Gore Hopes New AIDS Pact Will Help Shake Protesters," *Wall Street Journal*, August 12, 1999: A24.

22. For a closer look at South Africa's own attempts to address the HIV/AIDS pandemic using a rights framework, see Gathii J, "Rights, Patents, Markets and the Global AIDS Pandemic," *Florida Journal of International Law*, 2002, *14*: 278–95.

23. Department of Trade and Industry, Press Release, "Joint Understanding Between the Governments of South Africa and the United States of America," Sept. 17, 1999. Available at www.polity.org.za/povdocs/pr/ 1999/pro9176.html Accessed June 11, 2003. Barber S, "US Remains Hostile to South Africa Drugs Act," *Business Day*, Sept. 27, 1999: 4. Black Radical Congress, "Africa-at-Large: Activists Lock Gore out of His Office, Criticizing SA AIDS Drugs Deal," *African News Service*, Aug. 25, 1999. Available at www.freerepublic.com/forum/a37c4c4fe58fa.htm Accessed May 25, 2005.

24. Barber S, "US Remains Hostile to South Africa Drugs Act"; Black Radical Congress, "Activists Lock Gore out of His Office, Criticizing SA AIDS, Drugs Deal." This did not, however, soften support within PhrMA and Congress for taking a tough line on South Africa.

25. Exec. Order No. 13,155, 65 Fed. Reg. 30,521, 30,522, May 10, 2000.

26. Gathii JT, "Rights, Patents, Markets and the Global AIDS Pandemic," pp. 752–63.

27. Gupta S, "Bush's Thompson Booed at AIDS Conference." Available at www.cnn.com/2002/ALLPOLITICS/07/09/thompson.aids.conference Accessed July 9, 2002.

28. Brown D, "Disease Fund Says Money Needs Grow; Global Effort Against AIDS, TB, Malaria May Need $20 Billion in 2007," *Washington Post*, October 12, 2002: A2.

29. "U.S. under Fire at AIDS Conference," CBS *News*. Available at www.cbsnews.com/stories/2002/07/08/health/main514417.shtml Accessed July 9, 2002.

30. Ibid.

31. Swarns RL, "African Nations Applaud Bush Plan to Fight AIDS Epidemic," *New York Times*, January 29, 2003: A19.

32. Ibid.; Swarns RL, "Free AIDS Drugs in Africa Offer Dose of Life," *New York Times*, February 8, 2003: A1; and Stolberg SG, and Stevenson RW, "The President's Proposals: AIDS Policy; Bush AIDS Effort Surprises Many, but Advisors Call It Long Planned," *The New York Times*, January 30, 2003: A1.

33. Stolberg SG, "Senate Approves AIDS Bill, Pleasing White House," *The New York Times*, May 17, 2003: A13.

34. Ibid.

35. Ibid., and Stolberg SG, "A Calling to Heal; Getting Religion on AIDS," *The New York Times*, Feb. 2, 2003: A1.

36. Russel S, "Fears, Cheers over Bush AIDS Pledge: Plan Shortchanges Global Fund, Activists Say," *The San Francisco Chronicle*, January 30, 2003: A5; and "AIDS Plan Other Hope; But Some Activists Worry Global Funds May Not Reach Victims," *Newsday*, NY, Nassau and Suffolk ed., January 30, 2003: A39.

37. Lobe J, "Activists Slam Bush AIDS Initiative." Available at www.aegis.com/ne ws/Ips/2002/ipo20611.html Accessed June 19, 2002.

38. Russell S, "AIDS Fund Payment Slashed: US to Contribute $200 Million Less Than It Did Last Year," *The San Francisco Chronicle*, Friday, November 19, 2004. Available at www.sfgate.com/cgi-bin/article.cgi?file=/c/a/2004/11/19/MNGSB9UAM21.DTL Accessed November 19, 2004.

39. "Bush's Broken Promise on Global AIDS," *Headlines*, May 17, 2005. Available at www.democrats.org/news/200505180001.html Accessed June 1, 2005.

40. Global AIDS Alliance, "International AIDS Conference, July 11–16: Taking Stock of the Global Fight Against AIDS." Available at www.globalaidsalliance.org/bangkokbackground.cfm Accessed June 1, 2005.

41. Doha Declaration on the Trade-Related Intellectual Property Rights Agreement & Public Health, at ¶ 6. It is also noteworthy that the USTR's office cited the Attaran and Gillespie-White paper at the Doha Ministerial meeting to make the argument that it was poverty, and not patents, that prevented access to essential medicines. See e-mail from Asia Russell to the essential medicines listserve of the Consumer Project on Technology, "USTR at TRIPS Special Council Meeting," September 19, 2001. Available at www.lists.essential.org/pipermail/ip-health/2001-September/001866.html Accessed June 1, 2005.

42. Doha Declaration on the Trade-Related Intellectual Property Rights Agreement and Public Health. The submission further noted that for "any TRIPS-related solution there would still involve a cost."

43. The IIPI describes itself as "an international developing organization and think tank dedicated to promoting sustainable economic growth in all countries through the use of healthy intellectual property systems..." Available at www.iipi.org Accessed June 10, 2003.

44. International Intellectual Property Institute, "Patent Protection and Access to HIV/AIDS Pharmaceuticals in Sub-Saharan Africa," 2000.

45. Ibid.

46. Lee Gillespie-White was the Executive Director of IIPI and one of the authors of "Patent Protection and Access to HIV/AIDS Pharmaceuticals in Sub-Saharan Africa." She teamed up with Amir Attaran a year later to write the article that gave poverty the spotlight as the leading barrier to

access to essential medicines. See Attaran A, and Gillespie-White L, "Do Patents for Antiretroviral Drugs Constrain Access to AIDS Treatment in Africa?" *JAMA*, 2001, *286*: 1886–92.

47. International Intellectual Property Institute, "Patent Protection and Access to HIV/AIDS Pharmaceuticals in Sub-Saharan Africa," p. 2.

48. Ibid., pp. 2–3.

49. Ibid.

50. Attaran A, and Gillespie-White L, "Do Patents for Antiretroviral Drugs Constrain Access to AIDS Treatment in Africa?"

51. Ibid., p. 1887.

52. Ibid., pp. 1887, 1889–90.

53. Ibid., p. 1891.

54. Ibid.

55. Ibid.

56. This endorsement by the pharmaceutical industry is perhaps best exemplified by a press release issued by PhRMA (the pharmaceutical industry lobby) soon after the Attaran/Gillespie-White paper. See PhRMA, "Health Care in the Developing World: Intellectual Property and Access to AIDS Drugs." Available at www.phrma.org/ip.access.aids.drugs.html Accessed June 10, 2003. On Attaran's link to the pharmaceutical company world and his criticism of access to essential medicines, activists, and advocates, see "Big Pharma's Favorite Academics and Opinion Makers." Available at www.cptech.org/ip/health/pharmadefenders.html Accessed August 17, 2002.

57. It is reported that the USTR's office cited the Attaran and Gillespie-White paper at the Doha Ministerial meeting to make the argument that it was poverty, and not patents, that prevented access to essential medicines. See e-mail from Asia Russell to the essential medicines listserve of the Consumer Project on Technology, "USTR at TRIPS Special Council Meeting," September 19, 2001. Available at www.lists.essential.org/pipermail/ip-health/2001September/001858.html Accessed July, 2003.

58. Morris J, Tren R, "A 'Free Market' Point of View." Available at www.pharmaceutical.patents.com/opinions.asp?ID=13 Accessed May 25, 2005.

59. Morris J, Tren R, "Patent, Not Real Villain in Blocking Access to Drugs," November 9, 2001. Available at www.businessday.co.za/bday/content/direct/1,3523,965575-6096-0,00.html Accessed June 10, 2003.

60. Attaran A and Gillespie-White L, "Do Patents for Antiretroviral Drugs Constrain Access to AIDS Treatment in Africa?"

61. Interestingly, Attaran and Gillespie-White noted that "poor countries have only the last resort of compulsory licensing ... which both TRIPS and the Paris Convention legitimately allow them to do so." However, the authors seem to suggest that compulsory licensing is not an option

until 2005, when the TRIPS Agreement comes into force in developing countries. Even then, the authors suggest the issue of access would only be restricted to access to new medicines – presumably those patented after 2005. See Attaran A, and Gillespie-White L, "Do Patents for Antiretroviral Drugs Constrain Access to AIDS Treatment in Africa?" p. 1891.

62. Finger JM and Philip Schuler, "Implementation of Uruguay Round Commitments: The Development Challenge," *World Economics*, 2000, *24*: 511. Available at www.econ.worldbank.org/docs/941.pdf Accessed June 1, 2005.

63. For an extensive authoritative expose of such policies, see Stiglitz JE, *Globalization and Its Discontents* (New York: Norton, 2002).

64. World Bank, "Investing in Health, World Development Report," 1993, p. 58.

65. Epprecht M, "Investing in Amnesia, or Fantasy and Forgetfullness in the World Bank's Approach to Healthcare Reform in Sub-Saharan Africa," *Journal of Developing Areas*, 1997, *31*: 337, 343–44.

66. Ibid.

67. Ibid., p. 344.

68. For an excellent analysis of the cultural and stigma issues related to the HIV/AIDS pandemic, see Dube S, *Sex, Lies and AIDS* (New Delhi: Harper Collins, 2000).

69. Sherwood RB, "Global Prospects for the Role of Intellectual Property in Technology Transfer," *IDEA*® *The Journal of Law and Technology*, 2002, *42*: 27, 34.

70. Attaran and Gillespie-White, "Do Patents for Antiretroviral Drugs Constrain Access to AIDS Treatment in Africa?" pp. 1886–92.

71. See McNeil, DG Jr., "W.H.O. Moves to Make AIDS Drugs More Accessible to Poor Worldwide," *The New York Times*, April 3, 2002: A6.

72. Ibid.

73. Ibid.

74. Nevirapine, which prevents mother-to-child transmission of the HIV/AIDS virus, costs U.S. $430 per 100 units in Norway (although there is hardly any market for it) and $874 in Kenya, where the need is desperate; ibid.

75. McNeil, DG Jr., "W.H.O. Moves to Make AIDS Drugs More Accessible to Poor Worldwide."

76. Ibid.

77. See, e.g., "Profiting from Pain: Where Prescription Drug Dollars Go," *Families USA*, July 2002: 1.

78. See, for example, "IRIN, Kenya: Focus on Lack of Access to HIV/AIDS Drugs" Available at www.irinnews.org/AIDSreport.asp?ReportID= 1429&SelectRegion:East_Africa Accessed May 25, 2005 (UN Office for

the Coordination of Humanitarian Affairs making certain observations on simple and rather inexpensive steps that the government has failed to take in the registration of AIDS drugs that might make them more accessible quickly and affordably).

79. Power S, "Bystanders to Genocide: Why the United States Let the Rwanda Tragedy Happen," *Atlantic Monthly*, Sept. 2001: 84–108; Lippman TW, "Albright Embarks on Africa Tour; She Acknowledges U.S., Allies Mishandled Rwanda Crisis," *The Washington Post*, December 10, 1997: A28; and Duke L, "Frustration and Envy over the West's Rapid Response," *The Washington Post*, May 7, 1999: A31. See also Bilder RB, "Kosovo and the 'New Interventionism': Promise or Peril?" *Journal of Transnational Law & Policy*, 1999, *9*: 153, 163.

80. Kristof ND, "What Did You Do during the African Holocaust?" *The New York Times*, May 27, 2003: A25.

81. "President Clinton Apologizes," *Associated Press*, March 25, 1998. Available at www.news-star.com/stories/032598/new_clinton.html Accessed June 1, 2005.

82. Riechmann D, "Bush Signs Bill to Help Fight AIDS Abroad," *Yahoo News*, May 27, 2003. Available at www.miami.com/mld/miami-herald/5950053.html?template=contentModules/printstory.jsp Accessed June 2, 2005.

83. Global AIDS Alliance, "International AIDS Conference, July 11–16: Taking Stock of the Global Fight Against AIDS."

84. UNAIDS, Report on the Global HIV/AIDS Epidemic 2002, p. 23.

85. Berger JM, "Tripping over Patents: AIDS, Access to Treatment and the Manufacturing of Scarcity," *Connecticut Journal of International Law*, 2002, *17*: 157, 158.

86. See WHO, *3 Million HIV/AIDS Sufferers Could Receive Antiretroviral Therapy by 2005*. Available at www.who.int/inf/en/pr-2002-58.html Accessed July 9, 2002.

87. Such a pill could combine AZT (Zidovudine), 3 TC (lamivudine), and a third drug such as nevirapine, abacavir, or efavirenz, depending on the particular patient. Other drugs on the WHO's essential drugs list include didanosine, indinavir, lopinavir, nelfinar, ritanovir low dose, saquinvir, and stavudine. See James JS, "'Trizir' Approved: Three Existing Drugs in One," *AIDS Treatment News*, Nov. 17, 2000, 355. Available at www.aegis.com/pubs/atn/2000/ATN35503.html Accessed May 25, 2005.

88. McNeil, DG, Jr. "W.H.O. Moves to Make AIDS Drugs More Accessible to Poor Worldwide."

89. Agovino T, "New AIDS Drug Raises Hopes, Fears," Aug. 22, 2003. Available at www.immunecentral.com/templates/info_template.cfm/6181/77/31 Accessed May 25, 2005.

90. Attaran and Gillespie-White, pp. 1886–92.
91. Joint Statement by Oxfam, Treatment Action Campaign, Consumer Project on Technology (CPT), Medicines Sans Frontieres (MSF) and Health GAP, "Patents Do Matter in Africa According to NGOs," Press Release, October 17, 2001. Available at www.accessmed-msf.org/prod/publications.asp?scntid=171020011428553&contenttype Accessed May 25, 2005.
92. Ibid.
93. Borrell J-R and Watal J, "Impact of Patents on Access to HIV/AIDS Drugs in Developing Countries," Center for International Development at Harvard University, Working Paper No. 92, May 2002, p. 2.
94. Baker BK, "Brief Analysis of Macroeconomics and Health: Investing in Health for Economic Development." Available at www.lists.essential.org/pipermail/ip-health/2001-December/002547.html Accessed June 10, 2003.
95. Ibid.
96. "An Advance for HIV/AIDS Treatment Access in Developing Countries: A Fixed-Dose Combination of Generic Drugs Is Validated in a Clinical Trial," July 2, 2004. Available at www.accessmed-msf.org/prod/publications.asp?scntid=272004153542&contenttype=PARA& Accessed July 15, 2004.
97. Report of the Commission on Macroeconomics and Health, WHO, "Macronomics and Health: Investing in Health for Economic Development," 2001, pp. 11–12.
98. Report of the Commission on Macroeconomics and Health, WHO, "Macronomics and Health: Investing in Health for Economic Development," 2001 and Rather D, "Why Do We Sleep as AIDS Epidemic Continues?" *Houston Chronicle*, March 2, 2002. See also Carter J and Gates B, Sr., "Pennies a Day Can Stop Spread of AIDS," Op-Ed, *Los Angeles Times*, April 7, 2002: M5.
99. Report of the Commission on Macroeconomics and Health, WHO, "Macronomics and Health: Investing in Health for Economic Development," 2001. See also Global AIDS Alliance, "Internationl Conference, July 11–16: Taking Stock of the Global Fight Against AIDS."
100. Lucas CP, "The Strength to Kill AIDS Lies within U.S.," *Newsday*, August 13, 2002: A27.
101. "Bush Begins Trip to Five African Countries," *U.N. Wire*, July 7, 2003. Available at www.unwire.org/UNWire/20030707/449_6231.asp Accessed July 2003.
102. "Africa: You Talk, We Die," September 30, 2003. Available at www.sas.upenn.edu/African_Studies/Urgent_Action/apic-093003.html Accessed May 25, 2005.

103. Jawara F and Kwa A, *Behind the Scenes at the WTO: The Real World of International Trade Negotiations/Lessons of Cancun*, 2nd ed. (London: Zed Books, 2004), pp. xxxxii, 249–257.

104. Ibid., p. xxxiii.

Notes to Chapter 20

1. Availability for this vaccine has also become a concern in the wake of shortages of inactivated influenza vaccine. Levine S, "Spray Flu Vaccine Comes in at a Trickle," *Washington Post*, November 13, 2004: B1. Available at www.washingtonpost.com/wp-dyn/articles/A46360-2004 Nov12.html Accessed November 2004.

2. Nonetheless, preventing influenza infection with any influenza vaccine has the potential to blunt the spread of infection in all ages through a herd immunity effect. Seeman BT, "Texas Flu Researchers Test 'Herd Immunity' Theory," *Newhouse News Service*, 2004. Available at www. newhousenews.com/archive/seeman102604.html Accessed November 2004.

3. Whalen J, Tam P-W and Luek S, "Vulnerable System Behind Flu-Vaccine Shortage: Struggle to Police Drugs Globally," *The Wall Street Journal*, November 5, 2004.

4. Treanor J, "Weathering the Influenza Vaccine Crisis," *NEJM*, 2004, *351*: 2039–40.

5. The National Vaccine Injury Compensation Program, Health Resources and Services Administration, U.S. Department of Health and Human Services. Available at www.hrsa.gov/osp/vicp/INDEX.HTM Accessed November 2004. "National Injury Compensation Program Marks Tenth Anniversary," September 30, 1998. Available at www.usdoj.gov/opa/pr/1998/September/453civ.htm Accessed November 2004.

6. Cowley G, "The Flu Shot Fiasco," *Newsweek*, November 1, 2004: 40–44.

7. "A Flu Vaccine Fiasco," Editorial, *The New York Times*, October 6, 2004.

8. Nearly 30 years ago, in January 1976, a memorandum was sent by the Director of the CDC to the Secretary of the Department of Health, Education and Welfare (HEW) stating that "liability problems may drive vaccine manufacturers out of business, and recommends that the Secretary support legislation to indemnify the manufacturers or to compensate all victims of vaccine." See Neustadt RE and Fineberg HV, "The Swine Flu Affair: Decision Making on a Slippery Slope," U.S. Department of Health Education and Welfare, 1978, p. 123.

9. "HHS Activities on Influenza," revised: October 28, 2004. Available at www.hhs.gov/nvpo/influenza_vaccines.html Accessed November 19, 2004.

10. "WHO Sets Flu Vaccine Summit Meeting: World Health Organization Sets Flu Vaccine Summit Meeting to Deal with Pandemic Threat," *The Associated Press*, November 1, 2004. At least 16 vaccine companies and international health officials met to plan for a possible new pandemic of influenza.

11. Barry JM, *The Great Influenza: The Epic Story of the Deadliest Plague in History* (New York: Viking, 2004).

12. Altman LK, "Experts Urge Greater Effort on Vaccine for Bird Flu," *New York Times*, November 13, 2004.

13. Reynolds G, "The Flu Hunters," *The New York Times Magazine*, November 7, 2004: 36.

14. La Montagne JR and Fauci AS, "Intradermal Influenza Vaccination – Can Less Be More?" *NEJM*, November 8, 2004, editorial. Available at www.nejm.org Accessed November 14, 2004.

15. Boyce N, "From Eggs to Cultured Cells," *US News & World Report*, November 11, 2004: 60–61. Available at www.USNews.com Accessed November 2004.

16. "Influenza Vaccines under Development," Protein Sciences Corporation, 1000 Research Parkway, Meriden, CT 06450. Available at www.proteinsciences.com/vaccines.htm Accessed November 2004.

17. Oseltamivir phosphate (Tamiflu®) inhibits an influenza enzyme that the virus needs for release of mature virus from infected cells, thus slowing viral spread. Available at www.tamiflu.com/ Accessed November 2004.

18. "No Requiem Yet for Vaccines," Editorial, *The New York Times*, November 7, 2004. Available at www.nytimes.com/2004/11/07/opinion/07sun2.html?oref=login Accessed November 2004.

19. Fauci AS, "Emerging Infectious Diseases: A Clear and Present Danger to Humanity," *JAMA*, 2004, *292(15)*: 1887–8.

20. Grady D, "Vaccine Works to Prevent Cervical Cancer," *The New York Times*, November 2, 2004. Available at www.nytimes.com/2004/11/02/health/02canc.html Accessed November 2004.

21. Primary prevention is practiced prior to the biologic origin of disease; secondary prevention is practiced after the disease can be recognized, but before it has caused suffering and disability.

22. The World Health Organization Smallpox Eradication Programme. Available at www.choo.fis.utoronto.ca/fis/courses/lis2102/KO.WHO.case.html Accessed November 2004; Fenner F, Henderson DA, Arita I, Jezek Z, and Ladnyi ID, "Smallpox and Its Eradication," World Health Organization, Geneva, 1988.

23. "Wyeth Waives Patent Royalties on Its Innovative New Bifurcated Needle, Aiding in the Delivery of 200 Million Life-Saving Smallpox Vaccinations per Year," 1968. Available at www.wyeth.com/about/period3.asp Accessed November 2004.

24. "Polio Will Be Finished by Year's End, Say Ministers of Health," *Bulletin of the World Health Organization*, February 2004, *82(2)*: 157.

25. This author served on a U.S. Public Health Service Interagency Group to Monitor Vaccine Development, Production and Usage in the early 1980s, when the shrinking number of U.S. vaccine producers was of concern. As part of this effort, a team of scientists from the FDA, NIH, and CDC made trips to Japan and Sweden to evaluate the pertussis vaccine made in Japan, and used in Sweden, as a replacement for a less effective pertussis vaccine made in the United States by a single supplier.

26. "Financing Vaccines in the 21st Century: Assuring Access and Availability," Institute of Medicine, August 2003. National Academies Press. Available at www.nap.edu Accessed November 2004.

27. A similar call for collaboration between the private and public sectors was contained in a white paper from the Infectious Diseases Society of America (IDSA) published and presented to the U.S. Congress in July 2004. The IDSA is campaigning for an environment that provides incentives for the pharmaceutical industry to continue the development and production of newer antibiotics to combat the continuing emergence of bacterial strains that are resistant to existing antibiotics. See "Bad Bugs, No Drugs: As Antibiotic Discovery Stagnates . . . A Public Health Crisis Brews." Available at www.idsociety.org/Template.cfm?Section =Home&CONTENTID=9726&TEMPLATE=/ContentManagement/ ContentDisplay.cfm Accessed November 2004; Belden H, "IDSA Warns: New Antibiotics Needed ASAP," *Drug Topics*, November 8, 2004. Available at www.drugtopics.com/drugtopics/article/articleDetail.jsp? id=132380 Accessed November 2004.

28. Klausner RD, Fauci AS, Corey L, et al., "The Need for a Global HIV Enterprise," *Science* June 27, 2003, *300*: 2036–39. Available at www. sciencemag.org Accessed November 2004.

29. Kremer M and Snyder CM, "Why Is There No AIDS Vaccine?" Center for International Development, Working Paper No. 11, Harvard University, October 2004.

30. "Incentives for Private Sector Development of an AIDS Vaccine," Policy Brief #2, International AIDS Vaccine Initiative, September 2004. Available at www.iavi.org/file.cfm?fid=1086 Accessed November 2004.

31. These rewards need not be monetary alone, for altruistic motives are also very powerful when reasonable financial stability is available. Government service, such as this author experienced at the Centers for Disease Control and Prevention (CDC), for example, can fulfill that condition.

32. The question of how less developed societies of the world may obtain increased availability and access to basic necessities of life and health is

far from settled, despite extensive efforts of the international community, led by the UN, World Bank, IMF and other multilateral organizations and nonprofit organizations, e.g., the Bill and Melinda Gates Foundation and a host of others.

33. Eviatar D, "Spend $150 Billion per Year to Cure World Poverty," *The New York Times Magazine*, November 7, 2004: 44–9. Dr. Jeffrey Sachs has proposed a plan to deal with world poverty, one of the most fundamental barriers to improved health.

34. Available at www.merck.com/about/cr/mectizan/home.html Accessed May 25, 2005.

35. "African Comprehensive HIV/AIDS Partnerships (ACHAP) in Botswana." Available at www.merck.com/about/cr/policies_performance/social/hiv_aids_partnership.html Accessed November 2004.

36. "In Uganda, a New Model for Training AIDS Health Care Givers: The Infectious Diseases Institute," in "A Prescription for Access," *Pfizer*, Spring 2004: 15–17. Available at www.pfizer.com/subsites/philanthropy/access/access_spring_2004.pdf Accessed November 2004.

37. "Uganda: HIV/AIDS Training Institute Opened," UN Office for the Coordination of Humanitarian Affairs, November 9, 2004. Available at www.irinnews.org/print.asp?ReportID=43777 Accessed November 2004. ("The material contained on this Web site comes to you via IRIN, a UN humanitarian information unit, but may not necessarily reflect the views of the United Nations or its agencies.")

38. "The Trachoma Initiative," in "A Prescription for Access," *Pfizer*, Spring 2004: 13–15. Available at www.pfizer.com/subsites/philanthropy/access/access_spring_2004.pdf Accessed November 2004.

39. Examples of these programs can be found at these Web sites, all accessed November 2004: Abbott laboratories, available at www.abbott.com/citizenship/access/global_access.cfm; Astra Zeneca, available at www.astrazeneca.com/article/10831.aspx; Aventis, available at www.aventis.com/main/page.asp?pageid=68343920040802140702&folderid=87579320040722095420&lang=en; Bayer, available at www.bayer.com/about_bayer/social_responsibility/international/page1288.htm; Boehringer Ingelheim, available at www.boehringer-ingelheim.com/corporate/corp/sr2003/corp_triple_bottom_line.htm; Bristol-Myers-Squibb, available at www.bms.com/sr/philan-thropy/data/2004_founda.pdf; Eli Lilly, available at www.lily.com/products/access/international_initiatives.html; Johnson & Johnson, available at www.jnj.com/community/international/HIV/index.htm; Merck, available at www.merck.com/about/cr/policies_performance/social/philanthropy.html; Novartis, available at www.novartis.com/corporate_citizenship/en/index.shtml; Pfizer, available at www.pfizer.com/subsites/philanthropy/access/access_spring_2004.pdf;

Schering-Plough, available at www.sch-plough.com/schering_plough/ corp/corporate_responsibility.jsp. Also see "Accelerating Access Initiative," available at www.ifpma.org/Health/hiv/health_aai_hiv.aspx.

40. The bottom line, however, is that for-profit companies must be just that – profitable, for without profits they will not exist. And while companies in the pharmaceutical industry, in particular, compared to other businesses, have a responsibility to be good corporate citizens, they will cease to exist without profits. Expecting less profitability from the pharmaceutical industry than other major corporations that are publicly traded will ultimately slow investment and threaten survival of the corporation, as so many other failed companies have demonstrated in recent years. Other authors here have examined and debated whether the pharmaceutical industry spends its resources wisely on research and development, advertising and marketing, and this is certainly a subject worthy of debate that the industry must take seriously, because public trust in the industry is essential for its long-term health.

41. Despite the conduct of premarket clinical studies of drugs and medical devices that involve ever larger numbers of participants, very rare side effects are not likely to be detected until widespread use of a marketed product occurs. This was the case in 1976, for example, when Guillain Barré syndrome was only detected as a rare side effect of "swine influenza" vaccination after nearly 40 million doses of vaccine had been administered. If an epidemic of this strain of influenza had, in fact, occurred in the United States in 1976, vaccination would likely have continued, because the benefits of vaccination would have been expected to provide a much greater benefit than the rare and nonfatal reactions to the vaccinations. See Neustadt RE and Fineberg HV, "The Swine Flu Affair: Decision Making on a Slippery Slope."

42. To "give first priority to the well-being of participants in research studies and patients who use pharmaceutical products and medical devices" is the first statement of the American Academy of Pharmaceutical Physicians Code of Ethics for the Practice of Pharmaceutical Medicine, adopted in 2001. Available at www.aapp.org/ethics.php Accessed November 2004.

43. As an example, the etiologic agent of Legionnaire disease was first identified at CDC in 1976, and early *in vitro* studies of antibiotic treatments were evaluated there. Similarly, HIV was first identified by scientists at NIH and the Pasteur Institute, and more than 20 antiretroviral (ARV) treatments subsequently have been identified by the combined efforts of both academic and private sector laboratories. Studies to demonstrate clinical safety and efficacy of these ARV products have benefited from collaborations of scientists and clinical investigators in both the private

and public sectors, whereas the commercial risk and liability remain with the companies bringing the products to market. Reform of tort laws could help to alleviate some of these legitimate concerns that industry may have for entry into product development, such as vaccines, where liability concerns do exist.

Notes to Part IV Introduction

1. See, for example, Harris, G, "At FDA, Strong Drug Ties and Less Monitoring." *The New York Times*, December 6, 2004: A1.
2. See Berenson A, "Despite Vow, Drug Makers Still Withhold Clinical Information," *The New York Times*, May 31, 2005.
3. This will no doubt raise some antitrust concerns, as do all efforts at industry self-regulation, but such considerations should not be an excuse for inaction where the public interest can be enhanced. See Santoro MA, *Note on Industry Self Regulation and Antitrust* (Boston: Harvard Business School Publishing, 1994).

Notes to Chapter 21

1. "River blindness" is caused by the parasitic filarial worm *Onchocerca volvulus* infecting the eye, leading to impaired vision and blindness from severe inflammation and scarring It is known as "river blindness" because it is associated with living near rivers where the black flies that spread the infection breed. The filarial worm can also cause debilitating skin infections.
2. Broder DS, "Health Care Hopes," *The Washington Post*, March 16, 2003, p. B7.

Note to Chapter 22

1. Scanlon TM, *What We Owe to Each Other* (Cambridge, MA: Harvard University Press, 1998), p. 224. See also, for example, Singer P, "Famine, Affluence, and Morality," *Philosophy and Public Affairs*, 1972, *1*: 231.

Notes to Chapter 24

1. Rowland C, "An Ailing Image: Drug Industry's Tenacious Price Protection Stirs Anger," *The Boston Globe*, July 11, 2003.
2. "Our Credo." Johnson & Johnson website. Available at www.jnj.com/our_company/our_credo/index.htm Accessed May 25, 2005.
3. Maxwell J, *There's No Such Thing as Business Ethics* (New York: Time Warner Inc., 2003).

4. Available at www.fda.gov/oc/ohrt/irbs/belmont.html Accessed May 25, 2005.

5. Available at www.sciencemag.org/cgi/content/full/305/5691/1695 Accessed May 25, 2005.

6. Available at www.oneworldhealth.org Accessed May 25, 2005.

Index